# The Shape and Shaping of the College and University in America

# The Shape and Shaping of the College and University in America

## *A Lively Experiment*

### Stephen J. Nelson

LEXINGTON BOOKS
Lanham • Boulder • New York • London

Published by Lexington Books
An imprint of The Rowman & Littlefield Publishing Group, Inc.
4501 Forbes Boulevard, Suite 200, Lanham, Maryland 20706
www.rowman.com

Unit A, Whitacre Mews, 26-34 Stannary Street, London SE11 4AB

British Library Cataloguing in Publication Information Available

**Library of Congress Cataloging-in-Publication Data**

Names: Nelson, Stephen James, 1947– author.
Title: The shape and shaping of the college and university in America: a lively experiment / Stephen
    J. Nelson.
Description: Lanham, Maryland : Lexington Books, 2016. | Includes bibliographical references and
    index.
Identifiers: LCCN 2015046093 (print) | LCCN 2016004351 (ebook) | ISBN 9781498515566 (cloth :
    alk. paper) | ISBN 9781498515573 (Electronic)
Subjects: LCSH: Universities and colleges--United States--History. | Education, Higher--United
    States--History. | Education, Higher--Aims and objectives--United States--History.
Classification: LCC LA226.N53 2016 (print) | LCC LA226 (ebook) | DDC 378.73--dc23
LC record available at http://lccn.loc.gov/2015046093

Printed in the United States of America

To Gettysburg College,
for the education and the foundation of inquiry bestowed,
and
Professor William W. Jellema,
for the scholarly challenge that
inspired this work.

# Contents

Acknowledgements      ix

Preface      xi

Introduction: The Land, Landscape, and Promise: Embarking in a New World      1

1    Religion in the Nation and the Academy      27

2    The University: What Is It and How Does Its Center Hold?      55

3    Contentious Compatibility and the Common Good: The University as Servant and Critic in a Democracy      83

4    The Purpose of the College: Clashes over Liberal Education and Ideas that Prevail      113

5    The Rise of the University: The Influence of Progressivism and the Social Gospel      153

6    Battles over Liberty, Academic Freedom, and Free Speech      183

7    The Disuniting of America and the University: A Reprise of Academic Freedom and the Threat of Balkanization in the Quest for Pluralism and Diversity      223

8    The Contemporary Ideological World of the McCarthy Era to Present: Political Rightness and Wrong-Headedness      259

Conclusion: A Coda: The Concept of a University in America and the Culture We Deserve      291

Bibliography      315

Index      321

# Acknowledgements

I have been watching and studying colleges and universities for over four-and-a-half decades, first as a college student, then as an administrator in the 1970s and 1980s, and since as graduate student and researcher of the college presidency and as a collegiate faculty member. I have had the privilege of writing five previous books, all about the college and university presidency. To have been able to continue publication of my scholarly interests and to have the opportunity of further informing our understandings of the college and university in America is something that I count as a blessing and the best of good fortune.

I continue to be indebted to a tremendously supportive and loving wife, Janet Cooper Nelson. She is always willing to listen attentively to the discoveries that I think I have made and the ideas I attach to them. More importantly, Janet adds her reactions and thoughts, and these always lead to me to reform and revise in ways that make the argument and narrative vastly more clear. Her dedication to the life of the university and its many constituents from her perch as Chaplain to the University at Brown University is unsurpassed. She has had a strong influence in shaping that fine university during a tenure there of over twenty-five years.

Susan Slesinger has worked with me as an editor for more than a decade, overseeing and making immense contributions to four previous books. She is enormously gifted and has been remarkably helpful at multiple steps along the way in my work and writing. She is a professional who knows her business and knows how to work with an author. I am extremely indebted to her for the collaboration and partnership in which she has engaged with me.

A dear friend of over fifty years and a tremendously accomplished teacher, researcher, and writer in his own right, Stephen Marini has been instrumental in my career as a professor and academician. In the early stages of conceptualizing this work, Steve was of help beyond measure in assisting with the shape of the content on which I have focused. He was also a special guide as I grappled with issues regarding the relationship of religion to the college and university and in American society. I am indebted to him for friendship, for the standard of inquiry and excellence that he has embodied and passed to me, and for his encouragement and support of my professional and personal life over decades.

I am also indebted to the Center for the Advancement of Research and Scholarship at Bridgewater State University for the provision of funding at a number of stages in the research, writing, and final production of the manuscript. First, they provided a faculty research grant through which I hired a research assistant, former Bridgewater educational leadership graduate student, Melissa McCann. Melissa searched, tracked down, and delivered to me documents, resources, and other materials connected to the extensive review of the literature and research that form the foundation of this book as a narrative. Melissa was thorough, prompt, and highly skilled in what she did for me, and I cannot thank her enough.

Second, the Center provided a small grant to support Susan Slesinger's editorial work with me.

Finally, Bridgewater provided further support through a Provost and Dean scholarship grant that enabled the hiring of another former Bridgewater educational leadership graduate student, Carol Moran, who contributed outstanding and thorough work to prepare the bibliography and index of this book.

Final words are in order about the journey that led to the production of this book. First, as noted in the preface, I have to thank my doctoral dissertation adviser at the University of Connecticut, Professor William Jellema, for planting the prospect in my mind that I might be capable of tackling a project of this size and scale. His wisdom and encouragement throughout my doctoral studies and his confidence since in my scholarly, research, and writing ability has sparked my commitment and undergirds everything that I have had the good fortune to produce, including this work.

Second, the broad sketch of this book was hatched in the late fall 2011. I began to outline what the book would include and what the extent of the research would likely be while on a sabbatical (again thanks to Bridgewater State University for that privilege, the first I had ever had) from January–May, 2012. Work continued that summer, and throughout the summer of 2013, on the research and reading. Writing commenced in the summer 2014 and was completed in the summer 2015.

Lastly, as also indicated in the preface, I am fully responsible for what I have chosen to cover in this book, the ideas concocted and presented, and the angle and perspectives that I have argued. You as the reader can judge the outcome of that work.

My modest goal is to have contributed just a bit about what we know and understand about the shape and shaping of the college and university in America. All of us who care about higher education in this country have a stake in that quest.

Stephen J. Nelson
Providence, Rhode Island
September 2015

# Preface

The foundation for this book derives from a number of sources. First, while a doctoral student, my advisor, Professor William Jellema planted the original seeds for this work by suggesting to me the prospect that I undertake a history of the college and university in America. He had in mind a true stretch. That was what I aspire to replicate but more importantly update the classic history of higher education in America by Frederick Rudolph, *The American College and University: A History*.

In no way did I have the ability or pretense then or now to reach for a work as comprehensive and fully researched as that which Rudolph created. More practically, at the time I had completion of the dissertation front and center, and knew I had found a scholarly passion for the study of the college presidency. I wanted to pursue that quest, its own narrow specialty slice of higher education in America. But that was what I desired as my short-term direction and commitment. I have been fortunate and blessed, in the ensuing two decades since, to publish a number of works about the college and academic presidency.

Nonetheless, Jellema's prodding and its implicit and explicit challenges remained in my mind. It became an idea that I knew I could not and did not want to duck.

Over time, the way I wanted to tackle this project began to take shape more and more precisely in my mind. That gestation over years brought into greater focus what would be required and involved if I were to follow through in this quest. I began to grasp a clearer picture of the research that would of necessity have to be untaken. More critically, what I originally viewed as the daunting nature of what would be demanded became more realistically something that I came to believe I was capable of doing. The result of that thinking, work, and writing is what you will find in these pages.

The structure of this book is a series of essays that are presented each as a chapter on topics and themes in the history of higher education in America. The ten chapters, including the introduction and conclusion, are linked under the umbrella of the book's title: *The Shape and Shaping of the College and University in America: A Lively Experiment*. The chapters are constructed as stand-alone, independent inquiry and commentary about that history. In one way of thinking, each essay can be conceived of as a scholarly article. However, the chapters or essays are intended to be read

*Preface*

as a whole, even though they can equally valuably be read individually by the selection that you as the reader might elect to make.

This book is not a chronological trek through the evolution, the shape, and shaping of the academy in America. It is rather thematic, revealing distinctive points of view of what has transpired, who and what have been the key players, and forces that have produced the college and university as we know it today. Some of the essays in this book unfold chronologically, others not so. The ones that are presented in chronological review cover certain eras and not others.

However, I have taken the liberty to begin and end selectively each of these treated issues and subjects chronologically. I take responsibility for the judgments that led to those choices. Nonetheless, I suggest that this is a wide-ranging tour of the forces and leaders that have swayed and shaped higher education in America.

The reader will observe a number of recurrent contentions and points of view throughout this narrative that are also of the author's choosing. But the standpoints chosen and the contentions made did not come about willy-nilly or out of thin air. The selective topics and issues that you read about in these pages result from years of working in and thinking about the academy and its leadership, about how and why events, policies, and decisions have unfolded the way they have, and about what the roads both taken and not taken are. These issues, points of decision and departure either back to the future in efforts to reclaim traditions of the past or away from traditional ideas and views and into new territory, are threads that I assert run through the history of the college and university in America.

My thoughts about the college and university in America and my judgments about how and why we are where we are today are based on a number of baseline assumptions. These include but are not limited to the following.

First, I iterate repeatedly the thinking of Kenneth Minogue in his classic work, *The Concept of A University.*[1] This book was written in the late 1960s and early 1970s on the immediate backside of the protests and upheavals in his native England, as well as the lurching about of colleges and universities in America from the late 1950s through the 1960s.

One of Minogue's most thought-provoking ideas is that for the university to remain the university it must maintain its unique foundations and identity among any and all other institutions of the nation, society, and culture.

Should the university become simply a social action organization, a politically geared or ideologically driven (to one viewpoint to the exclusion of others) constellation of ideas and constituents, or an institution dedicated to right every wrong that it sees in society (not to get into how its constituents would arrive at a monochromatic view of those problems), then the university would no longer be the university. Rather by going down that path, the university would morph, maybe irretrievably, into something else that, while maybe of institutional value to a nation or a society, ceases to be the academy qua the academy.

In line with Minogue's ideas, throughout I take note of the remarkable contribution to our thinking about the university brought to us by Cardinal John Henry Newman in his *The Idea of the University*. Of particular emphasis is his notion that the academy is and must be guided by "first principles," that is, the focus on a culture of the intellect and the pursuit of the intellectual foundations of knowledge. These are the essentials of what it is for the university to be the university. These values must remain both preeminent and be firmly held to in order for that heritage to be sustained.

In many ways Newman and Minogue are compatriots, linking arms in the battle for the university. Neither man knew about the forces of political correctness, as they came fully into their being in the latter twentieth and early twenty-first century. However, both of them, in previous eras of the mid-nineteenth and mid-twentieth centuries respectively, could sense the precursors of political correctness and the corrosive influence of ideology in the academy.[2]

As John Turner notes: "Curiously, Newman's vision, despite its potential for religious interference, possessed a wider sphere for intellectual freedom in the university than the vision of those who conceive education as capable of radically transforming the pride and passion of human beings."[3]

What Newman succeeded in doing, and one of the fundamental premises of the story about the college and university that follows in these pages, was that he:

> thus set himself and the institution whose idea he articulated against the ideals of utility and useful knowledge and consequently made the distinguishing value of the university its apparent *uselessness*. The usefulness, indeed the higher calling, of the university was its very lack of direct social and economic utility. That transcendent uselessness . . . has preserved much of the freedom of university life.[4]

Minogue would heartily endorse this concept of the university, echoing as it does his own.

Second, I firmly believe that when we examine the sweep of the history, evolution, and advancement of the college and university in America, the more things change, the more they stay the same. That is, the fundamental foundations, convictions, beliefs, and creed of the university have changed little if at all throughout the nearly four hundred years of the college in America.

Size, scope, and scale have changed dramatically as a result of the growth and progress of American society and life in the Republic. But we lose a sense for the basic foundations of the college and university when we allow ourselves to get caught up in what appear to be changes etched in stone that are themselves transitory, regularly modified, and subject to continual change.

Connected to this belief is a critical view, admittedly bordering at times on resistance, in my thinking about the jeremiads swung at the university throughout its history. Undoubtedly, many of these commentators and critics have substantive points of view and their criticisms have occasionally resulted in progress and vital changes in the course of the college and university.

However, when we encounter these critics what needs to be stated, as I contend at many junctures, is that there are different angles and interpretations about these different views, jeremiads, and criticisms. That is, regardless the intense, negative critical judgments that some commentators and naysayers have uttered about the college and university in America, things are nowhere near as bad today or in any previous era as these critics would have you believe.

Rather, the sky has not fallen. The degradation of the academy has not taken place. Corrosion and erosion are not everywhere to be found. The basis of the academy in America is fundamentally that which has historically been the case. Further, the university qua the university is fundamentally intact to the roots of its historic heritage.

Lastly, the most recurrent themes and core undergirding of the university in America revealed in these pages include: The role and relationship of religion and religious beliefs and passion in the academy; struggles and debates over the place and value of the liberal arts; the role of the university as both critic and servant of society and the nation; the demands and intrigue of academic freedom, free speech, and liberty; the relationship of liberal arts colleges to major universities; the need for colleges and universities to maintain centers that can hold, and the corollary threat that disunity and balkanization pose to the academy; and the pressures and battleground of ideological points of view, and the arguments of often poles-apart contenders seeking to control the academy and its agenda and purpose.

As the reader, you and other observers and commentators are welcomed to think differently about the assumptions, underpinnings, and values at the foundation and the development of the college and university. However, despite those differences, we no doubt would agree that these are the essential principles of the academy: the critical role of debate and dialogue; the search for knowledge and investigations based on opinions rooted in learning; and the prospect that explorations about the past hold the potential to shed vital light on the present and maybe even to guide the future.

The suggestions made in these pages are designed to add to that discussion and exploration, and you are invited to engage in that conversation and journey. Thus what is suggested in these pages is done with forethought, intentions based on decades of examining colleges and universities, their cultures and the leaders and shapers of them as institutions and as a force in the nation and the society. But these offerings are made with great humility, a sense of context and relative importance captured in the words of A. Lawrence Lowell, president of Harvard.

After his distinguished presidency, Lowell concludes the preface to his compendium of speeches and writings during his tenure with the following statement that reflects the spirit with which I offer this book to the reader: "Any constructive labor is in the nature of a work of art, and no one is more aware of the defects of what he has done than the artist himself. When he has finished his picture, as well as his skill permits, he takes it, and hangs it up beside the altar, saying, I am sorry that it is not better, but in the time for work allotted it is the best that I could do."[5]

## NOTES

1. Kenneth Minogue, *The Concept of a University* (Berkeley and Los Angeles: University of California Press, 1973).

2. Ibid., 114. Minogue offers a definition of "ideology" as "the conversion of religious or political demands into an academic idiom." Throughout the pages of this book, oft-noted mention of ideology and ideological ideas and thinking are based in Minogue's definition.

3. Cardinal John Henry Newman, *The Idea of a University*, ed. John Henry Turner (New Haven, CT: Yale University Press, 1996). John Henry Turner essay, "Newman's University and Ours," 282–301, 289.

4. Ibid., 291, italics author's.

5. A. Lawrence Lowell, *At War with Academic Traditions in America* (Cambridge, MA: Harvard University Press, 1934), ix.

# Introduction

## *The Land, Landscape, and Promise: Embarking in a New World*

The relationship of the college and university in America to the Colonial commonwealths and later to the Republic and nation has from the beginning been tangled and provocative. At the same time the emerging and later new nation and its colleges and universities have always shared strong bonds of joint interest. They hold common and mutually reinforcing fundamental beliefs, values, and principles. In general, albeit occasional dust-ups to the contrary, America's colleges and universities and the nation they inhabit have remarkably suited each other's desires and investment in the commonweal.

The life of the college and university, like the nascent Republic and nation of which it was born and in which it has thrived, has continually fashioned and promoted its interests and existence in a custom profoundly interwoven with the life of the nation. As mutually invested partners, their relationship and the shape and shaping of the college and university spawned have, from the get-go, been a lively experiment.

Less than a scant two decades passed before the first settlers in a new, unknown land quickly founded the first Colonial College at Harvard. Thus was born this story of the college in America with it all its intertwining, internecine twists and turns. Colleges were to be servants of social and civic life. However, from the outset, even if at times in unwanted ways, they quickly and often forcefully also served as critics of society, of culture, and of the birth, emergence, and advance of the nation itself.

The emerging Republic, comprising the independent colonies and their respective public and governing frameworks, possessed a creed constituted of fundamental values and beliefs: its own religion. This creed would later be fully affirmed and codified in the Revolutionary War and Constitutional era. However, the crucial elements of this civil religion, which at its formation could later be called the religion of the Republic, were in the mix from the initial landing of the Pilgrims and Puritans in Massachusetts Bay, and as fellow settlers landed and formed in the other colonies of America.

This civically religious set of social, political, and cultural ideas were interposed, absorbed, and shot through the founding of Harvard and the

1

other eight Colonial Colleges that would follow, the last founded just as the about to become Republic faced a Revolutionary War that would make it a nation, "the first new nation,"[1] in a new land.

However, it would not be until nearly the end of that first century of higher education in America, nearly sixty years later, that the second college, William and Mary, was to be founded in 1693. Then only one more, Yale, would be added before Harvard reached its centenary. These early decades of the commonwealths and colonies, and the environment these nascent colleges infiltrated, are often romanticized. A close examination of the civil and religious foundations of the Puritan settlers in Massachusetts Bay can help us avoid the trap of sentimentalizing what went on.

The crucial, cardinal stipulation is that religious and cultural restrictions were the dominant characteristic of the Massachusetts Bay Colony where Harvard was founded by Puritans and Congregationalists. As we shall shortly see in greater detail, there is no mistaking these theological, faith-inspired foundations and the strong religious reign that was the cradle John Winthrop and his Massachusetts Bay colonists wrought.

They had sought freedom, most decidedly religious freedom from rule of their British homeland, and of the church and clerics who sought to control them. But when they had their shot as the religious and political—the two nearly impossible to sort out as befits a theocracy—leaders in a new land, they exerted their will with force, and at times with vengeance.

Sidney Mead, the eminent American religious historian, preferred to describe his discipline as "religion in American history."[2] The title of this book and its essayist style are modeled on his work, making me heavily indebted. Mead establishes in unvarnished terms the tenor of these Massachusetts Bay denizens and their handling of dissenting opinions. This is the initial crux of the issues at hand in understanding how the college in America commenced.

In a seminal chapter, "From Coercion to Persuasion: Another Look at the Rise of Religious Liberty and the Emergence of Denominationalism" in his groundbreaking book *The Lively Experiment: The Shaping of Christianity in America*, Mead argues that "The Puritan theocrats on the Charles soon had one important aspect of the meaning of the great space available thrust upon them." Probably to their horror, "They discovered that while they might protect their won religious uniformity by banishing all dissenters, they could neither keep the banished from settling in neighboring Rhode Island . . . nor prevent every wind from the south carrying their contagious ideas back to the Puritan stronghold."[3]

Furthermore for the exiles who with Roger Williams sought refuge in Rhode Island, the reality was that "the zeal of the dissenters, far from being dissipated by banishment, was truly enlarged by the knowledge thus forced upon them that even the long arms of civil and ecclesiastical authority could not encompass the vast spaces of the new land."[4]

These refugees took heart in what the new land of America, space and distance, would accord them. Whether intentionally or not, their mere presence over the border to the south would stand as a display of independence and as a permanent beachhead of contrast with the theological culture left behind in Massachusetts. The Rhode Island refuge also became the fertile ground later on for the founding of Brown University which incorporated the civic establishment of religious toleration within its gates.

This theocratic mentality indeed lay at the roots of Harvard College. Thus, at the birth of the academy in America, there were to be early compromises about freedom of expression, what later would be called free speech, liberty, and academic freedom, and the free flowing dialogue presumed at the foundation of the university. In addition and critical to our inquiry, these features shape a welcome to the earliest ideological battleground of political, or in this case much more chiefly theological correctness.

However, early dissent contested some of these assumptions. Those who sought control of Puritan society and of Harvard got push-back from a most ironic source. Mead highlights the part of the story over which they had no control. That is, the dreaded British "Crown, in giving its consent to Rhode Island's 'lively experiment,' with 'full liberty in religious concern' in the new Charter, gave official sanction to the scandal of Massachusetts Bay and forestalled future attempts on the part of the Bay Puritans to impose their kind of theocratic order on the neighboring chaos."[5]

The contention that follows in this and subsequent chapters is that the history of the college and university is a lively experiment akin to and paralleling that reflected in the earliest seeds and in the historical unfolding of the quest and challenge of religious freedom in America.[6] I further assert that the religion of the Republic, the creedal articulation of the Constitutional framework, and the ideals, beliefs, and principles of its civil and civic formulations, is shot through the emergence of the college and university in America. In a further twist, in recent times the religion of the Republic has emerged as "the" religion of the academy (more about this in a moment).

To what extent has the religion of the Republic found its way into the academy, at times meandering under the radar screen and at others more obviously fundamental in the foundation and framework of the college and university in America? A case can and will shortly be made for the existence of this relationship. In a corollary fashion the case also exists that the college and university in America has developed its unique counterpart to religion of the Republic, in this case what I have chosen to call a religion of the academy.

I recognize that the idea that there is a religion of the academy will be viewed as highly speculative. Understand that the intent is to provoke debate about the degree to which this proposition possibly holds water.

However, this idea, regardless its probity, merely hints at territory constituting a larger argument, one much less speculative. The assertion that follows is, I believe, seminal to understanding the history of the college and university in America: How have higher education and its institutions been shaped, and how have America's colleges and universities symbiotically shaped the nation and culture of which they are a part.

That overarching proposition is: Religion and religious affections and beliefs, in large measure those of Mead's religion of the Republic, have played both essentially veiled as well as substantively overt roles in the decisive formation of the college and university in America. This assertion will be fully elaborated in the chapter that follows. However, for the moment a capsule summary will flesh it out further for our present purposes.

The nascent creed of the young commonwealths that were to come together to found a Republic was freighted with core principles and beliefs, the overwhelming majority of them heftily theological, biblical, and obviously Christian. Indisputably these polities and their cultures developed simultaneously with the development of the college in America and the convictions and beliefs that were at the core of the academy. These two original institutions of the colonial era—the thirteen commonwealths and their colleges—came about side by side, each imbued with the values of the other. Especially it was the basic foundation of an emerging democracy and its social, public culture that created the environment in which the college and university developed.

This was the milieu that first shaped the college and university in America. A simple but frequently overlooked characteristic of this state of affairs is that the incipient values and principles that came to be at the crux of the Republic and later of a nation have continued to this day to have the same core influence on its colleges and universities.

In the early 1970s, LeRoy Moore suggested that the development of Mead's religion of the Republic in the twentieth century could well reveal further its relationship in this contemporary era to the university in America. "The story of this religion [of the Republic] in the twentieth century would undoubtedly focus significantly on the university which in so many respects displaced the church," Moore notes, citing Michael Novak "as 'spiritual center' . . . [and] source of guidance and legitimation' in our society. . . ."[7]

Novak's notion about the total eclipse of church was way ahead of its time. His predicted prospect that the university would displace the church as the "spiritual center" of American society remains yet largely unfulfilled, and may be simply a testimony about how the temper of the

1970s affected thinking, rationality, and presumptions about the pace and direction of social change.

While Novak's idea might appear today as an overreach well outside mainstream thinking, there is credibility about the ways the academy, living up to its highest ideals, can be construed as, and often is, a "spiritual center" of society and culture. The notion of the university as a social and culture center, maybe spiritual depending on how that term is understood, is not far-fetched as the history of the university can well attest from Bologna on, not to mention from the shorter history of its American days in the spiritual roots of Harvard. We need go no further than this same college in its later life as a full-blown university, with its own *Harvard Redbook* report of 1945 as evidence.

The authors of the faculty report that was the *Redbook*, addressing the demands of education and especially a "general education" to uphold democracy and democratic principles, contend that "A successful democracy (successful, that is, not merely as a system of government but, as democracy must be, in part as a *spiritual ideal*) demands that these traits and outlooks be shared so far as possible among all the people."[8] If democracy itself is a "spiritual ideal," and the university is to undergird its foundations through a regimen of general education, then presumably there is at least some spiritual component to the curriculum and learning, i.e., the place itself that generates that education.

The 1960s were times when Novak, no doubt like many others, became caught up in the ascendency of the university as a cultural force, due to its role as center of protests against the Vietnam War and civil rights. This political and social prominence no doubt led him to predict that the university would somehow supersede the church (Novak combining and collapsing denominational distinctions to argue a claim of the "church") as a national and cultural "spiritual center."

However, even if an overreach, Moore and Novak were on to something. That something is the overlap in creed, philosophy, and principles between the American nation reflected particularly in its religion of the Republic, and its colleges and universities as they were spawned and as the nation provided the landscape in which the academy thrived.

We will observe the character of this relationship at many points in our story. This connection between the political and social commonwealths that were the colonies and the early academy in America was at times mutually reinforcing and at other times one breeding friction and divisiveness. But regardless the level of meddling in each other's affairs, the religious tenor and temper of the different colonies was instrumental in the religious foundation of the Colonial Colleges.

Evidence of this intertwined colonial connection between what could be called the "state" and the growing diversity of religious sectarian forces, and how they pushed their style of higher education, persisted for some time in the nation's early history. Beginning in the late eighteenth

and through the early to mid-nineteenth century, attention to the demands of the "state" coupled with sectarian pushes and tugs remained as
considerations at the foundation of many in the generation of colleges
that were the offspring of the Colonial Colleges.

## THE MAJOR ERAS OF THE COLLEGE AND
## UNIVERSITY IN AMERICA

This era of the early years of the nation was religiously shaped and characterized originally by the First Great Awakening prior to the Revolutionary epoch, and later by the Second Great Awakening coming right
after the founding of the Republic, and into the early to mid-nineteenth
century. This period featured the birth of the new nation, ever-expanding
sectarianism, and the expansive founding of new colleges. These forces
moved both collectively and independently. Through it all, the relationship between the religion of the Republic and the sects of the new nation
continued to be one of unrelenting competition.[9]

The sects operated in an environment that allowed them to do what
they wished in a new nation that was the first in history to provide a
constitutional guarantee of not just religious toleration, but freedom of
religious expression. Thus each sect and denomination worked competi-
tively to assert and to prove its prescription for salvation.

Part of this competition was played out in the proliferation of denominational and sectarian colleges. Higher education institutions became one
battleground, arguably one of major consequence, as the religious sects
engaged each other seeking prominence, geographic hegemony, and cultural influence. The aspirations to build schools of learning were rooted
both in the beliefs of the sects and denominations, and in the nation's
convictions about what education could and must do for the lives of
individuals, and through them for society.

The individual identities of the Colonial Colleges were honed by this
continuing contest among competing sectarian factions, and their political, religious, theological, and ecclesiastical ideas and ideals. While
messy, these confrontations pushed each college to establish an identity
that distinguished it from the competitors.

As the next generation of colleges was founded, this competition set
up an expanded battleground between and among the sects and denominations of the Republic and the new nation as they clawed and scrapped
their ways to acceptance and notoriety. The denominations—Baptists,
Methodists, Lutherans, Presbyterians, Congregationalist, Mennonites,
and others—created what they each believed to be unique college cultures.

These religiously grounded campus worlds were designed to lure
their "faithful" to their gates. Of course, once they got the students inside,

the college's goal and promise was to protect, nurture, arguably educate, but more critically secure them, and by connection their families, in the denominational belief and practice.

During the Revolutionary War and Constitutional era of the latter eighteenth century, the Colonial Colleges observed and integrated the goings on in their midst. But they had also been contributors over a century and a half in creating and conveying to the forefront the now embryonically codified creed, beliefs, and values of the infant Republic—what was already its seminal "religion"—as the new nation was birthed.

The thread of religious influence and the canopy of the religion of the Republic thus woven into the fabric at the beginning has continued to be at stake as the decades and centuries of higher education institutions in America unfolded. Much later on, and ahead of our story, the Civil War created for both the nation and the academy a time of reflection about where the country was headed comparable to that at the founding.

The Civil War proved to be a major moment when the democracy of the still young Republic, presumed to be able to avoid such a divisive test, was forced to confront its creed, to figure out how to live it out with more integrity and to mature as a nation as a result of being propelled by its own failures onto the scaffold.

Colleges and universities at times transcended the warring, brother-against-brother world of that war. Many campuses had in their midst significant numbers of students from both the North and the South side by side, as roommates and fellow academic compatriots, and campus denizens. But the young colleges and universities, many of them barely decades old, were mired in the conflict.

Higher education institutions certainly could not deny their complicity in the slavery bargain drawn up in the Constitutional founding, and in the stands they had taken or failed to take over time concerning slavery and the life of blacks, both those on the plantations and those who were free. Colleges and their leaders and supporters were cast in the middle of arguments about whether slaves should be freed. Also, there were forever the difficult, if not impossible, to answer questions about the paltry numbers of matriculated black students.

Then there were the nagging questions both in the Antebellum and Reconstruction eras about what stood as the responsibility of educational institutions and of society for the plight of black Americans, not to mention aspirations for equality of both free and enslaved blacks. On top of these ethical and moral quandaries, the reality was also that conscription into the ranks of military service on both the Union and Confederate sides decimated student enrollments at all colleges.

Still later the Social Gospel and the accompanying Progressive Era of the burgeoning industrial age and revolution of late nineteenth and early twentieth centuries featured the involvement in higher education of a new and sophisticated class of leaders from the corporate and business world. The Social Gospel appeal fashioned the impetus and challenged these business tycoons to put their social and moral consciences and compasses on full display by founding and supporting the emerging research universities.

As a group these business moguls and philanthropists were leaders enlightened by the Social Gospel movement. Many of these barons of industry were "true believers" of the Christian moral preaching of the day, committed by personal faith to support colleges and universities as part of the push for social progress and reform.

Meanwhile as these new players in higher education got onto the stage, likewise the college presidents, faculty, alumni, donors, and other players at the colleges and universities that had existed for decades, and in some cases centuries, began pushing similar Social Gospel-inspired changes in education. These fellow leaders and educators were similarly exhorted by the temper of times. They ramped up the shaping of their institutions both internally and as viewed by external constituents to be more explicitly responsible than previously for the common good and for building a better society.

The principles and beliefs of the religion of the Republic and its democratic ideals as well as these overlapping and mutually reinforcing principles in the academy continued to be at stake throughout the twentieth century. In the span of six decades there were continual battles over patriotism and the confrontation with an array of real and imagined enemies.

In the run up to both world wars, but especially World War II, colleges and universities, their presidents, and faculty were caught up in debates about intervention versus isolationism, and about who was patriotic and who was not. The two world wars, as had the Civil War, decimated student enrollments. Many students never returned, though the GI Bill helped to ensure a college education to many others who survived and wanted to complete a college education.

A jarring dose and tragic regime of fear and repression were spawned on the back edge of World War II and as the Cold War took root. McCarthyism, despite its short reign, held sway dealing damage to academic liberty, freedom, and free speech.

Well-intentioned campus leaders, faculty, and outside political actors, some less well intentioned or even decent, squared off over loyalty to country, oaths, and recriminations about Communist Party and other feared personal and political affiliations. Epigrammatic lines from the McCarthy era such as "have you no shame," and "how do I get my reputation back" tragically typified the times in and outside the gates of the academy.

Lastly, as the tumultuous twentieth century moved further beyond its mid-point, the Vietnam and Civil Rights era of the 1960s and early 1970s became a social and cultural battleground. These times were yet another moment in the life of the nation and of college campuses pushed willy-nilly on center stage when many of the values and beliefs of American democracy were urgently contested within as well as outside the gates of the academy.

As a direct result of reactions and counter reactions discussed later, the 1960s era became a larger point of contention after its days than during. In the years since, the battles of the 60s and 70s have continued to be played out in ever more pronounced, at times bizarre and chilling, ways for the body politic.[10]

The unsurprising byproduct is that the combatants across the political and political correctness gamut relentlessly and cynically challenge each other's character, intentions and motivations both in- and outside the gates of the university. The result is frequent reliance on ad hominem attack to make political hay rather than informing civil discourse with intellectual substance and ideas.

In an ironic twist, these ideological forces, with equal conviction about the "rightness" of their beliefs and views (not to mention the high value of victories they believe to be within their grasp), are reminiscent of the bygone religious, sectarian battles for prominence and control of the academy. Those were times when the college was transparently used as a vehicle of social, cultural, and political dominance. This was the theological and philosophical modus operandi of the leaders of the Colonial Colleges and of the denominational sectarian folk establishing church outposts in the colleges of the early to mid-nineteenth century.

Interestingly, the twentieth- and twenty-first-century ideologues in the academy, equally on the Left and the Right, while not espousing religious beliefs per se, similarly view themselves and their enemies as reduced to camps of believers and non-believers, saints and heretics of that earlier bygone era. In ways that today's factions reflect but never acknowledge, they likewise go about their business misusing and distorting what the academy stands for.

As the twentieth century closed and the twenty-first dawned, renewed global crises, the specter of terrorism, and economic body blows have also concomitantly called into question the ideals of the nation's religion, and the religion and creed of the academy. Many of the issues at stake remain understandably inchoate, yet fully to develop. Thus a quest to suggest lasting trends could be viewed as a fool's errand.

However, other contemporary issues are rooted in both recent and the longer term history of the nation's colleges and universities. Taken together with the pivot points we have been discussing, we can derive a further sense for how the college and university in America has gotten to where it is and the lively experiment that marks that journey. As has been the case, the changing cultural, political, and social landscape of the United States and the foundation of the religion of the Republic continue to undergird the foundation of the academy in America.

What is the nature of this civic framework and its relationship to the academy? Who are the leaders, personalities, and commentators, and the issues and crises that have shaped America's colleges and universities? What have America's colleges and universities believed about themselves? To what degree and in what ways have they made contributions to the nation and society? What has been the relationship of America and its religion of the Republic, and of other religious forces, to the colleges and universities of the nation?

## THE UNIQUENESS OF AMERICA AND ITS
## COLLEGES AND UNIVERSITIES

The landscape of the Republic and of the American nation that was built on its republican foundation is distinctive and powerful. The American college and university is born in and out of a land, a time, a space which, as the world looks at this nation and as it looks at itself, has ever been declared unique.

America has always had the view, from the inside out and the outside in, that it was different from other countries. Foreign and domestic commentators have delivered interpretations about what America is and who is the American. These include, to name just a few, Alexis de Tocqueville and Jacques du Crevcour from abroad, and Thomas Jefferson, James Madison, Ben Franklin, and Frederick Jackson Turner from homefront.

What are the distinctive qualities that make up America? How are they connected in contiguous and compatible ways to the beliefs, values, and creed of its colleges and universities? In what ways do these mutually reinforcing qualities create the land and culture in which the colleges and universities of the nation find themselves, and in return permit the academy to have a hand in shaping that land and culture? How do the creed, beliefs, and values that form the lively experiment of the commonwealths that became the Republic and nation, manage to sit side by side with the mission, convictions, beliefs, and soul of the lively experiment of the colleges and universities of America?

The litany of the distinctive qualities that shape and form the American nation, and its higher education institutions, is arguably lengthy. However, a few characteristics that stand out, though subject to debate, are nonetheless prominent.

## AN ERRAND IN THE WORLD
## OF THE WILDERNESS

First, the pioneer colonists and inhabitants of the initial decades and century played their hand in a wilderness that fashioned the colonies, commonwealths, and their institutions. The idea of an "errand in the wilderness" was set at the outset of the journey and saga of the colonists and their commonwealths. Perry Miller offers a complicated yet invaluable series of comments about the emerging Republic in its eighteenth- and nineteenth-century face. Miller contends a major battle line in the "errand in the wilderness" was between "*the* American theme, of Nature and civilization."[11]

Miller defines Nature as an embrace of the natural world, the land, the forests, the wilderness, granted to human beings by God. Civilization is the taming of that wilderness in order to create society and to establish a polity. He reminds us of the recurrent theme that as civilization was wrought, the natural order was changed and in some cases desecrated. The winner is clear: Miller asserts that though "'Jeffersonians' [had] distrust of cities . . . the founders had no qualms about doing harm to nature by thrusting civilization upon it."[12] Thus, part of the errand became a necessity to tame the wilderness, with the colleges playing a role, rather than to accommodate to its powers.

The notion of "errand," for the colonists "in the wilderness," was not the pedestrian concept of going to get something and to return. Rather it was going out, not to return but to be on a journey about which they were duty-bound by God. Because of their beliefs, the colonists had a fervent sense of their obligation to be on this errand. It was not an ordinary errand. It was a challenging prospect. The errand was assumed to present obstacles to be overcome. And the players would become better people, better souls as a result of taking up this journey.

Without going overboard, the root of "to educate" is in part to be "led out." Indeed it could be argued that the first settlers were actually on a journey that was about their education as people. Their "educations" in England and elsewhere in the Old World no doubt informed their thinking about the "errand" in educational terms. Their founding colleges early on in that journey reflects the importance they attached to education as *the* prescription to enlarge human understanding, to craft a rational and just polity, and to better both the individual and society.

Further, theirs was a sacred errand, a righteous errand in which there was no delineation, as would be distinguished today, between the sacred and the secular. Those notions, for better and worse, were collapsed. Miller highlights the way John Winthrop argued this assumption in his classic sermon, "A Modell of Christian Charity," preached in 1630 (nine years after the first settlers in Massachusetts Bay and just six years before the founding of Harvard) to his followers onboard ship on the way to the New World.

Miller has little doubt about what Winthrop meant. The colonists would and should organize themselves to live and become a polity "'under a due form of Government both civil and ecclesiastical.'"[13]

Connected to the journey into a wilderness land, the first settlers and colonists, and even later the Founders of the nation (not to mention the founders of the Colonial Colleges) created an ethos that reflected the openness of the land, along with the pragmatism and practicality the environment necessitated. Generally, though not across the board, this meant resisting absolutes and ideology.

However, there was that obvious underside to the Pilgrims, Puritans, and early Massachusetts Bay inhabitants. Winthrop's preaching to his fellow travelers what they were and ought to be stands in stark contrast to American notions of pragmatism and adaptability. That is those governing the commonwealth were, in response to Winthrop's exhortations, to be dedicated believers, creating a social, cultural, and political state visibly grounded in faith and theology. Their ideas and conduct were to be similarly individually and communally rooted.

Miller describes that commonwealth as "the pure Biblical polity set forth in full detail by the New Testament . . . no denominational peculiarity but the very essence of organized Christianity." Thus what Winthrop's notions of "a due form of civil government meant, therefore, become crystal clear: a political regime, possessing power, which would consider its main function to be the erecting, protecting, and preserving of this form of polity." Miller contends that "This due form would have, at the very beginning of its list of responsibilities, the duty of suppressing heresy, of subduing or somehow getting rid of dissenters—of being, in short, *deliberately, vigorously, and consistently intolerant.*"[14]

Unsurprisingly this polity produced unintended offspring. Roger Williams proves to be unacceptable in the eyes of his fellow citizens. But mercifully both for him and for the Massachusetts Bay Puritans and Congregationalists who refused to tolerate him, there was a place to go across the immediate border to the south.

The Winthrop group used their strong beliefs to produce a college of their own with the founding of the first, Harvard (1636). Nearly simultaneously, because land and space "solved" the lack of tolerance accorded him and in order to avoid a likely severe punishment, Williams moved on with his fellow Baptist exiles. They found the Providence Plantations. This became Rhode Island, and much later the home of another alternative to Harvard, Brown University (1764).

Decades after Williams' expulsion, but ahead of the founding of Brown, Yale (1701) comes about because there was not enough room at Harvard for a recalcitrant batch of Congregationalists who no longer bought the Winthrop founding polity and theology. Meanwhile the Episcopalians of Virginia, with great unanimity and no opposition to speak of, certainly no Roger Williams in their midst, founded the second Colonial College, William and Mary (1693).

Thus geographical space and physical separation of warring parties became the ready solution to any problems that threatened to heighten controversy and contention. Certainly being able to push infidels out or having a place for them "voluntarily" to go helped to insure uniformity and at least superficial unanimity in the home commonwealth.

Religious, and along with it in a world where sacred and secular were collapsed, political, social, and cultural toleration did not exist. Yet contentious people and their ideas could still co-exist because separation and distance were there to be had. If you didn't like what someone was doing or represented, and or they didn't like you, you could simply march to another piece of the wilderness and expand the errand.

This ethos perforce affected the developing colleges and universities both overtly and covertly, because, if for no other reason, they emerged *in medias res*.

## RELATIONSHIP OF DEMOCRACY AND CULTURE

A second major distinctive characteristic of the American landscape is the intersection of democracy and culture. It took a while for this connection to develop to how we might think about it today. Early on in theocratic Puritan Massachusetts Bay, its citizens might have thought of themselves as democratic, at least compared to the reign of the King and the monarchy they had fled. But their version of democracy did not possess the ideals and expectations that formed later regarding diversity and difference.

However, from the beginning the nascent democratic ideas existed that would lead to the early Republic. These ideas became codified in the Constitutional era when the principles, values and beliefs, what comprises the creed of the United States, were formalized and affirmed.

The relationship of culture to democracy in the Republic and the nation is a chicken and egg proposition: Which to a greater degree engineers or underpins the other? Which if either of these social forces— culture or democracy—is a priori? Is this relationship merely symbiotic, both sides getting their say in relatively equal and balanced measure? Is democracy able to exist and be the political system in only certain types of cultures? Culture is the stuff of certain values and beliefs. Do those values and beliefs and the principles on which they are based precede the development of democratic principles and ideas? Or vice versa?

Edward Purcell takes a shot at these complex questions and the issues embedded in them. He utilizes the thinking of John Dewey and Jacques Barzun to explore the relationship between democracy and culture. However, as we will see, both of these men's ideas skirt the chicken and egg problem.

Dewey's ideas about the relationship among democracy, culture, values, principles, beliefs, and morality evolved over time. Summarizing that evolution, Purcell suggests, "Whatever one thought about the foundations of morality," Dewey reasoned, "strong individual and communal values in fact existed . . . such values arose out of a general cultural matrix which characterized every society. The crucial practical problem." And herein lies the rub of the chicken and egg issue, "confronting democracy, then, was the discovery of what kind of culture produced democratic institutions."[15]

Citing Dewey's further considerations, Purcell continues: "The problem of freedom and of democratic institutions . . . is tied up with the question of what kind of culture exists, with the necessity of free culture for free political institutions."[16] Many from Plato to Dewey have wrestled with this issue. Dewey comes out on the side of the contention that when a "free culture" comes about—the how's and why's of that not a simple matter—it is essential for it to have "free political institutions," all presumed foundation stones of democracy.

Free culture and free political institutions are organizing attributes for a democracy and democratic institutions. There might be other types of political organization, such as a radical libertarian society or a full-blown anarchy, in which it could be argued that things are "free," even if in total chaos, but that is another matter for another time.

Dewey concludes about the chicken and egg that "political institutions are an effect, not a cause."[17] If we buy Dewey and Purcell's interpretations, their assumptions attach to how America, its democratic foundations, and culture have been joined to its colleges and universities. The college, beginning in the early years of what would become the Republic, was an ideal, even if not always in reality presumed to be a "free institution" based on a "free culture." Here the foundations of higher education even in their early formation in America and of the American nation are absolutely overlapping and mutually reinforcing.

In parallel fashion, Purcell turns to Barzun in his *Of Human Freedom.* Barzun believes that democracy, rather than "an institution or a set of institutions . . ." is an "atmosphere and an attitude; in a word—a culture." This means that "Democracy is thus originally the result and not the cause of our deep-seated desire for diversity, freedom, and tolerance."[18] These characteristics—diversity, freedom, and tolerance—are at the core of the academy in America, not to mention in many of its forbears in Europe. Thus the college in the United States became at the outset a force for the fundamental values essential for a democracy.

From the get-go the landscape of what became the American Republic possessed these qualities. As both the college and university developed hand in hand with an emerging democracy and democratic nation, the Republic that was America came to pass.

These fundamental values of diversity, freedom, and tolerance have always remained at the foundation of both the nation and its colleges and universities. These values along with others that the academy features—intellectual inquiry, search for truth, the value of liberal education, open debate and dialogue and many more—are accepted as shot through the heritage of the university and are of equal importance to a democratic society.

Much of our debate today in and outside of the gates of the academy focuses on the degree to which we are still able to tolerate and to embrace these values. We will probe the dimensions of this problem and these controversies in full detail in a later chapter about free speech, academic freedom, and liberty in the academy. For now suffice it to say, sometimes we do, and sometimes tragically we don't.

Purcell ends his inquiry with summary thoughts. He asserts that regardless which are preeminent— the chicken and egg conundrum irresolvable despite the shots of Dewey and Barzun—both America's cultural as well as its civic and democratic principles and values, even beliefs, are all equally normative for American society.

Of interest in light of our discussion and narrative, Purcell draws a concluding connection that few others make and that places the university's role in our culture on a large pedestal. That is, in addition to its other cultural and democratic values, the culture, definition, mission, and ideals of the academy qua the college and university in America likewise stand as normative for American society.[19]

The only times when these normative qualities have been challenged, in Purcell's thinking, are in moments of deep crisis (e.g., the Civil War, World Wars, McCarthyism, and the conflicts of the 1960s). Only in such instances, and we might add since his writing events such as the September 11th terrorist attacks, are the normative assumptions embedded in America's culture and in its democratic foundations opened up for debate. Only then is change in these assumptions and values even contemplated, and this usually only by the most radical political elements.[20]

Thus when we consider this second characteristic unique to the American landscape—the close joining of its culture and democratic civic and political life—there is more than a hint of a crucial connection between the nation and its institutions of higher learning. That is, these clear principles and values of society, culture, and the public square are interwoven with and mutually bolstered by the beliefs and creed of the college in the era of the Republic and beyond.

## AMERICAN INDIVIDUALISM AND PATHWAYS TO EDUCATION

Another facet of what distinguishes and makes America unique and in part answers Crevcour's question of "Who is the American?" is a quality that many have noted: the citizen as individualist. This notion embodies the profound sense of autonomy and individuality that the first settlers through successive generations possessed. At the same time, individual-

ism in America does not contest, rather tends to uphold, even complement, communitarian needs and public virtue.

The American trait of individualism embraces the impulse to do it
"our" way. For generations, Americans have come to and inhabit a land
where little of the previous confines of space and of ways of living are in
play. Even where previous traditions remain at hand, they are scrutinized and subject to change in ways that would not be the case in a
homeland. Such is the effect of the new land of America on the beliefs
and conduct of waves of individuals who have come here.

Any immigrant can claim this distinguishing feature of America: i.e.,
everyone is an immigrant. Individualism, the "you can do it your way"
ethos, is a part of the lure that attracts people to this land. It is the reality
they find, and it is a normative impulse that they take on in adjusting to a
new place.

Another characteristic of the individualist in America is the lure of
choosing the path of becoming educated. The first Pilgrim and Puritan
settlers and those who inhabited other colonies and commonwealths had
the desire for education in their bones. They knew the value of education—a model many brought with them from England and elsewhere—
and the need to continue to educate themselves and successor generations.

The founding of Harvard just fifteen years after the arrival of the first
settlers in Massachusetts Bay is no accident. Neither was the founding of
the other Colonial Colleges, despite the tiny population of the colonies
from which interested students could be drawn; the million-population
threshold was not reached until 1750.

Long before Jefferson's entreaties about the essential need for an educated citizenry in a fledgling democracy born out of the Constitutional
era, the business of education was important to the development of the
Republic. The people and their commonwealths that were to become the
United States got into education early and often. They did so in unique
and innovative ways, especially when their actions, and the institutions
and schools they founded, are contrasted with the educational formulas
of their original homelands: In America, as education evolved it became
more public, less elitist, more for the common man and woman than
anything known in the Old World.

Because the colonists and founders believed in the common "man" in
ways that the monarchies of Europe did not, public education for the
masses beginning at grammar school was viewed as critical. Education
was something that could and must be done. This urgency about the
meaning of education began well before the nation got into the business
of major public federal funding of schools later in the mid to late nineteenth century.

Jefferson's views about education have been romanticized and subject
to misinterpretation. Be that as it may, he believed that for a democracy

to function, let alone flourish, an educated populace was indispensable. Absent that, citizens could not become sufficiently informed, and therefore would be subject to the actions of charlatans, to tyranny, and to problems corrosive of democratic decisions and process.

Furthermore, a body politic without education would not be capable of understanding what was needed, how individuals and communities should act, and how to shape a corporate existence. Thus there would be little hope for concerted, communal action, the exertion of the commonweal, to deal with issues and problems.

Viewed from the outside in and the inside out, the approach that the Colonial commonwealths and the founders at the nation's birth undertook in education contrasted fundamentally with their European forbears. Embedding education in the fabric of society, and public investment that supported it is another characteristic unique to the United States; it also contrasts with the social and educational heritage of the Old World.

From the beginning, education was critical to America's unfolding story as a nation. The seeds of education were implanted in the early colonies of New England and the Mid-Atlantic (less so and not until later in the South). Leaders of society were committed to the idea that education was an essential building block for individuals in fulfilling their lives and for a civil society in pursuing civic good.

Jefferson got out of the box early to make good on his interest in higher education, founding the University of Virginia as the nation's first truly public university. He did this in reaction to William and Mary, a college that he viewed as nearly public given its strong financial support at the time from the Virginia Colony.

A similar push for public university education came in another form from an idea of George Washington's. He and others proposed and sought, though it never happened, a centralized National University in Washington, DC. Its mission would have been to teach, inspire, and inculcate democratic values and political theory. In fact Washington's idea withered in the face of concern that it would feature central (federal) control. Another fear was that this university would establish intellectual uniformity harmful to the free exchange of ideas and to the development of a diverse array of higher education institutions.

All of this was enormously practical in the Jeffersonian tradition: uneducated masses would upend the democratic aspirations of the lively experiment that was underway. The earliest colonists' and the nation's founders' belief in education was connected to fundamental assumptions that education, through the values and beliefs it inspires, held the potential to shape society and culture.

That is not a European notion. It is a uniquely American notion. It is a commitment and an intention absolutely at the center of the lively experiment of the nation and of the academy in America.

## THE NATURE AND
## BATTLES OF INTELLECTUAL IDEAS

The last American characteristic bearing on the life of its colleges and universities is the relationship of religious and theological intellectual ideas to ideological arguments and polemics in the academy. In one sense this is an evolutionary aspect of the story of the college and university in America. That is, the Colonial Colleges were based in deeply held, in many cases uncompromising religious, Christian, sectarian beliefs.

Religious players from college presidents to their faculty, including the citizen leaders and public officials who supported these schools, ascribed to religiously based intellectual beliefs and accordingly led these first higher education institutions. As founders and leaders, they were invested in establishing and sustaining colleges that furthered the existence of sectarian and denominational ideas, and of religious—again sacred and secular collapsed—ways of thinking.

The story about how the intellectual ideas at the heart of the academy were closely connected to the life and development of the Republic is captivating. A brief review of the relationship of colleges and universities to the religious and philosophical intellectual ideas of the colonial era augments our narrative. Later the role of religion in the shaping of America and of its colleges and universities will be addressed at length.

J. David Hoeveler is a guide and provocateur about the manner in which religious intellectual ideas were significantly at stake and at the heart of debate during the colonial days and in the formation of the Colonial Colleges. He confirms impressions noted previously about the religiously formulated faith and belief, on occasion theocratic, nature of the nation's earliest colleges as they reflected the polities, theologies, and religious passions of the commonwealths from which they emerged.

Hoeveler asserts that the Colonial Colleges "were political to the core."[21] Given the ideal picture of the university qua the university as a place that should not be "political," the conclusion could be drawn that therefore these colleges were not true to "the university" ideal traditionally defined. However, delving deeper, the American story of the state of the college in the early decades and in the first century or more of its formation is more nuanced.

Hoeveler contends, and herein an important distinction, that the politics of these institutions, those that their presidents, faculty, and even students engaged were "politics of the intellect." That is, "A college's very identity embraced a position often painstakingly secured through elaborate argumentation, within an array of religious opinion, theological discourse, and denominational prescriptions that proliferated in the seventeenth and eighteenth centuries."[22]

Thus, though Hoeveler describes the Colonial Colleges as "political to the core," the reality is more nuanced. The image is more of educational institutions and their founders and leaders, albeit fervently sectarian and forcefully theologically energized, hacking out fundamental territory, but doing so nonetheless on the ground of thoughtful engagement of ideas. Viewed this way, the philosophy and actions of these institutions and their leaders are more in tune with the traditional underpinnings axiomatic in the foundation of the college and university.

Consequently it can be argued that these leaders and founders maneuvered in a fashion that was at its heart quite close to that of time-honored educators and their classic formulations of the university; that is, the Colonial leaders, presidents, and faculty, engaged in argument and discourse about ideas. They did so within distinctive frames of theology and belief. However, there were wide varieties of perspectives within even those silos.

The nuance is that these educators were willing to tussle with each other and dedicated to the outcome of that discourse. These leaders and founders wrestled with each other about their ideas and differences, and in the process they created their colleges.

However, we must resist overreach in this interpretation of how and why the founders of these commonwealths and of the tiny Colonial Colleges did what they did. Hoeveler's overall contention about what he calls the "Intellectual Founders" is that they sought to "establish authority in institutions," from their churches and schools, including colleges, to the commonwealth.

We have previously noted that the ideological battleground in the academy in America was foreshadowed at the outset. Regarding the launch of the first higher education institution—though this little college, Harvard, could hardly at the time be considered a higher education institution as we now know them—Hoeveler concludes that, "In establishing Harvard, the Intellectual Founders secured an institutional base for orthodoxy."[23] Thus the ideological battleground in the academy was put firmly in place from the inception of the first college in America.

On the other hand amid all of this shape-shifting, Hoeveler's judgment about the nine Colonial Colleges underscores the notion that their struggles, individually and their gamesmanship with each other, were fundamentally intellectual quests and fights. "The American Colonial Colleges grew amid the intellectual warfare of the seventeenth and eighteenth centuries," Hoeveler argues, "and they contributed to it." These colleges "partook of denominational struggles, sometimes within those denominations to which they belonged, sometimes within the contests for power and influence that set Protestant groups against each other in this period."[24]

Notwithstanding these ideological power struggles and tensions, most of that in the water of how they functioned and hacked out their identities, the Colonial Colleges primarily upheld the traditional heritage of the college as a place of inquiry, intellectual engagement, and character formation. In the colonies this meant good citizenship along with sectarian purity, and moral and ethical rectitude.

As these colleges fashioned themselves and in the ways they contended with each other, they did not violate the fundamental tenants of the college qua the college, or what would later be associated with the university. Ironically, despite all their wrangling Hoeveler believes that as a group their curricula "suggest a stark and unexciting uniformity."[25] However, he thinks even this unity has another feature.

This colonial era as "one of contest, of intellectual warfare both within and between the nine institutions," unfolded as it did because these first colleges "always looked out for their own particular publics." Certainly they had to, for "Indeed those publics created them."[26] Whether out of necessity or intentional design, or a combination, the formula for their existence was rather simple: "The colleges came into being, usually, when a religious denomination, or faction within it, had acquired sufficient self-consciousness and a particularized intellectual tradition of its own to give it institutional expression by way of a college founding."[27]

All and all, Hoeveler believes that developing individual identities in this way was not only a necessity but something in the end quite healthy. He asserts that, "Usually, in fact, these histories reflected both intramural and intermural conflict. Partisan confrontation was nothing new, then, when the American colleges entered into the revolutionary years of the 1760s and the events that carried the colonies into war against England in the next decade."[28]

Concluding his thoughts about how the Colonial Colleges got to be what they were and how they functioned at the origins of their era, Hoeveler ventures into the impact of their existence on the emerging identity of the Republic and nation. We will unravel the story of the relationship of America's colleges and universities to the religion of the Republic in great detail in the next chapter.

However, Hoeveler offers a glimpse and serves as a bridge to that inquiry. In the process he unveils yet another conundrum. In a return to his notions of "politics of the intellect" versus more straightforward, unvarnished political ideology, he concludes that as a result of engagement in the "politics of the intellect," the Colonial Colleges "evolved to become expressions of American nationalism."[29]

Furthermore, Hoeveler adds that the public rhetoric, writings, and leadership of elite graduates of the Colonial Colleges in the decades, years, and days prior to the Revolution do not lead to the conclusion that one could "describe the results as an American ideology as such." He believes, again pushing a prima fascia assumption, that "'American intellectual culture,' then provides a better reference than 'ideology' in describing the legacy of the American Colonial Colleges."[30]

The bottom line: The founders and other major public figures and thinkers who cut their educational teeth in the colleges were independent intellectual leaders, not rank ideologues representing narrow sectarian interests.

This means that "one is at pains to imagine the American Revolution and the creation of the new republic apart from the intellectual culture fashioned in these years. Those who founded the Colonial Colleges did not generally speak in nationalistic terms." Essentially the leaders of these colleges created classical curriculum and "filled their libraries with Christian literature, books on modern philosophy and science, and Whig political theories." As a result, Hoeveler believes that regardless what might have been intended and whether anyone envisioned this outcome, "In the middle of the eighteenth century, the collegians who studied them [these books and sources] created new documents of American nationhood."[31]

Hoeveler is focused on the heritage and shaping of the Colonial Colleges. He does not extend his argument about ideology and the "politics of the intellect" to possible connections to today's ideological landscape in the academy. But let's take a shot at doing so.

Hoeveler argues that the Colonial environment, both inside each commonwealth and as they related to each other, featured clashes of doctrine related to institutional identity that indeed mattered. These differences distinguished one place from another. Hoeveler finds that these displays of identity formation and the civil societies that were thus shaped, along with the colleges that were founded and established by these civil polities, were fully rooted in the "politics of the intellect."

The question is: What became of these early clashes of the "politics of the intellect?" What happened when the original theological and religious rule was eclipsed by less out-rightly sectarian controls? Are there contemporary vestiges, skeletons in the closet, of these primordial battles? A number of conclusions can be drawn.

First, we can conclude that there were clear ideological debates at the very beginnings of the academy in America. Hoeveler believes the first ideological controversies and battles were about a "politics of the intellect" rooted in theological ideas that were also at the foundations of social policy, of the commonweal, and of the commonwealth. He does not attempt to sanitize this picture.

However, Hoeveler contends that at their heart these were academic, intellectual scuffles about ideas. Even in their most extreme forms, they were not corrosive to historical notions about the foundations of the academy and the traditional concept of the college or university. In short, heated intellectual ideological argument was carried out without violating the ideals of the academy.

Second, Hoeveler's story runs through only the founding of the Colonial Colleges. His "politics of the intellect" provided the ground for how the mission and intentions of each of the colleges were hacked out. It is a story about the *raison d'être* of the ways these fledgling academies branded themselves, and how they viewed and related to each other. Here we find that in the beginning, the colleges in America were bulwarks dealing with competing forces, philosophies, theologies, and authorities of the day.

Hoeveler does not trace what happened in the aftermath of these very determined college founders getting their way. We don't know what he thinks about the degree to which their successors relied on the "politics of the intellect" to maintain themselves. The guess would be that these theological and philosophical ideas predominated for some time. He also doesn't get beyond the century and a half that he covers: Harvard, 1636 to Dartmouth, 1769.

These were the nine pre-Revolutionary forays into higher education in the new land. What happened in the Revolutionary epoch and beyond is another chapter in the story, though one that evolved on the foundations of the Colonial Colleges.

But we do know that as this chapter unfolded other competitor institutions, mostly also sectarian, emerged especially in the years of the Second Great Awakening. This was when, as previously noted, even more denominations entered the fray and proliferated throughout the now states and territories yet to become states of America. This was the time when the life and culture of the new nation moved into westward outposts.

It is reasonably conceivable that Hoeveler's "politics of the intellect" continued to be the way defined ideologies remained evident as higher education moved into its third century, that is from the early decades of the nineteenth to mid-century and beyond.

If we were to speculate when that ethos changed, it is likely toward the end of this antebellum era and into the Civil War and Reconstruction years. This was when research universities entered the playing field. That impetus resulted from both the import of the German model in places like Johns Hopkins and Cornell Universities and the initiatives under the Morrill Land Grant. This was the time when the earliest colleges matured and began to develop broader, less theologically driven, world-views.

At some point in this historical era, certainly by the early decades of the twentieth century, Hoeveler's colonial, theological, highly sectarian "politics of the intellect" was eclipsed. As our story unfolds we will speculate further about what may have replaced them, and how post the "politics of the intellect," politics and ideology in the academy evolved over time in America.

There is a third conclusion that can be drawn about this evolution of the "politics of the intellect," about the question of what became of Hoeveler's assumptions regarding the original modus operandi of the academy in America. That conclusion is that his era, and however long it lasted, stands in stark contrast to what is experienced today in the opening decades of the twenty-first century.

The contemporary scene within and outside the gates of colleges and universities, in contrast to the "politics of the intellect," is characterized more by the existence of politics for the sake of politics, what I call the "politics of ideology." What tends to be perpetuated now is ideological contention absent the ideals of Hoeveler's "politics of the intellect."

In the eyes of many critics and commentators, and with ever-increasing polemics in recent decades—the late 1970s or earlier to present—the out-rightly political has overtaken previous notions of how civil discourse and academic, scholarly inquiry are supposed to be conducted. Today, the modus operandi and modus vivendi are strongly characterized by clashes of polemical personalities carrying dyed-in-the wool assumptions and hard-edged political positions both in the academy and in the society in and around the gates.

The reality of life today in the academy, and in the media and other worlds outside the gates, can readily be contended as treating us more to politics that simply feature straw men and proxies as vehicles to argue points, and to jockey for power and influence. An idealistic interpretation could argue that these jockeying forces, at least within the academy, feature intellectual ideas undergirding their political passions and persuasions. However, it is easy to conclude to the contrary when confronted with arguments made for no reason other than rhetorical flourish and the hope to score ideological and political points.

The difference that distinguishes this picture of our contemporary scene of politicized battle of ideologies from Hoeveler's "politics of the intellect" may appear small. It could be contended that there is no difference at all; that is, to claim that Hoeveler's Colonial College world was every bit as out-rightly ideologically driven as ours and that his "politics of the intellect" is a chimera.

Such as there is a difference from his time to ours, the pivot point rests on a two-fold set of assumptions. The first is that Hoeveler's belief that the "politics of the intellect" transcended the ideology of theological and religious clashes is questionable. Second, that what I am calling the more contemporary "politics of ideology" generally lack foundation in intellectual ideas and thought, but are rather mere politics for their own sake.

If these assumptions are accurate, the difference is significant. If these assumptions don't hold, the space is quite narrow between Hoeveler's era of the "politics of the intellect" and the contemporary world of the politics of ideology.

However, even marginal change in the role of ideology from the eighteenth century to today suggests a threat to the fundamental values of the university. In either case, the role of ideology in the academy is a feature of where we are and how we got here. This analysis is also crucial to any assessment of the present-day battles for control of the university.

In this latter case, the "politics of ideology," especially absent commitment to the classical ideals of academic and intellectual inquiry, place the identity and future of the university qua the university at risk. The danger is that the university as we would like to think we have known it, erodes to a place where ideologies fight for ascendancy and control. The academy would then be defined by whatever political force "wins" at any point in time and is thus enabled to enforce its ideological bent.

I am proposing that there is a difference between ideological battles fought out by the "politics of the intellect," rooted as they were in theological, religious, and philosophical ideas, and the "politics of ideology" that are blatantly political. This leads to an ideal wish that even if elusive is worth pursuit. That ideal is the aspiration to re-instill a culture in the academy in which ideological differences and controversies are engaged on the basis of philosophical ideas and genuine discourse about intellectual deliberation.

The philosophical positions and ideas in the academy today would of course be cast in non-sectarian terms. Nonetheless even when the expression of beliefs and convictions get close to the religious grounding of a bygone era, they would nonetheless be argued in line with the fundamental ideals and heritage of the college and university. This battleground of ideas would be preferable to academic discourse shot through with politics alone.

We have witnessed the initial results of disintegration of supposedly academic conduct and public rhetoric in the present ideological battleground. The result of ideological warring parties with little quarter for the views of the other side has born extreme costs in- and outside the gates of the academy. Further, it is certainly not the tone of intellectual inquiry, search for truth, and embrace of diverse viewpoints historically and ideally situated in the bedrock of the university.

## NOTES

1. Seymour Martin Lipset, *The First New Nation: the United States in Historical and Comparative Perspective* (New York: Basic Books, 1963).

2. Sidney E. Mead, *The Old Religion in the Brave New World: Reflections on the Relation Between Christendom and the Republic* (Berkeley, LA, and London: University of California Press, 1977), 106.

3. Sidney E. Mead, *The Lively Experiment: The Shaping of Christianity in America* (New York: Harper and Row, 1963), 24.

4. Ibid.

5. Ibid., 26.

6. "A lively experiment" was how John Clarke and Roger Williams characterized the impetus of the petitioners who were to be the founders of Rhode Island when they appealed for a charter from the King of England. See Mead, frontispiece.

7. LeRoy Moore, "Sidney Mead's Understanding of America," *Journal of the American Academy of Religion* 44, no. 1 (March 1976): 133–53, 148. As an important aside, Moore's dissertation advisor was Sidney Mead, and Moore was my advisor in my master's thesis. I am clearly indebted to both and can only hope that my ideas are as worthy as are theirs.

8. Harry R. Lewis, *Excellence Without a Soul: Does Liberal Education Have a Future?* (New York: Public Affairs, 2006), 53. Italics mine.

9. For a tour de force description of this tangled relationship, see Mead, *The Old Religion in the Brave New World,* especially his opening chapter, 1–31 in which he lines out the argument that is the remainder of the book.

10. See Stephen J. Nelson, *Decades of Chaos and Revolution: Showdowns for College Presidents* (Lanhman, MD: Rowman & Littlefield, 2012).

11. Perry Miller, *Errand into the Wilderness* (Cambridge, MA: The Belknap Press of Harvard University, 1964), 205. Miller's entire essay, "Nature and the National Ego," (204–16) is an extended commentary on these themes and worthy of reading.

12. Ibid., 207.

13. Ibid., 5.

14. Ibid., 5, italics mine.

15. Edward A. Purcell, Jr., *The Crisis of Democratic Theory* (Lexington, KY: University of Kentucky Press, 1973), 211.

16. Ibid., 211–12.

17. Ibid., 212.

18. Ibid., from Jacques Barzun, *Of Human Freedom* (Boston: Little, Brown and Company, 1939), 40.

19. Ibid., 256–58.

20. Ibid.

21. J. David Hoeveler, *Creating the American Mind: Intellect and Politics in the Colonial Colleges* (Lanham, MD: Rowman & Littlefield Publishers, 2002), ix. Hoeveler's work is an extraordinarily well-researched and narrated journey through the original nine Colonial Colleges, and the heritage, context and foundation on which each were built.

22. Ibid., x.

23. Ibid., 28–29.

24. Ibid., 241.

25. Ibid., 347.

26. Ibid.

27. Ibid., 347.

28. Ibid., 241.

29. Ibid., 348.

30. Ibid., 349.

31. Ibid.

# ONE

## Religion in the Nation and the Academy

Religion has played a vast role in the history of the college and university in America. This bearing prompts an inquisitive proposition about that role. The proposition: The religion of the Republic has been a crucial thread throughout the history of the college and university in America. This civil religion emerged in its nascent, pre-Republic form during the days of the Colonial Colleges, developing as a public creedal underpinning of the commonwealths and the civic polities that later became the "united" states of the nation.

Added to this notion is the proposition that the religion of the Republic has today replaced the "church," (more about this in a moment, but the quotation marks indicate the proviso) in the classic three-legged stool of the state, the "church" or religion, and education, including the higher education of America's colleges and universities.

Consider this proposition as a lens through which to view the college and university in America, one which, by providing a fresh angle, can enlighten our thinking about the formation of the college and university.

### THE RELATIONSHIP OF RELIGION TO THE COLLEGE AND UNIVERSITY IN AMERICA

Religion was the most conspicuous feature in the founding of the colonies. A snapshot history of events and players sheds light on our understanding of the relationship of religion and of the religion of the Republic to the college and university in America.

As noted, the religious foundations of the original colonies ranged from heavily theocratic to domination by one, or at most two, Protestant denominations or sects. In this seventeenth-century era, the Protestant Reformation is barely over a hundred years old. Therefore these denominations had yet to be formed as distinctively as became the case decades and centuries later.

However, despite their youth in the new land, lines of demarcation between Protestant denominations were already significant. At the same time, the New World afforded convenient geographical separation and distance. More severe competition among the sects and denominations emerged later on.

For example, Massachusetts Bay was the haven of the Puritan-Congregationalists; Virginia of the Episcopalians; Pennsylvania of the Quakers; Maryland of Roman Catholics; Rhode Island of the renegade Puritan, later to become Baptist Roger Williams; and Connecticut of other splintered Congregationalists led by Thomas Hooker from Massachusetts. Some of these colonies, including the heavy-handed theocracy of Massachusetts Bay, had mandated public taxes paid by the citizenry to support "the church," regardless of whether the tax payer was a member or not.

The similarity among the colonies was that they were comprised of distinctive denominations and in many cases run by highly sectarian leaders. With fervently religiously inspired civil and civic polities, it is no surprise that there were equally strong ties between religious influence and these commonwealths, and the Colonial Colleges founded in their midst.

Crucial to our story is the manner in which religious influence was carried into the colleges that were established in the colonies. Higher education quickly became a vital building block in the bulwark to fortify citizens and the "state" in the wilderness of the new land. Thus colleges were crucial in the quest to secure and to sustain the colonial life and prosperity.

This generally Protestant Christian sectarian constellation (Roman Catholic influence in Maryland excepted, and they had no hand in founding a college in the colonial era) remained the overriding predominant religious force in the development of colleges throughout early decades of the establishment of the Republic. However, an even greater sectarian influence in the culture of colleges came to the fore as the denominations entered direct geographic competition as the Republic spread westward in the colonies and beyond to other territories, soon to became states.

At that time in the early antebellum and Second Great Awakening eras, an increasingly diverse and swelling proliferation of Christian sects and denominations entered the fray. A large part of this growth directly resulted from the now constitutionally established freedom of religion, not mere toleration of religious differences. Thus, if one believed something ever so slightly different from the beliefs of the next-door neighbor, he had constitutional rights to found his own religious sect and to go about freely evangelizing.

The original constitutional idea of founding one's own religion was the particular genius of Jefferson and those who bought his views about religious freedom. That is, Jefferson intended this competition, even the degree to which it quickly developed from the get-go. Jefferson's democracy was to be a political system sans a state church. Religious freedom as widely pursued as possible was indispensible to preserve the democracy and government he envisioned.

Jefferson and many fellow founders were committed to avoid the establishment of a state church, the role the Anglican Church played in the homeland of England. This stance grew from firsthand experience of how an ecclesiastical seat of power competed and challenged the standing government and its politics. Thus the founders made sure that the Constitution would prevent "establishment" of a national church or religion.

With the corollary invocation of religious freedom, the sects were free to be founded, to proliferate, to thrive, and to compete with each other. In the eyes of the founders this was an indispensable alternative to the prospect of sectarian energies, especially in the form of a "state church" competing with and challenging the state. Openly permitted, even encouraged to compete with each other, the founders knew well where the sectarian passions would have to be directed: fighting for individual group survival.

We divert slightly from the central theme of our story, that of the shape and shaping of the college and university in America. But not far given that the churches, sects, and denominations exercised their respective and distinct (even if not radically different) religious beliefs as the core of their aspirations for higher education. The result was that Christian Protestant religious beliefs and convictions imbued the missions, purposes, values, beliefs, and ideals of the earliest colleges in America that followed immediately in the footsteps of the religious foundations of their Colonial College forbears.

Hence in the post-Constitutional, antebellum period, the sects used the founding of colleges and the battles for student enrollment as the way to serve the interests of their followers. What better way to exhibit seriousness of commitment and purpose than to provide religious education for the children of believers in the pursuit a college education? Founding colleges was also an avenue for the sects to advertise particularistic denominational beliefs and ends.

In the process of rushing to found colleges, the sects and denominations upped the ante in their competition with each other. Interestingly this included the Catholics, through the Jesuits founding Georgetown College in 1789. However, the religious identity of the colleges and of course of the nation still remained broadly Protestant Christian for most of the first half of the nineteenth century.

As the settlements marched westward, numerous denominational, sectarian campus beachheads were established throughout central and

western Pennsylvania, Ohio, Illinois, Indiana, and elsewhere in the Midwest. This development accelerated through the opening decades of the
nineteenth century. This was especially true in the 1820s and 30s as passions of the Second Great Awakening became more evident. The Roman
Catholics joined the fray in the frontier inhabited heavily by the Protestant sects and denominations by founding Notre Dame in 1844, though
this was nearly a half century after Georgetown's creation.

Major competition unfolded when the public universities marched
onto the scene. The first major public universities coming to the fore at
the mid-point of the nineteenth century challenged this Protestant sectarian hegemony for campus supremacy. No longer would Protestant sects
and denominations have exclusive province.

These new universities by definition as public institutions did not
have specific religious roots and religious interests at their foundations.
However, that did not preclude them from identifying with the religious
tenor of the country and that of its other colleges and universities. At this
point in the mid-nineteenth century the religious character of national
culture and of the campuses was shifting from being dominated by Protestant sectarianism to a broadly mainstream protean Christian, and
shortly Judeo-Christian identity.

Soon the major research university arrived in a number of forms. The
major push of public universities resulted from the Morrill Act in 1862,
Cornell University (1865) one of the first out of the chute. However, it
would be decades before the early impact of the universities founded as
"land grants" would be felt.

Johns Hopkins (1876) is often cited as the first import of the German
research university to the United States. The University of Michigan, another example of the German university, though founded in the early
nineteenth century (1817), did not take on the makings of a major public
university until the mid-1840s after it had moved from Detroit to Ann
Arbor.[1] Its first president, Henry Tappan, was not appointed until 1852,
marking the inception of the university as it has been known in the century and a half since.[2]

The religious cultural attachment of the American college and university reflecting the nation evolved toward a more inclusive Judeo-Christian, rather than specifically Christian, character. Thus these newly established institutions, mostly larger universities, were not afraid of being
viewed as Judeo-Christian, the label assumed as the major religious identity in the country. However, these mid to late nineteenth-century universities, public and private, avoided any prospect of being tagged as sectarian or denominational even where they might boast of Judeo-Christian
trappings.

Thus we find many of these research universities pushed back against
religious influences by clearly fashioning themselves as intentionally
non-sectarian. This no doubt (as we will see momentarily from Cornell's

Andrew White's stinging comments below) reflects the fact that the ambitious sectarian and high evangelical era, particularly heralded by the Second Great Awakening earlier in the nineteenth century, had run its course.

The mission of the research universities embraced the rhetoric of objectivity, science, and discovery to a greater degree than was the case with the Colonial Colleges and the colleges immediately founded in their wake. Thus, the founders of major research universities wanted and needed to convince themselves and the public that the full, free inquiry and pursuit of truth and knowledge, yoked as the core of the research university, was their uncompromising goal.

Ideological, sectarian religious thinking coupled with its inevitable prejudices could not be permitted to enter this academic circle of the "new," emerging research universities. There could not be any hint of partisan control of curriculum, appointments, or the pursuit of instruction and knowledge. Cornell's charter, for example, drew the distinction that it would be free of specific institutional religious orientation. Like Brown University earlier, Cornell's charter states that, "Persons of every religious denomination, or of no religious denomination, shall be equally eligible to all offices and appointments."[3]

Frederick Rudolph notes Andrew White's, Cornell's first president, sarcastic comment that the pre-Cornell history of American higher education was "the regime of petty sectarian colleges."[4] However, Rudolph quickly dissects White's diatribe, challenging aspects of the foregoing argument that the Protestant sects and denominations had for decades been in a cutthroat competition, vying with one another by using the founding of colleges as the vehicle to battle each other.

Rudolph chooses to substitute for "the regime of petty sectarian colleges" rather the "regime of the religiously-oriented college."[5] The reason "'religious-oriented' is more satisfactory" to Rudolph "than 'petty sectarian' is that White's phrase did not accommodate the paradox that while most colleges of the period were founded by denominations, they were also forbidden either by charge or public opinion to indulge in religious tests for faculty or students."[6]

The result was that "the nineteenth-century American college could not support itself on a regimen of petty sectarianism." This was the case for a couple of reasons: "there simply were not enough petty sectarians or, if there were, there was no way of getting them to the petty sectarian colleges in sufficient numbers. The high mortality rate of colleges in the first half of the nineteenth century was proof that petty sectarianism did not pay off."[7]

Rudolph asserts this moderate take on what had been going on during the Great Awakening and in the engaged sectarian battles. He points out that this assessment was especially true in the race to found colleges as bulwarks of faith and practice in targeted geographic locales. His proposition is that many of these colleges, whether legally permitted, refused actively to argue for discriminatory practices, pitting their religious views and identity against those of others.

However, there is little doubt that in practice things did not always work out so neatly or clearly. And Rudolph, unlike Sidney Mead, is a historian of higher education in America, not a historian of religion in America. Rudolph has a piece of the puzzle, yet it is a piece that may not fully account for the deeply partisan and passionate sectarian differences that were well in the mix.

Furthermore, we should note that in the allegation about "petty sectarian colleges," White was merely taking stock of the context of what had been going on, probably since the founding of Harvard, but certainly in the earlier decades of the nineteenth century and the Second Great Awakening. That is, sectarianism, whether petty or a monopoly approach to founding colleges, had been holding sway.

White believed there was sufficient evidence for his assessment about the threat posed by sectarian forces. He saw them as attacking Cornell as "a stronghold—first of ideas in religion antagonistic to their own; and secondly, of ideas in education likely to injure their sectarian colleges."[8] He obviously didn't think that these sectarian groups could topple Cornell, any more than they had been able to stop its creation. But they were obviously about in the land. Non-sectarian higher education leaders perceived the threat caused by sectarians to be tangible, and thus issued jeremiads such as White's against it.

At the same time, as an educator and new university president White was also well aware that at this point in the nineteenth century, sectarianism's province over the direction of the American college and university had probably reached its apex and was in decline. No matter other debates about White's intentions, sectarian influence was clearly waning.

Henry Tappan, a fellow major and public university president, echoes White's sentiments. Tappan too saw the sectarian forces amassed at the gates of the academy, hurling criticism at what he and White were trying to build. Tappan has no problem with Christianity as an overarching identity for the university. The trouble was that sectarianism with its "either-or," and "our way or the highway" mentality, especially in its most extreme forms, threatened hopes of a commonweal.

Tappan asserts that, "The University [of Michigan] as an institution of the state, open to all the people of the state, and affording to them the means of the highest education, is a symbol of the essential union of all religious sects, and of all political parties."[9] In the ideological competition of today, that ideal might look naïve. It may have been so in Tappan's time. But he wields it nonetheless. Tappan's ideal contends that the university is a center of society, a centrist institution that can, as he puts it, be "an essential union" of competing interests and ideas.

Amplifying on this unity theme, Tappan adds: "We are all Christians, we are all American citizens." In a critical piece of advice worthy of attention from the academy of the early twenty-first century, particularly in the continuing era of political correctness that began in the 1970s, Tappen concludes:

> Whatever may be our differences, we have a common agreement—a common interest in the great subject of education.—It is the part of wisdom to preserve the University intact from the questions on which we differ, and to maintain and foster it purely as an educational institution.[10]

Here is a major university president, in the early days of the advent of the research university in America, making a crucial argument about what the university should be. Tappen's message is clear: If the historic tradition and foundation of the university is to be preserved, the university must be the university. It cannot risk falling into the trap of allowing ideological argument to tear at its foundation, thereby turning the university into simply one other institution in society, no longer the university.

This primarily Judeo-Christian cultural tradition that Tappan urges continued to be the overarching, generally accepted religious signature of American society and of its colleges and universities from this latter portion of the nineteenth through much of the twentieth century. Throughout this period, the Judeo-Christian heritage was at least the majority affiliation of the nation, even if not necessarily the belief or practice of a majority of citizens.

Nonetheless, the Judeo-Christian cultural tradition served as a foremost bond for the nation. Even if not acknowledged formally, colleges and universities, public and private, large and small, of this time affirmed this tradition as a significant part of the foundation of how they understood who they were.

Even out-rightly nonsectarian universities still broadly identified with the Judeo-Christian tradition as the commonly assumed religious basis of the nation. This included those such as Johns Hopkins, and later in the nineteenth century the University of Chicago and Stanford, of course along with the increasingly numerous public universities of all sizes and shapes. In the latter twentieth and into the twenty-first centuries, the Judeo-Christian label has gradually been stretched in a more inclusive, multi-religious way, enfolding belief and faith traditions such as Islam, Hinduism, and many other major world religions.

Some argue that the religious glue of America can today more appropriately be collectively labeled as the Abrahamic tradition, combining at least Christian, Jewish, and Muslim traditions. However, even that is not sufficiently inclusive, as so many major religions fall well outside that nexus. However we might characterize it, the United States has certainly become arguably more multi-cultural. This place that has been a magnet for the "tired and poor" from nearly every nation, has also become extraordinarily more multi-religious.

Suffice it to say that the college and university in America has come a long way in nearly four hundred years from its highly sectarian, denominational, exclusively Protestant roots and heritage. Harvard is no longer a sectarian, Puritan-Congregational College and University. That may be its heritage, but Harvard is many years removed from searching for minister-presidents from Congregationalists (today's United Church of Christ).

Brown University was never Baptist run, though it did have an enormously close relationship with the Baptists throughout its history. After all, its first non-Baptist minister president was Henry Wriston in 1937. He was Brown's eleventh president; ten predecessors over its first 175 years were ordained Baptist clergy. But Brown is unlikely, and then probably only as an accident, ever again to have a Baptist minister as president.

The many denominational colleges [e.g., Gettysburg (1832) Lutheran; Kenyon (1824) Episcopalian; Duke (1838) Methodist, the list could go on] founded during the Second Great Awakening may still officially acknowledge their denominational "tie." But those connections are today barely a shadow of what they once were. Such religious links are no longer as strong as they once were and will not in any near future return to the stature of earlier days of towering denominational control and identity.

Even Catholic colleges face challenges regarding the tension between maintaining strong religious ties and the identity of their Catholic heritage with the demands of what it is to be the university. No one grappled with this issue more comprehensively and distinctively than Cardinal Newman.[11]

His take was essentially a coming of age for Catholic education, an argument that the preeminent goal had to be insuring that the university be the university, no matter attachment to Roman Catholic theology and belief. Newman, for example, believed that theology had to be part of any university, part of the curriculum, not unto itself, but so that it along with other fields of study and inquiry would be forced into intellectual dialogue and argument.

By definition American Catholic universities are quite clear about the religious nature of their campuses and support of Catholic beliefs and faith. However, for the most elite Catholic schools such as Notre Dame, Georgetown, and Boston College, this becomes more complicated as they strive at the same time to present a public face of adherence to the traditional principles of the university.

Their religious identity is not in doubt. Nonetheless to be major players, these Catholic universities must simultaneously take great pains to recruit and to retain highly diverse and scholarly research-oriented faculty, as well as to matriculate significant numbers of students from non-Catholic or non-religious traditions. Roman Catholic colleges and universities reflect and imbue the continuing influence of Cardinal Newman: that they be true, whatever else they do, to the fundamental tenets of the university.

Are religious identities and practitioners drawn from all manner of world religions evident at today's colleges and universities? Absolutely, represented by vast religious diversity of students, faculty, and in the leadership of head chaplains (of the university, deans of the chapel and such by title) along with chaplains—rabbis, priests, ministers, imams, and the like—dispatched to serve these major religious traditions and the organizations that support them on campus.

This is a previously unprecedented level of intentional acknowledgement of religious diversity in campus life. As noted, much more than in the past, this is the multi-religious face of the multiculturalism spread throughout the nation and its campuses in the last fifty years and more.

This contemporary take on religion on campus—most accurately described as multi-faith, multi-religious—reflects and represents where American society finds itself at the beginning of the twenty-first century. Indeed it well has been this diverse for a longer period of time than is often conventionally projected. That is, assertions about what is a majority are based on superficial assumptions. Such judgments risk ignoring the greater diversity shot through all societies and cultures.

Certainly today no mainstream college president (excepting those leading purely evangelical, Christian colleges) could come close to claiming as Tappan did that "We are all Christians, we are all American citizens." They could substitute "we are all multi-religious." However, that meaning while more inclusive than Tappan's—though he was not fully accurate with the assignation that "we are all Christians"—is nebulous, bordering on meaningless.

Presidents today might arguably use the second of Tappan's phrases, "we are all American citizens." However, due to the global reach of universities and colleges, that too fails to represent the variety of nationalities on most campuses today.

This reality further underscores the scale of diversity, evident religiously and geographically, that is the world of higher education today as compared to previous history. Nonetheless, despite the great diversity of students on most college campuses, the American college and university's "when in Rome do as the Romans do" style reflects the fabric of the nation, influenced by that milieu.

## RELIGION, THE RELIGION OF THE REPUBLIC,
## AND THE LIFE OF THE ACADEMY

The influence of the religion of the Republic began before the actual Republic in America was constitutionally formed. As the first settlers and their commonwealths gained a foothold in a new land in the prior century and a half, the nascent core beliefs and civic creed of what could later be called the religion of the Republic were tangibly emerging. At the nation's founding in the last decades of the nineteenth century these beliefs, principles, values, and traditions were legally formulated and constitutionally implanted. From that point this creed formally constituted what could then be called the religion of the Republic.

There are varied interpretations of the role of religion in the foundations and development of the emerging Republic. What went on for the nation religiously, also influenced the shape and shaping of the college and university. A further unique aspect of America is the additional role that its religion of the Republic played in the life and formation of the academy.

What evidence is there for this proposition that the religion of the Republic has always been a deep current in the water underlying the denominational and sectarian, and later more inclusive religious traditions that floated on the surface of the life of colleges and universities throughout their history in the United States?

To understand the complexion of this story, we need to grapple with a number of questions. First, what is the formed nature of the religion of the Republic? Second, what is the relationship of this civil religion to the shape and shaping of the college and university in the United States?

There are key facets to this latter question: How the religion of the Republic provided an underlying, organizing thread throughout the formation of the college in America. How this religion paralleled the more conventionally acknowledged denominational and sectarian religious inclinations in the nation and in the academy. How and in what ways this civil religion in America contributed to the framework of the role of religion in the academy.

Finally, we explore the prospect that the religion of the Republic today is in the forefront as a commonly agreed religious identification and presence in the foundation of the college and university in America.

Recapping what we have seen, the nutshell history of religion in the academy initially featured the fervent sway of denominational, sectarian religion. Next, colleges and universities took on religious identification as more broadly Christian and slightly later Judeo-Christian. Later and into recent times, the academy's religious identity is now multi-faith, with even its secular values drawn broadly from religious principles. These evolutionary religious characterizations have been continuously accompanied by the religion of the Republic in the foundation of the nation and in similar fashion of the academy.

That is to say that the religion of the Republic primarily lurked beneath the surface of the sectarian, denominational, Roman Catholic, Jewish, and other religions as they individually and corporately contributed to religious history of the nation. This civil religion had its own formative credibility and visibility. That is the religion of the Republic complemented and undergirded organized religious institutional life and traditions in America.

However subsequently, and here is the unique slant I suggest, the religion of the Republic gradually—conjecture about when in a moment—displaced the role these combined religious traditions played as the third leg, nominally the "church"—the other two legs: the state and education—of American society and culture. These diverse religions had long comprised the religious culture of colleges and universities and complemented normative values in academic and campus life. But over time, the religion of the Republic became even more prominent as the religious "faith" furnishing that role.

It is beyond our scope to say precisely when this religious state of affairs came about. However, suffice it to say that it was a gradual process, likely a century or more in the making, for America's civil religion to become the primary religious underpinning in the academy.

Hazarding a guess, it can be argued that the post-World War II patriotic rush coupled with the desire to build American society after the war, quickly followed by the tumultuous events of the 1960s and early 1970s, pushed the religion of the Republic into a prominent position, religiously grounding the academy. Not coincidentally, this is when the civil religion and an array of comparable terminology first came to the fore, and a slew of ideas about it were developed, in no small measure, as a result of Robert Bellah's and Sidney Mead's ground-breaking thinking, both in the auspicious year, 1967.[12]

The religion of the Republic is the national religion of the America. It embraces the nation's creed, its belief system, and its commonly agreed principles and values. These are the ideals that constitute the nation's founding documents—Declaration of Independence, the Constitution, and the Bill of Rights—and the theology, traditions, and homiletics that have grown up and developed, embellishing and extracting meaning from this seminal framework.

The religion of the Republic is an organic religious faith and constellation of beliefs. It is ever subject to reinterpretations necessitated when those ideals have been forced, usually in times of decisive national crisis, to the center of controversy, debate, and social, cultural and political divisions. It is particularly at those points that the "creed" has undergone scrutiny, questioning, and resulting reinterpretation about meaning.

There exists a crucial overlap in the beliefs, convictions, and values of the academy in America with these core tenants of the religion of the Republic. Examples and the particulars of the reinforcing faith declarations abound.

One is the assertion that all people are created equal and that they are endowed by a Creator, defined as one might wish, but pretty clearly what the Deist founders meant, with unalienable rights. Folks in the academy might stint on the "Creator" notion, but they will likely assert that something exists, whether out there or more down to earth, grander than and transcending human beings.

Added to those notions is belief in "life, liberty, and the pursuit of happiness," values that underscore the central importance of the individual in American society and in the academy. At the same time there is the strong inference, if not outright belief, that people are placed on the earth to do good, to improve their own fortunes and those of their fellow human beings, society, and culture. That society is supposed to progress and problems are to be solved or at least ameliorated.

Under this canopy, men and women are expected to advance the human prospect and to improve society and culture as we know and inherit them. Education serves to magnify and enhance this prospect. The common good, the commonweal, is to be pursued, though that quest will of course always be in persistent tension with the rights, privileges, and interests of the individual. Finally, democratic principles are the way we adjudicate or at least ameliorate that tension, and our social and political conflicts and controversies. All this is engaged in the aspiration of maintaining a generally free yet secure society.

The list could go on. But the simple, though frequently ignored point is that it is no accident that the college and university has developed as it has given the social, political, cultural, and ideological climate in which it has grown since the founding of Harvard in 1636.

Benjamin Franklin asserted, an idea no doubt shared by most fellow founders, that there were a dozen or so universal, eclectic, and commonly agreed beliefs, even faith statements, that nearly every religion embodied to one degree or another, and on which they tend to concur.

Franklin's ultimate tenets include a belief in a Deity; that this power is a force for good; that men (and women) have had "life and reason" bestowed (rights and abilities not earned or deserved) on them; that there is something in the human being that leads to devotion or worship; that the best way to honor the Creator is to do good in the world; and that the many virtues in which Franklin would seek refuge throughout his life, including his "13," are in one way or another exhorted by the Deity on creation and are standards of behavior human beings are driven to uphold as their part of the bargain.[13]

Franklin was convinced that these are "the" overarching beliefs that bring people together. Further, these beliefs have the capacity to convince even those from divergent, at times hostile, religious quarters, that they share a common lot. Arguably those involved with and who uphold the fundamental traditions of the academy, in Franklin's time and today, would be in majority agreement with these beliefs, ideas, and ideals.

Those in the academy obviously divide on notions of belief in a Deity, some perfectly comfortable and others not. They might be in some accord about a transcendent force. But denizens of the college and university would likely agree that people should—and in the case of the academy, be specifically educated to—do good work toward human and social progress, and to fulfill themselves as individuals and human beings.

We have been probing questions about the role of religion in the nation. Getting more specific, how and in what ways has the religion of the Republic developed throughout that history? How does that history connect to our primary interest in examining the shape and shaping of the college and university in America?

To examine these and other questions, we turn again to Sidney Mead's insights about religion in American history. Our emphasis is on the relationship of religion to the "state" in America, the development of the religion of the Republic, and the connection both of sectarian religion (in all its forms, shapes, and sizes from Puritans to Muslims) and of the religion of the Republic to the shape of the college and university in America.

Mead, a historian's historian, notes the challenges of every quest at historical inquiry. He asserts that, "Every historical study is an attempt to provide a satisfactory answer to the question that bugs the author."[14] Paraphrasing what was Mead's question and applying it to our narrative, the question before us is: What is the nature of the college and university in America today, and how did it get that way?

When facing complex questions in historical inquiry, Mead was haunted by Alfred North Whitehead's insight, that "'the prominent facts are the superficial facts,' the froth on the surface of history." Mead adds that, "it is also true that only after the prominent facts of one's immediate subject have been ordered out of the primordial chaos . . . can one suggest to his audience the nature of the gulf stream in history on which they float."[15]

Mead's thoughts are critical to our story. These ideas pivot around the issue of the relationship of religion to the foundation of the college and university in America. Some of this thinking bears more directly than others on our story. However, all of this thinking is important in this quest to understand the basis of how and why the college in America is what it is, and of the issues, developments, changes, and challenges it has chronically confronted. Without assuring that we can identify the "gulf stream" on which other parts of our inquiry "float," that is our quest.

## HOW RELIGION UNFOLDED IN
## AMERICA ABSENT A "CHURCH"

One concern, first and foremost, is to understand what is meant by use the term "church" in America. There never was "one" church, but rather numerous sects and denominations running about the land. As Mead notes, when the United States emerged "It was a new kind of commonwealth in Christendom religiously, primarily because the founders had realized that if there was to be a *United* States made up of the heterogenous (*sic*) thirteen colonies, it could have no nationally established church such as fourteen centuries of Christendom's teaching had held was essential." [16]

The reality that there would be no nationally established church in the new land as it became a nation cannot be lost on what this meant for America's colleges and universities. After all, the academy had grown up in the Old World, in the previous setting of "Christendom religiously." The previous and only known "churches" and "states" of that world were recast with remarkable difference in America. The colleges and universities in this new land had to adjust to an American religious climate.

Thus the milieu of the academy's nearly six-century relationship to Christendom from the founding of the university at Bologna in 1088 to the founding of Harvard in 1636 has changed. This does not mean that the fundamental values of the academy were at risk or absolutely had to change in the new land. However, with religion playing the different role in society and culture that it did and would in America, a new balancing act was required of its colleges and universities.

The changes that were wrought did not come overnight. In reality it would take from the founding of the original colonies to the formation of the Republic in the Constitutional era for the nation to frame the way it would deal with religion as a wholly different, "new kind of commonwealth in Christendom religiously."

Even though adaptations were inevitable in the way Christendom was to be religiously involved in the state, initially the thought was that nothing much would change. Mead suggests that "All up and down the colonial coast the idea and expectation of the first planters . . . was that the ecclesiastical forms developed through centuries of experience in Europe would be perpetuated in the New World."

Though there were some changes in the new land, "Everywhere charters, laws, and instructions (with the exception of Maryland and, later, Rhode Island) demanded religious uniformity," falling into the Old World pattern, "but nowhere as clearly as by the founders of Massachusetts Bay. . . ." [17] By and large the Colonial Colleges were born in these commonwealths, their "states," that were heavily religiously formed and structured.

While college founders had undeniable autonomy on many fronts, this water of "religious uniformity" was all around them. Thus, they fashioned and articulated their respective missions and purposes in response to these religious realities and the people leading and inspiring the religious climate. We know that the pressure of the religious culture around it had an enormous effect on Harvard. This in turn affected other Colonial Colleges as they hacked out their identities reacting to Harvard's example for navigating religion and religious passions.

## THE ENLIGHTENMENT'S SOCIAL, POLITICAL, AND RELIGIOUS IMPACT

Second, Mead is a strong advocate for the role of the Enlightenment as the major force altering the course of the seventeenth and eighteenth centuries. Mead is convinced that there exists a religion of the Enlightenment. It is not a stretch to argue that this religion became a strong force in the shape of the academy in America. This alone is not a unique assertion, as the college in the Old and New World emerged as the institution we know today from the Enlightenment's social, cultural, and political, not to mention religious, underpinnings.

However, I am further suggesting that this religion of the Enlightenment is also the basis for the academy's own brand of a civil religion in America. (This too is not a stretch as it was Enlightenment contributor Jean-Jacques Rousseau who originally hatched the notion of civil religion).

Mead's understanding of the religion of the Republic relies in part on Crane Brinton. Mead notes Brinton's contention that:

> The basic structure of Christian belief survived, however, not without heresies and schisms, until, roughly in the late seventeenth century when there arose in our society what seems to me clearly to be a new religion, certainly related to, descended from, and by many reconciled with, Christianity.

Brinton then cuts to the chase adding that "I call this religion simply Enlightenment with a capital E."[18]

Most members of the academy would likely endorse Brinton's religion of the Enlightenment as instrumental in the creed of the university. Brinton clearly draws this connection: "Sufficient to note finally that the Enlightened," read the denizens and constituents of the college and university, "share a teleological view of man's place in the universe summarized in words like progress and evolution and that again the Marxists with their thoroughly eschatological concept of the classless society come closest to a quite definite surrogate for the Christian heaven—but a heaven to be on earth, and in a relatively near future."[19]

Brinton adds that even "For the less radical Enlightened there may well be no such Marxist utopia in sight, but the Enlightened faith is surely always optimistic about the possibilities of an increasingly happier life for all men on this earth."[20] Life, liberty, and the pursuit of happiness was how this "Enlightened faith" was inculcated in the creed of the Republic. It is no leap of faith to recognize the connection and thus acclaim of these values part and parcel in the academy's mission, purpose, and its aspirations for individuals and society.

This faith of the academy, this religion of the academy, runs deeper. Brinton adds that while many in the "educated and privileged classes" cannot accept a "Christian transcendental world view, cannot accept as real in any sense the Christian City of God," yet they "do expect, long for, sometimes firmly believe in, a City of Earth transformed—usually by the grace of science and reason—into a City of God built of, for, and by human beings. . . ."[21] Here is where even unbelievers, those academics with a world view as absolutely as possible crafted in scientific, objective terms, still in Brinton's mind have a faith in a better world and view themselves as responsible for creating it.

What could be more true to the aspirations of the university than "progress and evolution," "faith [is] surely always optimistic about the possibilities of an increasingly happier life for all men on this earth," and "the grace of science and reason."? If America was in Lipset's terms the "first new nation," surely the academy in America was the "new university" borne exclusively from the groundbreaking intellectual frontiers of the Enlightenment.

For Mead these developments are nothing short of a larger revolution that overarched the Revolutionary era. He concludes that, "What is most significant historically is that for the first time in Christendom the people of a commonwealth were offered an authentically religious alternative to orthodox Christianity, and their right to accept and propagate it defended by civil authority." This meant that it was "the theology of the 'Enlightenment' in Brinton's sense that legitimated the thrust of the Declaration and the constitutional structures of 'the first new nation' in Christendom."[22]

Thus the Enlightenment for Mead and for our story is a cornerstone event. It is the Enlightenment that produced a cascade of ideas that permeated thinking about religion, politics, and the commonweal. This revolution included the world of education, the stirrings inside and outside the gates of the emerging Colonial Colleges and the generations of colleges and universities that followed.

## THE INTELLECTUAL MIND
## ECLIPSES THE RELIGIOUS MIND

Next is Mead's take on the tension and battle between the religious mind and the intellectual mind in the colonial, Great Awakening, and early antebellum eras. Mead believes that the "polarization of the religious and intellectual lives of the country becomes increasingly evident from around the middle of the eighteenth century," marked by Harvard's rebuke of the Great Awakening, New Light preachments of George Whitfield—a head versus heart confrontational battle if ever there was one—in their midst in 1744.[23]

He contends that this "drift apart," decades later, "becomes clearer with the launching of the often-called 'godless' state universities beginning in the 1790s to rival the denominationally controlled colleges."[24] Among other examples, he includes a revisionist interpretation of the iconic Dartmouth College case.

Putting the nail in the coffin of the further collapse of the religious influence at the heart of the Colonial Colleges, Mead turns the Dartmouth College Supreme Court Case inside out. To Mead, the Dartmouth College decision "which turned back the attempt to gain state control of the private colleges," as most would agree, was actually "a Pyrrhic victory, for it implied that independence of the private colleges from denominational as well as state control and helped pave the way to ever more complete separation of education from its religious roots."[25]

A watchword of colleges and universities of America is their desire for autonomy. This characteristic is among those that make higher education in the United States the envy of the world. Autonomy is coveted, whether from governmental interference as was clearly at stake in the Dartmouth case or as the basis for maintaining independence from other outside forces—denominational forces, the courts, associations of critics, even cabals inside the gates—that seek to control a college or university.

Mead is a realist about what happened in the Dartmouth decision. He views it at best as a mixed blessing. This view is juxtaposed to the oft thought claims of outright victory in which Daniel Webster's "small college but there are those who love it," was a David slaying a Goliath.

On one hand, yes Dartmouth was able to maintain control over itself, being able to claim the name "College" rather than be forced to be Dartmouth University under New Hampshire State control. On the other hand maybe this is beware what you wish for, because now the door was opened, in Mead's interpretation, for colleges and universities to claim their freedom from religious and denominational constraints and control.

Cheerleaders for religious ties for universities and colleges will find cause for consternation in Mead's take away that the Dartmouth case signaled "ever more complete separation of education from its religious roots." But Mead is really only being realistic about the fact that these religious roots in many colleges and universities would have lasted only so long, even at heavily religiously based institutions.

Whatever the case, rapid or gradual, complete or marginal collapse, religious influence where it exists in the academy must be navigated along the idealistic lines of Cardinal Newman's "the idea of the university," otherwise it undermines the core principles and values of the academy. In Mead's reading, the college and university in America, to the degree it was originally constituted and run by the denominational forces, steered a course from the mid-eighteenth century onward toward greater attention to upholding the classic fundamental purposes of the university.

## THE ACADEMY FROM COERCION TO PERSUASION

Mead's fourth point about the religious features of the American landscape is original and perceptive. That view is that over time, America and American religious influences evolved from coercion to persuasion. How does he understand coercion versus persuasion, and how did this transformation happen? And what was the effect of this change on the academy in America?

One of Mead's prominent questions is the degree to which public and political coherence, government order and control, and the attendant social and cultural forces of the commonwealth and nation are reached by coercion versus persuasion. These provocative questions apply to the university now as well as throughout its history.

Mead makes clear the connection of these issues to the concerns of the university noting that ". . . as long as there have been humans *as* humans, the necessity to work at creating communities and universes of discourse has been recognized and made tangible in initiation rites and educational systems."[26] Space does not permit a detailed account of Mead's conclusions.[27] Suffice it to say that Mead reveals the rapid shift from religious uniformity to religious toleration to full-blown religious liberty in the colonial era, particularly in the half century from the First Great Awakening to the Constitutional Convention.

This evolution dramatically changed the way sects and denominations viewed each other, and their individual and mutual prospects. Inevitably this progression translated into the commonweal in the form of Constitutional guarantees not simply of religious toleration, itself a rather new thing, but of religious liberty, a unique, original American contribution to its polity and as a new "good" for other nations and civic communities, including the college, to follow.

The shift from coercion to persuasion was profound for society and for the academy. Coercion had meant: we or someone will tell you how to live and behave, your soul and spirit as well as your citizenship at risk for failing to obey and comply. That way of doing business was replaced by persuasion: we agree to our mutual right to believe and do as we wish. We will not simply put up with—merely tolerate—each other. More critically, we will argue out differences of opinion, even belief itself.

This temperament seeped into the fabric of the academy, for example in no religious litmus tests at the founding of Brown, the University of Pennsylvania, and Columbia to mention just a few.

However, the tension between coercion and persuasion is by no means settled. In the heat of ideological battles, especially in the contemporary era, many in the academy, including well-intentioned college presidents, provosts, deans, and other senior administrators, along with esteemed faculty, trustees, and other key stakeholders, end up disregarding persuasion. Rather to get their way they substitute coercion in various guises, stifling free speech and discussion as just one fateful consequence. This choice, used as a short cut to reduce or even more foolishly in the hope of eliminating conflict, is as flawed as it is errant.[28]

## HOLDING SOCIETY TOGETHER: KNITTING WITH A CIVIL RELIGION

If we are not to be held together politically and socially by coercion, then how does the center hold? How does the commonweal get established and, more to the point, is it sustained? What then knits society, a nation, or the academy together?

These questions bring us to Mead's next point of description of American society and the role of religion in it; specifically, how the religion of the Republic, the civil religion of America, developed and imparts order and meaning to culture and civic life.

Unsurprisingly, Mead turns to de Tocqueville's notions in *Democracy in America* that any society, in order to function, must have its people accept "dogmatic beliefs, that is to say, opinions which men take on trust without discussion." What this means is that "If society is to exist 'it is essential that all the minds of the citizens' be 'held together by some leading ideas; and that could never happen unless each of them sometimes came to draw his opinions from the same source and was ready to accept some beliefs ready made.'"[29]

What could be more simple yet so complex to do? The difficulty is highly pronounced, especially absent coercive forces. That is, if people are not to be compelled, then they must be lured, impelled, or propelled to hold the center, to hold together socially and culturally. Thus mutually acceptable, "beliefs ready made" are absolutely critical to the commonwealth.

Into this muddle strides civil religion. What does this religion do for us? To answer that question, Mead turns to Robert Bellah's view of

"American Civil Religion." For Bellah, "It is one of the oldest of sociological generalizations that any coherent and viable society rests on a common set of moral understandings about good and bad, right and wrong, in the realm of individual and social action."[30]

This is the starting point. However, the critical need that brings civil religion into the picture is that "It is almost as widely held that these common moral understandings must also in turn rest upon a common set of religious understandings that provide a picture of the universe in terms of which the moral understandings make sense."[31]

Though ahead of our story, note the dilemmas that the university in America has faced in recent decades. One thing is clear: Great danger lurks from a dearth of some set of beliefs, "common moral understandings," maybe even "religious understandings" out of which the "moral understandings make sense." It is here, among other places, that the absence of even minimally commonly agreed to beliefs has made the battles of ideologically opposed wings of the academy much more difficult and damaging than might otherwise be the case.

Nothing happens or exists in a vacuum. That is certainly the case in the development of college and university in the American colonies, in these early commonwealths of the emerging Republic. Bellah and de Tocqueville assert the essential need for prima fascia, commonly agreed ideas, principles and beliefs. Colleges and universities as institutions and their multiple constituencies must rely wittingly or not on commonly agreed notions about moral issues. These are the ground for navigating individual and corporate controversies and crises, and for fashioning the social and cultural architecture.

To a profound extent, the academy buys into Bellah's "American Civil Religion." Its values, principles, and beliefs provide the common ground essential for holding the center. Despite ideological polarization, a reality always with us, the civil religion in the academy forms a creed and faith that willy-nilly, all sides, no matter their differences, grant credibility and substance.

## IDEOLOGY AND IDEOLOGICAL
## BALANCE IN THE ACADEMY

The role of ideology must be confronted in any discussion of a religious creed and system of belief. The civil religion, especially as it relates to the college and university, is not an exception. As an ideology it carries its own baggage, even as it critiques other ideologies and theirs. These realities lead Mead now to another point that extends the way the civil religion, his religion of the Republic, functions in America.

Delving into this complex set of issues, we must be clear about our understanding of ideology. In wrestling with ideology, Mead cites John

Higham's assertion that ideologies are "those explicit systems of general beliefs that give large bodies of people," clearly the inhabitants of the college and university, "a common identity and purpose, a common program of action, and a standard for self-criticism."[32]

Every college and university has, to use Burton Clark's classic assignation, a "saga."[33] Higham understands saga as a historical, but also continuously lived out and refashioned, chronicle that unifies and makes meaning for any institution, including colleges and universities. However, there is also a difference between "saga" and ideology.

Higham suggests that "Being relatively formalized and explicit, ideology contrasts with a wider, older, more ambiguous fund of myth and tradition," Clark's elements of saga. Ideology "includes doctrines or theories on the one hand and policies or prescriptions on the other. Accordingly, it links social action with fundamental beliefs, collective identity with the course of history. . . ."[34]

We have witnessed in the academy, especially in the last five or six decades or longer, the influence of ideology frequently in extreme forms. The more the breaches between constituencies, the more vulnerable any community or institution is to the vagaries of the ideological forces in its midst, and the greater the potential that those forces will be unleashed.

But this circumstance would not surprise Higham. He realistically asserts that, "Arising in the course of modernization when an unreflective culture fractures," as many would argue and agree has been the case in contemporary culture within and outside the gates of the academy, "ideology provides a new basis for solidarity."[35]

Higham extends Mead's and other religious historians' beliefs about civil religion and the way it developed in America. Sectarian, denominationally dominated religious vantage points evolved to something more comprehensive as ". . . eighteenth-century Christians developed an intellectual framework that accommodated unprecedented diversities."[36]

Higham calls this framework, analogous to the civil religion, the "Protestant ideology." As a new variation on the Protestant religious story in America, the Protestant ideology incorporated two forces existing side by side. These were, on one hand, the "specific creeds and confessions [that] adorned the more formal, visible level." Meanwhile and on the other hand, "At a deeper level, unaffected by the class of creeds, dwelled the inclusive truths, which required neither debate nor strict definition."[37]

These intellectual considerations and "truths" emerged as a unifying force eclipsing sectarian and denominational pressures as the dominant Protestant and later Christian and Judeo-Christian ethos of the land and the ground of the continuing formation of the academy. Higham's concluding idea about this evolution is that "As time passed, theological doctrines acquired a largely honorific, ceremonial status in America's pantheon of religions. The basic ideology stood guard, and one could question its tenets only at the risk of heresy."[38]

The way this mix of religious ideas and beliefs got into the water was rather simple. What happened was that "In actuality secular life was suffused with a pan-Protestant ideology that claimed to be civic and universal." While this ideology "Pledged to leave private beliefs undisturbed, it was vague enough so that increasing numbers of Jews and Catholics could embrace it. But it infused a generalized piety in school textbooks and civic oratory."[39]

In short order, regardless specific religious affiliation, passion, and duty most everyone, regardless religious faith and belief, got on board. Unsurprisingly, this emerging secular religion—the religion of the Republic or American Civil Religion—found itself, among other locations, lodged in the foundations of schools, including colleges and universities.

Paralleling and mutually reinforcing each other, this faith system grew up with the emerging college and university from the Civil War on. What evolved, alongside the advent of the research university and the proliferation of universities inspired by the Morrill Act, was a reliance on the technical, on technology, and the resulting bureaucracies that were shot through the Industrial Revolution and the Progressive Era. This intellectual-technological ideology eclipsed, especially in the academy that inspired it, the Protestant ideology and the American ideology.[40]

Higham claims that with "Their ends already fixed in their hearts," as a result of the ideologies that had supported and sustained them, "Americans adopted technical means without fear of personal loss. Thus technical integration spread under the shelter of the American ideology; and the resulting innovations were embraced as ever more powerful instruments for attaining familiar goals."[41]

Coupled with the development of the Progressive, Social Gospel eras was a rapidly increasing emphasis on a college and university education and especially on research in the university. As a consequence, ". . . American intellectuals became more humble about the limitations of their own spare culture and more aware of common problems emerging in all industrial societies." The subsequent temperament was that, "For solving these problems the insufficiency of the old republican faith became painfully apparent."[42]

The impact of these changes on the American ideology that had grown from the Protestant ideology was clear and dramatic. Again the university was at the crux of what developed.

Higham claims two alterations took place. One was a "revised definition of freedom." In this case individual rights came to be viewed "as a function of participation rather than autonomy. Not the absence of legal restraint but the capacity to share as widely as possible in the common good of the whole society makes us free and equal."

The second was that "progressive intellectuals thought," here again represented by the founders and faculty of both research universities and even the colleges of the day, "scientific techniques can take the place of universal a priori principles. To identify the common good, we may rely on scientific inquiry." Moreover, "Since it is both flexible and objective, science can build a self-correcting mechanism into the American ideology."[43]

This ideology has steered American society and culture, and been the grist for the "new" mission and purpose of the university in the twentieth and into the early twenty-first centuries. For better and worse, reliance on science, technology, and the goods and ideas they produce presumed to build up the common good, has attained this high, exalted pedestal-like position within and outside the gates of the academy. Among its impacts that we will later explore is how this framework of assumptions set off curricular and other battles about the mission of the university in the last century and more.

Thus, the university and its growth closely paralleled and inspired this next turn in the road for how America and Americans viewed themselves and their prospects. There is certainly a chicken and egg issue, but clearly these were times of symbiotic, reinforcing developments.

The industrial, corporate, and entrepreneurial magnates and tycoons of the Progressive Era heavily invested personal wealth and reputation to found and expand the university foundations of the nation. Corporately they were captivated by the technical values and bureaucratic ideology of the age. As Higham underscores, these were the very tenets viewed as holding the nation together.[44]

However, there was for Higham an underbelly to these technical, bureaucratic, and science-dependent developments. As a creature of his times of the late 1960s and early 1970s, Higham feared the consequences for the nation and the society of overreliance on unchained technology and science.

What gave him pause was the corrosive effect of how smitten American society had become with technical and scientific thinking and beliefs. That is, the notion that "technical organization," and here intense critics of the contemporary university and how it has gotten to where it is would no doubt be in fervent agreement, "is essentially undemocratic. Not equal rights but the hierarchical articulation of differentiated functions is its working principle"[45]

Risking an unrealistic solution, Higham suggests a reintegration of the historic cultural attachments and identities at stake for American society and by inference for the academy. He assessed American culture of the early 1970s as involved in a "continuing struggle to bring the primordial," that of the parochial, exclusive group identity, "the ideological, and the technical dimensions of culture into some kind of counterpoise with one another."[46]

Higham claims each of these "adhesive forces . . . has something to contribute to our complex society; and each of them survives within it." Synergistically, "we may raise to a new level one of the great and endur-ing principles," again "at the heart of the aspirations of the university," of our ideological heritage: the importance of diversity, "the value of countervailing power."[47]

The academy is shot through with this faith, and the beliefs and val-ues undergirding it. Higham's injunctions underscore the demand on the university to rely on its heritage of balance in a climate so marked by the stresses and strains of diversity and difference.

### REPRISE: THE RELIGION OF THE ENLIGHTENMENT, THE RELIGION OF THE REPUBLIC, AND THE RELIGION OF THE ACADEMY

Mead's final point about the relationship of religion to the foundation of the college and university in the United States returns to the power of Enlightenment thought on the political, cultural beliefs of American soci-ety. Mead is unequivocal that the "mainspring of that [our] Republic," is "that the theology of the Republic is that of 'Enlightenment'" as the histo-rian Crane Brinton defined it.[48]

The overlap of the prevailing values of the Enlightenment with the core values of the academy of the seventeenth and eighteenth century is undeniable. This assertion is not new news. However, it is not stretching Mead and Higham too far to conclude that the religion of the Enlighten-ment and the "theology of the Republic," were readily exported into the academy as a theology or religion of the "university."

We come full circle. These religious underpinnings of America's emerging commonwealths of the colonies were also at hand in the Colo-nial Colleges. Sure there were varying degrees of religious influence. But throughout the original colleges, religion was shot through discussions, debates, and founding blueprints. We cannot tease religious influence out of the evolution of the Republic, the different body politics, and the civic and common good. Certainly if religion was an influence in the social, cultural, and political fabric and its institutions, it had to be in America's colleges and universities as well.

The foundational ground of the college and university in America is unique. Three overlapping factors indeed stand out. It was out of the fabric created by these factors, certainly joined by others, that the acade-my has grown and flourished in the United States.

First, and most ground breaking and original, was how America em-braced not mere religious (and by inference other forms of individual and group identity) toleration, but for the first time in human history, relig-ious liberty and freedom. Of all the things that were and are America, this is arguably the single most profound. Mead is clear about the reality of what was put in place at the Constitutional founding of America: "For the first time in Christendom there was legal *religious freedom* as distinct from [mere] toleration in a commonwealth."[49]

Second, further equality and notions of equal opportunity were baked into the American cake, as was the embrace of diversity. As proclaimed at the foot of the Statue of Liberty, to mark America's second century as a nation, the country always embraced the message, if not the reality, of "give me your tired, your poor."

Third, diversity was not to be feared. Rather arguments at the founding of the nation implanted the notion of "*E pluribus unum*." The "many" was a good. Diversity that recognized a uniting creed and banner would strengthen and solidify society. There could be a commonweal and the common good even with a diversity of players, identities, and constituencies.

Paralleling the contests between and among the proliferating religious sects and denominations were the colleges that first dotted the American landscape. Despite religious influences, these educational institutions had autonomy over what they chose to be. As with the sects and denominations, the colleges also lived or died in a competitive environment.

That continued later on when state and federal funding supported both public and private colleges and universities through grants, financial aid, and other support. Regardless of the variations in government support, a free market competition has always served to winnow and improve the education offered to citizens. That free market competition is yet another feature making American higher education the envy of the world.

This competition and diversity contributed willy-nilly to the remarkable variety that was and is the college and university in America. As the history of the colonial era moved into that of the Revolution and the Constitutional eras and then well beyond, it became evident that the college and university in America would have no universal, externally enforced stamp of conformity, uniformity, or control.

Rather what we have had both for better—certainly one reason the United States is the envy of the world for higher education—and at times for worse is these many boats navigating on their own bottoms. There are particular, as well as broadly complementary, missions and purposes. But the bottom line is choice in an open marketplace.

Some of the battles inspired by competition have caused problems. But at other times the passions and dedication connected to strongly held beliefs and values have guided individual institutions through difficult passages. One result is that the entire mix of colleges and universities in America is better off for its diversity, for competition over ideas, and for the strength that derives from well-won if not well-worn identities and claims of service to citizens and constituents.

Arguably there is a religion of the academy, a religion constituted of both the historic intentions of the university, but also fashioned in the crucible of the religion of the Enlightenment and the religion of the Republic. There certainly have been the religions and the religious-like fervor of various ideologies in the college and university in America from the get-go. In the latter case, contemporary iterations of ideology for the sake of ideology alas tear at the fabric of today's campuses.

Thus the battle today, admittedly a battleground that has always been, for the soul of the university reduces to a simple question: The degree to which the university maintains fundamental beliefs and values against critics and pretenders, some might say infidels, who would overtake it. Religion and religious wrangling in many guises has ever been part of the mix.

## NOTES

1. http://alumni.umich.edu/about/university-of-michigan-history.
2. http://bentley.umich.edu/research/um/umpresid.php.
3. https://trustees.cornell.edu/cornell_charter.pdf, 2.
4. Frederick Rudolph, *The American College and University: A History* (New York: Alfred A. Knopf, 1968), 68.
5. Ibid.
6. Ibid., 69.
7. Ibid.
8. Richard Hofstadter and Wilson Smith, eds., *American Higher Education: A Documentary History*, Volume II (Chicago: The University of Chicago Press, 1961), 557–58.
9. Ibid., 543.
10. Ibid., 543–44.
11. Cardinal John Henry Newman, *The Idea of a University*, ed. John Henry Turner (New Haven, CT: Yale University Press, 1996).
12. See especially Robert Bellah, "Civil Religion in America," Daedalus (Winter, 1967), 1–21 and Sidney Mead, "The Nation with the Soul of a Church," Church History, XXXVI (September 1967), 1–22.
13. Benjamin Franklin, "Articles of Belief and Acts of Religion," http://franklinpapers.org/franklin/framedVolumes.jsp?vol=1&page=101a.
14. Sidney E. Mead, *The Old Religion in the Brave New World: Reflections on the Relation Between Christendom and the Republic* (Berkeley, Los Angeles, and London: University of California Press, 1977), 1.
15. Ibid., 6.
16. Ibid., 16, Italics authors.
17. Ibid., 22.
18. Ibid., 28. Quote is from Crane Brinton, "Many Mansions." *The American Historical Review* 69, no. 2 (January 1964): 309–26, 315.
19. Ibid., 315.
20. Ibid.
21. Ibid., 316.
22. Mead, 29.
23. Ibid., 30. The vehement nature of the conflict is captured in the Harvard Faculty Rebukes Whitefield statement. Whitfield is charged with "Enthusiasm," and with great irony given their own theologically specific and theocratic roots, the Harvard faculty proclaims that "Hence such a Man naturally assumes an Authority to dictate to others, and a Right to direct their Conduct and Opinions; and hence if any act not

according to his Direction . . . he is presently apt to run into slander, and stigmatize them as Men of no Religion, unconverted, and Opposers of the Spirit of God." To make matters worse, of both their beloved Harvard and Yale, they note the disastrousness of Whitefield's claim that "As for the Universities, I believe it may be said, Their Light is now become Darkness, Darkness that may be felt." http://declaringamerica. com/harvard-faculty-rebukes-whitefield-1744–exerpt/ (unpaginated).

24. Ibid.

25. Ibid.

26. Ibid., 36, italics authors.

27. For full elaboration of his ideas and argument, see Sidney E. Mead, *The Lively Experiment: The Shaping of Christianity in America* (New York: Harper and Row, Publishers, 1963), "From Coercion to Persuasion: Another Look at the Rise of Religious Liberty and the Emergence of Denominationalism," 16–37.

28. For a perceptive and prescient account of this tendency and its corrosive results, see A. Bartlett Giamatti, "A Coda: The Codification of Us All," in *The University and the Public Interest* (New York: Atheneum, 1981).

29. Mead, *The Old Religion in the Brave New World*, 60. Mead takes Bellah's quotes from Robert Bellah, *The Broken Covenant: American Civil Religion in Time of Trial* (New York: Seabury Press, 1975).

30. Ibid.

31. Ibid.

32. Ibid., 153, fn. 28. The Higham citations are found in John Higham, "Hanging Together: Divergent Unities in American History," *The Journal of American History* 61, no. 1 (June, 1974): 5–28.

33. Burton R Clark, *The Distinctive College: Antioch, Reed and Swarthmore* (Chicago: Aldine, 1970).

34. Mead, *The Old Religion in the Brave New World*, 153, fn. 28.

35. Ibid.

36. Higham, "Hanging Together: Divergent Unities in American History," 5–28, 12.

37. Ibid., 12–13.

38. Ibid., 13.

39. Ibid.

40. Ibid. 19–20. For the full elaboration of Higham's assertion, see 20–28.

41. Ibid., 20.

42. Ibid., 23.

43. Ibid., 24.

44. Ibid., 19.

45. Ibid., 26.

46. Ibid., 28.

47. Ibid.

48. Mead, *The Old Religion in the Brave New World*, 71.

49. Ibid., 76, Italics authors.

# TWO

## The University

*What Is It and How Does Its Center Hold?*

Colleges and universities like all institutions confront the pushes, pulls, and pressures of politics, culture, and social forces in and outside their walls. There is no way around the tangles their sages and historical times present, not to mention personalities and persuasions arrayed to criticize as well as to support their fortunes.

How colleges respond to these forces dictates the degree to which they endanger or defend fundamental mission, beliefs, and values. For the university to be the university it must uphold core principles, maintain a steady rudder, and stand in a center that holds.

In short, the existence of the university hinges on the ability to fulfill its duty to the heritage of the academy: a unique institution in society and culture dedicated to preserve the best of the past, to pass knowledge and civilization to the next generation, and to pursue wisdom and learning. To be that institution for society, the university must handle challenges and lures that distract from and undermine pursuit of these core ideals. Otherwise, when the university fails at this task, its identity is altogether lost. In that circumstance, the university is nothing more than merely one other social or political institution of society.[1]

Noting the timeless foundation of the university and college in America, Frederick Rudolph concludes, "a college develops a sense of unity. . . . where there might otherwise be aimlessness and uncontrolled diversity. A college advances learning; it combats ignorance and barbarism. A college is a support of the state; it is an instructor in loyalty, in citizenship, in the dictates of conscience and faith." Lest these aims appear ethereal, pie-in-the sky, furthermore "A college is [also] useful: it helps men to learn the things they must know in order to manage the temporal affairs of the world; it trains a legion of teachers."[2]

Thus throughout its history: "All these things a college was. All these purposes a college served."[3] Nonetheless, despite Rudolph's unified and unifying image, the college in America has always meant different things to different people. Interpretations and understandings about what the university is and what it should be are legion. At times these differences are highly contested and fought out. The reality is, present decades by no means the exception, ideological pushes and pulls, and political demands have ever been a piece of the scene of the American college and university.

## THE NATURE OF IDEOLOGY AND ITS
## TUGS ON THE CENTER OF THE ACADEMY

There is nothing to be feared about ideology in and of itself. Ideology and ideological thinking are a natural outcropping of human interactions, reflective of people and their ideas. Ideology results from the sorting of the themes and tropes of human experience, and from individual, communal, and institutional encounters in social, cultural, and political life.

However, ideologies can create problems and mischief. Among those difficulties: the degree to which we fall prey to the effects of ideology, especially the erosion of discourse and debate when harangue displaces listening; how unrestrained ideologies corrode the ideals of the academy; and the energy consumed in navigating between and among ideologies, all the while trying to acknowledge individual human passions.

These dilemmas create crucial questions for the academy. Observers and denizens of the university readily acknowledge the existence of ideology and ideological thinking in their midst. In many ways, what would life inside the gates be without it? However, a critical firewall must be maintained: The university cannot concede ideological beliefs and assertions displacing the principles and values of the academy that inspire the search for truth and that undergird free debate and discussion.

Ideology is a term that can get thrown around all too easily without needed definition. Before using ideology and ideological thinking further, we need a working concept to inform our thinking. A number of thinkers generate ideas that collectively shape the definition of what constitutes ideology. What then might we assert as the broad contours of ideologies and ideological thinking?

Herbert McClosky, drawing ideas from Daniel Bell, Edward Shils, and Lewis Wirth, suggests that ideologies are "*systems* of belief that are elaborate, integrated, and coherent, that justify the exercise of power, explain and judge historical events, identify political right and wrong, set forth the interconnections (causal and moral) between politics and other spheres of activity, and furnish guides for action."[4]

Colleges and universities reveal their beliefs, even their ideologies, in mission statements, charters, sagas, and policies. However, universities must tread a fine line to make clear that the fundamental tenets and basis of the academy—freedom of inquiry, research, search for truth, and the like, as Hutchins notes—are not overridden by ideologies grounded in nothing more than rancorous politics, long-drawn-out argument, and blind beliefs.

This of course is no small task. The lines are finely drawn and the slope slippery when "solutions" about ideology result in infringement of academic freedom and speech (see the rush to speech codes in the late 1980s and early 1990s), litmus tests in hiring, and orientation programs that indoctrinate about ideas rather than set the grounds to debate them, to name just a few.

McClosky extends the nature of ideology in general to the specifics of "American democratic ideology."[5] Noteworthy is the overlap between "American democratic ideology" and the tenets about which the academy and those connected closely to it would heartily subscribe. Furthermore, his take about American ideology dovetails with what we know about the ideology of the religion of the Republic and its congruence with Enlightenment and American democratic thought.

McClosky's ideology of American democracy includes "such concepts as consent, accountability, limited or constitutional government, representation, majority rule, minority rights, the principle of political opposition, freedom of thought, speech, press, and assembly, equality of opportunity, religious toleration, equality before the law, the rights of juridical defense, and individual self-determination over a broad range of person affairs."[6]

Who in the academy, in any college or university, be they on the political Left, Right, or Center, from any academic discipline or persuasion, or with any other social and cultural rift, would oppose these time-honored, publicly acknowledged creedal propositions? These are beliefs. These are values. Their common characteristic is that they transcend partisanship and petty distinctions. This stands in stark contrast to the stock and trade corrosive use of ideologies in the academy, a pattern that left unchecked can destroy its very existence.

John Diggins's view of ideology differs from McClosky's, who by comparison appears anodyne. McCloskey offers a measured definition of ideology that fits the normative political forces in the academy and in society. He presents an even-handed approach, capturing a universal sense about competing ideologies and what people do with them. His thinking about ideology, particularly the "American democratic ideology," is not pejorative and tends to a view of ideology that is its social application.

To McClosky, ideologies are useful, essential, and unavoidable. People can possess ideological thinking without abandoning their critical faculties. Ideologies in this view are not antithetical to free inquiry and debate especially as they are ideally engaged inside the gates of the academy.

By contrast, Diggins's interpretation of ideology is more pejorative. It possesses an edge. This is especially the case regarding how ideologies function in the hands of political actors and activists, and in the movements they generate in society as well as in the academy.

Diggins's concept of ideology poses a threat to the academy, whereas McClosky's does not. Diggins believes ideological thinking is less prone to the rational, more appealing to the heart rather than the head (recall the Old Lights vs. the New Lights of the Great Awakening). Ideology in this interpretation is atavistic as well as activist.

Underscoring this point, Diggins argues that ". . . ideology is the release of thought from abstract contemplation; its criterion is not intellectual consistency but emotional intensity; its appeal is not that of esthetics but of power. The dynamism of ideology is such that it functions less as philosophy than as the activization of philosophy."[7]

There are unending debates about whether ideological forces and pressure intensified in the academy beginning in the 1960s, thereby threating the university's ability to hold the center. That story line is magnified by tales of conservative forces that used the political correctness cudgel of the late 1970s and through the 1980s against what they viewed as a takeover of the ivory tower by forces of the Left.

This impression has a ring of truth. The 1960s and early 1970s were tumultuous in- and outside the gates of the academy. Indeed what transpired piled upheaval on upheaval. The Left appeared to be in ascendency. The Right looked for payback.

The litany of offenses that the academy had committed was lengthy. It became a repeated mantra of vociferous critics of the university. The wrongs were the stuff of continuing rants: Curricular "innovations" displacing traditional subjects and Western civilization thought, recruitment of minority faculty and students, relaxation of long-held standards of social policies governing student life, perceived abandonment of moral standards, and changes in the decorum of college communities. These and other indiscretions left many in and outside the gates gaping in horror at what was happening.

These changes produced backlash by those—the political Right, advocates for "law and order"—seeking to uphold traditional social and moral values. Conservative alumni and trustee constituencies, joined by a bevy of commentators decried the destruction of the academy. Though it was by no means alone, the repeated confrontations that Dartmouth College had with the student run but conservative alumni and major outside-funded *Dartmouth Review* stands as just one example of the reaction of the Right in the 1980s and 1990s to the alleged takeover of the university by the Left in the 1960s and 1970s.

However, while the battles of those times were highly visible and made-to-order for the media, especially television, they were really nothing new on the landscape of the university. Their legacy was long, winding, but ever-present in the academy.

Douglas Sloan reminds us how the early- to mid-eighteenth-century ideological debates of the Great Awakening echo through eras and epochs since. Against the backdrop of the 1960s and early 1970s upheaval, Sloan believes that any modern denizen "who makes the initially difficult effort to get inside the conceptual world of eighteenth-century religion, may find himself looking at intellectual and educational issues that bear a surprising resemblance to those of his own time."[8]

Reflecting on the campus tensions of contemporary times, Sloan remarks that in the Great Awakening:

> For example, student dissent, struggles over the control of educational institutions, charges of anti-intellectualism, and counter-cries of intellectual elitism, debates concerning the social purposes and uses of education, disagreements of priority in the proper relationship between character and knowledge, discussions of the nature of human psychology and the roles of intellect and emotion, issues of academic freedom—all were present.[9]

If Sloan is right, there is little difference between this litany and what many critics in the latter twentieth and early twenty-first century wring their hands about as destroying the academy. Further, Sloan's linkage of the movements of the First and Second Great Awakenings to contemporary ideological struggles in the academy opens the door for conjecture about the characteristics of today's political, cultural forces.

If we reduce the primary tension today as between the political Right, conservatives, sometimes called neo-conservatives, and the Left, the liberals, progressives, in light of the Great Awakenings how might we construe the current divide? For example, who would be the revivalists— generally choosing the heart over the head—of the Great Awakening days, viewed as anti-intellectual, and who would be the anti-revivalists, viewed as intellectual elites? Who stands for character and who for knowledge?

Sometimes it seems that both sides—the Left and the Right—simply exchange blows at times reversing roles with respect to each other. At times one will operate from the head, the other from the heart. Then they switch. Likewise, one side will at times behave like anti-intellectuals, challenging or ignoring tradition, while their opponents look like intellectuals, guarding the standards of academic life and scholarship. Then they switch and invert who is on one side and who on the other.

These warring parties also change positions like chameleons, depending on issues and circumstances. Who are the Philistines—those generally viewed as anti-intellectual—in the present battleground and posing a threat to holding a center? Are they those guarding the gates from intrusion by anti-political correctness forces? Or are the forces of the Right attacking curricular changes, diversity initiatives, and a decay of moral and other values the Philistines arrayed at the gates? Who are the revivalists in the current struggle and who the anti-revivalists?

The rapid media pace and output of contemporary culture also tends both to oversimplify rhetoric and action and to turn positions, especially as caricatured by the opposition, into chimeras. The reality however is much different. Today's ideological struggles are much more nuanced than often characterized. In similar fashion, the clashes of the Great Awakenings echoing through decades and centuries were equally nuanced.

The bipolar struggle of the Awakenings between the revivalist and their traditional, more hidebound anti-revivalist counterparts is remarkably similar to the situation today. In both instances, and as the case in ideological battles, it was all about opposing sides fighting for control in order to put in place their assumptions about society, and how it should be shaped. Both sides believed they were more in the "right" than the other. Each felt they were entitled to get their way and that their victory would ensure the best interests of society, culture, and education.

Sloan notes that from their beginnings in America, "Educational institutions had always provided one of the central bulwarks of civilized life . . . but their function was traditionally one of maintaining and strengthening an already accepted ideal of social organization." A curious by-product of these early religious dust-ups was that the revivalists provoked a change in the approach to education, including the world of higher education, over which they battled.

This change was one that even they did not anticipate. That is, "In the Great Awakening a subtle but extremely important shift began to take place, from an essentially conserving to a more dynamic view of the role of education in society."[10] The revivalists, for all their throwback-appearing style, actually ended up being the revolutionaries, the change artists. It was they who shifted education from its hidebound, elitist, and less-than-fully accessible persona to an open, pliable, forced to adapt and be adaptable version of its former self.

These sectarian, denominational struggles at the foundation of the college in America began at the outset and persisted at least into the latter days of the Second Great Awakening in the mid-nineteenth century. Those battles, as we have seen in Hoeveler's ideas about the "politics of the intellect," shed a lot of heat, and only fractions of light. However, even if the revivalists, as Sloan implies, were not forthrightly intent on changing the substance of the role of education, that ended up being what they, as an unintended consequence, triggered.

## PUBLIC PRESSURE AND INVESTMENT IN THE
## FORTUNES OF HIGHER EDUCATION

The nation's colleges and universities over time were viewed less the province of private interests and constituencies and more a focus of public interest investment. The academy could still occasionally be a fiefdom for control and the willy-nilly wielding of power and influence. However, as the nineteenth century unfolded, education became increasingly more secularized, even as it still retained religious trappings as evidenced by public colleges happily embracing the Christian and Judeo-Christian religious culture of the nation.

But the sectarian battles among religious groups also unwittingly opened the door for increased emphasis on and pressure for greater development of public higher education. A historical snapshot captures this evolution.

Julian Sturtevant, a Yale undergraduate and Divinity student and Congregationalist, after serving on the faculty of Illinois College, became its second president in 1844 and held the post for thirty-two years.[11] Sturtevant argues that Illinois was never interested, either as Congregational or Presbyterian—its two denominational affiliations—in being a sectarian institution. Rather it wished to view itself as broadly Christian. However, sectarian aspirations and pressures from amassed denominations of this era in the Midwest gave Sturtevant and his college little choice but to jump into the fray and fly its denominational colors.

Sturtevant resisted pressure for education to be turned over exclusively to the public. However, he acknowledged that the colleges which competing denominations had founded, each looking for a foothold in small cities and towns, were often of questionable quality. Many external critics whole-heartedly agreed.

This opinion, Sturtevant was aware, opened the door for the critique that only the public is capable competently to run colleges and universities. The downside for Sturtevant and no doubt many of his Christian, sectarian college leaders was that religion, Christian principles, and morality were as a result driven to the margins of higher education.

Commenting in his autobiography about the culture of Illinois, Sturtevant alleges that early on public opinion was nearly unanimous in the belief that the development of higher education institutions should be carried out and controlled by religious bodies and their people rather than to be founded and controlled by the state and its authorities or for that matter by any political body. Thus the principle on which Sturtevant's institution, Illinois College was based, its attempt to be broadly

Christian rather than exclusively sectarian, was met with nearly universal approval by the Illinois body politic. [12]

Due to the internecine battles between and among the denominations, this sectarian struggle created a resistant if not hostile public climate. "After a time intelligent and patriotic men, seeing the denominations entirely incapable of uniting for a great undertaking and even weakened by internal dissension," Sturtevant sorrowfully remarks, "began to despair of colleges founded on the voluntary principle, and to turn toward the state as the only hope for great and well-equipped seats of learning." [13]

Sturtevant adds that the Christian colleges of the day still were the fortresses that society could depend upon to uphold the moral and religious convictions about which most churches were in agreement. However, due to concerns about quality and no doubt fear of overzealousness, many citizens began to react and divisions arose about the role that Christian colleges could well play in society. This loss of faith in the *raison d'être* of these schools served further to weaken core notions about the voluntary principle that in the first place had supported and made attractive these denominational colleges. [14]

What these denominational divisions led to, in Sturtevant's opinion, was that Christian leaders "have thus unwittingly consented to divorce the higher education from religion. We [in America] wisely separate the church from the state, and then foolishly give over into the hands of the latter the control of our institutions of learning. This is one of the most bitter fruits of our sectarian divisions—a result whose final consequences," Sturtevant remarks with more alarm than ever materialized, "no man can foresee." [15]

Nonetheless sectarian influence had been besmirched. The door was opened further for a more rapid rise in the position and influence of the public college and university.

In the wake of the ideological battleground of this era, the public, the citizenry, the public sector was thrust into the role as primary navigator of society's best educational interests. The public, as opposed to battling sectarian interests, was increasingly looked to for the sound grounding of the mission and purpose of these higher education institutions. In the prior two hundred years of the college in America, that had not been either the debate or the case.

The damage to the private college sector wrought by public forays into higher education was not as vast at Sturtevant feared. Private colleges, including and most primarily religious founders and supporters, could point to many positive results of their efforts. Overall, their good work undoubtedly outweighed the bad.

However, the Morrill Land Grant movement and act gathered impetus in reaction to this denominational battleground. Little imagination is required to reinforce the trope that higher education, left to the devices of religious sects, would fail to produce the heft the nation called for from its educational institutions.

The now fully emerging nation would need and require a higher education "system" with a center that could hold, that could be depended upon. The country also had to depend equally on individual colleges and universities to have centers that could hold, rather than ones with nothing more than the *raison d'être* of sectarian and polemic discontent.

The nation, though still young, developed and changed rapidly in the early nineteenth century. A number of otherwise isolated forces joined willy-nilly to shape both the country and the academy. The continuing religious influences of the two Great Awakenings, the second in the latter eighteenth and early to mid-nineteenth century, were as we have seen among those factors.

Added to these challenges and responses sparked by arguments about religious beliefs and their educational and social interests, Americans became more riveted on social mobility than had been the case in the colonial and Colonial College era. Education began to be viewed as instrumental in upward social progress. Higher education complemented the nation's meritocratic vision of how people gained the power to climb and to contribute in society. The opening decades of the nineteenth century were a seminal time for the nation and for its colleges and universities.

In 1820s and 1830s the tug between the elitism so characteristic of colleges and universities and a newly emerging pulse featuring the common man and upward mobility became more evident and pervasive.[16] The question for the colleges and universities was which side of the argument they would be on. Would it be, on one hand, relying on elitism, a meritocracy but one to which only the few would have access? Or on the other hand, would they embrace a more democratic, common man culture that would downplay elitism and underscore greater accessibility?

Among the forces at work, the Jacksonian era became a major influence on the colleges of the day. Frederick Rudolph highlights the pressure that this political climate placed on the colleges. They had previously been able to be as relatively isolated as they wished and to resist selectively these social forces. But now they found themselves in the maelstrom of changes wrought by Andrew Jackson's presidency and by the dramatic cultural shifts of which he was in part architect, in part bellwether.

The Jacksonian *laissez-faire* approach, "allowed all the incompetence, variety, and final achievement which were associated with competitive American enterprise, and in that respect allow the colleges to suffer the results and to reap the benefits of their own decisions." At the same time "It set up a barrier against Jacksonian extremists while permitting the colleges to indulge in the Jacksonian mood of enterprise, competition, and opportunity, in the Jacksonian mood, which substituted competition for monopoly and opportunity for privilege." [17]

In this new era for America, colleges might still be elitist and rooted in the fruits of privilege. But they needed to appear less that way. Nevertheless, colleges remained vulnerable to criticism from a citizenry skeptical about just how much their doors were open to those wanting in for no reason other than social mobility. These were the folk, common people who were not alumni legacies, were not caught up in the status of the college environment, and who had highly practical reasons to want more education.

Thus Rudolph concludes that "Until the American people were fully convinced that their society was fluid as [Philip] Lindsley [Jeffersonian and President of the University of Nashville] argued, until they were adequately assured that their customs and their institutions supported a high level of mobility, they would continue to view the colleges with suspicion and contempt." [18]

The reality of the period was that "education in America was to be a remarkable means of social and economic mobility. As yet, however," despite urgings otherwise of presidents and founders of colleges such as Philander Chase at Kenyon, George Ticknor at Harvard, "higher education was not called upon to perform this function in any large-scale way." [19] But changes in the way colleges and universities conducted themselves were clearly underway. The Second Great Awakening, coupled with Jacksonian democracy, led the way.

## HOLDING THE CENTER: TRADITIONAL
## AND NEW PATHWAYS FOR THE PUBLIC GOOD

What would the center of the academy be with these new pressures teeming? How would colleges and universities navigate their fortunes such that both tradition and change would be joined, rather than being at odds, in mission and purpose? In comparison, the first two hundred years of the college and university in America appeared as a time of minor change and challenge. That was a pastoral era about to be displaced by a Civil War, by increasing public interest in education, by the rise of the major research university, and by the breaking forth of the Industrial Revolution.

Despite this upheaval in the social framework of a still fledgling democracy, the gap between the rich and the middle class remained a major issue of the mid-nineteenth century. College presidents were not far from the fray. Among the main jousters were Charles Eliot at Harvard and James Angell at Michigan.

Rudolph characterizes minister-president Angell's view that, "The state university was the bulwark against an aristocracy of wealth: it was the inevitable and necessary expression of a democracy society; it was Christian equality in action."[20]

Angell minced no words in defending this territory, an argument as poignant then as it is today. Sure that he was on the right side of history, Angell's bottom line was simple: There was not "anything more hateful, more repugnant to our natural instincts, more calamitous at once to learning, to people, more unrepublican, more undemocratic, more unchristian than a system which should confine the priceless boon of higher education to the rich."[21]

Angell was smack in the middle of the sea change as the research university jumped onto the stage of American higher education in the mid-latter part of the nineteenth century. Joining Angell to form this new breed of presidents were Charles Eliot, holding the rearguard at Harvard but putting his own stamp of new ideas on even then a very old place, Daniel Coit Gilman at acclaimed Johns Hopkins, and Andrew White at Cornell.

These leaders laid sizable markers that were dictating the shape of the emerging university. Their actions in the realm of the university in turn had a large effect on the college idea in America. The liberal arts colleges, the small colleges, were forced to adjust to these major new players on the block: public as well as private, large institutions with concrete aspirations and ideas about who they were, and with leaders who were hacking out territory on canvas of their creation. The university was leading the way; the colleges had no choice but to respond and adapt.

The first Board of Trustees of newly formed Johns Hopkins specifically recruited Gilman from the University of California, Berkeley (after just two years as its president) to lead the university. Educational leaders across the nation applauded this choice. It turned out to be quite the fit, another of the lengthy presidential tenures of that day, Gilman's running from 1875–1902.

In his inaugural address, Gilman captured the university in surprisingly traditional rhetoric, echoing the long-held values associated with the American college. Hopkins was to be a research university modeled on those in Germany, closely following that heritage. However, in the eyes of its founding president, Johns Hopkins in intent, if not mission, would be seamless with the educational foundations of the college in America.

Gilman claims that his university's objective is "to develop character—to make men. It misses its aim if it produces learned pedants, or simple artisans, or cunning sophists or pretentious practitioners." This motif was very in line with the traditional values of the colleges in America, beginning of course with the colonial forbears. Gilman underscored the point adding, "Its [Johns Hopkins] purport is not so much to impart knowledge to the pupils, as to whet the appetite, exhibit methods, develop powers, strengthen judgment, and invigorate the intellectual and moral forces."[22]

Bookending his tenure in a farewell address, Gilman still uttered similar themes. But at the end of his run, he also echoes Angell's concerns about the higher, more transcendent aspects of the university, especially in a society that should be republican, democratic, shall we say "Christian." Delivering his speech on Washington's birthday, Gilman cites the first President of the United States' vision for the "establishment of a University *in the central part of the United States,*" a location Gilman associates with John's Hopkins which, had it existed in Washington's day, would have been in the "central" United States.

Gilman interprets Washington's urgings as still on the mark over a century later in addressing critical issues at hand for higher education in relationship to the nation's needs. Washington's plan for a university was a prescient attempt to cut off the worst consequences of ideological, partisan wrangling, as well as to highlight the importance of equality and access to education. Gilman believed Washington's aspirations for a national university were befitting of the transcendent goals that any university or college would want to claim.

The national university was to be where Washington believed "youths of fortune and talents from all parts of thereof" in the young budding nation, would "free themselves in a proper degree from those local prejudices and habitual jealousies which have just been mentioned, and which when carried to excess, are never-failing sources of disquietude to the public mind, and pregnant of mischievous consequences to this country."[23] To Washington, the negative consequences of ideology unbridled and unchecked by knowledge, education, and socialization to the demands of the commonweal, had to be avoided.

Washington saw that divisions that could mark destruction of the commonweal and the common good in the emerging Republic, testing every ounce of its mettle and endurance. As the founding president of the first higher education institution established truly as a research university in the United States, Gilman invokes the belief of the first president of the United States that a national higher education institution could serve as a solution to ideological rancor and division.

Gilman's thoughts are uttered not quite four decades after the Civil War, a crucible for the nation that exhibited the tragic consequences of threats to the social fabric that Washington knew were there. The nation's colleges and universities had not—a burden beyond the expectation of bearing—managed to save the country from this crisis and disaster of civil war. Washington's ideal, his utopian hope, that education would somehow serve to overcome prejudices, jealousies, disquiet, and mischievous consequences, failed to be realized in the century between his time and Gilman's departure as Johns Hopkins president.

The prospect remains debatable about whether the ideals of Washington's university could ever have delivered the promise he envisioned. A related question is the degree to which the colleges and universities of the nation have collectively responded to Washington's hope that through higher education the youth of the nation would be able to "free themselves in a proper degree from those local prejudices and habitual jealousies."

That ideal remains something for the higher education community to ponder. This aim is within the province of the historical purposes of the academy. Furthermore, pursuit of this quest can be viewed as especially pertinent amid the contemporary world of overly simplified ideological thinking and cultural, political polarization. These forces are at least as pronounced today as anything Washington imagined about the nation of his times or in any era in a dim future he could have conjured.

Nonetheless, Gilman is a realist, as too was Washington. He viewed the turbulent times of his day as no different from those throughout history. Such times demand that the finest minds do what they are able to bring order out of chaos. In the process, those minds, the educated and yes no doubt the elite, engage the battle for civility and decency.

Turbulence was clearly on Gilman's mind when he delivered a lengthy address at the 1898 dedication of a new library at Princeton. The Spanish American War was going on, the Civil War just three decades in the nation's rear view mirror, and Reconstruction had been at best marginally beneficial, and in many ways a failure.

In this talk, Gilman asserts that "Human progress is usually heralded by fire and sword, hunger and thirst. . . . History warns us that in our new career we may anticipate perplexities, embarrassments, blunders, a neglect of principles of efficient civil service, the rivalries of churches, the wasteful and perhaps fraudulent expenditure of vast sums of money, and attempts to engraft the system of spoils on the unsophisticated and unwary." Then on a personal note, he reveals, "I dread conflict. Nevertheless, I believe that the American people," here the voice of optimism crystal clear, "through their errors, perplexities and sins, will rise to the situation before them. . . ."[24]

The college and university in America was shifting and changing throughout the nineteenth century. A confluence of social, religious, cultural, and political features amplified, in large measure caused, this rapid movement. This evolution became even more pronounced as the research university set its foothold. However, if Gilman and Angell are indicative of fellow presidents, at least rhetorically as well as practically, the goals of a higher education in America, the principles of what a college or university stood for, remained firmly rooted, if not timeless.

As with many university leaders over centuries, Gilman is evangelical about the university, about its place in the world, and about its duty to civilization. Returning to the University of California at Berkeley for the

Inauguration of Benjamin Wheeler as its president, Gilman invokes the university's grandest ideals and aspirations. He leaves no doubt as to the necessity for the university to be a strong influence, even to rule, for the betterment of humanity and for the good of the world.

"Let us study the progress of human civilization," Gilman urges, "remembering that by ideas the world is governed. They are stronger than kings in council, or representatives in Congress; more enduring than Bills of Rights, or written constitutions, or governments, or treaties, or creeds: they bind together men of different speech, of different races, of different parties;" Lest nothing be left behind, Gilman adds that ideas "give unity to human purpose; they promote human progress: and *universities are the exponents of these civilizing ideas.*"[25]

The size and scale of these research universities, accompanied by expanded access and opportunities offered to increasingly socio-economically diverse students, altered the landscape of higher education in the latter decades of the nineteenth century. However, the grander intentions of the academy, the presumed value of a college education, albeit with dust-ups over curriculum and demands for more vocational education and training, remained remarkably unchanged: they serve as a positive force for society, the nation, and civilization, search for truth, use ideas to better culture and humankind, and, in Gilman's words, to be "the exponents of these civilizing ideas."

## ROBERT HUTCHINS AND HIS CRITICS:
## IDEALS AND IDEAS ABOUT THE UNIVERSITY

In its ideal state, what is it that the college and university is supposed to be? How does the university manage to defend itself against those who would form it as something very different from the university qua the academy?

Many have thought long and hard about this issue.[26] Though by no means a leader without vast critics, Robert Hutchins, president of the University of Chicago from 1929–1952 is one of the most avant-garde, high-profile thinkers and leaders of the university in the twentieth century. He followed in the footsteps of the research university founders and early presidents of the late nineteenth century. But Hutchins' vision was in critical ways at odds with their philosophies and visions.

Hutchins was no milquetoast. At times arrogant, always forceful, and both very right and very wrong about many issues facing the university, there is no mistaking the take of his arguments about what the university must be and what it must not allow itself to become.

Horrified by what he viewed as ill informed, ill-gotten designs characteristic of the nineteenth century's altered landscape of the college and university, Hutchins was determined to rectify what he believed were horrific mistakes and errors. He knew what it would take to hold the center. However, the only way he could see that happening was if it were on his terms, with no negotiation or capitulation to any opponents.[27]

Hutchins minced no words in conveying his convictions about the university: "A university is a community of scholars. It is not a kindergarten; it is not a club; it is not a reform school; it is not a political party; it is not an agency of propaganda."[28] Many leaders and commentators of the university would heartily endorse these sentiments. However, many of those in Hutchins time and in ours willy-nilly walk a contrary path. When the academy becomes distorted so that its ends belie supposed fundamental values, the university becomes the anathema that Hutchins feared.

The politics of the day ever lurk outside the academy. That is simply a reality, nothing harmful or untoward in itself. The danger comes when the university succumbs to a takeover by these forces inside the gates of the academy. The politicization of the university, the capitulation to wrangling ideologies and political views of whatever persuasion—liberal, conservative, Left, Right, and any combination—is the outcome that Hutchins, Kenneth Minogue, and many others have consistently warned against.

Hutchins captures what is at stake. "Freedom of inquiry, freedom of discussion, and freedom of teaching—without these," Hutchins argues, "a university cannot exist." These are the principles of the university. The danger is that "Without these a university becomes a political party or an agency of propaganda. It ceases to be a university." The university must be riveted on its purpose, existing "only to find and to communicate the truth. If it cannot do that, it is no longer a university."[29]

The predicament for Hutchins and for the academic community is profound. That is, there are always forces at the gates whose very presence, if not intent, work to shape the university in ways counter and destructive to its purpose. These pressures became more pronounced in the modern era as a result of corporate and governmental influence, with their overlapping agendas focused as they are on their own interests and not those of the university.

Left to these devices, the university is no longer the university. It will be shoved, shaped, and distorted into something else, whether by design or default, at the hands of these forces that Hutchins believed simply "didn't get it" about what the university must be.

Hutchins never shirked from his responsibility to make clear what the university should be. For him this was a challenge that simply had to be confronted. The dangerous, undermining forces that he believed lurked in the academy in reality exist, no matter the era and the players. Any academic community can and should take cues from his warnings. Hutchins drew a line in the sand: If those in the academy are not going to defend it, who will?

Immediately after departing the Chicago presidency in 1951, Hutchins pulled together his grandest ideas and schemes for the university, no small task when you elect to title the book, *The University of Utopia*. Hutchins's thinking reflects this era of momentous tugs of ideology created by the early days of the Cold War and the heart of the McCarthy assaults on liberty and academic freedom.

However, the alarm he sounds transcends the peculiarities of these times. The onus was not only on educational leaders, but also on society. The university had to take the lead in being true to its foundations.

But it could not win that battle completely on its own. It had to rally other leaders in the nation and society to its cause. "Unless we can figure out what education is and what a university is, and unless we can build up a tradition in this country that supports these conceptions," Hutchins argues, "education and the universities will always be at the mercy of those who honestly or for political purposes seek to make them the protagonists of their views." [30]

Nonetheless, Hutchins cuts his opponents more than a bit of slack. He indicates that this takeover of the university can in some cases be done "honestly," though obviously also in other instances for nothing better than bald "political purposes." Regardless, even those who try to shape the university as a "protagonist for their views" are still guilty of damaging the university's foundations, even if their motives are not directed at political takeover.

However, Hutchins's attempt at throwing a bone to his opponents finds him guilty of suggesting a distinction without a difference. No matter the motives for trying to shape the university in ways counter to its fundamental creed and purposes, the end result is the same. The overall ground of Hutchins's warning is profound. It is something about which the academy must regularly take stock.

Hutchins saw chaos in his midst. He believed this chaos created a lack of coherence within the university, and for the university as a power in society and the nation. He is not the first person to fall for the shibboleth that chaos automatically dictates disaster. Change had taken place in the university and college, not only in the nineteenth, but continuing and amplified in reaction to the new forces of the twentieth century. Hutchins's view of the landscape was based in reality. But the solutions were not as simple as he depicted and fellow educators countered by taking the challenge to him.

One educational leader who jousted with Hutchins was Harry Gideonse, president of Brooklyn College after a professorial career at Rutgers, Chicago (overlapping with Hutchins's presidency), and Columbia universities. [31] Gideonse entered the fray of the debate about the university, what it was or was becoming, and how leaders and the university should react to the public jeremiads of Robert Hutchins and of Abraham Flexner, and Thorstein Veblen in the earlier decades of 1900s.

Whether the players of the time realized it or not, the future shape of the university for the remainder of the twentieth century was at stake. It was not a time for shirking the responsibility of public debate or for ignoring the notion that ideas matter. Hutchins had his. Gideonse made clear that he had his as well.

Gideonse's critique admits that the university likely no longer coheres as it once did. He understood that there exists in- and outside the gates of the academy a degree of chaos, but he avoids getting into a debate about what is cause and what effect. Gideonse chalks up more chaos and less coherence as the reality of a more complex, less homogenous nation.

By the early decades of the twentieth century the nation had grappled and grown, been stretched by its ever-increasingly diverse population and the assault that science and the Enlightenment had wrought.[32] Gideonse is simply not surprised, and nowhere near as concerned as Hutchins, that increasing diversity and intellectual breakthroughs had generated challenges to the coherence of the university

Gideonse (in *The Higher Learning in a Democracy*) takes Hutchins head on arguing that Hutchins fascination with the core of medieval theology were not born out of its intellectual foundations but rather in a shared, common faith of its devotees. For Gideonse, the problem with Hutchins was the desire for the university to turn back the clock and embody the theology of its the medieval history and forbearers while judging the present generation in the academy and in society as "faithless" and one with "no stock in revelation."[33]

Among Hutchins's vulnerabilities were his assumptions that American society, including the college and university, were in a state of decay. Only implementation top-down of his ideas based in Aristotelian and medieval assumptions about knowledge and the university could save things.

Gideonse goes to this core issue of Hutchins's contentions. He points to the major problem in Hutchins's thinking: A desire to return the university in America to a medieval model. The battle between Gideonse and Hutchins was one of a romanticized vision of the past versus the demands of modernity. Gideonse turns Hutchins's thinking on its head concluding that his assumptions about metaphysical first principles for the university demanded the same degree of reliance on revelation as medieval theology.[34]

The Hutchins-Gideonse argument was very simply one of old versus new. On one hand, there was the desire, highly romanticized, for a by-gone era however good it was or could be. In contrast stood the notion that the university, even if muddling its way through, was sufficiently strong and coherent to make sense of itself, thus defining an identity and reaffirming its role in society. If it could do those things, it would have no problem in being able to endure. And if that ended up as the outcome, Hutchins's fears would be revealed as overreactions.

Willing to accept what Hutchins staunchly resisted, Gideonse suggests that what was happening in modern culture, even if it was considered to be as Hutchins and other critics argued disintegrating and in
radical decline was neither brand new nor insurmountable. Any problems in the culture of the day were not result of intellectual foibles and
errors but rather the necessary trade-off from greater reliance on citizens
and the values to which they chose to adhere as individuals. These individual choices and convictions were not ones for the state, the body politic, or the college to be involved in or to be made for people. And if the
individual were to be so confined the result would be an obstacle to
academic pursuits and scholarly inquiry.[35]

In contrast to Hutchins, Gideonse argued that the contemporary
world was complex and unstable. Therefore the old, seeming to Hutchins, tried-and-true means and ends of intellectual life and values, simply
no longer obtained. Thus for Gideonse, and in a slam at Hutchins's approach, the prospect for contemporary culture and for the university is
that taken as a challenge, philosophy held the prospect of clarifying and
developing the values by which individuals and society were able to live.
In the contemporary world this organic and synthetic approach to knowledge stood and would continue to stand in stark contrast to Hutchins
dictatorial approach based on his unrelenting belief in a "discarded meta-
physics."[36]

Historical hindsight does not afford the luxury of "what if's." In this
case "what if" Hutchins's vision for the university had been wholly established in the mid-twentieth century? Or even "what if" a handful of
colleges and universities had followed his vision (arguably colleges such
as St. John's Annapolis have done so)?

We do know that Hutchins's ideal university was not to be set up in
any way that would make its shape pliable or adaptable. In fact, Hutchins's assessment that the university had already adapted far too much to
changing times was the source of his demand to alter that course.

To his credit, Hutchins risked his ideas in the public square. He
thought long and hard about them. He had a consistent rationale for the
value and importance of his vision for the university. He sought to push
the college and university's identity in a certain direction. However, by
the mid-twentieth century, the university had evolved as a result of
events and decisions made in the middle of the previous century. That
evolution was not about to be stopped, even by someone of Hutchins's
passion and chutzpah.

However, the ledger of who won and who lost reveals a complicated
picture. The outcome of these debates doesn't produce a simple account
of winners and losers.

On one hand, Hutchins managed to slow down and to shift partially
the course that the university was on. Pieces of what he argued and
hoped for—classical, traditional curriculum, use of the great books, pre-

serving the undergraduate college rather than have it be swallowed up in the large footprint of the university, and emphasis on the Socratic meth-od—were preserved not just at Chicago, but elsewhere in higher educa-tion.

On the other hand, despite these victories, Hutchins's critics and op-ponents also carried the day. The university had become an increasingly large player in the national consciousness. With its high profile, and its research and other public apparatus, the university was now playing a more instrumental role in what society needed and wanted. It had be-come a key institution dedicated to the betterment of the lives of citizens and contributions to the common good.

But even with these as its *raison d'être*, the university, more so than frequently thought, joined the historical reputation of the college rather than eclipsing and burying it. In this way Hutchins, though not primarily focused on saving the liberal arts college (though he clearly advocated the liberal arts), ended up with an admirable victory as the colleges of the nation have continued to thrive rather than be gobbled up by the research university and its educational quests. When all the dust had settled, Hutchins had some wins; his opponents also had theirs.

## THE COLLEGE AND UNIVERSITY TODAY: CONTEMPORARY INTERPRETATIONS OF TRADITION AND CHANGE

Any coherence that the university and college enjoys in the contemporary era has been hard won. Any holding of the center is not something to be taken for granted. College presidents, other academic and faculty leaders, professors, trustees, alumni, and outside supporters must remain com-mitted to the cause of maintaining the identity of the university qua the university. Otherwise that will not happen, and the fears of Hutchins, Angell, Gilman, and others will be realized: the university becomes just another, in Hutchins's words, "political party or an agency of propagan-da," or social agency or organization, however noble the cause and goal.

John Gardner, one of the major thinkers and contributors to the uni-versity in the mid-twentieth century, knew well centripetal forces on the academy, particularly in the tumultuous times of the 1960s. Regarding the recurrent crises of the university, he suggests: "If the college or uni-versity is to preserve its character as a community and forge for itself a distinctive identity and role in the vast clutter of scholarly, scientific, and instructional activities that will characterize our evolving technological society, it will have to have a considerable measure of internal coherence and morale."[37]

In many ways Gardner's "clutter" has become more severe in the five decades since his comment. One need go no farther than the proliferation—a blessing and a curse—of scholarly publications, unending re-search much of questionable point or worth. Then there is the matter of the technology of computers and the internet—again blessing and curse—and the questionable, certainly not fully examined, educational value of virtual teaching and learning and of massive online course work. Gardner barely knew of "clutter."

However, Gardner does not expect the clutter to disappear. Rather he argues the antidote is "internal coherence and morale." This is a not simple, but yet it is a critical challenge for the academy. Coherence and morale do not happen by default. They are crafted only through inten-tional effort and sustained thinking. The desire for coherence, and morale as well, connects to the values asserted by holding the center in the acad-emy. In short, locating and holding the center is the avenue for keeping the greatest number of constituents of the university as highly engaged as possible over a substantial period of time.

Gardner reflects his times, the march from the post-World War II era of unbridled growth, hope and expectation in the university, to the chaos and rancor of the 1960s. But his advice about what needs to happen to accomplish "internal coherence and morale" applies equally in any era.

He asserts that reaching this goal of coherence is crucial to the for-tunes of the academy and requires a corporate effort. This ". . . means that trustees, administration, faculty, and students are going to have to admit that they are all part of one community—distasteful as that may be to some of them—and they are going to have to ask what they can do individually and collaboratively to preserve the integrity and coherence of that community and to regain command of its future."[38]

At one level, Gardner's counsel aligns with assertions that all institu-tions and organizations in order to be healthy and prosperous must rely on buy-in and investment from members of their communities. This is true regardless—certainly much the case in the academy of how varied and diverse those constituents.

To an extent there is a "chicken and egg" aspect to what Gardner suggests. Which comes first: community and culture, around which con-stituents gather and rally, or that members of an institution work first to exert the force of their interests and personalities in order to shape a coherent whole, a commons that satisfies those interests?

Centripetal forces have always been in- and outside the gates of the academy. Gardner has an antidote to counter chaos and the threat of dissembling. That is, the effort must be to maintain "internal coherence and morale" through the goodwill of constituents of the college and uni-versity who understand what is at stake and thus are willing to accept their duty to "preserve the integrity and coherence."

This could be viewed as wishful thinking. But wishful or not, it is a critical aspect of the university's capacity to retain its identity as the university, and to sort through passing fads and navigate the serious challenges it faces.

The demand that the university play a role in the common good, in the welfare of society, has always been a part of its *raison d'être*, especially in America. The Colonial Colleges, whatever their particular and peculiar theological and cultural bents, and desire to do it their way, shared this understanding about why they existed and what they should do.

This mission outside the gates is one defining purpose and identity of the college and university. Though a more global era seems to be upon us today, the press for the university to contribute to the human good abroad, as well as at home, goes back more than a century, if not longer.

In assessing the state of the university a decade after the conclusion of his presidency at Stanford University (1992–2000), Gerhard Caspar finds timelessness in Daniel Gilman's remarks 135 years before. Gilman's propositions reflected then mid- to late nineteenth-century global initiatives of American educational leaders. Casper believes then and now that the global reach of the university creates part of its identity.

Caspar notes "At the founding of Johns Hopkins University in 1876, its first president, Daniel Coit Gilman, spoke about American involvement in promoting higher education institutions in Japan, China, Lebanon, and Egypt. . . ." Why bother doing this? What was the point? Betterment of humankind and morality are in the heart of Gilman's litany. Caspar underscores the basis of the university for Gilman: "What is the significance of all this activity? It is a reaching out for a better state of society than now exists; it is a dim but an indelible impression of the value of learning; it is a craving for intellectual and moral growth. . . ."[39]

But Caspar is not done. He adds more of Gilman's aims that define the university in its global reach but apply at home as well. These features of the university and its initiatives were as important in Gilman's day as they are in ours.

In Gilman's words, the significance of the university's activity on this global front:

> is a longing to interpret the laws of creation; it means a wish for less misery among the poor, less ignorance in schools, less bigotry in the temple, less suffering in the hospital, less fraud in business, less folly in politics; it means more study of nature, more love of art, more lessons from history, more security in property, more health in cities, more virtue in the country, more wisdom in legislation, more intelligence, more happiness, [and last and interestingly] more religion.[40]

Stanford was one of the major research universities to be established in the mid- to late nineteenth-century era. Understandably a cheerleader for his home base of Stanford, Caspar highlights what is distinctive about the academy.

He takes note that Stanford's founding grant "referred to 'promotion of the public welfare' as the purpose" and, in 1902, Jane Stanford elaborated in a flowery speech to the Board of Trustees, "The moving spirit of the Founders . . . was love of humanity and a desire to render the greatest possible service to mankind. The University was accordingly designed for the betterment of mankind morally, spiritually, intellectually, physically, and materially."[41] We can be easily distracted about the purposes of the contemporary university by the ways they have bettered themselves "physically and materially." That is all true.

But Caspar, former president, denizen of the twenty-first century, bolsters his definition of the university relying on Gilman's rhetoric about "intellectual and moral growth," and on Jane Stanford's ideas about moral, spiritual, and intellectual, albeit also physical and material, benefits and betterment. Caspar could readily cite other social benefits of the university—medical advances, technological innovations, embrace of diversity, or many other accomplishments that are broadly part of human betterment. But he does not. Instead, Caspar unapologetically relies on rather traditional, certainly fundamental, values and beliefs at the foundation of the academy.

Like Stanford, Columbia University has a rich and longer history. When Stanford was only a few decades old, Columbia launched the first "contemporary civilization" requirement (1919) in the country. In addition, this storied institution is home of such professor luminaries as Daniel Bell and Jacques Barzun and their writings about Columbia and the university writ large, not to mention the nearly fifty-year presidency of Nicholas Murray Butler.[42]

Following in their footsteps at Columbia, Andrew Delbanco has thought long and hard about the state of the American university, now in its twenty-first-century garb. Delbanco goes "back to the future" to the answer a question crucial to the degree to which we are able to know whether the college and university can hold the center, the question implied in the title of his book: *College: What It Was, Is, and Should Be.*

Delbanco believes that an examination of the European, British, clerical, and church roots of the university and college in America leads to rejection of those who believe there is nothing of value in the past. "In our own time, when some colleges seems to have less than a firm grasp on their public obligations, such precedents—from both the era of religion and of Enlightenment—should not," Delbanco urges, "be cause for embarrassment but for emulation."[43]

Using humor to underscore the traditions that should be embraced, Delbanco suggests that, "If you were to remind just about any major university president today that his or her own institution arose from this or that religious denomination, you'd likely get the response of the proverbial Victorian lady who, upon hearing of Darwin's claim that men descend from apes, replied that she hoped it wasn't so—but if it were, that it not become too widely known."[44]

The extent of religious heritage in the college is not quite as universal as his claim portrays. However, there is more than a grain of truth to it. We have observed the religious roots of even many public universities, not to mention the religious heritage of many private universities and colleges. Additionally, the religion of the Republic religiously undergirds the expanse of the academy.

We have come this far in our story about the foundation of America's colleges and universities without mentioning one of its major traditions: noblesse oblige. On the score of noblesse oblige, Delbanco is highly critical and highlights a vacuum that should be cause for alarm. His concern is that noblesse oblige, the idea that college graduates owe something to society as a result of the opportunity they have been given in becoming educated, is in serious eclipse.

He asserts that many of the "best" colleges "have now arrived at a conception of themselves that is the reverse of where they began." That is, these colleges "now seem to discount" a belief once firmly in place "that courage and selflessness are democratically distributed virtues (something I believe, that many people learn in war), and that with privilege comes responsibility."[45]

This criticism is spot on. Certainly many colleges and universities have in recent decades developed elaborate emphasis on community service, volunteerism, and internships geared to the public good. However, much of this reduces to resume-stuffing for students, i.e., not done for reasons of giving back, but rather for the purposes of enhancing personal profiles in order to make them more attractive to prospective employers or for graduate school admissions.

Delbanco calls for something much different. He covets a return— much of his critique is about return—to a true sense of noblesse oblige, college students and graduates developing a deep understanding of what they owe to society as a result of the robust gifts and opportunity their education affords them.

Further, noblesse oblige is something unique to the university, a special aspect of what makes the university what it is (though Delbanco does suggest that noblesse oblige is also ironically taught in military service and war). Thus a re-embrace of noblesse oblige is crucial for the university to be true to its heritage.

Sounding like a secular evangelical of the academy's heritage, Delbanco returns to the theme of religious roots in the colleges of the nation. His belief is that there is a near consensus among critics of the academy on the left and right of the political spectrum that "our oldest colleges have abandoned the cardinal principle of the religion out of which they arose: the principle that no human being deserves anything based on his or her merit."[46]

In the political ideological framework of much of today's debates about the academy, coalescing of opinion is infrequent. But Delbanco is onto something on the point of noblesse oblige, on the idea that merit does not dictate entitlement. About this aspiration, if he is correct, even those at loggerheads on other social and cultural issues—political correctness apologists and attackers alike—can find common ground.

Delbanco is not short on overarching social commentary that connects to what colleges are doing and not doing in today's climate. His challenge is that regardless the sources of the disintegration in the social fabric and in supports for notions of giving back, the college must re-grasp traditions such as noblesse oblige that have in the past served them and society well.

The glaring shortcoming of today's colleges that Delbanco and others highlight is as important as it is complex: "by failing to reconnect their students to the idea that good fortune confers a responsibility to live generously toward the less fortunate, too many colleges are doing too little to help students cope with this [contemporary] siege of uncertainty."[47]

Furthermore, this aspiration connects to the core to which the academy should be dedicated. This because "One of the insights at the core of the college idea—indeed of the idea of community itself." Delbanco no doubt believes an ideal, "has always been that to serve others is to serve oneself by providing a sense of purpose, thereby countering the loneliness and aimlessness by which all people, young and old, can be afflicted."[48]

Delbanco's tour of where the college finds itself today simultaneously reveals cause for concern but also hope that ambitions of the past can be re-established. He advocates a shift in focus from the fads of recent decades and the ideological debates they have inspired. In place of these distractions, Delbanco calls for recapture of the fundamental principles of the academy.

His conviction is that these principles will enable the university to restore a crucial part of its bygone stature. At the same time, from this foundation the university could in more fundamental ways address a number of critical issues—diversity, equity, curricular wrangling, which political faction is controlling the academy—on its docket but often these too producing nothing more than mere distraction.

Of course, absent the convictions and actions of college presidents, key faculty leaders, and trustees dedicated to follow Delbanco's prescriptions, the danger is that nothing will happen. With the vital traditions of the college at stake, the prospect that those in positions to come to the rescue would do nothing is a daunting possibility.

No review of the meaning and identity of the American college and university would be complete absent the thoughts of a great president of the twentieth century. Hannah Gray was president of the University of

Chicago from 1978–1993, arriving in the post over twenty-five years after Hutchins's departure. She peered with consternation and veneration over her shoulder at her predecessor, Robert Hutchins.

Citing a moment in Chicago's history, Gray captures the chutzpah of Hutchins. The piece of Chicago history in question was Hutchins's roll of the dice with his trustees fifteen years into his twenty-plus-year presidency.

In a "Trustee-Faculty" dinner speech in January 1944, Hutchins sought trustee approval of his plan to vest in the president all authority for the academic life, program, and policies of the university. He contended that this autocratic authority would actually and paradoxically, but more a point of rhetorical argument than reality, lead to "a more democratic community by reducing the preponderant power of the senior faculty and extending the same rights to those previously excluded from the faculty senate."[49]

Hutchins's argument was that democratic, consensus-seeking decision-making was creating a stranglehold on the university. The institution had become subject to a tyranny of a minority in the form of its senior, longest tenured faculty leaders. Hutchins sought to rectify that misfortune and believed that vesting more authority in the president was the way to do that.

Convinced of his own genius, Hutchins demanded total control over the university's academic culture. He conjured a grandiose solution to a problem of questionable scope. However, his public overture posed a real threat to Chicago and its culture. What would have happened at Chicago if the trustees had somehow been convinced to go along with Hutchins?

The bottom line was that Hutchins's idea ran counter to common sense about what is truly involved if the center of the university is to be held. That task is not as simple as Hutchins felt. It certainly can't be brought about by the control and dictatorial power of a president alone.

Gray is fully aware of the ideological nature of the Hutchins's philosophy and intent. In her mind, Hutchins's actions posed a peril that went beyond his proposal. She views his initiative not as a singular event, but rather as in character with the arrogance of his presidential temperament.

Hutchins tried to wrap his plans in the veil of democracy and democratic principles. That his ideas aspired to democratic ends is a highly debatable proposition. In fact the opposite can be argued: that his suggestion was absolutely undemocratic in vision and intent. Furthermore, if the trustees had agreed, the outcome would have produced a highly ideological end—Hutchins's authoritarian ideas holding sway over the way Chicago would have been run.

We can be fairly certain that even such an outcome would not have been the end of the story as reaction and retaliation to Hutchins would undoubtedly have set in and the consequences for Chicago would have been unimaginable.

Gray acknowledges the high-sounding rhetoric in Hutchins' dinner speech to the trustees and faculty. Hutchins claimed his "crusade" to be directed at accomplishing the purpose of the university, a purpose that "is nothing less than to procure a moral, intellectual, and spiritual revolution throughout the world," no minor visionary he. At his core, Hutchins believed that "The whole scale of values by which our society lives must be reversed if any society is to endure. We want a democratic academic community because we know that if we have one we can multiply *the power which the University can bring to bear upon the character, the mind, and the spirit of men.*" [50]

The university as a force for human and societal salvation is an admirable end. We know that Hutchins's passion arose from overwrought belief that depravity and decay had invaded the gates of the academy, as well as being shot through society outside. That his views resulted from such fears does not diminish his aspirations for what the university could and should fulfill. The problem was Hutchins's solution: placing in the college president the power to make over authority and decision-making in the academy.

Shaping "the character, the mind, and the spirit of men" is a worthy goal of the university. The irony of Hutchins's idea is that he would have manipulated power from authority in the presidential pulpit to get the university to that end. Investment and collaboration by others, the involvement of the university community and its constituencies in pursuing this commendable ideal, would have been nearly eliminated in Hutchins's university and worldview.

Sparing little in her criticism of her predecessor, Gray offers withering judgment: Hutchins's desire strove "to impose an ideological conformity threatening to the intellectual freedom at the core of the university." [51] Nothing could be more destructive to the fundamental principles and values of the academy than this type of kingly rule. A university with a center that holds cannot endure leadership with such animus about the free-flow of ideas and debate, and such calculated embrace of "ideological conformity."

What have we been saying? Simply that the university needs to be the university. It cannot allow itself to become something other: a political force or institution with a partisan political agenda; a social agency notwithstanding how elevating and meaningful the social ends sought; or worse an ideological battering ram abusing the university's reputation in the marketplace of ideas.

If the university can be true to its beginning foundations and to the fundamental beliefs and values traditionally associated with it, then the university gains respectable coherence. It is that coherence that forms a center. With that center the college and university can fulfill its duty to educate students, to challenge them to give back to society, and to contribute through all its the resources to human betterment.

The ultimate question, then, is whether those who guide the university can muster sufficient wisdom to shape the university as wholly different from other institutions in society and to possess the moral convictions to steer it to fulfill that role and vision. Triumph of that vision in the future as in the past delivers a prescription for Delbanco's proposition and question: "The college and university: What is it and what should it be?"

## NOTES

1. For extended discussion about the necessity for the university and its leaders to hold the center see: Stephen J. Nelson: *Leaders in the Labyrinth: College Presidents and the Battleground of Creeds and Convictions* (American Council on Education Praeger: Series on Higher Education: Westport, Conn., 2007), Part 2: The Contest for the Middle: Can the Center Hold?, 67–144, and Stephen J. Nelson, *Decades of Chaos and Revolution: Showdowns for College Presidents* (Lanham, MD: Rowman & Littlefield, 2012), especially Chapter 8, Ideological Follies and the Soul of the University, 155–74.

2. Frederick Rudolph, *The American College and University: A History* (New York: Alfred A. Knopf, 1968), 13.

3. Ibid.

4. Herbert McClosky, "Consensus and Ideology in American Politics," *The American Political Science Review* 58, no. 2 (June 1964): 361–82, 362, italics authors.

5. Ibid., 363.

6. Ibid.

7. John P. Diggins, "Consciousness and Ideology in American History: The Burden of Daniel J. Boorstin," *The American Historical Review* 76, no. 1 (February 1971): 99–118, 112.

8. Douglas Sloan, *The Great Awakening and American Education: A Documentary History* (New York and London: Teachers College Press, 1973), 2.

9. Ibid.

10. Ibid., 47–48.

11. *American Higher Education: A Documentary History*, Volume I, Richard Hofstadter and Wilson Smith, eds., (Chicago: University of Chicago Press, 1961), 237. The material that follows is taken from this source from 237–40.

12. Ibid., 240.

13. Ibid.

14. Ibid.

15. Ibid., 242.

16. Rudolph, 212.

17. Ibid.

18. Ibid., 215.

19. Ibid., 217.

20. Ibid., 279.

21. Ibid., 279-80. From James Angell, *Selected Addresses*, 49.

22. Daniel Coit Gilman, *The Launching of a University*. With new Foreward by Francesco Cordasco. (New York: Garrett Press, 1969), viii.

23. Ibid., 130-31, "Resignation: A Farewell Address" (February 22, 1902).

24. Ibid., 216. "Books and Politics—An Address on the Completion of a New Library Building at Princeton University."

25. Ibid., 233, italics mine. (October 25, 1899).

26. Among the most insightful, especially regarding the threat to the university posed by ideologies and ideological forces, see Kenneth Minogue, *The Concept of a University* (Berkeley and Los Angeles: University of California Press, 1973).

27. See Stephen J. Nelson, unpublished paper, "President Robert Hutchins' Designs on Education and the University: Imposing Provocateur or Mediocre Prophet?" Presented at the Eastern Educational Research Association, February 2014.

28. Robert Hutchins, *No Friendly Voice* (Chicago: University of Chicago Press, 1936), 5.

29. Ibid.

30. Robert M. Hutchins, *The University of Utopia* (Chicago: University of Chicago Press, 1953), 83.

31. Gideonse was joined by numerous thinkers and writers who argued publicly with Hutchins in writing and from the rostrum. Again, for a full review of these personalities and what they had to say, see Stephen J. Nelson, unpublished paper.

32. *American Higher Education: A Documentary History*, Volume II, Richard Hofstadter and Wilson Smith, eds. (Chicago: University of Chicago Press, 1961), 947.

33. Ibid.

34. Ibid.

35. Ibid.

36. Ibid.

37. Gilman, x. Cited from John Gardner, in Alvin C. Eurich, ed., *Campus 1980* (New York: Delacorte Press, 1968), 8.

38. Ibid.

39. Gerhard Caspar, "The Search to Know—What? Reflections on the Purposes of the University Curriculum Workshop" The Van Leer Jerusalem Institute, May 27, 2010, 2, 1-14.

40. Ibid.

41. Ibid., 3.

42. Daniel Bell, *The Reforming of General Education: The Columbia College Experience in its National Setting*. With Forward by David B. Truman (New York: Columbia University Press, 1996) and Jacques Barzun, *The American University: How it Runs, Where it is Going*. (New York: Harper and Row, 1968).

43. Andrew Delbanco, *College: What It Was, Is, and Should Be* (Princeton, NJ: Princeton University Press, 2012), 66.

44. Ibid., 65.

45. Ibid., 137.

46. Ibid., 138.

47. Ibid., 148.

48. Ibid.

49. Hannah Holborn Gray, *Searching for Utopia: Universities and Their Histories* (Berkeley: University of California Press, 2012), 17.

50. Ibid., italics mine.

51. Ibid.

# THREE

## Contentious Compatibility and the Common Good

### *The University as Servant and Critic in a Democracy*

On the occasion of his inauguration as president of the University of Michigan, Harold Shapiro chose for his address the title "Critic and Servant: The Role of the University."[1] Critic and servant concisely captures the expectations the college and university in America has borne over centuries. From the smallest liberal arts colleges to the major research universities like the institution Shapiro was about to lead, the academy in America has shouldered this burden and exerted this clout.

The nation's higher education institutions are supposed to uplift society and to contribute in ways that will better the fortunes of citizens and the nation. At the same time, often in the same breath, they are expected to criticize traditions, dogmas, and the way things are done, and to contend for necessary changes regardless who or what might be offended in the process.

Shapiro asserts that, "The relationship between the modern university and society is very complex and fragile because of the university's dual role as society's servant and as its critic." Amplifying the demands, he adds:

> On the one hand, the university has a responsibility for training and research functions that serve society's current economic and cultural life. On the other hand, the university has a fundamental responsibility to criticize society's current arrangements and to construct, entertain, and test alternative ways of organizing society's institutions, alternative approaches to understanding nature, and alternative visions of society's values.[2]

Michigan and its major university counterparts hold high profiles in the public eye. Thus the judgment of the public targets, pro and con, concerning how they fulfill these roles, given the university's large footprint in the American higher education world.

However, the colleges of the nation, even the smallest, are not exempted from equal expectation to be both critic and servant. These schools contribute to society as servants and critics in direct ways paralleling the research university. As with major universities, the graduates of small colleges move into professional lives in society and into graduate education at the universities. From these perches, students produced by the colleges and universities serve both as individuals and as members of communities and institutions in lifelong roles as both critics and servants of society and the nation.

Shapiro rightly underscores the complexity and fragility of this university role as critic and servant. By nature this is a tense relationship, one fraught with the danger of litmus tests being posed and fingers being pointed from outside the gates in, and from inside the gates out.

Society in the form of government, legislatures, and politicians, but also citizens, can urge on the university that certain people of certain stripes, or certain policies and types of research do not belong inside the gates. Hiring the "wrong" faculty and engaging in research that doesn't pass moral muster or political tests, can readily lead to withholding of public approbation and to cuts in funding.

Likewise colleges and universities can step over the line of their presumed objectivity and neutrality, a critical quality that the university must exert in its quest to maintain a high stature as a unique institution in society. The academy fails the test of this duty to strive for impartiality when it institutionally enters the political fray, takes sides, decries one ideological camp or another, or denies public figures a speaking platform because they don't measure up to some standard.

This is a fine line, because to be a critic of society requires the university to broach concerns and to lift the veil on social and political issues that otherwise would be glossed over. However, the university can only bring concerns to the fore from the platform of its fundamental foundation in inquiry, search for truth, and engagement of research regardless where those lead. When the university slips down the slope to behave and to lead otherwise, it risks its very identity as the university.

For the university to be critic and servant requires of it a tough skin. But likewise, society and its movers and shakers, politicians and public commentators must have equally tough skin to hear the messages that the university might deliver, even as those same constituents outside the gates expect to luxuriate in the benefits that the university's servant role produces.

What is it that makes all this work? How is the complexity and fragility of the university's sway in society to be navigated such that the critic and servant role can be filled? How does all this happen, particularly in a democracy which at one and the same time argues for freedom of thought, individuality, and public engagement, all the while having to maintain itself and its public with an aura of security, safety, and stability?

The pivot point for Shapiro is the overlapping ideals in- and outside the gates—for our colleges and universities and for American democracy—of the use of reason, the free play of ideas and thought, and toleration of differing points of view. Shapiro believes that "society's support" for the servant and critic role "has been ultimately sustained by faith in rationalism, faith in knowledge and science, and the resulting notion of human progress," all features that we see repeated in any appraisal of the university's historic foundations.[3]

Added to this is an Enlightenment and certainly American idea, what Shapiro characterizes as "one of the most distinctive ideas of Western civilization," i.e., "the idea that nature, by itself, cannot achieve its full potential. Rather, what is needed is a mutually beneficial interaction among nature, science, and humankind." The glue for all of this is that "The university plays an increasingly central role in this process." Concluding this argument, Shapiro declares that this material progress and expansion in knowledge connect to an even transcendent end: the university's role in "progress in the moral and spiritual sense."[4]

Standing Shapiro's view on its head, it must be noted that if the university reneges on its promise and on the challenges of "faith in rationalism, faith in knowledge and science, and the resulting notion of human progress," then it loses the ballgame. It is no longer the university. In that case, the creed that these beliefs constitute no longer exists as the bridge between the academy and the society of which it is a part. Given the stakes, even more than the university is lost as well.

## REVOLUTIONARY EPOCH: THE BIRTH OF EDUCATION'S ROLE IN AMERICAN SOCIETY

The seeds of the connection between education and the body politic, both in mutual self-interest and in contentious compatibility, were sown early in the American colonial environment. Picking up the story in the decades immediately following the Revolution, Bernard Bailyn underscores the closeness of this relationship.

Of particular interest is his interpretation of the implications of the nation's educational system at all levels. He believes that among its purposes, education enables citizens to become political and moral agents as individuals and as the body politic. In addition are the pushes and pulls for a society that, having shaped the environment in which schools and colleges were born, then finds itself continually swayed by that creation.

These foundation stones say much about how the college and university have undertaken the mantle of critic and servant, and how the nation has greeted the ways those roles have played out.

Bailyn bolsters the notion that in the pre-Revolutionary era, sectarian, denominational groups behaved as though they had no choice but to dive into the education game for reasons of their own survival. Exercising commitment and involvement in education was the way to promote themselves and to establish their heritage and pass it on to rising generations. In this way these religious groups would sustain the present influence they exerted into that future.[5]

To accomplish that task, these denominational and sectarian groups had to operate on a plane on which "Persuasion and nurture would have to do what compulsion could more easily have done."[6] But, Bailyn argues, in full agreement with Sidney Mead that there was to be no compulsion; there would be in Mead's terms, a movement from "coercion to persuasion."[7] Separation, diversity, and continuing schisms were the rule of the day. Thus each denomination, every sectarian group had to look out for its own folk and its own interests. Herein lies further evidence that the polemics of ideology were embedded in America's colleges and universities from the get-go.

However, these sectarian and denominational impulses, rooted as they were in self-interest, led de facto to de-emphasis of the commonweal of the body politic. The state and its interests were at most a second thought, if not subjects of no consideration at all. "The members of such groups participated in a continuous enterprise of indoctrination and persuasion, an enterprise," Bailyn contends, "aimed no longer at unifying society but only at aiding one group to survive in a world of differing groups."[8]

This penchant of the sects to put their interests socially and politically ahead of those of the commonwealths, colonies, and subsequent states had a further sway in how these denominational, sectarian forces perceived and used education. "Education, so central to their purposes, was deliberate, self-conscious, and explicit. . . . Education," for the sects and denominations, "was an act of will."[9]

With such a will-to-power in their approach, the first and foremost purpose of education was to be certain the needs of the religious group were met. Servanthood to society, though not to be avoided altogether, was at the same time not an intended purpose or consequence of education and the educated life.

At the same time, regardless the activity of these sects and denominations, the state ruled and reigned supreme in matters of education. The magistrates and other public officials were separate from the clergy, and the state licensed, provided authorizations, and otherwise controlled the arc of the educational climate and system of education (as it could be called such).

However, this did not mean that the role of the college as critic was taken off the table. If Bailyn is correct, this story of education, the college and university included, in America society has been remarkably seamless for decades, even for centuries.

Bailyn claims that as education in America emerged from the Revolutionary epoch, its character remained the same as it had been nearly since the nation's first colonial days. That is, in the post-Revolutionary period the foundations American education had developed from its beginnings in the New World were "Confirmed rather than disturbed by the Revolution," thus passing "into the nineteenth century as it had developed in the colonial period."[10]

What then was that already-formed character that Bailyn argues stayed put even after the upheaval of Revolution?

Taking a step back, Bailyn believes that education is not completely autonomous of society; rather, "education not only reflects and adjusts to society," but additionally "once formed, it turns back upon it and acts upon it." Here is education as full-blown servant and critic, exerting influence and authority on society, on the polity, on the nation. Bailyn believes that "The consequences of this central transformation of education had," even by this Revolutionary epoch, "significantly shaped the development of American society."[11]

Nonetheless, Bailyn does not view this role of education in the nation's early history as played out so much institutionally, but rather that education's influence on society was born out by individuals as a result of their schooling. His view of the relationship of education, especially through its graduates, with society is nuanced. Bailyn's understanding about this relationship connects to individualism in a democracy as an American phenomenon.

There are many unique characteristics of the American character, certainly among them this notion of boundless energy, creativity, and pragmatic aspirations. Education undergirds and jump-starts these individualistic, national traits. Out of this relationship and the scene of post-Revolutionary America, Bailyn believes two critical developments occurred, both of which bear on higher education's role as servant and critic.

The first was that "education in this form," Bailyn's notion of education not only reflecting and adjusting to society but acting on it, "has proved in itself to be an agency of rapid social change, a powerful internal accelerator." The way education produces this result is by "responding sensitively to the immediate pressures of society it has released rather than impeded the restless energies and ambitions of groups and individuals."[12]

The second development in Bailyn's view was that "education as it has emerged from the colonial period has distinctively shaped the American personality; it has contributed much to the forming of national character."[13] Thus in the big picture, what happened?

Much of what we witness transpiring in the academy, equally a curse and a blessing, and for good and for ill, finds its roots in Bailyn's assumptions. Here is where the rubber meets the road in terms of the impact of the individual in American society.

"What was recognized even before the Revolution as typical American individualism, optimism, and enterprise," Bailyn argues, "resulted also from the processes of education which tended to isolate the individual, to propel him away from the simple acceptance of a predetermined social role, and to nourish his distrust of authority." What ensued was that "The transformation of education that took place in the colonial period," at least with us at mid-twentieth century and likely to today, "was irreversible. We live with its consequences still." [14]

## THE DELICATE BALANCE OF
## THE UNIVERSITY IN A DEMOCRACY

College presidents and other commentators have debated at length the purposes of the college and university in its relationship to American democracy and society. Understandably, they generally agree that the needs of democracy have to be met; that the university, regardless public or private, exists in part at the pleasure of society and the state. However, within that overarching goal and expectation, a number of contentious, in some cases mutually exclusive tensions and controversies inevitably arise.

For example, to what degree is the university an elitist institution, a gateway for those already at the top of society to go on and to be secure in these positions of control, power, and influence in society? Democracy and democratic values imply the common man, equitable access, and the diversity that comes with those aspirations and beliefs. James Angell once described the University of Michigan as existing to provide an "uncommon education for the common man." The "common man," regular folk and citizens, presumably have a meritocratic shot at upward mobility and social-economic success in a democracy.

However, are there limits to how far the borders of the academy are to be stretched in order to meet the ideal of including everyone? That is, what are the dangers of watering down mission, purpose, curriculum, and the demands of intellectual inquiry and academic research if the university either decides or is forced to take all comers?

American democracy has always pursued venerated ideals about the relationship of the citizenry and society. What is considered democratic today may be different from the times of Harvard in the early 1600s. But the values and saga of democracy in America remain remarkably unchanged throughout centuries and the challenges presented in different eras.

The democratic creed of American society is much in the nation's bedrock. That foundation is a defining feature of its colleges and universities as well. The consequent role, as Shapiro notes, of the academy as critic and servant of that democracy and society, is complicated by the expectations, responsibilities, and constituencies entailed.

The nation's aspirations, especially as a democracy, have always been an experiment. Louis Menand captures that quest:

> The Constitution "is an experiment, as all life is an experiment," [Justice] Holmes wrote in a famous dissent. That is what Lincoln said in the Gettysburg Address; democracy is an experiment the goal of which is to keep the experiment going. The purpose of democracy is to enable people to live democratically. That's it. Democracy is not a means to something else; there is no higher good that we're trying as a society attain.[15]

The academy in America is likewise an experiment, and the basis of its experiment is revealed in its relationship to the nation, to the Republic. Democracy, according to Menand, is the highest good that the nation of America is trying to attain. Thus, as the college and university functions as servant and critic, it shapes that aspiration through both its service and its criticism.

## ANDREW JACKSON: THE COMMON MAN VERSUS THE ELITE

Only a few decades into the history of the nation, the voice of the common man came to the fore from the late 1820s through much of the 1830s in the form of Andrew Jackson and his presidency. Jackson represented a pushback against elites and elitism. To him and his supporters, the educated, those whose economic and political status had put them in charge, had hermetically sealed American society from the influence of those who had not been able to break into the ranks of educated and into the seats of power.

Jackson shook all of that up. He was not going to let a wall stand between the common man and the social, political, and cultural benefits over which an elite had claimed and perpetuated a monopoly.

At the very time that the Yale Report of 1828 was arguing for the academy to maintain a traditional curriculum, to hold onto the role of education in the "discipline and furniture of the mind," Jackson was taking hold of the country in his run for President on a platform of opening up the windows, of challenging the hide-bound, and calling the nation to practicality and pragmatism. Maintaining the academy in the face of the Jacksonian onslaught would be no easy task and change was inevitable.

It is no surprise that in a democracy, those who were feeling excluded, whether they actually wanted in or not, would attack the exclusive nature of the college, bringing criticism about its head. Richard Storr describes this early nineteenth-century scene and this confluence of competing pressures: "The college had the strength of a small but hard-shelled nut, and it needed this strength. For even unintentionally exclusive groups invite attack in a democratic society." [16]

What was going on was a new wrinkle for the college in America, especially in its role as critic and servant. The pressure was intense. Defending the college with its built-in elitist qualities now had to be carried out before an increasingly invested and critical public.

"It is perhaps no accident that the classic defense of the traditional college course, the Yale Report of 1828, appeared just as Andrew Jackson was about to give his name to a type of democracy which had no patience," Storr argues, "with the traditional ideal of training for political leadership." The problem for the academy under this new scrutiny was profound. In the Jacksonian arena, "Privilege was taboo; and the colleges, if they did not expressly support privilege, did represent a formalism which could easily be mistaken for it." [17]

However, the Jacksonian Democrats were not alone in this press on the academy. The conservative forces of the day were also promoting the idea that the college, however private it might look, needed to embrace a significant public purpose.

Samuel Ruggles, a lawyer, politician, and board member at Columbia College (later University), produced a pamphlet in the early 1850s, "The Duty of Columbia College to the Community." In it Ruggles offers a traditional view of the academy, but unmistakably one that underscored a high public purpose. He demanded that even if the college wanted to be an ivory tower, it could not hide behind its walls, and had to understand that part of its mission was the betterment of society.

Storr's interpretation is that in this era "the college was a public, not a private, institution;" thus for Ruggles, Columbia, and by inference other schools "owes a peculiarly high and sacred duty—not only faithfully to discharge its trust, in educating individual students," but to do so "to advance the moral and intellectual dignity of the community itself—to become an element of our social system, felt in all its workings, modifying the culture and elevating the character of all around us." [18]

These themes of the public role and conscience of the university continued to unfold throughout the latter decades of the nineteenth. They were amplified by the Social Gospel and Progressive eras, and provided a platform from which the university would experience increasing public demands as the twentieth century opened.

## CHARLES W. ELIOT: REFASHIONING
## THE UNIVERSITY IN SERVICE TO ALL

In 1869, Charles Eliot began a titanic forty-year tenure at Harvard. The Civil War had been over for less than a five years. The advent of the research university was only beginning. The Social Gospel was still a few decades hence.

But the challenges to the country and to the university following the tragic events of a nation tearing at its own seams were profound. This was especially the case as the nation grew to its next phase in maturity and stature. Part of that process was a recapitulation of the revolution in thinking about the common man that Jackson had inspired. New occasions would teach new duties to the university. Eliot was a major figure who led the way. Eliot shifted the ground of debate, such as he could, to be more on the university's turf, rather than letting it be played out by Jackson's agenda.

Eliot's accession to the presidency at Harvard at the young age of thirty-five was met and joined by colleagues, youthful presidents of other major research universities of the time: Andrew White (age thirty-four) inaugurating Cornell in 1968, Daniel Coit Gilman (age forty-five) at new Johns Hopkins in 1876, and James Angell (age forty-two) at the University of Michigan in 1871.[19]

This bevy of university talent and leadership left an enormous footprint on American higher education and on American society. As we have and will see, these leaders were servants and critics par excellence, and the universities they led were shaped in the image and vision of these presidents.

In the era on the backside of Jacksonian democracy, when one might have thought the college in America would be moving toward a strong dose of pragmatism, ironically, in the view of Eliot's biographer, Hugh Hawkins, "The ideal which Eliot raised for the American college was rigidly non-utilitarian."[20] Eliot would become a university-builder at Harvard, and through its leadership he would create the same impact on other higher education institutions. To pull off such a sea change, Eliot had to summon the grandest practicality.

But Eliot was also a man of ideas. Even his views about choice in the curriculum—introduction of electives—while revealing a pragmatic urge were in the end idealistic, because to Eliot's mind they underscored the point that college students were capable of crafting their own courses of study. Hawkins asserts that Eliot believed, "The college should be dominated by the ideas of 'formation and information of the mind,' broad culture, and 'the love of learning and research for their own sake.'"[21]

Hawkins points out, for the university and for Eliot, "This remarkable amalgam included the discipline-and-furniture rationale developed in the Yale Report of 1828," which Eliot might normally have been thought to oppose, as well as "traditional humanism, and even the research ideal." In Hawkins view, this led Eliot to conclude, "one thing the college was not: it was not practical or utilitarian."[22]

Eliot's impact on American higher education is without parallel or match in leadership and influence. Hawkins cites George Herbert Palmer, who went so far as to propose that Eliot not only brought the university to a new maturity, but more significantly embedded it within the fabric of the nation. Anointing Eliot to near sainthood, Palmer believes that, "'To him more than any other man . . . America owes it that her system of higher education is no longer a thing apart by itself, a sort of [']] Ark of the Covenant ['] too sacred to be touched, but a normal part of the life of the nation as a whole.'"[23]

Eliot's idea of the university, of higher education in a democracy and for a democratic society, balances two worldviews that pose risks inside and outside the gates of the academy. Hawkins captures the poles that Eliot believes must be avoided. "There is a danger in an elitist theory of society that it will require a passive population, obedient and apolitical. Eliot," Hawkins declares, "did not want this any more than he wanted control given to the 'fierce passions of the multitudes.'"[24]

The former danger is a return to an aristocratic, fiefdom-like society. The latter peril is to permit a tyranny of the majority. Because of its foundational principles, the university had to stand opposed to both dystopian possibilities.

However, navigating between these two poles is never a simple task. In the end, Eliot and others inside the gates knew that to fulfill its duty and purpose, the academy had to maintain its foundations as a privileged institution. The university is, after all, a distinctive institution in society. Its ability to maintain that identity and to use that platform in order to be both critic and servant to the society and the nation rests on carving out that unique position: exclusive but not disconnected, elite but animated by noblesse oblige.

Hawkins captures how Eliot navigated this fine line. He knew that the academy would produce an elite, well-educated class, what Hawkins labels as "scholar-experts." At the same time, Eliot was aware of the society and political order beyond the bounds of the academy.

Thus even as Eliot hoped for the best for individuals and for that social order, Hawkins believes Eliot simultaneously knew that, "Meanwhile the university would protect itself from the leveling tendencies of equalitarianism. *The university could serve the democratic society best by remaining somewhat separate and privileged. It was for the people, but not of them.*"[25]

## THE COLLEGE AND "THE NATION'S SERVICE"

Woodrow Wilson led Princeton as president (1902–1910) before his time as President of the United States. Wilson was passionate throughout his career about public service and the public good. At Princeton he stressed these themes and puts flesh on the bones of Ruggles's duties of the university.

In a fall 1909, *Scribner's Magazine* article, "What is a College For?" Wilson cuts to the chase: "The college is for the use of the nation, not for the satisfaction of those who administer it or for the carrying out of their private views." Wilson rivets on the distinction between the transcendent purposes of the university and the mundane, prone to foibles views of presidents or, for that matter, of professors. The reality not to be lost is that "They may speak as experts and with a very intimate knowledge, but they also speak as servants of the country and must be challenged to give reasons for the convictions they entertain."[26]

Wilson's philosophy places a hedge on the voice of those in the college and university. However, he is not arguing in the least for censorship. Rather in- and outside the gates the call is for debate and discourse. Rational argument must prevail. Whether for its presidents, its faculty, or even its students the university must provide the foundation for logical dialogue, must use its resources to set that example and create that environment.

Those in the academy are entitled to their opinions, their convictions. However, those ideas must be based in reason and sound thought. Otherwise, all is simply so much rhetoric, so much heat with no light.

Wilson then gazes into a crystal ball. He presciently warns about how politics and ideology can unfold from intellectual tangles and academic arguments no matter how innocuous the discourse might appear. This danger would grow as the twentieth century developed. Wilson's worry was that even out of concerted debate, "Controversy, it may be, is not profitable in such matters, because *it is so easy, in the face of opposition, to become a partisan of one's own views and exaggerate them in seeking to vindicate and establish them. . . ."*[27]

To Wilson, the only thing more dangerous than a one-sided debate, where one party gets its way, is an argument in which the wrangling between two sides results in more polarized partisanship as both get more stuck in their ways. This risk is heightened in college culture when dueling academics become more wedded to their causes.

Democracy demands debate and dialogue, as should the academy. The college and university cannot control what goes on in the society and national culture around it. However, the academy can control how inquiry, discussion, and the exchange of ideas are handled within the gates. America's colleges and universities need to be mindful of how and in what ways they contribute to national culture. How the university conducts itself determines how its voice is heard as servant and critic.

Even with its elitist baggage, Wilson believed that an education, especially a higher education, made a profound difference both in the lives of individuals and in society through the contributions that men and women who were products of the academy would make to the nation.

Most in- and outside the gates of the college and university would agree that education is presumed to have some impact on society. However, a nagging issue confounding the university's image is the degree to which the university is viewed as standing to preserve and to defend tradition versus the degree to which it is an agent of progressivism and change. The academy for centuries has been criticized for being both too conservative and not conservative enough, and for seeing its purpose as too much or too little focused on conserving.

Wilson stands traditional understandings of conservatism and conserving on their heads. The way Wilson sees things the conservation of life relies on growth. In the absence of growth, life will decay and be destroyed. Thus progress in life and for the body politic is elemental and natural. The challenge then for the academy in serving both individuals and society is to nurture that attitude toward growth and progress in life and to translate progress as crucial to conservation and conservatism.[28]

However, the logic of the Wilsonian analysis is that the nation is at risk when its fortunes are left too greatly in the hands of those not exposed to the college life. Without schooling, people are left bare and barren with only habits, not knowledge, to understand and to comprehend the past. Absent the education that can be only found in schools, citizens and the body politic will be left to be guided only by desires and instinct in order to judge what is right as guides to the future. Thus the duty of America's colleges is to serve the state by building up in its citizens the capacity to recollect and to provide the foundation for the essential value of memory.[29]

This task of maintaining culture and passing on to future generations the best of the past requires national and civic corporate memory. It is the only way citizens are enabled to grasp the times in which they live and the issues of the day in the broad context that such understanding demands. This is the duty that the college must fulfill, on its own behalf and that of the nation.

The role of the college and university is unmistakably crucial, its service to the country is clear. The *raison d'être* of the college is manifold and multi-faceted. It should provide the country with men and women who understand and are able to confront both failure and success. The college should prepare students and citizens who are able to discern transcendent and long-lasting tendencies from those more transient in the moment. Most importantly, the service of the academy is to provide the context and grounding of knowledge and understanding about how generations before have lived and the principles they have passed forward to the present generation.[30]

## THE IDEALS OF THE ACADEMY
## AND THE SPIRIT OF DEMOCRACY

After his presidency at the University of Chicago (1929–1951), Robert Hutchins set about to describe the university in its ideal. He had nearly twenty-five years of experience in his presidential post, tumultuous though it often was. Hutchins never went small when he could go big. In this case that is what he did, reflected in the title of his book, *The University of Utopia*.

Hutchins feared that the servant role bore the danger of shrinking the university to nothing more than offering an education reduced to practical, training-oriented purposes. This prospect had to be avoided at all costs. Regardless the outcome as servant or critic, amid the pressures to the contrary, Hutchins's Utopians, "have never been misled into thinking that technical training from the elementary school onward can create industrial power. They do not believe that science is the only knowledge worth having. They are not confused about what makes a country strong."[31]

We know that Hutchins was an inveterate idealist, though he also had his highly practical side. But when confronted with a polarized choice between education as responsible for nothing more than vocational, professional training and preparation, and education as stimulating the life of the mind, Hutchins unrelentingly steered to the latter.

That is not to say there was for Hutchins no place in the academy for formal, career-oriented education. It was simply that this training was to follow stimulation of the intellect and immersion in the world of ideas, the task of the undergraduate college and in Hutchins's world, the use of the great books.

Professional training on the backside of an undergraduate education was a fine and necessary idea. But it was the province of graduate schools—engineering, medicine, business, law—to prepare students, while it was specifically in the laps of business and corporate sector to train recruited employees in skills required in their marketplaces.

So what were the "Utopians" to do in maintaining the university? How were they to be critics and servants of the nation, a role that Hutchins fully endorsed as responsibility demanded of higher education in America?

Hutchins had a spiritual side to his expectations about higher education. He decried the decay and depravity of American society. Expressing fears about the nation's future, he claimed the country to be in dire need of a moral and spiritual revolution. In his mind it was education, and especially in the academy, that was going to lead the nation on the path of reformation. This was a bound duty—critic and servant—of the university. Without it America would lose its faith, fail and be destroyed.

So it is no surprise that Hutchins characterizes the Utopians, read: Americans, as having in their fiber essential doses of the spiritual, the moral, and loyalty to country. The entire educational experience, not just that of higher education, was critical to make that happen.

Hutchins asserts that the Utopians "rely on the patriotism, moral fervor, and intellectual capacity, which, they hold, gives them the ability to meet any new situation with intelligence and decision. Their hope is to be wise and to become so through their educational system."[32] The good Utopian used education to prepare for giving back, for building up and for maintaining Utopia.

This interplay of wisdom with democracy, a Jeffersonian idea and ideal if there ever was one (this despite Hutchins jousting with Jefferson's thinking including in this book), is critical to Hutchins's declarations about the role of the university in America. The Utopians could be and needed to be as practical as they were by nature idealistic.

But Hutchins would settle for nothing less than the highest ideals of the educational system. In his paradigm, education's role is to prepare the citizen, the student, through exposure to ideas, through pursuit of intellectual curiosity, and through learning in the proper classical curriculum inspired by the greatest forbear thinkers and writers.

Thus, in the face of any call to the contrary for practical needs to take priority, the Utopians "never allow themselves to be annoyed by such slogans as adjustment to the environment or meeting immediate needs, because they have sharply defined the purpose of their educational system." The goal of that system is "to promote the intellectual development of the people."[33]

In terms of who should provide education, there would be no deferring to the church, religion, or the family. To Hutchins, the business of education was too important to let amateurs rule. "The Utopians think that intellectual development is too important to be left to amateurs; and, since they are devoted to democracy," an a priori loyalty, "they do not see how they can maintain and improve their democracy unless every citizen has the chance to become as wise as he can."[34] The important matter is that of wisdom, and that education is the sole force to deliver this value to society, consequently contributing to build up the democracy and thereby the nation.

But for Hutchins and others committed to the historical foundation of the academy, the pathway to fulfill this aim of the university is fraught with snares. Always confronting the platform on which the university stands lurked the slippery slope of how easily the academy could unsuspectingly be taken over and altered.

The task of being what it needed to be, the university qua the university, involved juggling the demands of a nation, even in a democratic civic polity, with the conventions of the academy. Those stresses and strains could place the academy at odds with society and thus threaten to undermine the university's mission.

Even the best-intended idea of a university that projected collapsing its foundations and purposes with those of the commonwealth and the nation posed risks and dangers. Thus, referring to Jefferson's aspirations for the University of Virginia at its founding, and one might include Washington's idea for a national university, Hutchins offers a cautionary slant.

He highlights the reality that:

> Since there is this exalted precedent for the attempt to make the American university a means of indoctrination in the common opinion, or even indoctrination in a partisan view of what the common opinion ought it be, it is not surprising that in religious, economic, and political controversy one side or another has often tried to take over the university.[35]

This danger to the university is magnified if the desire for indoctrination is coming from the nation itself, from the power and authority of even duly elected, supposedly informed, leaders and legislators.

It is one thing when ideological camps attempt to dictate to the university what it is to be a servant and what it is to be a critic. It is wholly another matter, and an even graver alarm, when public officials push on the university litmus tests of all and any sort, i.e., as was endured in the McCarthy era and to an extent in the post-September 11 decade plus. When this happens, it is the public, not an ideological cabal, pushing its doctrinaire vision of the proper "common opinion" and using the university to accomplish that purpose.

Nonetheless Hutchins, despite his penchant for cynicism and pessimism, draws a conclusion that reveals the positive overlap for him in the aims of the nation and the aims of the academy. He echoes the confluence of the beliefs of the Republic and the beliefs of the academy discussed earlier.

Hutchins describes these commonly-held values: "The leading articles of the American faith are universal suffrage, universal education, independence of thought and action as the birthright of every individual, and reliance on reason as the principal means by which society is to be advanced."[36] These timeless values are those as well of the academy, certainly the college and university in America.

Thus, when the university plays its role as critic and servant, it sings from the same hymnbook of beliefs and values held to be primary and beyond question by the nation. Whether in support and service of the nation or critical of its course and decisions, the best the university can be is rooted in the highest ideals embodied in American values and tradition.

World War II unraveled stability around the world, threatened American fortunes, and caused rethinking of education's role at the foundation of democracy. Nicholas Murray Butler at Columbia had decried the failures of American preparation for World War I. He warned that getting caught so unawares should never occur again, only to have another world war catch his country napping once more less than two decades later.

To Butler, education, the university sector shared great blame for this miscalculation. The university had duty then and had to bear that obligation in the future to make certain the nation would not again find itself so vulnerable and ill equipped.

As World War II wound down and its conclusion became clear, President James Conant established a select faculty committee at Harvard to address the role of education in a democracy. Like Butler, Conant felt that America's educational system had let the nation down in failing more fully to understand democracy and the threats arrayed around it. The Harvard committee's *Redbook* outlined the ways in which American democracy should be better prepared to protect itself, especially through a renewed and refashioned educational system from grammar school to college and university, against similar future threats.[37]

Hutchins shared the perspectives of these contemporary fellow university presidents. The last years of his tenure at Chicago overlapped with World War II and its immediate aftermath of domestic and international rebuilding and of the Cold War. These times shaped his view of the university. They no doubt led him to hatch his notions in the early 1950s of the University of Utopia in Utopia. At the same time, Hutchins had an arguably larger vision of the university than one simply grounded in the times in which he lived. For him, the role of the university had salvific power and strategic influence in the fortunes of the nation.

With the Second World War still underway, Hutchins expressed views that undoubtedly in his mind transcended those times. After all, we know that Hutchins believed there were many crises and threats to the university, to American culture, and to the land. A world war was just one of those crisis times, albeit in this case the most contemporary and presently gripping.

Hutchins is unalterable about what the university owes the nation. "Candid and intrepid thinking about fundamental issues—in the crisis of our time this is the central obligation of the universities," Hutchins signals. Colleges and universities could not duck the duty at hand: "This is the standard by which they must be judged. This is the aim which will give unity, intelligibility, and meaning to their work." Knowing what Hutchins believed the university must inspire, the aim is sure: "This is the road to wisdom. Upon that road the American university will regain its own soul and bring hope and comfort to a distracted world."[38]

The rise of Fascism, Nazism, and other destabilization in Europe in the run-up to war and of World War II presented a major national threat to the United States. In light of these developments and the threat posed, it is no surprise that the times spawned a rush to turn to the university for response to these issues and to save the nation. The servant role of the university, for the moment checking being a critic at the door, was front and center.

The tenure of Henry Wriston, President of Brown University for nearly two decades from the mid-1930s to the early 1950s (1937–1955) overlapped with that of Hutchins, Butler, and Conant. Wriston joined the fray, further asserting a voice from the college presidential pulpit to debate in the land.

Tensions were in the air: What could a democracy tolerate and withstand in the face of such threats, and what did the nation need from the academy? It was a time of high-pitched focus on democracy and its fortunes, the country still understandably fragile less than a century removed from its test in the Civil War.

The university and its leaders did not shirk from shaping the debate about their duty and about how the nation should act. However, this rhetoric and activity contained more than a little self-interest: if you don't say what should be done and what you as the university will do, then political leaders, social commentators, and corporate barons and their interests will do that job for you and order you to do their bidding.

In commentary about events and about the place of the university in the maelstroms of his day, Wriston is nuanced. Even in the tense and trying times of the 1930s, with the war not yet broken out though its rumblings blatant, Wriston navigates a middle path. He points out that things are not as extreme as they appear—historical perspective is our friend—and affirms that the university, if true to itself, cannot allow collapse of its grandest ideals simply because some jeremiad makes them appear easily expendable.

Wriston stakes education to its traditional roots, a crucial perspective amid the social and political forces, and changes of his day and of any era. He argues that change and complexity were no different in these times than at any previous era. Wriston felt the claims made by many commentators that there existed differences of one era compared to another were simply unfounded. The presumed differences—our time is the worst time—were based in failure to examine events and pressures in relative perspective, or worse were spun from intentional distortions.

Wriston tackles one of the repeated refrains of his day that "Democracy is in danger," alleging that this assertion is simply not true. He inverts the issue, claiming that democracy is by nature always a dangerous proposition. A democratic state is constantly at risk because of its emphasis, stressed in the academy, "upon the individual and his inalienable rights, against the state and its supreme power," and its dedication "to the proposition that liberty is more significant than security."[39]

Democracy then and now ever battles over the tension between assertions of individual freedom and liberty against the aspirations for a united commonweal and for the common good. As Wriston points out, and as the pressures following September 11, 2001 confirm, the pivot point and dilemma is clear: the proposition in the ideal, but one so very difficult to maintain, is that "liberty is more significant than security." The reality is that "Men moving freely, acting freely, speaking freely, and controlled primarily by self-discipline," traits that the university inspires and that those educated within the gates learn, "will come into conflicts that directly jeopardize security."[40]

Critics in Wriston's time and in any time find an easy target in education, and especially higher education, for doing little or nothing to contribute tangibly to society. However, Wriston argues that Jeffersonian notions about education "mitigating" these dangers inherent in democracy are real, and adds the assessment that, while "Education has not done all we desire, it has been far from bootless."[41] The investment of the university as servant and critic, while not perfect, has been felt, especially when the nation needs it most.

What has stayed the same and what has changed? Little, to Wriston's mind. Regarding contemporary complexity and politics of his day, Wriston's response is rooted in his beliefs about what the university can do to offset these difficulties. "The basic problems of politics are the same today as always—" Wriston argues, that is, "to induce men to use reason instead of passion, to select men of public spirit instead of political leeches for public office."[42]

The academy is a complex but unique institution in American society. Its ideals are animating, albeit if not as universally embraced even within the gates, as might be desired and hoped.

Nonetheless the university has persisted. If Wriston is correct, the academy "has been far from bootless" in the face of the demands and challenges of his age, and we might suggest of any age. To continue his metaphor, when the university puts its boots down, its function as servant and critic to the nation and to the building of the spirit of democracy is played out for all to see.

The Wriston take on contemporary times and culture did not line up with what Hutchins believed was happening. In contrast to Wriston's view that there was little change or difference in the 1930s era from previous times, Hutchins was convinced that their era was markedly dissimilar. He simultaneously longed for a bygone era while he feared the confluence of threatening ideas and events that were surrounding him and the academy.

Wriston was the positivist, the optimist, and the cheerleader for the college and university and for the state of American democracy. Hutchins was jaded, pessimistic. Though he wanted the academy to be what it could and as what it had to be for the sake of society and culture, Hutchins was also shot full with alarm at the way things were.

Hutchins ever pondered the relationship between what he called "the higher learning," that is the academy and democracy. He wanted the university to undergird democracy. But in the same breath, he bemoaned the culture of his times, jeremiads that could easily be transplanted to the twenty-first century.

He knew that the founders, especially Jefferson, firmly believed that the "services" of education and the university were "indispensable to democracy." But Hutchins warned that the founders "could hardly have foreseen how acute the need of them [those services] would be today." The problem is, and this is where Hutchins's belief that life in contemporary times was dramatically different from previous eras came to the fore, "They cannot have anticipated the terrific storm of propaganda from every quarter that now beats upon the citizen." [43]

In a comment that could be ripped from the headlines of the political correctness world of the later twentieth and early twenty-first century, Hutchins rails that the nation's founders:

> cannot have expected a government by pressure groups, groups able and willing to drive into oblivion anyone who opposes them. They could not have imagined that the day would come when individualism would mean: Look out for yourself, and the devil take the community. [44]

In addition to threats on the academy from the barrage of propaganda and agitprop from political pressure groups, indeed connected to these destructive forces, Hutchins joined a long-standing group of critics decrying this thread of an anti-intellectual streak in the culture, national life, and psyche of America. Hutchins believed that the university in the twentieth century and even earlier had a duty to use its heft as a critic of society by standing at the gates of the academy to defend against the constant assault of anti-intellectualism.

Anti-intellectuals were Philistines, threatening the university in every aspect of its mission and aims. If the university dropped its guard even slightly, the price paid would have been irreparable. Desiring to hold the line, Hutchins excoriated the anti-intellectual forces for the undermining of the academy, a threat that their very presence engineered.

The looming disaster was obvious: "An anti-intellectual attitude toward education reduces the curriculum to the exposition of detail." Hutchins believed the anti-intellectuals' modus operandi presumed nothing less than capitulation to their reading of culture and notions of what the culture should be. For these opponents of the academy, "There are no principles. The world is a flux of events." In Hutchins's mind, the anti-intellectual response was simple: "We cannot hope to understand it. All we can do is watch it." This way of dealing with society, culture, and any influence that the university might exert, "is the conclusion of the leading anti-intellectuals of our time."[45]

Hutchins viewed the anti-intellectuals as people who had no faith in the past. Thus their penchant to ignore where humanity has been was not, in the mindset of the anti-intellectuals, any sort of problem. In stark contrast, the university stands to preserve the past, to pass on the best of what has been known and experienced to future generations.

To accomplish that end, Hutchins based his ideas of the university in the classic curriculum and in traditional, rational thinking. These were his values. This was the antidote to the anti-intellectual wringing of hands about events they believed to be swirling out of control.

The problem was that, "to anti-intellectuals, rational values are worthless; they are based on the past. They cannot be valid for the future, because man and his world are changing." In a stinging criticism, using his bully pulpit and the university's role as critic, Hutchins argues that the anti-intellectuals would settle for the following: "A curriculum of current events, without reference to the intellectual and artistic tradition that has come down to us from antiquity, is the only possible course of study which anti-intellectualism affords."[46]

Of all the assaults that Hutchins believed the university needed to gird itself against, the anti-intellectual tradition in American thought was the hugest. This was because the culture of anti-intellectuals was, by its roots, at polarized odds with those of the university, i.e., everything that the university stands for, the anti-intellectuals dispatched as unimportant, and of no value. That reality led Hutchins to declare that these forces "must be repudiated if a university is to achieve its ends."[47]

Hutchins captures the university's retort to this anti-intellectual undermining of a culture of ideas and principles. Ever aware of the duty of a university president, he contends that the university's "buildings may be splendid, its endowment adequate, and its faculty notable; it may have achieved unity, liberty, and clarity in its organization. Its mechanics may be perfect." But at the end, the university "is nothing without an abiding faith in the intellect of man."[48] It is this platform in the foundation of the university that creates the leverage for it to be of service and to utter its criticisms to the society and the nation.

The debate about whether the times for the college and university in Wriston's and Hutchins's era had changed significantly or were really not wholly different as compared to previous ages was more than just an academic exercise. Hutchins was of the view that the times had changed, that the threats to the university were as great if not greater than at any time in its history. Despite whatever changes he felt had occurred, and he certainly thought they were almost exclusively for the worse, Hutchins's answer to each change was to rely even more firmly on back-to-the-future emphasis on the traditional philosophy and foundation of the university.

Wriston and Hutchins disagreed over the degree to which the climate in which they found themselves was a new world, whether the pace of change and the extent of international turmoil and threat to the United States were unparalleled or merely the way things have always been. However, as university presidents and leaders they agreed on the compass: that ideas would win out and would solve problems, and that reason had to overcome the simplistic solutions of passion.

Their debate is important in our time as we look back to their era. Suppose that society, culture, and national needs that the academy faced in the 1930s were not so markedly different in their times from those of previous eras, which is the Wriston position. Then it is plausible to argue that there has been less change in the three-quarters of a century between then and today than commentators think.

This battle of ideas about the value and extent of change, and its bearing on the present and the future of the academy would continue to be waged. On one hand the university then and now has to push back against the passions of those who hanker for change for its own sake.

At the same time, the university must counter the passions of anti-intellectual forces that surround the gates and who work to seduce those desperate for easy answers to social and cultural problems. This is especially the case when the simplistic answer is to argue that out-of-control forces are overwhelming any intentions designed to reduce chaos, and that the best course of action is therefore to dumb down everything and everybody. To engage these battles and to protect the university against these forces of anti-intellectualism and reductionism is fundamental to the foundation of the university and is crucial to sustain to the bond of the academy with society and the nation.

## CONTEMPORARY REALITIES: THE UNIVERSITY CONFRONTS SOCIETY AND THE "STATE"

A major line of argument asserts that American society—and this easily extended worldwide—confronted an unprecedented wave of revolution and clamor in the 1960s and 1970s. Whatever happened and however these times were indeed "new," the issues in the public square had effects on the college and university, and on what society, buffeted as it was by the events of the day, expected of the academy.

J. M. Cameron, a Canadian educational philosopher, suggests that the tumult of the 1960s and early 1970s had in fact an extreme effect on society and the university. The university during that era, as in any time, simultaneously reflected the surrounding society, even as it put an imprint on it.

A long-standing aim of the university is to hold culture together by passing to future generations the best of what is known and has been brought to us in the present. This task was complicated by the centripetal and cataclysmic events of the decade of the 1960s and early 70s. The danger arising out of this tumult compels Cameron to conclude that, "If our society suffers from what is in modern jargon called an identity crisis (perhaps it ought rather to be called a quiddity crisis), it is because this line" reaching back to the oral traditions of antiquity, "is frayed though not perhaps quite cut." [49]

If, as Cameron believes, American society was going through a quiddity crisis, a crisis to its bones, to its very nature and essentials, the academy was experiencing the same. However, context is important. Wriston thought that his era of the 1930s and 40s was not as unprecedentedly terrible as some of his colleagues believed. We have to maintain equal perspective about the 1960s and its impact on the university. Although they were highly dramatic and high-profile times for the academy and society, were the 1960s that much different from previous eras?

Federal financial support for America's colleges and universities increased significantly in the wake of World War II. Governmental involvement at these levels of capital, financial, and budgetary support was a new thing. These dollars came in various forms: the GI Bill; investment in science, engineering, and technology spawned by the Cold War and the arms and space races; and support for capital building projects, and other financial assistance, including greater aid packages for students. These entanglements generated by the increasing monetary ties between the government and the academy grew by leaps and bounds through the 1950s and continued in the early to mid-1960s.

In addition, tensions between the university and the "state" were high, perhaps unparalleled in the 1960s. The issues at stake—the Vietnam War, race and civil rights, equality and equal opportunity, women's issues—were debated in the public square off-campus.

But to a great degree the focus was on those debates and how they were handled in the ivory tower on campuses across the country. On the front burner: student decorum and behavior, public protests of all sorts, security and police actions, professors stepping beyond an exclusive role in the classrooms to become advocates for political positions, and administrative and political leader backlash. [50]

Much of that debate was in the form of protest, demonstrations, teach-ins (often in a veneer of the academic but in many cases simply opportunities to promote one point of view) arrayed against the government, its policies, and its ties to the corporate and industrial complex, especially as those were instrumental to the military and to the war effort. In this unmistakable time of crisis, the lines between the academy and the nation were drawn and sides taken. Positions were not as polarized as frequently portrayed, but to the extent that they were, a climate for reasoned discourse and debate was torn asunder.

As a result, crucial differences developed in the relationship of the ivory tower to the surrounding society and nation in the 1960s. The strains seemed grander and the stakes greater compared to previous eras, chiefly in the university's role as servant and critic.

Because of the influx of taxpayer money into the university, citizens grew to have a new and larger stake in the academy, especially at public colleges and universities. Those opposed to what they saw going on inside the gates became increasingly critical about where their money was going. Supporters of the university, those more satisfied with the use of their taxpayer dollars, often failed to see any urgency in coming to its defense when sieges by the opposition should have appeared obvious.

Savvy politicians such as Ronald Reagan, in his run for and tenure as governor of California, and President Richard Nixon stirred the pot of opposition to the university. Using their bully pulpits, they extolled the virtues of "law and order," called on presidents to exert their authority over their campuses, and vilified protestors—the students and professors inside the gates. In return, these national leaders hit upon great political capital by making the academy out to be the bad guy and an isolated, marginal voice against the Nixon-Agnew "Moral Majority" on the national stage.

In this environment and with these pressures at its gates, the university was still applauded, even encouraged, in its role as servant—produce engineers and scientists, beat the Soviets in the Cold War and the Space Race, give us lawyers and corporate leaders. Meanwhile, the university was little tolerated for criticizing and opposing the government, especially on issues of the war and race, and for permitting transgressions of the norms of social and cultural life as a result of unchecked, unchained student, as well as faculty, behavior.

In such a climate, Cameron returns to none other than Cardinal Newman's notion that "a University is an intellectual power," and therefore, "as such a power is likely to be from time to time obnoxious to the national state, always jealous of powers that exist over against it and have claims to the exercising of an independent authority."[51] Only with this unmuzzled authority is the university able to act as servant and critic. Absent this autonomy, having to capitulate to governmental or any outside constituency's pressures undercuts the concept of the university qua the university, or, in Newman's terms, its stature as "an intellectual power."

The passage of time over the last four decades from the mid-1970s has resolved few if any of the problems spawned by the 1960s. Today, the politics are perceived as more coarse, more tense, and more polarized. In the academy, numerous issues kicked off in the 1960s have persisted as problems and as failures of a search for common ground.

These issues include affirmative action and matters of equity and access; diversity—how and in what ways it should be addressed; continual reductions in federal and state support and its financial implications, even with a citizenry demanding increasing control and influence; escalating expenses and tuition increases, and what to do about them; battles over curriculum; an increasingly complicated and interlocking nexus of government, corporate and business interests, and the degree of control they exert; and liberty, free speech, and academic freedom—how to uphold these ideals.

These controversies and unsolved, potentially unresolvable issues are debated in a polarized and overwrought climate and by a set of players who engage each other in a death-grip. That is, overarching this litany and using these issues as cannon fodder is the continuing ideological struggle between Left and Right, conservatives and liberals and their proxy battles fought and brought inside the gates of the academy.

However, as the distance from that era to our own lengthens, we gain perspective about those times and ours. Andrew Delbanco takes an interesting angle on where the college and university finds itself with respect to democracy and American society in the contemporary era. His is a unique and consequential assessment of what the academy is today and how it got here.

Assessing the array of forces bearing in on the gates of the academy, Delbanco stresses the vital importance of its true foundations. He echoes Cameron's "quiddity crisis," asserting that, as a result of this storm of contests and controversies in recent decades about its ideals, the identity of the college and university is at stake. To Delbanco this issue is, at bottom, existential. He declares that, "The American college faces a great many serious challenges—from the fiscal to the ethical and even, it might be said the existential—but it is too precious an institution to be permitted to give up on its own ideals."[52] In his tour of how the college developed and secured these ideals, Delbanco proclaims that its beginnings are lodged "in a spirit poised between hubris and humility." Delbanco pushes the underlying religious origins in the academy. He acknowledges that his "view of the continuing pertinence of its religious origins may seem at odds with the intolerance of the clerics who founded it." The authority of these leaders was diminished by a shortsighted combination of "blindness, self-deception, and cruelty."[53]

Not exactly a good way to found an institution that is supposed to be intellectual, to be based in the pursuit of knowledge, and to be the repository of the best of culture and social values.

Yet for all this wrong footedness, Delbanco contends that the highest values underlay even these religious zealots. This means that, in building the foundation of the academy, "when they were true to their convictions (are we sure that we are more so?), they tried to honor their cardinal belief that God in his omnipotence, not man in his presumption, determines the fate of every human being, and therefore that no outward mark—wealth or poverty, high or low social position, credentials or lack thereof—tells anything about the inward condition of the soul." [54]

Delbanco argues that his religiously based lens for understanding the academy is difficult to accept in the modern era. However, for those who find those religious ideals as outmoded, something tied to a bygone era, Delbanco has a substitute set of beliefs and principles for understanding the foundations of the academy.

That solution is a similar set of values and beliefs embedded in democracy. This creed is nothing less than democracy's proclamations about human equality and about how doors should be open to common folk in a fashion equal to the access presumed to be the privilege of the elite.

"If an old, and in many respects outmoded, religion seems an improbable touchstone for thinking about education today," Delbanco suggests, "perhaps a more plausible one is democracy." The rationale for this assertion leads him to reiterate the overlap of principles between education and democracy, many of which are the same principles aligned in the beliefs of most religions. For example, as a starting if not first principle for the academy, "Surely it is an offense against democracy," Delbanco notes, "to presume that education should be reserved for the wellborn and the well off." [55]

As evidence, the historian in Delbanco steers him to Emerson in his classic Phi Beta Kappa oration in 1837 for counsel about the academy and what it should be. In that address, Emerson implored that:

> colleges can only highly serve us when . . . they gather from far every ray of various genius to their hospitable halls, and by the concentrated fires, set the hearts of their youth on flame. . . . Forget this, and our American colleges will recede in their public importance, whilst they grow richer every year. [56]

For Emerson as well as for Delbanco, that "public importance" is the role of the academy as servant and critic in a democracy. Absent that, the college succeeds only in isolating itself, and the society which it is supposed to serve is diminished for want of the academy's force in its midst.

Emerson's era did not have on its radar the diversity and affirmative action pressures of the latter twentieth century. Nonetheless, his expectation of the college has a universal ring. For Emerson and the halcyon days of the Enlightenment in which he lived, democracy and the shaping of its principles were linked to the values and beliefs that education could inspire. Delbanco proposes as exemplary, Emerson's idea of the grasp of the colleges: that they "should reach far, wide, and deep for their students and allow them, by their convergence, to ignite in one another a sense of the possibilities of democratic community."[57]

In the contemporary political correctness era, a litany of tendencies run counter to Emerson's idea of the academy. The ideological battleground has produced the penchant to dumb down the college and college life, to create an intellectual, social, communal, and of course political culture that holds the least possibility of being offensive to any and all, and to guarantee that everyone is ensured the capacity to remain inside a personal, individually designed comfort zone.

Aware of these threats, Delbanco proposes an antidote to these forces that given half a chance will make over the university into something no longer recognizable as an educational institution. The solution is as old as the college ideal. Delbanco argues simply that standing for this ideal is the only avenue to a proper understanding of what education is and what it should do.

In the process, citizens and the body politic gain a more liberally educated comprehension of society and the culture that surrounds us. The resulting presumption is that, with a more wise understanding of education's role and importance, the forces of civic culture and the body politic will better understand how to let the university be the university.

That is not a blank check for the university to do as it pleases. Rather such an understanding would yield a more commonly held agreement about what the ideal of the academy is and what it should do.

Delbanco's idea of the college demands front and center consideration. Presidents, trustees, faculty, and others concerned about the future of the college need to take his prescription to heart and to act on it. His formula is simple:

> A college should not be a haven from worldly contention, but a place where young people fight out among and within themselves contending ideas of the meaningful life, and where they discover that self-interest need not be at odds with concern for one another.

If that vision can be pulled off, the dividends are profound: "We owe it to posterity to preserve and protect this institution. Democracy depends on it."[58]

Not only does democracy depend on this concept of the academy, but more importantly the university and college depend on it to secure their identity. When the university focuses on Delbanco's straightforward ideas, it simultaneously and crucially pushes back against the political correctness fervor that now, well into the second decade of the twenty-first century, remains unrelenting.

This is a challenge that has from time immemorial confronted the academy. However, we also know how pronounced these threats to the traditional basis of the university have been in the polarized ideological battles of the last thirty-five years. It is during that time that political correctness was first used and has continued to be honed as a cudgel by the Right. But we also know that this battle merely continued what began in the prior two decades, beginning in the early 1960s when the Right began to believe that the academy had been overtaken by the Left.

Thus we are six decades into this round of ideological controversy that weakens and rejects the democratic foundations of the academy and the nation. For the university this means two things.

One is that the university must be increasingly vigilant not to morph into simply one more political, social institution with a pre-conceived agenda that is pushed within and outside its gates. The other is that only by sustaining this level of vigilance is the university able to uphold its fundamental principles and stature for the sake of the commonwealth.

By maintaining this vigilance, the university can be an institution based in the search for knowledge and truth, and in the preservation and passing on to future generations the best of culture and history. That foundation creates for the university a pulpit and a voice in the public square as both servant and critic.

John Kemeny, president of Dartmouth College from 1970–1981, always preached about a university that would fulfill this mission as critic and servant. Throughout his tenure, he delivered insightful messages in annual opening convocation addresses. In one of those talks, in the fall 1978, Kemeny's voice presses the demands of the university as critic and servant. His theme: the complex world that Dartmouth and its students were living in and needed to be prepared to address.

Kemeny urges the students, faculty, and the Dartmouth community not to "listen to the siren song of simplistic solutions. The world is complex, the world is frustrating, the world is very fascinating—take it as it is, do not live in a fantasy world." As a citizen of the university and American society, this means "Face the problems the world presents to you. And, above all, use your years at Dartmouth to prepare yourself for that day when you can help make this a better world."[59]

Kemeny and Shapiro, presidential voices in the ivory tower, in public utterances only three years apart, knew well and used their bully pulpits to hack out the territory of the college and university as servant and critic. They followed in a long American tradition—a unique quality of the American university compared to its counterparts in other parts of the globe—that voices the need in a democratic society that its universities function with this dual purpose: critic and servant. Those who have followed and will follow in their footsteps must do likewise.

## NOTES

1. Harold Shapiro, *Tradition and Change: Perspectives on Education and Public Policy* (Ann Arbor: University of Michigan Press, 1987), "Critic and Servant: The Role of the University," April 14, 1980, 111–17.

2. Ibid., 112.

3. Ibid.

4. Ibid., 112–13.

5. Bernard Bailyn's *Education in the Forming of American Society* (Chapel Hill: University of North Carolina Press, 1960), 40.

6. Ibid.

7. Sidney E. Mead, *The Lively Experiment: The Shaping of Christianity in America* (New York: Harper and Row, 1963), "From Coercion to Persuasion: Another Look at the Rise of Religious Liberty and the Emergence of Denominationalism," 16-37.

8. Bailyn, 41.

9. Ibid.

10. Ibid., 47–48.

11. Ibid., 48.

12. Ibid.

13. Ibid.

14. Ibid., 49. Later in this book, Bailyn makes a complicated argument about the relationship between the evolutionary development of denominationalism and denominational pressure to exert a unifying force on society and culture, and the state, the emerging Republic during the colonial, Revolutionary, and post-Revolutionary eras. As Bailyn characterizes it: "[But] the growth of religious toleration and the separation of church and state were phases of a more general phenomenon whose central characteristics emerge with peculiar clarity when the focus of study shifts to education. For education was still thought of in the eighteenth century as a proper responsibility, if not a direct function, of the state, and of a state whose role was positive, expressing a separate, dominant interest apart from the particular concerns of groups within the population. No educational activity could be entirely 'private' for none was legitimately independent of the state; and at the higher levels—secondary schools and colleges—the force of the state was manifest in its exclusive capacity to license teaching and to bestow the legal immunities of incorporation. In the denominational complexity of eighteenth-century America this traditional role of the state was threatened. A common interest of minority groups developed to neutralize the state, to deny its right to a separate interest dominant over all others, and to create of its benefits not privileges but rights." 107.

15. Louis Menand, "How the Deal Went Down: Saving Democracy in the Depression," *The New Yorker* March 4, 2013, 71, 69–74.

16. Richard J. Storr, "The Public Conscience of the University," *Harvard Educational Review* XXVI, no. 1 (Winter 1956): 75, 71–84.

17. Ibid.

18. Ibid., 76–77.

19. Hugh Hawkins, *Between Harvard and America: The Educational Leadership of Charles W. Eliot* (New York: Oxford University Press, 1972), 49.

20. Ibid., 43.

21. Ibid. The quotes of Eliot are from his article, "New Education" in the *Atlantic Monthly* (1869).

22. Ibid.

23. Ibid., 52.

24. Ibid.,167.

25. Ibid. Italics mine.

26. Woodrow Wilson, *College and State: Educational, Literary and Political Papers (1875-1913)*. Ray Stannard Baker and William E. Dodd, eds., Vol. II (New York: Harper and Brothers, 1925), 160.

27. Ibid., italics mine.

28. Richard Hofstadter and Wilson Smith, eds. *American Higher Education: A Documentary History*, Volume II (Chicago: University of Chicago Press, 1961). 689, quote from "Princeton and the Nation's Service," 1896 in *Forum*, XXII (December, 1896).

29. Ibid.

30. Ibid.

31. Robert M. Hutchins, *The University of Utopia* (Chicago: University of Chicago Press, 1953), 20–21.

32. Ibid., 21.

33. Ibid., 55.

34. Ibid.

35. Ibid., 81–82.

36. Ibid., 102.

37. *General Education in a Free Society.* Report of the Harvard Committee (Cambridge, MA: Harvard University Press, 1945).

38. Robert M. Hutchins, *Education for Freedom* (Baton Rouge: Louisiana State University Press, 1943), 101-102.

39. Henry Wriston, "A Critical Appraisal of Experiments in General Education," in *The Thirty-Eighth Yearbook of the National Society for the Study of Education, Part II, General Education in the American College,* Guy Montrose Whipple, ed. (Bloomington, IL: Public School Publishing Co., 1939), 289.

40. Ibid.

41. Ibid.

42. Ibid., 302.

43. Robert Hutchins, *No Friendly Voice* (Chicago: University of Chicago Press, 1936), 4.

44. Ibid.

45. Ibid., 37.

46. Ibid., 38.

47. Ibid., 39.

48. Ibid., 39–40.

49. J. M. Cameron, *On the Idea of a University* (Toronto: Published in Association with the University of Saint Michael's College by University of Toronto Press, 1978), 5.

50. For an extensive review of these times and the stresses on colleges and universities and their presidents, see Stephen J. Nelson, *Decades of Chaos and Revolution: Showdowns for College Presidents* (Lanham, MD: Rowman & Littlefield, 2012).

51. Cameron, 8.

52. Andrew Delbanco, *College: What it Was, Is, and Should Be* (Princeton, NJ: Princeton University Press, 2012), 171.

53. Ibid.

54. Ibid.

55. Ibid., 172.

56. Ibid.

57. Ibid.

58. Ibid., 177.

59. John G. Kemeny, Convocation Address, September 17, 1978, 6. In a prescient line in this speech, Kemeny notes regarding debates about nuclear power: "Yes, I am scared about the possibility of a nuclear accident. Yes, I am scared about the possible impact of nuclear power plants on the environment. Yes, I am scared that a group of terrorists may get enough plutonium to put together a nuclear bomb." (2). Less than nine months later, Kemeny would be charged by the President of the United States, Jimmy Carter, to head up the Three Mile Island Commission to investigate the nearly catastrophic accident at that nuclear plant. And of course we also are aware of the other dangers that Kemeny raised as concerns.

# FOUR

## The Purpose of the College

*Clashes over Liberal Education and Ideas that Prevail*

The history of the college and university in America pivots greatly on battles waged from the get-go over the purpose of a higher education. Those arguments are per force rooted in understandings of curriculum. What is in the best interest of students and of society? What should be the course of study for a college student? Why, from both the perspectives of students as well as from those of the institutions that purport to educate them, invest so much in that education and in that preparation for life and work?

This story is complicated. As with all tangles shaping the college in America, the story about how a liberal education has been understood, and about the curricular ideas and required courses designed to deliver liberally educated individuals, is marked by twists and turns. It is a history revealed by reoccurrences of thought-to-be settled debates, and by the realities of unexpected frontiers as new times and challenges have been confronted.

Titanic college presidents have been major figures in these debates, weighing in and attempting to place their footprints both on their institutions, and on the trends and interests of society and of the Republic. Faculty from the institutions these presidents have led, and from others around the country, along with educational commentators and scholars from all quarters of the nation have been drawn to the fray.

For the first century and a half of the era of the Colonial Colleges in America, few differences separated and distinguished the original nine colleges. Although they had separate foundings and some founders who hoped to create substantively unique institutions, the Colonial Colleges were in the main quite similar. They all relied on the traditional curriculum that had pervaded the British and other European colleges and universities for centuries, which these founders willingly imported to the new land.

But even before the Colonial College period ended in the Revolutionary War and Constitutional eras, original understandings about the role of the curriculum and the intentions and aspirations of a college education had begun to change. Those periods at the end of the eighteenth century marked the beginning of more than a century of new interpretations about a liberal education.

As those years unfolded, ever-weighty debate was protracted about how a college education should be constructed and delivered, and what its purposes and thus those of a college, ought to be. In the process, the later emergence of major research universities and the academic world of these large-scale institutions challenged the smaller liberal arts colleges of the Republic. No one prevailed to the exclusion of others, but all were inevitably changed and had to accommodate the swirl of developments in this evolving world of American higher education.

## JOHN WITHERSPOON: CIVIC INSPIRATIONS AND LEADERSHIP FOR THE REPUBLIC

John Witherspoon was the first herald of new thinking about the colonial curriculum. When he took over the helm as Princeton's (then the College of New Jersey) president in 1768, the college accepted the mainstream view of a liberal education and the purpose of a college generally endorsed throughout its colleague Colonial Colleges of the pre-Revolutionary War era.

Witherspoon emigrated from Scotland, entered Colonial America, and took his place on stage at a moment of flux and fear. The Revolutionary War and the establishment of the nation loomed on the horizon. When he arrived as its president, Princeton was just over twenty years old. Brown, the seventh college in America, had been founded just four years before; the founding of Queens College, which was to become Rutgers, had happened two years prior; and Dartmouth College was founded a year later, thus rounding out the nine Colonial Colleges. The colleges were small in size, scale and enrollment, and quite young as a group.

Witherspoon took not only Princeton, but the colony of New Jersey and the rapidly emerging Republic, by storm. He was a leader on a mission and a force with which to be reckoned.

After graduation from Edinburgh University, "Witherspoon became a leader of the traditional Calvinist opponents of the Moderate Presbyterians, who aligned themselves with the high culture and political interests of Britain."[1] He came to America solely to assume the position as Princeton's president. He used his position to introduce "the study of Scottish moral philosophy and rhetoric in an effort to broaden the curriculum and make it more responsive to the social and intellectual needs of the generation who created the American republic."[2]

When Witherspoon took the helm at Princeton, increasing pressure was building in colonial society about its essential needs. The young Republic and its citizens had to be prepared to meet the challenges of the pre-Revolutionary period and of sharp struggle between the colonies and the motherlands. At the top of the list was the need for the citizenry to be nurtured with a substance and style of civic duty equal to the demands of the day. Greater dedication to the common good was markedly critical.

The Colonial Colleges fashioned the critical arena in which crucial political and social traits could be formed. Witherspoon embraced the challenges confronting the colonies and his fellow citizens. He lost no time in quickly asserting himself as a new American.

A testimony of his leadership was the clear match of rhetoric and action, significantly influencing the curriculum of one Colonial College. Witherspoon took up the challenge of supplying a fresh angle about the nature and demands of a liberal education and what a college curriculum should deliver. That change in the philosophy of the curriculum at Princeton had an impact on a generation or more of students. His approach was embedded in belief in Scottish moral philosophy.

However, more critically, Witherspoon's claim on his fellows at Princeton and on the nascent nation was an urgent call for interlocking public engagement in the political and social spheres of the emerging Republic. Furthermore, what went on at Princeton was not lost on his fellow college presidents and on the culture of the other colleges of the day.

Witherspoon is unique among America's college presidents. He was forty-five when he assumed the Princeton presidency, serving until he was seventy-one years of age, when he died in office in 1794. In his first decade in a new land he became the only clergyman and the only college president to sign the Declaration of Independence and also the only person with these bona fides to participate in the Continental Congresses.

In 1896, over a century after the end of Witherspoon's tenure and life, Woodrow Wilson commented shortly before his Princeton presidential appointment that under Witherspoon's leadership, the "College [Princeton] seemed 'a seminary of statesmen rather than a quiet seat of academic learning' during the founding."[3] Jeffery Morrison expands on Wilson's characterization adding that, "it is safe to say that no single educator in early America matched Witherspoon's record of making politicians and patriots."[4]

Such assertions about Witherspoon's legacy are absolute. He fostered public conscience and purpose as a result of the curriculum and culture he shaped at Princeton. The litany of Princeton students from Witherspoon's tenure who went on as graduates to positions of authority in the public square as legislators, judges, Supreme Court members, presidents of the United States, and other high-level civil service is legendary.

Witherspoon's philosophy, born out of the Scottish Enlightenment, infused his thinking and belief about education. His Scottish, Presbyterian roots ran deep and formed the beliefs that he injected into Princeton's foundation and purpose. These values inspired his view of the purpose of the college and made Princeton what it was during his time as president.

The imprint of Witherspoon's beliefs about education on Princeton and beyond to the American college is clear. To Witherspoon a college education "is also of acknowledged necessity to those who do not wish to live for themselves alone, but would apply their talents to the service of the Public and the good of mankind." This means that "Education is therefore of equal importance in order either to enjoy life with dignity and elegance, or employ it to the benefit of society in offices of power or trust."[5] Few statements more fully capture American attitudes and the core beliefs of its colleges and universities about the crucial purpose of a higher education than this.

The Princeton curriculum of Witherspoon's days was still in a nascent state, but it was rooted in the classic traditions that all the Colonial Colleges sought to embody in the education they offered. However, it is clear Witherspoon's ideas about civic commitment and duty transformed the generation of students who came through Princeton's gates during his tenure and for decades to follow.

That new tradition, brought into play less than 150 years into history of the college in America, now spun the curriculum as students consumed it into something that was intended to move them "to enjoy life with dignity and elegance, or"—more likely Witherspoon really meant, to "employ it to the benefit of society in offices of power or trust."[6]

Witherspoon's philosophy of education and his understanding of its role in the commonweal came in confluence with the increasing demands of America as it grasped for greater self-governing and self-sufficiency. This capacity was critical as the colonies shifted their sights on nationhood and on the reality of being a Republic. Witherspoon wanted Princeton graduates to be people and citizens who would live their lives in his mold. He sought an imprint on students as contributors to civic life in the manner he so strongly believed to be critical for them and for the nation.

The emerging American nation and its colleges were primitive in Witherspoon's day and that of his group of founders and their immediate heirs. The existing canvas for them had little on it. Thus there were profound opportunities for Witherspoon and his colleagues to put down strong and lasting imprints on the academy and on the liberal education tradition.

Morrison traces backward the long-range outcomes of the dots that the Witherspoons of the world created in this spare framework. Morrison turns to a quote (unattributed) of de Tocqueville that reveals the connection between the earliest contributions in the shape of the college and university in America to what we see today.

Tocqueville argued that:

> If we could go right back to the elements of societies and examine the very first records of their histories, I have no doubt that we should there find the first cause of their prejudices, habits, dominating passions, and all that comes to be called the national character. . . . America is the only country in which we can watch the natural quiet growth of society and where it is possible to be exact about the influence of the point of departure on the future of the state.[7]

Tocqueville's logic about the formation of a nation and state parallels that of the university in America. That is, Tocqueville believes the establishment of this "new" nation can be tracked from its earliest beginnings. That history includes its colleges and universities, the academy in the Republic. These likewise sprung from the fabric of the emerging nation. The colleges were for sure transported and copied from their Old World forbears. At the same time, the college in America did not begin and it certainly did not develop as a wholly intact branch of those European and British universities.

Rather the American colleges and universities are largely unique. They are the distinctive face of a new academy in a new nation. Their histories were played out by a few at first, and then later by myriad players. The work of these leaders and their institutions, though sketchy in its earliest seventeenth-century history, is still well known and documented. And this university in America is not fully like that in any other country of the world, whether those earlier universities in England, France, and Italy, or later ones in other nations.

As Witherspoon and other actors and events exerted a will on arguments about the purpose of the college in America, we can connect dots and form a sense both for what developed over time and for what we inherit as an outcome. Witherspoon was one of the early shapers, not only of Princeton, but of his cohort Colonial Colleges and of those that followed on their heels as the eighteenth century concluded and the issues of the nineteenth emerged.

## OVERLOOKED SLANTS ON
## THE DARTMOUTH COLLEGE CASE

The Dartmouth College case that ended up before the Supreme Court is recognized as a moment when the autonomy of private educational institutions in America was preserved. That take is certainly the case.

However, more was going on than a simple instance of a stand for autonomy and control as this complicated and lasting tale in the history of higher education in the United States unfolded. More fundamentally the Dartmouth College case is equally important for its impact on debate about the purpose of the college, and in particular who and what should determine the direction and aspirations of a college or university.

Eleazor Wheelock founded Dartmouth in 1769. On his death in 1779, his son, John Wheelock, succeeded as president. In a pre-Jacksonian era, the younger Wheelock attempted to wrestle control away from the Dartmouth trustees. At his invitation, the New Hampshire state legislature passed a law changing the name from Dartmouth College to Dartmouth University.[8]

Upon learning about the junior Wheelock's action, "An infuriated board of trustees thereupon promptly removed Wheelock from his three connections with the college, from his positions as president, professor, and trustee."[9] This was a ringing aspect of the battle: To maintain elite control of the college by its board rather than having the institution be run by the state on behalf of the common citizen and the public. The Dartmouth board willed out over its president, despite the affections that his family name otherwise inspired.

The case kicked to the Supreme Court and led to Daniel Webster's, one of the College's most famous alumni non-graduates, memorable comment that Dartmouth was "a small college" nonetheless "yet there are those who love it." If the younger Wheelock was a casualty, his demise was ultimately for a good cause for Dartmouth and normally presumed equally positive for American higher education as well.

In crafting the Court's decision, Chief Justice John Marshall remarked that:

> Dartmouth College was not a civil or public institution, nor was its property public property. Dartmouth College was indeed a private eleemosynary institution with an object to benefit the public, but it was not a public institution under public control. Therefore, the charter of Dartmouth College was a contract, a contract which the New Hampshire law of 1816 violated by substituting the will of the state for the will of the trustees.[10]

The Court's finding had lasting effects. Frederick Rudolph points out that in the wake of the Dartmouth decision, public funding of colleges and universities, even those that were public institutions, was stalled for nearly a half century. That period persisted until the Morrill Land Grant Act was passed and the gates were open for the founding of then true state universities.[11]

Rudolph concludes that the conventional thinking is that the Dartmouth College Court "decision put the American college beyond the control of popular prejudice and passion;" read, the emerging and reigning years of Jacksonian democracy.

In a high-wire act, however, Rudolph dangles both feet over the edge. On one hand, Rudolph notes in the negative that the Court's finding, "assured the further alienation of the people from the colleges," though he quickly adds the good news on the other hand: "but on the evening of the Jacksonian movement it [the Dartmouth case] also put the colleges beyond the control of people who *understood neither the colleges nor their problems.*" [12]

The battle of the Jacksonians and their appeals for the preeminence of the common man and of the people of democracy were only just beginning. As that maelstrom was about to unfold, Rudolph declares that the Dartmouth case went in an opposite direction: it laid out territory that preserved elite control over private institutions.

However, fast-forward to today as we witness issues of control and of who knows best for the college and university. These matters are by no means solved and have not been slid to the side.

In today's era conservative forces, ironically, despite their libertarian streaks and their belief about the take-over of the academy by the political Left, seek control of public institutions. The battle waged since the 1960s, if not longer, has been to influence colleges and universities in order to bend them to the social, political, and cultural purposes of one political faction or another.

Many public university presidents today are left to struggle with boards and governing bodies, not to mention the posturing and parading of legislators and citizens, who Rudolph characterizes as constituted of "people who understood neither the colleges nor their problems." The Jacksonian era rebounds with influence in our day.

Rudolph believes the Dartmouth College case became a hedge against the conservative Jacksonian forces that otherwise would have meddled further in the world of higher education in the middle decades of the nineteenth century. But that is not where interpretations of the Dartmouth case end.

Sidney Mead shifts reading of the oft-lauded Dartmouth College case to its effect on religious control of colleges. He begins his assessment of the foundation of the academy decades earlier in history, asserting that the "polarization of the religious and intellectual lives of the country becomes increasingly evident from around the middle of the eighteenth century," marked by the dustup between George Whitefield and Harvard University in 1744. [13]

On that occasion, as the itinerate preacher Whitefield was finding his way around New England and elsewhere, the Harvard faculty took a stand against his screeds leveled at the academy. Lest we think finger pointing today goes over the top regarding judgments about who are the forces of the light and who the forces of the dark, these folks did it for real.

The Harvard faculty note that Whitefield went:

further still, when he says, both of Yale College as well as ours, "As for the Universities, I believe it may be said, Their Light is now become Darkness, Darkness that may be felt. What a deplorable State of Immorality and Irreligion has he hereby represented Us to be in!"

The Harvard faculty quickly add, defending themselves if not Yale, "And as this is a most wicked and libellous Falshood [*sic*] (at least as to our College) as such we charge it upon him" (95).[14] Whitefield believed this "drift apart," the "polarization of the religious and intellectual lives of the country," became "clearer with the launching of the often-called 'godless' state universities beginning in the 1790s to rival the denominationally controlled colleges." In a unique claim, Mead alleges an unintentional but nonetheless critical effect of the Dartmouth case. That is, the Dartmouth College decision:

> which turned back the attempt to gain state control of the private colleges, was a Pyrrhic victory, for it implied that independence of the private colleges from denominational as well as state control and helped pave the way to ever more complete separation of education from its religious roots.[15]

Mead harkens to a time that once was, an era of great influence of religious affections over the definition of the purpose of the college. However, regardless of the Dartmouth College Supreme Court decision, the eclipse of that era of strong religious influence in the academy—something Mead appears to bemoan—would have occurred in any case.

Nonetheless, this religious, denominational authority was not washed away in an instant. Knowing what we know happened as American society became more secularized, even in the opening decades of the nineteenth century, religious force in the academy, including its sway in denominational colleges founded throughout the middle of the century, was sure to wane over time.

Although education did not become completely separated from its "religious roots," the academy, including the direction and purpose of the college, was not standing still in the mold of the Colonial Colleges, and of their founders and founding visions. The prior strength of religious influence was not to enjoy that grip forever. However, Mead's example of Whitefield and Harvard reminds us that religious influence in the academy, unless conducted along the ideals of Cardinal Newman and his belief that theology and religion had to wrestle with any and all other academic subjects and disciplines, can undermine the fundamental principles and values of the academy.

## THE YALE REPORT OF 1828: A BULWARK
## FOR TRADITIONAL PURPOSE

The Yale Faculty Report of 1828 is a signal declaration in the history of the college and university in America. The report hacks out territory that for its time and well into the future, arguably to the present, is distinctive regarding the purpose of the college and the value of a higher education for students and their lives as graduates.

Douglas Sloan urges a reset of the clock in order to view the Yale Report in the era of its time.[16] His complaint is that to understand its contribution and meaning, we have to sort fiction from fact, or better mythology, that has developed over centuries.

Sloan believes:

> The Report, actually a thoughtful, responsible attempt to consider the place of the undergraduate college in the totality of the American educational scene, did not differ in any of its essentials from the views held by most of America's foremost champions of university reform at the time.

Rather than some revolutionary statement, the Yale authors argued simply to delineate the undergraduate college as distinctive from graduate or professional schools, but still retained the purpose to prepare students for further study after their undergraduate days.[17]

The Yale authors had no idea what the evolution of the research university, even in its nascent mid- to late nineteenth-century form, would bring to the American higher education scene. But they sought urgently to protect the college as the academy.

The Yale Report in no uncertain terms draws a line around what the undergraduate life is supposed to be and what a college education must accomplish. What was at stake for Yale and others in the earlier part of the nineteenth century was that a college, undergraduate education, with all its requirements and trappings, was designed to "develop the intellectual skills and instill a foundation core of knowledge necessary for all higher learning."[18]

The oft-quoted statement of the report, was notion that two objects of a college education are the *"discipline* and the *furniture* of the mind."[19] Regarding "mental discipline," Sloan concludes that the Yale Report steered a wide berth of getting bogged down in the revivalist tendencies of the day or resting on throwback, bygone notions. Rather the report pivots on the idea that its concept of mental discipline was based on the generally held and accepted understandings of the day about cognition and mental capacity. Noting the broad acceptability of the report's contentions, the essential point is that nearly all educational thinkers of the time would have been in agreement with the authors' notions mental discipline.[20]

The Yale Report, and the century-long debate it inspired, also high-lights two issues that a number of college presidents and other educators and faculty continued to argue.

One was the degree to which undergraduate students had sufficient maturity to be responsible for the formation of their own education. The second was the connection of the curriculum—what type, what require-ments—to student matriculation and enrollment. That is, if a college edu-cation was viewed as a nice, theoretical opportunity, but one that was primarily of no use in the "real" world, then who would show up?

This was especially the question on the minds of less elitist citizens who didn't value education as the only avenue to economic advancement and security. While not denying that a college experience was a badge of social status, this constituency was less prone to value a higher education solely for the purpose of getting ahead. In the minds of some commenta-tors, these two issues—the capacity of students to guide their own educa-tion and which curriculum would attract the most students—while inde-pendent of each other, were also linked.

The authors of the Yale Report felt and pushed back against pressures and rumblings from those who urged practical change in the shape of a college education. They clearly contend that initiatives to broaden the curriculum beyond its traditional basis, and to permit students to elect courses and to determine their academic path was mistaken and mis-guided. The Yale faculty believed that the relationship of the student to a curriculum prescribed for them was all tied up with the issue of charac-ter. This is the high road they took.

Despite the ivory tower silo that was Yale—the same of course for any college or university in any era—the authors of the report of 1828 were aware of public concerns about the attractiveness of a prescribed, tradi-tional curriculum. Their response is simple regarding the relationship of the emphasis in the collegiate culture on an elevated character and whether necessary levels of student enrollment could be maintained. That is, in the face of criticism and fears to the contrary, the Yale Report asserts that, "Without character, it will be in vain to think of retaining them. It is a hazardous experiment, to act upon the plan of gaining num-bers first, and character afterwards . . ."[21]

The battle line, the Yale Report argues, that must be held is the idea and ideal of the collegiate experience. The authors press contentions that they believe must prevail if the academy is to remain true to its founda-tions and heritage. In the minds of the Yale professors, a college should be rigorous in its expectations, and be willing to prescribe for students what they should learn and how it is they become educated. The more the institution is inclined and able to follow this course, the more likely the college will attract students of character and will thus have the oppor-tunity inspire them to be people of high character.

There was fork in the road in 1828. The fork had existed in preceding decades in the history of the college and university in America. Yale chose to urge colleague colleges to be institutions of character by clinging to the curriculum the way it had traditionally been framed. However, the other branch of the fork in the road was dramatically clear: Colleges without character would collapse if they shifted their curriculum from the traditional offerings to a menu of student choice for no other end than to attract a wider diversity of students and concomitantly to increase enrollments.

Some argued that the Yale Report was pie-in-the-sky, that the practical realities of the emerging economic and more diverse vocational training demands required a shift in what an undergraduate education should be. Here again, the Yale authors relied on their interpretation of long-standing national and higher education assumptions about the merit of a college education in the preparation of students as citizens in society. Their answer to critics who wanted the curriculum to become more elective was that the traditional approach the Yale Report advocated had not only stood American society and the academy well in the past but was critical to the future as well.

The Yale faculty view was that fundamental academic foundations could not be abandoned. If they were, it would be at the nation's peril. They believed a classical education and education in the classics remained essential to the political and economic framework of society. These assumptions about the importance of education were put forth at the outset of the founding of the new nation and its emerging Republic.

The report does not ignore the practical claims exacted on colleges. Rather it boldly acknowledges the historical and contemporary demands of the merchant and business classes and their goals of leadership prominence and ownership of property. To those who believed the Yale authors to be pie-in-the sky, the retort was simple: equal doses of the pragmatic with the philosophical underpinnings of the value of a college education.

At bottom line, the college can and should be interested in both the most practical demands of society, while still educating each rising generation of students to be of the highest stature of learning, of citizenship, and of stewardship. Graduates could and likely would be wealthy and secure, but more importantly they had to be committed to the common good.

Concerning the students walking into and out of the gates of Yale or any college, the Yale Report argues that college students should gain an education based in the essentials of a liberal education. This foundation was designed to ground the students both as undergraduates and the lives they would lead after graduation on paths of building up society and culture. Rhetorically they assert that isn't it the purpose of college education to develop students who be able "to move in the more intelligent circles with dignity, and to make such an application of their wealth, as will be most honorable to themselves, and most beneficial to their country?"[22]

No doubt this rhetoric is wrapped in elitism, whether by pre-ordained social and economic status or by the meritocratic pathway that the academy in America was presumed to make possible. However, that is logical. Yale, like Princeton and its leadership pipeline that Witherspoon inspired, or so many other of America's budding colleges, knew its students, who they were, and what they could and did become.

The Yale authors argue that the nation's future must be directed by the intelligence, ability to think, and the style of discipline that provides "a steady hand at the helm."[23] Yale was duty-bound to produce such citizens and leaders for the American Republic.

The contrast about what Yale must do and what the nation must have is well defined. The threat posed by those within the gates of any college choosing retreat from expectations generated by the traditional demands of the classic curriculum was obvious. The Yale Report is unstinting that nothing less than the finest education was required. Anything less was weak tea that was not what the country and society demanded. Thus their conclusion: "Where a free government gives full liberty to the human intellect to expand and operate, education should be proportionately liberal and ample."[24]

## FRANCIS WAYLAND: PRAGMATIC
## NECESSITIES IN THE CURRICULAR MARKETPLACE

The Yale Report of 1828 injected major assertions into the curricular debates of the early to mid-nineteenth century. It highlighted fears about what would result if college leaders and faculty succumbed to the pressure of fashioning the curriculum to be more open and student-engineered. Should the collegiate course of study become something that could willy-nilly be subject to student self-selection, disaster would loom for sure.

The Yale authors were concerned about the erosion of the character of the academy. They predicted the reciprocal loss that would result from offering a less rigorous education and from simultaneously attracting students who would relish avoiding "the *discipline* and the *furniture* of the mind." Yale or any college that elected to follow this course would lose its character. College leaders who capitulated to this path would be making the worst of decisions.

Sure enough Francis Wayland strode onto the stage as president of Brown University in 1827, just as the Yale Report was being constructed and shortly before its public release. As his tenure unfolded, Wayland tackled headlong the report's notion that college students were too immature and shortsighted to decide their own courses of study. He saw no problem with a radical change in what had been for slightly more than a half-century the traditional curriculum at Brown or for that matter with similar change at Yale or anywhere else.

Wayland planted his feet in public arguments in the 1840s about the collegiate curriculum, culminating with his proposed curricular changes at Brown University. As a prelude to what he would propose to the Brown trustees (the Corporation), Wayland wrote a major commentary, *Thoughts on the Present Collegiate System in the United States*, published in 1842.

In this tract, Wayland covers a wide waterfront. Among his concerns is the—sound familiar?—cost of a higher education. He addresses this problem in the related context of the degree to which a university or college education should be viewed as "popular" among the populace and citizenry.

Wayland believed that popularity had to follow first doing the right thing, not be a driver of curricular changes. In order to have an education that would be popular, meaning that parents would want to send their children and that students would want to come into the gates of the college, it was essential to present education as prized for both the present and the future. A college education had to be presented as of worth to society and to the lives of graduates. In addition Wayland was deeply concerned and committed to present education not only as of great value, but also as universally available.[25]

Wayland walks a tightrope. He wants popularity for the college— Brown or anywhere else—shamelessly in order to boost enrollments. Wayland and Brown waved a flag to get attention in the ranks of citizens who previously thought college was not something they wanted or needed, that a higher education was something for only the elite few. He proposed gaining that status by doing the right thing. He presumed this could be attained with the best interests of the college in mind. The balancing act was to have Brown remain a prestigious, highly regarded institution while at the same time broadening its appeal.

However, more crucially, Wayland believed that a college education as a popular thing to do had to be convincingly conveyed to the mind of consumers, that is, citizens, parents, and students. In Wayland's world, these constituents were there to be convinced that a higher education was a good thing, something they should desire, rather viewed as simply a highbrow notion for the elite of society and nation.

To Wayland's mind the game was simple. He believed Brown and any other college that might follow his strategy had to be transparent about the desirability of increasing the popularity of a college degree and of swelling enrollments. As for his approach, Wayland urges that the rationale undergirding his purposes be clear to the university's constituencies. The public had to understand the reasons for the education that was to be offered. It was the content of an education at Brown that would carry the message to the public. Making the university increasingly popular was the goal, but Wayland knew that increasing popularity had to follow from the changes in the college curriculum and its purposes that he hoped to inspire.[26]

The public could not be treated with condescension or taken as fools. Wayland sought the approval of fellow citizens, but knew that he could only gain that by conveying the good that he sought to provide to them. The roll of the dice that Wayland was willing to make, and convinced Brown to undertake, was based on a simple premise: that by making "fellow men wiser, and happier, and better" he and Brown would succeed and flourish.[27]

This was the business that Wayland wanted Brown to be in. Whether anyone would follow his lead did not matter. In fact he would be very happy if he got a lock on the attention of the public and on his aspiration to increase the matriculation of their youth, and their sons and daughters, to Brown.

However, beyond his marketing strategies, Wayland's primary notoriety is for the changes he argued in the undergraduate curriculum and course of study. In addition, joined by others before and since, he was also highly critical of the secondary education preparation of college-bound students. He was convinced that the nation's colleges would be improved by raising their requirements for admission. If the bar of these standards could be made higher, then prospective students would be forced to spend more years at the grammar school level.[28] As a result secondary students entering college would both be better prepared academically and also more seasoned about their vocational interests.

This educational critique was intertwined with his interests for the college and for undergraduate education. He believed he could get communities and the nation to raise the standards of secondary educational preparation as a building block.

Pragmatically, if more sons and daughters of the citizenry came to view a college education as being in their futures, then the public could be pushed to invest more greatly in more sound secondary education as the preparation to get more students to pursue further study at the college level. Wayland argues for the net of the higher education institutions to be cast more broadly. He wanted more students and their families who previously might not have been interested in pursuing a college education to be encouraged to apply and attend. If the doors of Brown and other colleges could be made more open and attractive to all classes of society, then better grammar level preparation to meet the higher admissions requirements could be more easily enforced.[29]

If the gates of the college, Brown and all other comers, were swung more widely open, Wayland reasoned that one positive result would be that the interests of students would be spread out well beyond the previously scripted regular course of study. There would be less crowding in more limited course offerings and students would then be freed to pursue their educational objectives more successfully than was often the case in a mindlessly, needlessly rigid course of study. With the undergraduate curriculum refashioned by Wayland's scheme, "Each course of instruction would stand on its own merits," and the purpose of the institution would be make all of its curricular offerings as valuable and well done as humanly possible.[30]

At last in 1850 Wayland put his ideas into a proposal for the Brown Corporation. His rationale was based on what he saw happening in the initial half of the nineteenth century.

To Wayland, the picture was plain: "We have produced an article for which the demand is diminishing." Today's hue and cry over colleges seeking to out-brand and out-market each other is nothing new. Wayland saw the same predicament for higher education that many fear today: "We sell it at less than cost, and the deficiency is made up by charity. We give it away, and still the demand diminishes. Is it not time to inquire whether we cannot furnish an article for which the demand will be, at least, somewhat more remunerative."[31]

Wayland's goal, and the Brown Corporation bought it for a brief time, was for the Brown curriculum to have greater appeal to the sons of farmers, who would leave the farm for an education only if it were designed directly to prepare them for the world of business and commerce. These folks were not about to be drawn to a college and its education simply for the idealistic sake of feeding their minds and stretching their intellects.

Wayland was well aware of the declining enrollment at Brown. He knew that lacking some change in the university's appeal, Brown would become an increasingly small, likely financially unsustainable island. However, in a profound irony his short-lived changes to the curriculum did not have the presumed effect of bolstering enrollments. As a result his experiment was rapidly abandoned as he departed the presidency of Brown in 1855. An alternative scheme for the collegiate curriculum and course of study had its very brief day, and whatever threat Wayland posed to tradition was abruptly in eclipse.

## THE IMPACT OF THE UNIVERSITY CURRICULUM ON THE COLLEGE: MAJOR PLAYERS ENTER THE FRAY

Wayland as a president and Brown as a still young and small college, not yet the foremost university it was to become, formed a bridge between the foray of the Yale Report into the curricular divide and the defining interests of the emerging big league universities of the land in the latter decades of the nineteenth century. Henry Tappan, first president of the University of Michigan, entered the fray when he landed in office in 1852.

Michigan was a major public university founded well ahead of its land grant Michigan counterpart, Michigan State University.

Tappan brought to Michigan the German model for a university that in the next decade was even more intentionally visible in the founding of Johns Hopkins University (1867). Tappan believed that the German model was the only way for Michigan to go.

He shaped Michigan so that "It would hold high the ideal of a true university of advanced scholarship, but it would also respond to popular needs." However, public taste would not predominate. Whether a whack at Wayland, the Jacksonians, or simply a critique of prevailing culture, Tappan claimed that his university would be "a powerful counter influence against the excessive commercial spirit, and against the chicanery and selfishness of demagogueism which prevailed in American society."[32]

Tappan's solution for a match of the university's curriculum and course of study with public desires aligned with Wayland's hoped-for goal. However, for Tappan the basis of the university had to be preeminent. Public ends could be addressed. Practical approaches to the education could be offered, and the ways the universities were able to do this could be applied vocationally and socially. However, the university would set the agenda. The cart could not be in front of the horse.

Tappan's vision for Michigan was straightforward:

> We shall have no more acute distinctions drawn between scholastic and practical education; for, it will be seen that all true education is practical, and that practice without education is little worth; and then there will be dignity, grace, and a resistless charm about scholarship and the scholar.[33]

As the university concept based on the German model grew throughout the latter decades of the nineteenth century, the debates among college presidents intensified. The Old Guard pushed to hold the gates against the threat believed to be posed by the New Guard advocates of the research university. In the footsteps of Tappan and in reaction to the founders of Johns Hopkins, James McCosh of Princeton, and Charles Eliot of Harvard engaged an intense public debate.

McCosh was absolutely dedicated to the traditional approach to curriculum and its social value. Eliot was the force, well-eclipsing Wayland, who brought the elective curriculum full bore into Harvard's educational approach and into public play in ways that set it in a position where its prominent place could not be ignored.

The two presidents grappled publicly with the implications of what Wayland had had set in motion against the backdrop of the Yale Report. Among other concerns were questions about the impact of the emergence of elective choice on the tradition-bound curriculum for the college and university. Again, there was the related question about whether college students were in any fashion capable of being responsible for making such choices and what, if they were permitted to do so, would be the outcome for the future of both education and society.

Eliot and McCosh duked it out separately, yet in the same public setting in New York City in February 1885. Things had come to a head. Two college presidents so plainly exposed and willing to risk their ideas in public debate is inspiring in any era, something that many yearn for today. Eliot was in a full court press for electives at the time firmly in place at Harvard, and McCosh, down the road in Princeton, was holding out for the traditional curriculum. Although grounded in each man's talking points, their exchange was nonetheless a full-blown intellectual argument.

Space does not permit a full exploration of the ins and outs of the Eliot-McCosh tangle. But elements of the debate provide a glimpse of the divide between them and in the larger public over electives versus the traditional curriculum.

The seventy-three-year-old McCosh more than carried the day against an opponent nearly twenty-five years his junior. In a great nineteenth-century joust between two university presidents, McCosh uses a para-doxical source to bolster his contentions. He notes that, while Eliot extols the German university and uses it as an example and model of what should happen for American universities, the Rector of the University of Berlin had asserted that, "all efforts to find a substitute for the classical languages, whether in mathematics, in modern languages or in the natural sciences, have been hitherto unsuccessful."[34]

Later in his talk, McCosh excoriates Eliot's leadership at Harvard, highlighting examples of courses of study in their catalogue and decrying, "There are twenty such dilettanti courses which may be taken in Harvard. I cannot allow that this is an advance in scholarship. If this be the modern education, I hold that old is better."[35]

In a final point McCosh makes a twofold claim. His educational concern is that the elective system was leading to premature specialization by young men (mostly men in those days, exclusively at Princeton and Harvard, but there were young women at many institutions including the fledgling women's colleges of the day). This problem of students making too many choices too early was exacerbated because so early in their educational careers they neither knew themselves or their true abilities.

As a result, McCosh challenges colleges to pursue the goal that:

> . . . all parts of a good college curriculum should be connected in an
> organic whole. Make a man a mere specialist and the chance is he will
> not reach the highest eminence as a specialist. The youth most likely to
> make discoveries is the one who has studied collateral subjects; the
> well gushes out at a certain point because the rains have descended on
> a large surface and entered the earth, and must find an outlet.[36]

The McCosh and Eliot debate, a wrangling engaged by other players over time, has had many twists and turns. Adversaries across the divide of the traditional versus the elective curriculum both muster arguments they believe are in tune with the ideals of educational philosophy, pedagogy, and of the presumed expectations about what individuals, students, and society need to possess in order to be equipped for learning and lifelong contributions. But their disagreements about how to get there remain.

At bottom, the McCosh-Eliot divide pivots on whether young adults, late teenagers, can be trusted to know what education is best for them. Educational leaders and commentators don't regularly go down this path today. We want to assume that college-age students are more highly sophisticated and mature compared to the cohorts of the last century. However, the reality is that the nineteenth-century claims about immaturity and lack of readiness in the young are more applicable to today's college scene than some might think.

The elective curriculum is based on assumptions that young adults know what they like and don't like, what they are good at and what they are not, and where they think they are headed in life and in the vocational, professional world. If college students can be assumed to make such choices wisely, then the reasoning goes that they should be free to do so. Why, it is argued, should college students waste time with educational content that has little bearing on who they are or what they might become? For that matter, what good is a rigid curriculum serving no purpose than to force on students course requirements that are not worth unnecessary academic and intellectual struggle?

The McCosh camp has ever argued otherwise. That is, young college students do not know what is in their best interest, and what it takes to prepare them to live full lives and to reach their highest potential. Therefore educators, educational leaders, and faculty have a duty to dictate what must be included in the college curriculum and in required courses of study.

These years spanning the three decades of the 1860s, 1870s, and 1880s proved critical because other voices joined to prevent a leader as influential as Eliot and at an institution with the footprint of Harvard from operating in a vacuum in the curricular discussions of the day. Noah Porter, president of Yale University (1871–1886) in his inaugural address paved the way for the McCosh position and joined with his colleague. Their tenures—McCosh at Princeton from 1868–1888—nearly identically overlapped.

Porter's inaugural is generally regarded as an argument against the elective system that was evolving about the land.[37] Porter's plea is that while there may be redeeming features of the elective idea, there were serious evils that it exposed. Joining the criticisms of other opponents of the elective system, he underscores the problem of the developmental level of the average college student. That is most undergraduate students do not have sufficient have maturity or the knowledge to be capable of making curricular choices about the relative value of the courses they elect to study or even how the majors chosen and courses amassed might bear on professional employment and the contributions they might be able to make throughout their lives.[38]

Supporters of electives believed that student choice in the course of study would support the choices about vocational interests and training that they were presumed to be able to experience as undergraduates. However, Porter and others opposed to elective curricula believed that wet-behind-the-ears young people would simply permit their feelings and the propensity to be drawn to what appears most pleasing to override the best judgments about what is required. Beyond the critique about choice over the content of knowledge being left to students are Porter's grander fears that this style of undergraduate education would destroy a common sense of purpose and shared life in courses and classrooms. Along with that educational and philosophical aspiration, the elective system could lead colleges into unnecessary expenditures and all-too great complexity in its academic offerings and how they are presented to students.[39]

Porter's concern reacts to the cultural formation of the nation circa the mid- to late nineteenth century. He pictured a degradation of society and culture resulting from too much student choice in the too important matter of their education and the knowledge base that was essential to undergird their learning and preparation for life. A core, liberal arts education, with required courses and study, were Porter's and his colleagues' antidote for these negative developments in the ethos of society.

But Porter's jeremiad transcends its era. It could equally be a response to similar handwringing in the early twenty-first century. How similar to the preachments of today is the core of Porter's complaint that "We have plenty of cheap glitter, of tawdry bedizenment and showy accomplishments; plenty of sensational declamation, coarse argument, and facile rhetoric; much moral earnestness which needs tolerance and knowledge, and religious fervor which runs into dogmatism and rant."[40]

Like McCosh, Porter rhetorically embraces the debate between his views about the fundamental wisdom of a structured curriculum and those of the proponents—Wayland, Eliot, and others—of the vanguard changes that the elective system was purported to bring about. Apropos the debate about the land, Porter views it not as a distraction loaded with negative implications for the academy, but rather welcomes "The breeze of public interest and public criticism, which is now blowing so freshly through the halls of ancient learning," that is the nation's colleges and universities, "can only bring health and vigor."[41]

Imploring decorum, Porter warns that "It were a craven spirit in the intelligent believer in liberal education that should falter in its allegiance to well-grounded convictions because these are sharply assailed." But for

Porter and his allies there would be no flagging of spirit and conviction. "Whatever is good in the old systems," Porter is confident, "will not only endure the scrutiny of argument and bide the test of experiment, but, as we believe, will justify itself to the best judgment of the men who form public opinion."[42]

At its fundamental center, this debate about the curriculum was waged over differing contentions of how to prepare students to find their greatest promise and aspirations, and to do so in concert with what society and culture demands and needs of them. Regardless the differences, all sides attacked the debate earnestly as critical to the future both of colleges and universities and of the students they presumed to educate. They leave behind a legacy characterized by civil discourse, even where stridency and passion were of necessity shot through.

This was a time when a still fledgling Republic was less than two decades removed from a crucible of crisis and strife. The events of the Civil War and the stark differences that spawned it presented a fork in the road. As the nineteenth century drew to a close, there was legitimate fear that the wrong choice about the undergraduate curriculum and what was to be required of college students could lead to corrosive consequences for individuals and for society. All sides to this public discussion of the liberal arts foundation at the basis of the college in America knew that stability and the best interests of society had to be a priority.

The nation's saga could have turned out differently. The future had been placed on the scaffold. The nation's aspirations for its founding principles and beliefs laid out in the previous "four score and seven years" of Lincoln's famed phrase, not to mention the ideals at the foundation of the earliest colleges founded two-and-a-half centuries earlier, dangled in the balance.

Thus, in this formative time of the latter nineteenth century, the stakes inside and outside the academy could not have been higher. Many assumed that what had been in place for decades and centuries as the college curriculum was working and was a proven approach of value to both students and society. Others believed that there had to be change in how a college education was fashioned and offered, especially and primarily if American society was as was deemed essential to grow, develop, and adapt to new occasions and duties. This was a fair and important debate to be plumbed, and it was one with no simple solution.

## THE TWENTIETH CENTURY: A TRIUMVIRATE EMERGES IN CONTINUING CURRICULUM TUSSLES

In broad-brush strokes, America in the mid- to late nineteenth century witnessed the eclipse of the classic, Colonial College curriculum, that which was defended in the Yale Report of 1828. There was a steady movement, ever resisted but with varying success, toward a different conception of undergraduate education perceived as desirable both for students and for the economic salability for the colleges and universities. At many colleges and universities, missions began to include, if not be superseded by, a capacity to provide the more sophisticated vocational preparation and training that the more elective curriculum was presumed to produce.

An added force in this environment, difficult to sort completely the chicken from the egg, was the advance of the German university model and its imitative as well as native variations that formed the university in America as the reality it was fast becoming.

Few if any educational, political, and faculty leaders of the early nineteenth century could have envisioned the evolving breadth of the major university and the force it exerted on the liberal arts college by the end of the century. The liberal arts college and the undergraduate, presumed liberal arts grounded colleges within major universities such as at Harvard, Yale, and others, came under increasingly critical scrutiny. At times this criticism bordered on assault over the justification of the existence of the liberal arts and of the liberal arts colleges, and their role as the placeholders of the more traditional curriculum.

Alexander Meiklejohn, first a professor at Brown University and later president of Amherst College from 1912–1924, was an outspoken defender of the liberal arts college and proponent of liberal education. In his essay, "What the Liberal College Is" (published in 1920), Meiklejohn navigates the polarized false choices so frequently associated in recurring curricular debates and in these assaults on the liberal arts college.

As ever the case, the horns of that debate and dilemma was the choice between education for practical applications—promotion of the social good but also for bolstering the professions and vocational training—versus education for its own sake. The former *raison d'être* is that of the elective curriculum advocates and the specialized training that the university, even in its undergraduate guise, could logically offer. The latter is the curriculum of the liberal arts and the liberal arts college, the turf Meiklejohn and his fellow leaders of these colleges roamed and defended.

Meiklejohn claims that knowledge is crucial primarily for what it contributes to other activities in human life. At the same time the avenue to reach this goal in the college is a full and uncompromising intellectual quest. For Meikeljohn, these two demands of what life and society requires and the intellectual demands of the college were not in conflict but rather are complementary and harmonious relation of means and ends.[43]

As an architect of college curriculum and its rationale, Meiklejohn circumvents conventional point and counterpoint thinking. His stand opposes arguments that the elective curriculum is the only way a university education could be shaped to address the demands of an increasingly

complex world. Declaring further the *raison d'être* of the undergraduate
college as a bastion of the liberal arts, Meiklejohn suggests that leaders
and faculty must emphasize and demonstrate how the intellectual foundations of the college are not opposed to practical interests and purposes,
but rather stand in opposition to what is impractical and short-sighted in
both the short and longer run of what is desirable in the academy and in
the world of work.[44]

Meiklejohn claims that the matter at hand is not a false choice between
practical and intellectual goals and ends. Rather it is a choice between the
aims of the short-run versus the long run. It is a tension between what
can be done in haste and in the interest of demands for immediate results
versus the capacity to aim for the best results. The dilemma of how the
academy presents itself is that success in the intellectual quests can take a
long time and to critics will seem more roundabout than is necessary. In
contrast the aims of the intellectual mind cannot be found in a rush for
quick results. Maintaining these values and convictions is crucial to the
argument of what the liberal college means to learning and human life as
well.[45]

The public debates of the times, including those between McCosh and
Eliot, and in the attitude Porter exhibited, reveal higher education leaders, college presidents in this instance serving up civility, rationality, and
more light than heat. Meiklejohn hacks out his territory in no uncertain
terms. However, rounding out his argument, Meiklejohn gives quarter to
his opponents. He claims, wanting to have it both ways, that the principle
of election in the shaping of the curriculum and in the course of studies
that students should be able to pursue should not be entirely discontin-
ued. What Meilkejohn wants is a full-throated inquiry about what is most
right and justified in the shaping of the scale of electives and choice in the
curriculum.[46]

At the same time, Meilkejohn does not shirk from a jeremiad about the
times. Dangers abounded and he compellingly stresses what was at
stake. The problem was that the college and its interests about the course
of study and the requirements of the curriculum determined by academic
leaders and faculty had to trump what those students might elect for
themselves if given the chance. The special interests of students could not
be permitted to override the fundamental educational goals that the college had a duty to prescribe and that had to be met.[47] Educational leaders
were obligated, duty-bound to step into the breech. Anything less would
be an appalling abdication of that responsibility.

The danger was that educators and scholars of Meiklejohn's day were
a large part of the problem for failing to establish clearly delineated educational policies to govern curriculum. Meiklejohn blamed the willing-
ness to permit students, unbridled choices in the college curriculum were
born in intellectual agnosticism, itself an intellectual bankruptcy. Much of
the failures of the day on the curriculum and elective battleground front

resulted from a denial of responsibility into which university leaders and faculty had fallen. [48]

He had no toleration for this state of affairs, and believed that educational leaders could not simply stand back and refuse or think themselves powerless to do anything about it. Meiklejohn's philosophy may look archaic. Nonetheless his fundamental concerns are as germane today as a hundred years ago when he hammered out his ideas.

To this day, at stake in curricular arguments is the question of whether college undergraduates can adequately determine the foundational courses to prepare them as educated people for life in society and in the world. Joining other critics of the elective system, while by no means the exclusive centerpiece, Meiklejohn is gravely concerned that traditional-aged college students lack of the ability to decide wisely and in short or longer range perspective the most informed path of their undergraduate course of study.

Meiklejohn was joined in his pushback of the march toward the world of the elective curriculum by another major force in American higher education: Robert Hutchins. Hutchins became president of the University of Chicago in 1929 at the remarkably young age of thirty.

Hutchins shared almost none of Meiklejohn's temperament and measured rhetoric. He aggressively made his arguments about the college and university and the curriculum it must have, woe to anyone who thought otherwise. [49] Hutchins cared little if at all what anyone, from colleague faculty and fellow presidents to anyone in the broader citizenry, thought of him and of his ideas.

Hutchins sought a return to his version of the classical curriculum for the university. He fingers Charles Eliot as the leader of the misguided elective curriculum. Hutchins excoriated Eliot, calling him "the great criminal" who "applied his genius, skill, and longevity to the task of robbing American youth of their cultural heritage." This was because Eliot, "held that there were no such things as good or bad," black and white thinking that was a bane of Hutchins, "subjects of study, his laudable effort to open the curriculum to good ones naturally led him to open it to bad ones and finally to destroy it altogether." [50]

Extending the critique of Meiklejohn, Porter, and McCosh, Hutchins decries the educational outcome that contemporary colleges and universities were producing: "Today the young American comprehends only by accident the intellectual tradition of which he is a part and in which he must live: for its scattered and disjointed fragments are strewn from one end of the campus to the other." [51]

Giving credit where credit is due, Hutchins is not far afield of Porter's complaint seen earlier about the college and society: "cheap glitter . . . tawdry bedizenment and showy accomplishments; plenty of sensational declamation, coarse argument, and facile rhetoric. . . ." However, Hutchins is further riveted on the gravity of the prospect that the Western tradition as it had been known had already fully eroded.

This disaster was more dangerous than fears over the incapacity of undergraduate students to be architects of their education and over prospects that elective curricula would fail to produce an educated cadre of students to meet the needs of society. Those were no doubt on Hutchins's mind. But the final reality is that "Our university graduates have far more information and far less understanding than in the colonial period"[52] Thus even if it had taken well over a century, the degradation of the academy was fully underway, and Hutchins believed the consequences were both real and likely to worsen in the decades ahead.

As Hutchins saw it, the "crucial error" of Eliot and his ilk "is that of holding that nothing is any more important than anything else, that there can be no order of goods, and no order in the intellectual realm." Eliot and elective proponents fell prey to the trap that "There is nothing central and nothing peripheral, nothing primary and noting secondary, nothing basic and nothing superficial." In short, what has happened is that "The course of study" under an Eliot regime, "goes to pieces because there is nothing to hold it together."[53]

But Hutchins does not stop there. His critique couples two things, one from an earlier time and another prescient of struggles later in his own twentieth century.

On one hand, Hutchins fears the anti-intellectualism remarkably reminiscent of a century earlier when Jacksonianism was afoot posing a clear threat to the academy and, in the eyes of many, to American society. On the other hand, Hutchins foreshadows how, even before it was hatched as a concept in the latter 1970s and 1980s, political correctness would mindlessly distort academic discourse and the fundamental values and foundation of the academy.

However, even beyond these disasters and conundrums, Hutchins was more horrified by the vortex created by the convergence of sentimentalism and the anti-intellectualism. This coupling was a timeless—his or anytime—threat. Hutchins viewed sentimentalism as "an irrational desire to be helpful to one's fellow-men. It sometimes appears as an ingratiating and even a redeeming quality in those who cannot or will not think."[54]

For Hutchins the problem was that "the sentimentalist is a really dangerous character. He distrusts the intellect, because it might show him he is wrong. He believes in the primacy of the will, and this is what makes him dangerous. You don't know what you ought to want; you don't know why you want what you want. But you do know that you want it. This easily develops into the notion that since you want it, you ought to have it." However, things do not stop there. Never one to duck hyperbole, Hutchins adds that in the sentimentalist silo, "You are a man of goodwill, and your opponents by definition are not. Since you ought to have what you want, you should get it if you have the power; here the journey from the man of good will to Hitler is complete." [55]

Hutchins could be criticized for going over the top with the Hitler reference, writing as he was in the early 1940s when Germany and Nazism were on the march. But as noted, Hutchins cared little what people thought of him, of his ideas and of his rhetoric. Regardless the hyperbole, Hutchins's point is well founded: the road to Hell is always paved with good, in his critique, "sentimentalist" intentions.

Furthermore as things turned out, the politically correct of the 1980s through the 1990s and into today's world of the academy, in addition to whatever else might ascribed to them, are in Hutchins parlance certainly sentimentalists. As he alleged about their predecessors, if Hutchins were around today he would clearly condemn political correctness advocates for the damage they bring to bear on the affairs and culture of the academy.

Despite the curmudgeonly jeremiads, Hutchins was at heart an idealist. He believed that his idea of the university and the education it should offer could inspire a "spiritual revolution." This was something that could come about only from "the reconstruction of the educational system" in America. [56]

Hutchins believed there was nothing wrong with the educational system. What was wrong was the country that produced and put up with what it had when a far-reaching commitment, effort, and investment could change dramatically the way that system worked. [57] At the university level, such changes meant that then graduates "might be ready to take their place in a community devoted to the achievement of the common good through reason." [58] This was after all the dream from Jefferson, Franklin, and the founders of the Colonial Colleges to those in Hutchins's time, including those opposed to his back-to-the-future curriculum.

Hutchins's proposal for the way out of this morass ironically pivots not on educational assumptions, rather on a quest rooted in religious imagery. This social "good" and "spiritual revolution" was to Hutchins a necessity because he judged the American people as "devoted to the acquisition of material goods by any means not too outrageous." [59] He predicted that the generation of graduates of his model of a university "might suffer the same fate as the martyrs of the early church. They might be that phenomenon horrible to American eyes, financial failures." But Hutchins believed the "blood of [these] martyrs might prove to be the seed of an enlightened nation." [60]

In an era that, retrospectively, was an even higher-stakes time than those of Hutchins's day imagined, he daringly advocated that the university was the only institution remaining that could save society and the world. In the middle of World War II, Hutchins's aspirations for the university and how it must serve society were plain.

"Candid and intrepid thinking about fundamental issues—in the crisis of our time this is the central obligation of the universities. This is the standard," Hutchins argues, "by which they [universities] must be judged." As a counter to his purist notions that the university should be detached from "the world," Hutchins asserts that the university should be in tune with the times, at least in times of crisis. "This is the aim which will give unity, intelligibility, and meaning to their work. This is the road to wisdom. Upon that road the American university," here Hutchins's religious-spiritual quest, "will regain its own soul and bring hope and comfort to a distracted world."[61]

The classical idea of the university, á la Cardinal Newman, was an enduring ideal. However, though Hutchins conveyed that idea in high sounding, grandstanding fashion, he was not naïve about the environment in which the university existed. At the end of the day, he believed the university's educational ideals could not be completely detached from the world in which it lived. There had to be a classical curriculum, grounded in the best of Western tradition. Students had to be exposed to this discipline and way of thinking. But even this grand ideal could not be removed from the realities of the demands, crises, whys, and wherefores of the world.

Rounding out this line of thinking, Hutchins returns to the idea that the nation gets the education it deserves. He reiterates that "The chaos in education with which we are familiar is an infallible sign of the disintegration of civilization; for it shows that ideals are no longer commonly held, clearly understood, or deliberately pursued." This is "the incredibly heavy burden which rests, even in total war, upon the universities." The challenge was that "If they [the universities] cannot carry it, nobody else will; for nobody else can." In this mission, he quotes William the Silent: "It is not necessary to hope in order to undertake, or to succeed in order to persevere."[62]

The times of the early and mid-twentieth century were a maelstrom of social unease, political fear, and apocalyptic thinking. This inspired many education leaders then, as many still do today, to assert that the onslaught of societal change demanded that the curricular advances of electives in the late nineteenth century had to be secured and sustained, even expanded.

Another college leader siding with Hutchins and Meiklejohn, responding to these pressures about change, was Henry Wriston. Wriston was president of Brown University from 1937–1955, overlapping nearly identically with Hutchins's 1929–1951 run at Chicago. It is as though the baton of responsibility to push back against electives was passed in the twentieth century from Meiklejohn to Hutchins, and in nearly the same breath to Wriston. The three spanned nearly fifty years of advocacy for the value of the classical, fundamentally grounded, albeit heavily Western tradition curriculum.

Wriston disputed the manner in which change was thrown about will-ly-nilly as an excuse and rationale to do things differently academically, and as a reason to alter the purpose of the university. To Wriston this social analysis was used as a default refuge for those wanting to sustain the curricular shift to electives of the previous century. Wriston would have little of this line of argument.

Regardless the swirling of events, Wriston contends that things were no different vis-á-vis change and complexity in his day than in previous times. To portray the early decades of the twentieth century as a radically different time was a distortion. Education had always played its role bolstering democratic foundations as well as stimulating refinements designed better to serve the body politic and the civic good. This was the case in good times and bad, times of perceived accelerated change and those of stability and the status quo.

The idea that a sudden, graver contemporary threat to democracy required radical change in the college curriculum simply held no water. Democracy by definition was a fragile civil system, and that had been the case throughout over 150 years of the nation's existence, not to mention over three centuries of a democratic experiment in the New World.

This era was a critical moment in the historical connection between American democracy and the nation's educational system, including its colleges and universities. Wriston argues that it is "Groundhog Day," that the country had seen this movie before. Alarmist claims that education must radically change in order to secure democracy were the most false of false choices.

Wriston's era was indeed intense and featured politics that called for the same infusion of sanity and rationality that many would argue about our times today. The addressing of these concerns about change and what is required of education and the university could not be done in a knee-jerk, unthought-out fashion. Short and longer-term needs and consequences could not be ignored.

The reality was that over-the-top political diatribe and cultural commentary did not begin in the 1930s, let alone in the latter twentieth and early twenty-first centuries. Examining the complexity and politics that had infiltrated "democracy," Wriston reminds us of previous invective in public discourse more excessive than that of his day, noting Thomas Paine's allegations that George Washington was an "apostate or an imposter" as only one glaring example.[63]

Wriston goes to great pains to appear even-handed. But note his assessment about what was going on about the land and with his opponents. His philosophy pivots on two points. The first has to do with notions of a "traditional" versus a more vocationally guided curriculum. "On the one hand are those who would cling to the traditional disciplines," Wriston acknowledges, "and on the other are those who would make an analysis of the students' present and future activities and found the curriculum upon the basis of those activities."[64]

However, Wriston contends, "one can argue it in either direction. Thus it may be held that it is absurd, in laying out the curriculum, not to follow the life pattern of the individual, or it may be argued that any activities analysis is so superficial in its characteristics, is so gross in its deductions, is so little related to the actual processes of each individual student that it is meaningless—often, indeed it seems as though those who would make an activities analysis are reverting," here the vital verdict, "to the old fallacy of the 'economic man' that the economist uses to dress up for classroom purposes, but who proved," Wriston's zinger about students under the curricular regimen in college classrooms, "to be nothing more than a dummy."[65]

But Wriston is not done, far from it. An undergraduate education is not an easy business. Wriston is terribly concerned about those who would steer the curriculum away from its essential difficult challenges and would seek to eliminate the reality that students have to work hard and might fail.

When students engage the curriculum, they must confront the need to change and to be tested. In a comment mirroring many critics today who believe the academy is being dumbed down, Wriston claims, ". . . there is a very strong tendency to try to take all the hazard out of education. A psychology that, if dominant, would destroy industry and sport—and life itself—has persuaded us that the experience of failure . . . is always a destructive force."[66]

The contrasting approach to those who sought a more student friendly, accommodating curriculum is clear to Wriston. His judgment is that "The 'quick and easy' promise is always the mark of the educational charlatan." That is, "There is no painless or safe method of acquiring knowledge, and the pursuit of wisdom is even more arduous and hazardous."[67]

Returning to the tugs of the divergent interpretations held by opposing sides about the state of the nation and what to do about it, Wriston argues that, "Efforts to control the future through the educative process are particularly disastrous if they are based upon a defensive temper." He adds that "If schools undertake by formal means to 'save' democracy, they are much more likely to destroy it."[68]

Addressing another concern of his era, like Hutchins, Wriston is prescient about what came to be called political correctness. He declares that, "To try to 'condition' the student into one form of faith, political, economic, or religious, is to assault, rather than support, the dignity of the individual. The propagandists," he further alleges, "will capture the schools if they can; any effort to establish uniform ideals simply plays into their hands—against the interests of the students, whose innate right it is to learn rather than to be 'conditioned.'"[69]

Although Wriston knew of Hutchins's reputation as a "propagandist" for his uncompromising stands, the two were bedfellows in the grander battle against those who would dumb down education and students. Wriston and Hutchins had as a common enemy those who wanted to manipulate the curriculum to address shorter-term interests and to cave in to the desires of both students and American society. The way out is Wriston's truism that "Much educational change consists in the rediscovery of old truths by seeking them along new paths."[70]

Wriston, Hutchins, and Meiklejohn lived in interesting times. They battled the march toward more electives in the curriculum. They used their leadership to challenge unbridled ideological pressures on the affairs and shape of the university.

Frederick Rudolph summarizes what was going on and what was portended regarding the continuing struggles over liberal education and how best to attain it in the decades of the early twentieth century. In the 1920s, general education courses, such as the Columbia contemporary civilization requirement (1919), were put in place to offset the emphasis on electives of the latter nineteenth and early twentieth centuries. The Wriston wing fought for general education "proposed to restore some balance, to revitalize the aristocratic ideal of the liberal arts as the passport to learning."[71]

Lest we think otherwise, the meddling of political correctness and of ideological pressure on colleges did not begin only in recent times. Donors arguing that they were entitled to handpick the holders of the chairs and how their money was to be spent, and colleges and universities feeling the pressure to comply with those demands have for better and worse been going on for some time.

These pressures are not simply a contemporary reality for the academy and its presidents. Underscoring this point and capturing the tendencies in the 1920s, Rudolph notes it was a time "when a five-and-ten-cent store millionaire would endow a chair of civil rights at Lafayette College and then complain that he was having difficulty hiring for the chair a professor prepared to sell the donor's political and social views."[72]

Rudolph indulges a litany of the ills and frustrations of the 1930s, eerily similar to today and the post-Great Recession of 2007 world, especially for the prospects for college students following graduation. Regardless whether colleges and universities were powerless over the realities of this climate of the 1930s, the social and political environment was what it was, and that was not a good time for either the nation or the academy. Rudolph pictures people out of work, wonders whether greater regulation could have offset the 1929 crash, and asks who was in charge, "who ran the country? Political bosses? Big businessmen? The people? The cynical, monopolistic press?"[73]

Regarding the battles between the traditional and the new emerging growth of knowledge, Rudolph highlights ". . . the motto of the University of Chicago: 'Let knowledge grow from more to more, and thus be human life enriched.'" Extrapolating the Chicago influence, Rudolph believes that, "By mid-twentieth century this motto had actually become the motto of all American higher education, symbolic of a consensus."[74]

Warring factions in the battle over liberal education—the advocates of electives and the proponents of a traditional curriculum—at least agreed that knowledge was supreme and was the duty of the academy to inspire. But they retained distinctive and often conflicting ideas about how to get there.

## THE BEAT GOES ON: 1960s UPHEAVALS AND THE LAST DECADES OF THE TWENTIETH CENTURY

As the twentieth century drew to a close, different interpretations arose over the impact on the formation of the university of debates about what constituted a liberal education and about the meaning of curricular upheavals. What had happened? What had these events meant and where might things go in the future? That era of the 1960s and 1970s, and the continuing tumult and political correctness debates in the 1980s and 1990s about curriculum and the future of the college and university, were unstable times. In that environment, it became even more difficult to be objective about what was going on.

A superior intellect and writer of the twentieth century, a professor, administrator in the tumultuous mid-1950s to the late 1960s—some argue the most adept senior university administrator never to become a college president—and prolific author, Jacques Barzun conjectures about where things were and where they were going for the university and for American society.

Barzun was a denizen of the academy. He lived his entire life there, knew its fallacies and ideological culs-de-sac as well as its fundamental intellectual powers.

At the same time, Barzun possessed sweeping perspectives that fashioned his critiques about education, about culture, and about the affairs of society. He stresses the challenges foisted on the humanities when colleges raced like lemmings over the cliff in efforts to reframe the curriculum on the grounds of the presumed value of electives.

Concerning the battle between knowledge for "professional or vocational use," on one hand, and "social or moral (or philosophical or civilizing)" on the other, Barzun declares that "One is know how, the other is cultivation." He claims that, "for some hundred years [beginning in the late 1800s] American colleges and universities have innocently confounded the two . . ." The problem is that these two ends "require distinct uses of subject matter and of the mind, and they cannot be fused into one."[75]

There were undeniable consequences for the liberal arts of this conflation of the vocational, the "know how," on the one hand, and the civilizing, learning for the sake of learning *raison d'être* of a college education on the other. Barzun was passionate about the humanities and was aware of the immediate and lasting implications for curriculum and for the course of college and university study resulting from tense debate over the purpose of an undergraduate education. There would be no guarantees where things would come out for the academy as a result of the clash between external pressures, interests and desires of society and the professions pushing to determine what college education should be and include, and what the college believed was its singular purpose.

Barzun claims that as the nineteenth century turned to the twentieth, colleges were pressured by natural sciences, business and corporate sectors, and "from growing technologies and the new self-conscious professions" to "rejustify their existence." Thus "in order to placate both the social demand for professionals and the scholarly demand for specialists, the colleges broke up the old classical curriculum and invented the elective system." Though he doesn't label Eliot as an evil force to the degree Hutchins did, Barzun lays all this at the feet of ". . . Dr. Eliot of Harvard who became its [the elective system's] great exponent; he was a chemist."[76]

However, Barzun does not let Eliot off the hook for living in the siloed world of the scientist that shaped his thinking about a college education. Eliot's world dictated that any scientist in the making would require three to six years of concentrated study in their field. Clearly that course of study would be bogged down by the requirements of a traditional curriculum. The Eliot approach was to let the budding undergraduate scientist, and really any other vocationally and professionally directed student, get about the business of pursuing the course of study that their interests dictated.

Meanwhile condescending to the worth of subject matter outside the sciences, "Eliot was quite content to see that same undergraduate take, outside his science, one semester of this and another of that for four years—perhaps four years of freshman work." The problem was, and this is so often overlooked even by sophisticated educators and educational thinkers, "The need to *build* a humanistic education in a controlled and rigorous way was forgotten, lost in the shuffle. The college curriculum broke into fragments and departments became small principalities competing for students and seeking prestige by specialism."[77]

Constructing a response to deal with the demands society placed on the academy, and how society's needs might be tackled, Barzun turns to Princeton's president, Woodrow Wilson for remarks made at the Association of American Universities at Madison, Wisconsin (a citadel as one of America's great universities of the early twentieth century). Wilson argued that "All specialism—and this includes professional training—is clearly individualistic in its object. . . . The object . . . is the private interest of the person who is seeking that training."[78]

For Wilson a college education as a social end had to fulfill a vastly larger purpose. The nation's colleges and universities existed to produce an intellectual foundation in each successive, rising generation of students. Anything less would fall short of the expectations the country had for its higher education institutions, as well as those that the academy held for itself.

Wilson assailed the trend fast becoming a reality in his era that suggested the academy could get by with something less than the fullest possible intellectual grounding and preparation of each generation of students to come through its gates. Even at the most practical level, as Meiklejohn had pointed out for years, the educated person with a reasonably honed intellect and knowledge was a predicate to whatever the individual would then go on to do in society, in business, commerce, or whatever his or her pursuit.

What was at stake for Wilson was "'the intellectual as well as the economic danger of our times'—an intellectual danger, because the merely trained individual is a tool and not a mind; an economic danger, because society needs minds and not merely tools."[79]

Wilson feared that the undergraduate products of a more decidedly vocationally geared education and curriculum would in their adult years and careers become individuals so "immersed in some one special interest that he no longer comprehended the country and age in which he was living." To counter that prospect, Wilson argued that, "the business of a college is to re-generalize each generation as it came on . . ."[80]

To preserve their identity but more for the good of society, colleges and universities had a duty to embrace this mission and obligation for the highest intellectual purpose of the education they offered. This is the time-honored notion that the job of the university is to pass the best of culture and knowledge to future generations. Wilson, Hutchins, Porter, Barzun, and others opposed to the elective curriculum knew this was the larger cause for which they fought. This was the battleground of the undergraduate college and curriculum throughout the twentieth century, the era of the academy in which Barzun had a front-row seat.

We draw toward conclusion of this journey about the purpose of the college and two centuries of battles over what constitutes a liberal education and how that ideal has fared amid the challenges and changes in the undergraduate college. An obvious point needs to be made: In the final analysis, all of this Sturm und Drang is about perspective.

Douglas Sloan offers a slice of that perspective, providing what for him was an aha moment in attempting to gather a more firm grasp about the more "ancient" history of American higher education, notably that period between the Revolution and the Civil War. Sloan's concern is rooted in two assumptions that he feels "warrant a closer look. First, most histories of the early nineteenth-century college are written from the perspective of the later university. Too frequently, for example, descriptions of life and learning in the colleges are taken uncritically from the leading advocates of late nineteenth-century reform."[81]

Sloan lists the usual suspects, among them Andrew White, James Angell, and William Rainey Harper, the presidents who pushed the advance of the research university and their takes on the undergraduate college and education of students. Regarding this roster of leaders, Sloan elaborates about who these men were as presidents. In an ironic twist they were actually opponents of the existing institution of the university. These men were champions of the new development of what was the nascent research university. They led the battles to have the institution that was this new university find its rightful place in American society, and that story unfolded throughout the closing decades of the nineteenth century.[82]

However, the political reality was that "These university men had every incentive while struggling both to gain a foothold for their fledgling cause and, after it had taken root, to justify their life-long endeavors, to portray their competitors [the undergraduate colleges] in less than complimentary light."[83] To Sloan, reliance on these interpretations has clouded the capacity of later historians to get an objective handle on what had gone on during the earlier formative stage of the colleges of the nation.

The zinger, the problem this mish-mash of viewpoints creates for the contemporary audience is clear. That is for Sloan, "The propensity of historians to mix the university reformers' pronouncements on the antebellum college indiscriminately with what might appear to be supporting evidence from the earlier period itself continues to flaw attempts to obtain some objective assessments of the college."[84]

The footprint, rhetoric, and stature of these early university leaders, for better and worse, must be acknowledged. They changed the higher education landscape in America, and they knew it. For Sloan, the problem is that the shadow of their arguments and perspectives obscures clarity about what happened to the undergraduate college as a result of the sway of these leaders over people and events in press to put the research university on the map of American higher education.

Pushing for a clearer picture, Sloan urges that what is needed is a deeper assessment of how the historical foundations of the early colleges were shaped. He is convinced that such an analysis will find that the reality of how these colleges developed has been repeatedly altered by the extent to which historians have interpreted and colored their early histories in light of later times when they began to be forced to react to pressures created by the rise of the research university and by the evolution and differences that had to be confronted by new social and cultural times and influences.[85] That is to say, the earlier history cannot be back-filled through the lens of the later generations of leaders and institutions, or education and social commentators that fought the battles and controversies in the latter time of the "emerging university" and "the incredibly fierce sectarian strife of the American churches of the 1890s."[86]

Sloan's second flaw that leads to misreading of the history of higher education in America is that the problem with "many of our accounts of nineteenth-century higher education is that they are cast as morality plays."

To a large extent many of today's battles are fought along the same lines that Sloan describes. That is the situation in which "Developments in higher education are portrayed as a mighty struggle that it's the angels of light on one side—everything that is liberal, progressive, democratic, and reform-oriented—against the legions of darkness on the other—the forces of conservatism, retrogression, aristocracy, and reaction."[87] The contemporary reality in political correctness debates is the tendency of rival factions to paint each other in these corners. Polarized views then reduce the current scene to nothing more than a battle between forces of good versus evil.

Sloan's view is that in the nineteenth century, the intentions of curriculum and curricular programs in colleges as well as other educational institutions, regardless whether they remained rooted in traditional shape and form or were reshaped by changing times, "revolved around one or more of three major concerns: religion, revivalistic or rational; science, basic or applied; and culture, genteel or popular."[88] He notes that these three concerns have both overlapping constituents (e.g., revivalists who embraced science) but also reflect distinctively different core beliefs.

Regardless how disparate these forces at first glance appear to be, taken together, "all claimed a vital connection with the basic emotional and experiential dimensions of individual life; and they looked toward the welfare of society as they conceived it. Whether through social reform or control, they sought to justify themselves as socially useful—utilitarian. This in itself makes the nineteenth century of special interest in light of present [late 1960s and early 1970s] cries for an individually and socially 'relevant curriculum.'"[89]

Sloan believes that the college in American cannot run from these roots. He believes it is essential to uncover what has happened in order to understand either his era of the 1960s and 1970s, or in any historical time where we are and why. Over time, a lot of energy has been expended in attempts to cover up and to distract attention from those origins. The reality of these roots often contrast starkly with idealized versions about what we would like to think happened historically. But attempts to air brush out of the picture more truthful perceptions about this heritage serve to perpetuate inaccurate accounts about the identity of the academy.

On aspect of this history that captures Sloan's attention is the tribalistic, sectarian backdrop of religious affections and leadership at the foundation of the college in America. He contends that "If the history of education stands in need of a study of the camp meeting as an agency of frontier education, it could probably also profit from an analysis of the college as a camp meeting." [90]

Many leaders contributed to this camp meeting ethos. However pure we might like to think the liberal arts to be, these denizens of the early 1800s clearly fuzzed the lines between curricular purity and religious, ideological passion.

Sloan takes particular note of Timothy Dwight at Yale who initiated the "great Yale revival of 1802" and Charles Finney at Oberlin (a professor of theology and president) as strong hands in the collapsing of the revival fervor into the core values and daily life of the colleges under their control. Finney went so far as to say that Oberlin "should make the conversion of sinners and the sanctification of Christians the paramount work and the subordinate to this all the educational operations." [91]

Meanwhile, the controversial, nativist Lyman Beecher drew his line in the sand. The relationship of education to religion and society and culture collapsed even more profoundly in his vision of the New World and for the academy in America.

Beecher urged that to secure the goals of the revival, to bring civilization and religious and civil liberty, the key, more than all the conventional religious trappings of prayer and preachers, was "the establishment of 'permanent, powerful, literary, and moral institutions,'" as he argued in his classic, *A Plea for the West*, read the colleges of the day. In short, "Revivalism provided the needed commitment, concern, and purpose; the colleges gave content and discipline to inspiration, and harnessed it to the cherished values of civilization." [92]

What if any difference is there between these early to mid-nineteenth and the late twentieth and early twenty-first-century skirmishes in the academy over ideological control and the battles for preeminence of one view over others in that struggle? They are finally of the same cloth: Maneuver the foundation of the college in order to create a patina for the foothold of ideological passions which will hold greater sway in society because the imprimatur of the academy has been laid on it.

One antidote to what was about in the land in the Dwight era at Yale and in the other revivalist forces of the Second Great Awakening was the Yale Report of 1828. Our story comes full circle. In his assessment of the classic Yale Report of 1828, Sloan's historical analysis tries to sort fact from fiction, the myths that developed from the realities over time.

Regardless the coherence that the "reforms" of the Yale Report tried to bring about, the nineteenth century was a dynamic era. Colleges and universities forever scrambled to address and to keep up with the changes of the times.

In this climate, Sloan suggests, "the late nineteenth-century university not only reflected but in a paradoxical way was born out of and shaped by growing lack of social and intellectual cohesion." "The emergence of the university and its successful functioning have been possible because its members achieved and maintained a consensus not around eternal verities," Sloan observes, "but rather around certain structural arrangements and working procedures both in areas of governance and academic life."[93]

Stating that, "all these problem areas have been perplexing," Sloan adds, "Yet as long as the consensus held, these problems could be tolerated as serious but not ultimately destructive."[94] Sloan's assessment about the previous century is correct in places. But the influence of his times—the tumultuous 1960s and 1970s and the curricular and other upheavals of those days—clouded his vision and skewed how he understood that earlier consensus, primarily because he hyped his era as different and more damaging than any previous.

With the 1960s crashing in and around the world of the academy, and caught up in the times, Sloan argues that "Now there are signs that the university consensus may very well be breaking. Its survival has been dependent on a balance of interests within and on a basic acceptance, or at the least toleration, of its functions by the larger society without. Undue conflict at either point would jeopardize its future; unfortunately, the demands of universal higher education and present social discord are simultaneously bringing both under pressure. Failure to introduce flexibility and diversity into a monolithic system, if such it be, can only heighten tensions."[95]

The nineteenth century consensus had always been tentative and arguably fragile. The 1960s challenged it mightily. But finally that consensus, though stretched to the limit, did not fail. The Sloan prophecy did not pan out in the way he was convinced it would.

Whether one thinks that the additions of greater "flexibility and diversity" in the academy were accorded their due, or that little changed in the 1960s and that the status quo ante obtained, the academy, its curriculum, and its fundamental purpose did not come apart at the seams. Even though it looked in the 1960s and early 1970s that the time had arrived for the long-standing consensus in the academy to come apart, it didn't.

That does not mean there was no upheaval or that patchwork solutions, some temporary and others permanent, were forced into play to staunch social and cultural tensions. But the major challenges and fears of Sloan's day—attempts to overthrow structured liberal arts distribution requirements, sea-changes to the governance and structure of the university, clarion calls for relevance in and out of the classroom, and excising of all Western, white male subject matter—did not permanently come to pass.

Though Sloan could not see it, the consensus he identified for better or worse has been and continues to be maintained now, more than forty years later. Indeed that consensus has endured despite the most sustained assaults against it both before the 1960s, during the tumultuous decades of the 1960s and 70s, and certainly since. That in itself speaks volumes for endurance and breadth of a consensus about undergraduate education and the college curriculum in American higher education.

We are approaching the four hundredth anniversary of the college in America, celebrated when Harvard marks that milestone less than twenty years from now. There is every reason to argue that the more things change, the more they stay the same. The liberal educational foundation of higher education in the United States, surviving as it has the winds of history and buffeting of social and cultural controversies, will very likely continue to exist in much its historic fashion and reflective of its fundamental roots well into the future.

## NOTES

1. Thomas Miller, ed. *The Selected Writings of John Witherspoon* (Southern Illinois University, 1990), 2.
2. Ibid.
3. Jeffrey Morrison, *John Witherspoon and the Founding of the American Republic* (Notre Dame, IN: University of Notre Dame Press, 2005), 48.
4. Ibid.
5. Ibid.
6. Ibid.
7. Ibid., vii. Quote is from Alexis de Tocqueville, *Democracy in America*, but page number not cited.
8. Frederick Rudolph, *The American College and University: A History* (New York: Alfred A. Knopf, 1968), 208.
9. Ibid.
10. Ibid.
11. Ibid., 210–11.
12. Ibid., 211. Italics mine.
13. Sidney E. Mead, *The Old Religion in the Brave New World: Reflections on the Relation Between Christendom and the Republic* (Berkeley, Los Angeles, London: University of California Press, 1977), 30.
14. Harvard Faculty Rebukes Whitefield, Boston, 1774, unpaginated. http://declaringamerica.com/harvard-faculty-rebukes-whitefield-1744-exerpt/.
15. Mead, 30.
16. Douglas Sloan, "Harmony, Chaos, and Consensus: The American College Curriculum," *Teachers College Record* 73 (December 1971): 221–51.
17. Ibid., 243.
18. Ibid.
19. Ibid., 244, italics in the original Yale Report.
20. Ibid.
21. Richard Hofstadter and Wilson Smith, eds. *American Higher Education: A Documentary History*, Volume I (Chicago: University of Chicago Press, 1961), 287–88.
22. Ibid., 288.
23. Ibid.
24. Ibid.

25. Ibid., 369.
26. Ibid.
27. Ibid.
28. Ibid., 374.
29. Ibid.
30. Ibid.
31. Rudolph, 220.
32. Ibid., 233–34. Tappan quote is from his *University Education* (New York: G. P. Putnam, 1851), 66.
33. Ibid., 234, Tappan, 69.
34. James McCosh, *The New Departure in College Education: Being a Reply to President Eliot's Defence of it in New York, February 24, 1885* (New York: Charles Schribner's Sons, 1985), 10, fn. 1.
35. Ibid., 12.
36. Ibid., 17–18.
37. Richard Hofstadter and Wilson Smith, eds. *American Higher Education: A Documentary History*, Volume II (Chicago: University of Chicago Press, 1961), 699. Hofstadter and Smith characterize it this way in the introduction to their brief, less than 2 pp. excerpt of his 37 p. magnum opus.
38. Ibid.
39. Ibid.
40. Ibid., 700.
41. *Addresses at the Inauguration of Professor Noah Porter as president of Yale University*, Noah Porter Inaugural Address (New York: Charles Scribner and Company, 1871), 28.
42. Ibid.
43. Hofstadter and Smith, *American Higher Education: A Documentary History*, 899–900.
44. Ibid., 900.
45. Ibid.
46. Ibid., 901.
47. Ibid., 901–902.
48. Ibid., 902.
49. For a detailed account of Robert Hutchins' philosophy and his public debates with colleagues, see Stephen J. Nelson, "President Robert Hutchins's Designs on Education and the University: Imposing Provocateur or Mediocre Prophet?", unpublished paper delivered at the Eastern Educational Research Association Annual Conference, February, 2014.
50. Robert M. Hutchins, *Education for Freedom* (Baton Rouge: Louisiana State University Press, 1943), 25.
51. Ibid.
52. Ibid.
53. Ibid., 26.
54. Ibid., 35.
55. Ibid.
56. Ibid., 59.
57. Ibid., 58–59.
58. Ibid., 63.
59. Ibid.
60. Ibid., 64.
61. Ibid., 101–102.
62. Ibid., 104–105.
63. Henry Wriston, "A Critical Appraisal of Experiments in General Education," *The Thirty-Eighth Yearbook of the National Society for the Study of Education*, Part II, General Education in the American College, ed. by Guy Montrose Whipple (Bloomington, IL: Public School Publishing Co., 1939), 302.
64. Ibid., 312.

65. Ibid., 312–13.
66. Ibid., 315–16.
67. Ibid., 316–17.
68. Ibid., 320.
69. Ibid.
70. Ibid., 321.
71. Rudolph, *The American College and University: A History*, 455.
72. Ibid., 454.
73. Ibid., 469.
74. Ibid., 481.
75. Jacques Barzun, *The Culture We Deserve*. Arthur Krystal, Editor (Wesleyan University Press: Middletown, Conn., 1989), 111.
76. Ibid.
77. Ibid., 111–12.
78. Ibid., 112. This address, "On the Importance of the Liberal Arts: Address to the Association of American Universities, was published in the *Journal of Proceedings* of the association's conference in 1910, Wilson final year as Princeton's president.
79. Ibid.
80. Ibid.
81. Sloan, "Harmony, Chaos, and Consensus: The American College Curriculum," 221–51, 225.
82. Ibid.
83. Ibid.
84. Ibid.
85. Ibid.
86. Ibid.
87. Ibid., 226.
88. Ibid., 227.
89. Ibid.
90. Ibid., 229.
91. Ibid., 230–31.
92. Ibid., 232.
93. Ibid., 249.
94. Ibid., 250.
95. Ibid., 251.

# FIVE

## The Rise of the University

### *The Influence of Progressivism and the Social Gospel*

Gazing retrospectively at the last half of the nineteenth century, it would be simple to suggest that what historically unfolded must at the time have been the obvious future outcome. At this time in American history, a young nation, just over a half-century old, resorted to a Civil War to resolve though not fully solve long-standing issues of race, slavery, and the basis of its economic life and foundation. The decades after the war were marked by the expansion of the Industrial Revolution and the development of business and corporate commerce that set the path for the twentieth century in America.

But of course for historical events and times such simple interpretations are never quite the case. We later come to think that what was happening had to be obvious. But as we know the development of issues and events in any historical era is never that clear to the contemporary observers experiencing what is transpiring. How could they possibly know what we later find out to be the case with the progression and unfolding of crucial markers in society and culture?

Who could have imagined at the mid-nineteenth century, on the cusp and on the immediate backside of the Civil War, that the development of major universities and their identity as institutions of research would shape higher education in America as it did? The Morrill Land Grant Act sparked an enlarged sector of public colleges and universities. States that had invested in public higher education were able markedly to expand their campuses and their impact. Other states now got in the game with both research universities and public colleges. In the space of just a few decades at the end of the century formerly small-scale universities became in short order major research centers.

153

Meanwhile an array of private universities, beginning with Johns Hopkins and followed by the likes of Chicago and Stanford, found their way onto the stage of American higher education. These three grew like Topsy and by the early twentieth century had become large-scale research enterprises.

What happened in this half-century period was unprecedented before or since in the pace and scale of development that occurred in the academy in America. A confluence of events and movements not previously arrayed as distinctively and forcefully combined to alter the higher education landscape.

The Industrial Revolution was now full-blown. The commerce and income it generated, and the concentration of wealth in the hands of the barons of industry, were new realities in politics and society. The political assumptions of the Progressive Era, and the theological and religious foundations of the Social Gospel era reinforced the newfound influence of the industrial and financial sectors.

Many of the new wealthy were born out of these political and religious traditions. The era was a time when these enlightened social and cultural forces persuaded business and corporate leaders that their financial wherewithal should be dedicated to social ends that would improve the nation and the world. Specifically, many of these barons of industry were both self-inspired and driven by others to support colleges and universities. These commitments grew because the benefits of education and learning were increasingly, more so than in previous eras, to be universally recognized as critical and ultimate goods for society.

There had previously been massive financial interests and philanthropy dedicated to the founding and the sustaining of many colleges and universities. The wealth at the inception of Harvard, Yale, Princeton, and so many others was not wholly different than that which undergirded the foundations of Stanford and Chicago.

But now, in the late nineteenth and early twentieth centuries, there were increased public pressure and widely accepted presumptions that wealth ought to be funneled to the best interests of society. What better way to do that than through the nation's colleges and universities?

The overlap of the Progressive Era with the development of the college and university in America in the latter decades of the nineteenth and into the early decades of the twentieth century is unique in its timeliness. Rather than the clash of traditions, principles, and ideologies in evidence at other times, this era in the history of the American college and university was marked by a distinct confluence and merger of like-minded people, leaders, and generally agreed intentions about what would make the nation and society a better place for all.

Rudolph defines this version of Progressivism as a "spirit which in one important manifestation revealed itself as a kind of middle-class sense of obligation, a readiness to bring American society to some new sense of its problems and its promises."[1] The university idea and the Progressive spirit were mutually reinforcing. They shared commitments to notions of service, to the value of knowledge and the development of skill, and to beliefs that education was a clear gateway for the betterment of individuals and of the commons.

Shaping what the university should do, this impetus tapped long-standing beliefs the academy held about the importance of noblesse oblige. "Both movements," that of the university and advocates for its ideals, and of those caught up in the Progressive Era, "would in a sense argue," Rudolph declares:

> for stability in society, for an equality of opportunity now challenged by labor unionism and socialism from below and by vast concentrations of wealth and power from above; both would serve the idea of inevitable material and moral progress and see the future as a place that would not only be bigger but also better.[2]

Such grand aims at this historical moment were now realistically on the horizon of the America. The purging of Civil War was in the rearview mirror, though its memories and effects echoed for decades and longer. The nation was caught up the business of industrialization, of the development of more sophisticated commerce, and of a more highly evolved economy with all the wealth, fortune, and material advances it embraced and produced. The question and the quest was how to understand these riches: what had the social, moral, and political obligations to do in any way with this newfound wealth and abundance?

In Rudolph's analysis, the sweeping impact of the trends of the nineteenth century for the American academy and American society are highly compelling. He claims that the nation's colleges and universities suffered from a disengagement and abandonment of long-held roots and heritage in the earlier nineteenth century. Rudolph does not speculate about the reasons for why the academy diverged from previous historical foundations and roots at this point in its history. However, with his assertions on the table, thoughts about that "why" are unavoidable.

One interpretation is that this break in the long-standing intersection of religion and the academy was an inevitable result of the helter-skelter growth of denominational colleges and their subsequent sectarian competition in the opening decades of the nineteenth century. Another possible cause for the breakdown of earlier traditions was that the uprooting of heritage and mores in the academy and in society resulted from the religious push of the Second Great Awakening, a time that produced a forced choosing of sides over evangelism, theological interpretations, and denominational controls inside the gates of the academy.

There are other speculations about the causes for Rudolph's assumptions about what happened to the college and university in the nineteenth century. Maybe the glue that previously held society and the acad-

emy together had been eroded as a byproduct of Jacksonian anti-intellectualism and individualism—all boats on their own bottom and what's in
it for me thinking. Maybe it resulted from the battle lines drawn throughout American society in the rush to the conflict of the Civil War and the
ravages that ensued over slavery, and the arguments that it spawned
about race, economic realities, and differing pro and con religious arguments.

Although Rudolph does not specify reasons or causes, his interpretation about what happened during much of the nineteenth century features the assertion that the Progressive Era, in an ironic twist, marked a
return to a former time for the academy in America.

He contends that "Before Progressivism called them to their ancient
obligation to service, the American colleges were lacking the vitality, the
close connection with society that had characterized the relationship between Harvard and the Puritans or, indeed, the relationship between any
of the colonial colleges and the colonial society that sponsored them. In
the nineteenth-century college," by contrast, "service was an ideal that
fought for attention with the self-seeking which the American experience
encouraged." What had happened was that "The colleges implored their
young men to give themselves to God, but fewer and fewer of them did
so."[3]

What changed was that during this era the culture of the college came
to be, at least to Rudolph's mind, marked by students engaging in "self-
seeking," using education unabashedly to get ahead, and getting one's
share of the pie. The nation's colleges by default and design abandoned
traditional notions of noblesse oblige and of the value of education simply for the sake of education. The nineteenth century thus produced a
situation in which "The colleges, in the end, could not argue persuasively
or successfully against success which, unless chastened by some sense of
philanthropy or modified by some rare sense of proportion, was likely to
be quite the opposite of service."[4]

Rudolph has one angle on what happened. But he overreaches in
alleging that the original, fundamental colonial impulses about education
had fully collapsed. More than Rudolph admits, throughout the nineteenth century there continued to be forces that maintained traditional
notions of education as something for its own sake.

These impulses were at times under siege and buffeted by countervailing forces then as they have been on numerous occasions since. However, those traditional foundations never went into anything approaching full eclipse.

That historical bedrock foundation of education in America included
the practical applications of education that leaders such as President
Witherspoon at Princeton urged. Witherspoon viewed education as critical to the formation of citizen commitment and the development of leadership in a Republic and democracy. This reality, what Rudolph de-

scribes as "the vitality, the close connection with society," of the Colonial College did not disappear or lose its purity overnight as the eighteenth gave way to the nineteenth century.

Even after the waning of the early- and mid-nineteenth-century era of rapid expansion of denominational colleges and of the Second Great Awakening, the religious and spiritual connections in the academy and in a college and in a university education by no means vanished. Nonetheless, the nineteenth century was a time of tumult and change. Thus Rudolph has cover for the contrast he sets up: that the universities established at the end of the century reaffirmed long-standing and colonial-rooted traditions that had for a time waxed and waned as still critical to the foundation of the academy in America.

## THE TRAJECTORY TO THE UNIVERSITY OF CHICAGO

Three or four decades prior to the founding of the University of Chicago, few could have imagined that a university could and would look as Chicago did. But the university as it was emerging in America was clearly headed into a rendezvous with destiny, whether of Chicago's ilk or university prototypes similar in scope and aspiration.

Laurence Veysey unravels an intriguing polemic that looks both backward and forward regarding the ways in which the university in America has been viewed through the eyes of the society. He relies on the more than two hundred years of the academy in America up to the Civil War and uses the crucible of the final decades of the nineteenth century as a further footing to assess how the university emerged into the twentieth.

Examining the university at the middle of the twentieth century, Veysey claims some have "speculated that, in our present age of enormous emphasis on skill, the university may soon become as characteristic an institution in America as the church was three hundred years ago." If that is an over-the-top mid-1960s claim, Veysey hastens to turn back the clock. "On the other hand, even since the late nineteenth century the better university campuses have maintained the character of oases," Veysey notes, "sharply set off from the surrounding society in many of their fundamental qualities and frequently the objects of deep-seated suspicion."[5]

Of course, the church ever could be argued to suffer the same allegations; that is, more on the "not of the world" side of the spectrum. Furthermore, because of fears about what hardcore belief systems do to people, the church came to be perceived from the outside by some as cult-like, and as a threat to social and political stability.

However, Veysey's larger goal, albeit skirting close to the edge of the historian's customary trap of fashioning the past as prelude to the future, is "to show how the American university developed in such a way that it could inspire with equal accuracy, both these opposing definitions of its role"[6]: that is, an academy that develops the skills that society so badly wants and needs, while at the same time is set off from that same society and its claims. This is the "critic and servant" role of the university, a vital yet bifurcated role for the academy.

Beyond Veysey's "opposing definitions of [the university's] role" is the task to focus on the university's image and *raison d'être*. That is, how has the university viewed itself? How do others, both critics and supporters, view the university in terms of the image it proclaims? What are the key traits that have defined the university for those outside and have been debated—academics will clearly always debate almost anything, including who they are—among those inside its gates?

The university is and always has been understandably fenced in by both external and internal forces beyond its immediate control. However, deliberation about the broad dimensions of its image opens the door for the university to show itself as a responsible actor. That is, the university does not have to sit passively by and to be framed by others. It can and should have a hand in determining its own course and fate.

Tussles in the push-me-pull-you world of divergent opinions among critical observers and detractors as well as fans of the college and university are inevitable. But engaging that debate is crucial and is something in the hands of the university.

Veysey measures the evolution of the university in the early to mid-nineteenth century. "Increasingly as the nineteenth century advanced," Veysey asserts echoing Rudolph's conclusions, "the moral, religious, and political scruples which had operated as powerful deterrents to the adoption of recent European intellectual forms grew weaker among an educated minority of Americans."[7]

This erosion of religious and political values created a climate fertile for the emergence of the research university. What happened was: "This leadership [of the university], separating itself from orthodox evangelical piety and continuing to reject Jacksonian vulgarity, became receptive to European scientific and educational developments which might offer a counterweight to the cruder tendencies manifested in the surrounding society."[8]

In seesaw fashion, the research university sector of American higher education—the newest kid on the block—moved toward a zenith while the fortunes of the long-standing heritage of the small college shifted to a nadir at the other end of the spectrum. The emerging major research universities were already consuming a large supply of the oxygen in the higher education world and in the competition for the appetite and monies of the populace. Now it appeared that they would take up even more.

Thus, in the late nineteenth into the early twentieth century, "Even the best such [small college] institutions, since they lacked large endowments, had to scramble for public support on an annual, almost daily basis." Not surprisingly the burden to staunch this financial bleeding fell, as it always had and would continue to be so, on the leaders of these colleges. This reality altered the way college presidents asserted themselves and their institutions: "Presidential rhetoric took its tone from these pressures." [9]

The contrast between the small colleges and the big players of the major universities could not be more striking. In those settings, presidents as "the advocate[s] of liberal culture," found themselves "protected to a certain extent by the prestige of the institution." In a further irony, this meant that rather than merely holding ideas for consumption inside the gates of the campus where a public would not be much the wiser, small college presidents had little choice but to discuss college aims in a "far more promotional tone." [10]

In this environment, small colleges and their leaders were at a philosophical disadvantage in the eyes of Progressives and promoters of the Social Gospel. Fairly or not, these Progressives deemed the message from these liberal arts colleges about social service as a "watered-down version of liberal culture. The [small] colleges could serve society best by retaining their emphasis on the liberal arts, taught from a moral point of view." [11] Advocates for Progressivism and for the message of the Social Gospel desired a much bolder reach for the transformation of society by its academic institutions.

For the most part, smaller liberal arts colleges continued to claim a moral basis as key to their missions and to the way they would keep a hand in the marketplace of higher education throughout much of the twentieth century and into the twenty-first. They had little choice. Though a box of sorts, this identity was superior to the alternative: being accused of abandonment of fundamental beliefs and principles about the value of education. To forsake this philosophical foundation would be their undoing if constituents came to believe that the liberal arts were being forsaken in favor of the skill-building, careerist orientations of the major research universities.

However, meanwhile, the major universities were not standing still. They were were developing an ever-expanding platform. Their shear presence posed threats to the historical, small colleges.

But sometimes the rhetoric of the leaders of the research universities, especially when that rhetoric became dismissive and disparaging, lit a fire at the small liberal arts colleges. Such was the case with Charles Kendall Adams. Adams was a student of Andrew White and on the faculty at the University of Michigan when White departed there in 1866 to become the founding president of Cornell University. Twenty years later in 1885, Adams would succeed White as Cornell's second president.

While on the faculty at Michigan in 1875, Adams argued that the proliferation of small, in most cases denominational colleges, was not strengthening the hand of America's educational system and fortunes. This was an edgy era in American higher education. State universities, proliferating as a result of the Morrill Act of 1862, were making their mark and establishing a beachhead in the array of the colleges and universities of the land.

When in doubt, don't hesitate to put the competition out of business. Adams's platform was "that every consideration of true policy requires that the interest of the people should be concentrated upon a limited number of the larger and stronger colleges and universities." As though this were not a sufficient effort to bury the smaller colleges, he adds that "We believe that these [larger colleges and universities] should be raised into such conspicuous preeminence that the smaller and weaker ones will cease to be regarded as on the same level or to be entitled to rank in the same class."[12]

These small colleges were welcomed to struggle and to try to stay around, and for the most part they have over the nearly century and a half since Adams's screed. However, beginning then they have had to navigate their fortunes in the shadow of these the state colleges and universities.

Over time equilibrium set in and has held over that century plus. Public education continued to be a staunch competitive rival to the smaller, private colleges for everything from student enrollments to the money hunt from public and private sources. This contest was a new thing that the small liberal arts colleges had not previously witnessed. Their survival required that they adapt and adjust.

## WILLIAM RAINEY HARPER AND JOHN D. ROCKEFELLER: A PARTNERSHIP FOR THE AGES AT CHICAGO

Nothing grows out of whole cloth. Historical precursors and foundations are inevitably rooted in antecedent issues and provocations that create later movements and trends. The development of the university in the latter decades of the nineteenth century and the leaders who seized the helms of these institutions, however new and original they might be characterized and at first appear to be, found their way into education and into positions of leadership for reasons rooted in the past. Richard Storr declares that the bevies of university leaders emerging in the post-Civil War era were drawn to education for its purported transcendent value to society rather than to "business where great fortunes were to be made and where such administrative talents as theirs would have been rewarded handsomely."[13]

His reasoning is simple: these men (and nearly exclusively they were men with exception of some women's colleges founded in this era that had women presidents) viewed university-building "as a form of public service" that as "public-spirited" leaders they were destined to perform. Storr argues that this cadre of leaders was attracted to university presidencies because of the heritage laid down by "earlier university reformers" who had "preached the evangel of learning as a means of national salvation. . . ."[14]

In the latter days of the nineteenth century, there arose a striking historical confluence of leaders and their desires, vision, and imagination. The most visible philanthropists among these leaders also controlled the mother lode of money essential to get an institution up and running. This confluence of leaders was most pronounced in the founding of the University of Chicago. However, Stanford University and the Leland Stanford family with its monetary and proprietary interests would argue themselves to be in a close second if not first place.

However, California was not the Midwest in terms of the development of industry, business, and finance in that era. Chicago was fast becoming a commercial and cultural hub. Thus Chicago was in the driver's seat to hit the big time as fully and rapidly as it did for the world of higher education.

Nonetheless it is essential to maintain perspective about the sweep of the development of the research university in this era, especially the role that major moguls of commerce and industry played. Money, moneyed interests, and class, and social and economic status have been a longstanding leitmotif throughout the history of the college and university in America. Thus the founding of Chicago, or Stanford for that matter, was by no means the first time money and those who held it, and the fortunes of the university converged.

This picture of the late nineteenth and early twentieth century was an outgrowth of an enduring tradition. The only difference with former decades and eras was that now the overlap of corporate, financial interests in the academy was greater than in previous times.

With heavily moneyed interests pouring into the academy, the criticism grew that the rich are getting rich, the poor poorer, and the overall landscape of the academy becoming one where only the well to do and well off can get in the doors. The hegemony of the elite inevitably raises the Jacksonian barbs about the systematic exclusion of the common man or woman from the gates of the academy and the goods of society.

Many latter twentieth and early twenty-first-century commentators about the college and university similarly wring their hands about the problems of income disparities and social stratification in the students matriculating to higher education. The fear is that academic institutions in the race for financial preeminence and status seeking only serve to exacerbate these socio-economic problems.

But this is by no means a new thing. The twenty-first-century college and university world is, by design and default, increasingly populated with greater numbers of students produced by elite, mostly private, but including many wealthy community public schools. To an extent greater than many wish were the case, these students are the sons and daughters of upper-income families.

However, again it is clear that today what we witness is only the most recent evolution of long-standing issues in the academy over equity, access, and whose money is able to buy what.

The founding of the University of Chicago sent shockwaves in a number of directions through the higher education community and the nation.[15] Chicago signaled that investments from the wealthy can create a large-scale impact in a very short period of time. The role of philanthropists in higher education and the large blocks of money they were able to put on the table to launch a new university and to put it so rapidly on the map was just one of the issues that the founding of Chicago sparked.

In the evolution of the college and university in America, Chicago's founding was a most dramatic scheme. It was the first institution founded solely as a major research university with funding by mammoth injections of money from Rockefeller and his millionaire friends among Chicago movers and shakers. That level of financial investment enabled Chicago quickly to establish its stature in the style of the German research university.

The undertaking was massive. As Chicago opened, its rise in scope, size, and prominence was meteoric. What happened overnight was unprecedented. Chicago was not going to be the ordinary start-up of a new university, slowly finding its way and making its reputation.

For example, by 1916 the city of Chicago had given "eight million dollars' worth of land and buildings and Rockefeller thirty-five million dollars' worth of endowment" to a university founded and opened less than twenty-five years before, in 1892.[16] If translated to 2014 dollars, Rockefeller's investment alone would today exceed 750 million dollars.

William Rainey Harper was just thirty-two years old when he became enamored with the founding of the University of Chicago and became its first president. Rudolph does not delineate the degree to which Harper was courted by John D. Rockefeller, or whether he simply became aware of the early planning, which was becoming public, and wanted to link himself to the emerging University's fortunes. Whatever the case, these two powerful men with the largest of egos knew that they could do business together. Once that die was cast, they set about on a transformative, mutually self-interested mission that resulted in the University's establishment.

Beyond its enormous Rockefeller wealth, but also as an early way to use it, as the University got underway Harper shamelessly adopted a bold strategy. He publicly announced his intention to raid the faculty ranks of primarily East Coast schools. This campaign was a massive scheme to lure to Chicago high-class professors, scholars and researchers, and other senior faculty from supposedly collegial, but now to Harper's aggressive thinking, competitor colleges and universities.

Harper's raids on other schools no doubt inspired the ire and disdain of the higher education world. What happened was that:

> . . . he undertook the greatest mass raid on American colleges in history. When he was finished he had collected eight former college or seminary presidents, including Alice Freeman Palmer of Wellesley; he had relieved Yale of five professors; he had swooped down on Clark University, torn by dissension and flew off with a majority of the academic staff, including fellows, instructors, and fifteen professors.[17]

Because of these schemes and manipulations, as Chicago opened its doors it was instantly on the map as a massive-sized institution as measured by enrollment, by numbers of professors, and by financial wherewithal. It was on a trajectory quickly to become comparable to many universities of the day. Chicago's nascent profile and the Topsy of its development were extraordinary. "Harper did so well that with [managing] a budget for a faculty of eighty," Rudolph declares, "he hired for the first year a faculty of 120." When the university opened, his students "came from thirty-three states and fifteen foreign countries and provinces: 328 undergraduates, 210 graduates, and 204 divinity students."[18]

Nonetheless, even as it rose as a research university of force, Chicago's fundamental stature sat as much in the long-standing tradition of the college in America as it did as a new entity based on the German and European university model. The effect of the Progressive Era, and of its complementary and overlapping Social Gospel preachments on the foundation of Chicago—despite being a major research university, one that didn't lose sight of the liberal arts and liberal education—cannot be lost. Lyman Abbott, a high-profile, outspoken Social Gospel preacher of the day, offers a critical perspective about the effect of these influences on the University of Chicago.

Abbott's voice is discerning about what the American university became as a result of the advent of Chicago. His thoughts, expressed in an editorial about Harper after his death in office as president, at the young age of forty-six and just fourteen years into his tenure and the history of Chicago, are as much exhortation as epitaph. Abbott's preaching about the too-brief legacy of Harper's reign and about these early years of the University of Chicago's launch, capture the sway of Social Gospel thinking and theology, and of Progressive Era political, economic, and social inquiry laid down in the latter decades of the nineteenth and the early ones of the twentieth centuries.

Contrasting the university in America with that in England where the college and university "revolved around culture, the production of gentlemen aristocrats," and with the German university grounded "in scholarship, in erudition, in the production of scholars," Abbott contends that the American university symbolized by Chicago "was a place where the emphasis was placed neither on culture nor scholarship, but on service, on the preparation of young Americans for active lives of service."[19]

However, this slant scratches only the surface of what Harper was as an icon of the college presidency, of his contribution to American higher education, and of what Chicago had already become. As any observer, Abbott had a lens through which to interpret the life of American society and the role of the academy. But this lens was not Abbott's alone. It was one shared by the large cadre of fellow Social Gospel believers and an array of protagonists for the values and principles of the Progressive Era.

Abbott's beliefs led him to view service as one of the distinctive characteristics embedded in the research university education at Chicago. This value in Chicago's mission distinguished it from its European counterparts.

On one hand this reading branded a Chicago education as a sacred quest. Some forty years later as Harper's successor, President Hutchins contended that the academy had a critical role to lead a spiritual revolution for the nation. Abbott's take that Chicago's foundational principles pivoted on a religious dimension of the education it would offer no doubt inspired Hutchins's pleas.

However, on the other hand, Chicago could be equally viewed as a typical research university. But even the picture of the university, the academy as pragmatic and practical is still reflective of qualities historically in the mainline, in the mainstream character of the world of America and of its colleges and universities.

Abbott drills further into Harper's legacy and the springboard provided for Chicago's sway about what an education could be. Probing its influence further, he speculates about the broader implications that Chicago spawned for the university in America at the dawning of the twentieth century.

Abbott contends that differences between Chicago and existing colleges and universities are ones "not of essence but of emphasis." In this rendering, the colleges and universities of America are not as monochromatic as conventional stereotypes often claim.

Although appearing to contradict his preceding distinctions about the English and German universities, Abbott fleshes out the picture of the American higher education that Chicago had entered. Abbott is understandably caught up in the beliefs and ideology of his Social Gospel theology and its complementary Progressive Era political pulls. These assumptions undergird his views.

That is, in addition to producing gentlemen, which is often thought of as the college's primary goal, the "older college[s] of the English type [also] produce scholars." Meanwhile "The newer college of the German type," primarily thought exclusively to produce scholars, "also produces gentlemen." Lyman, cheerleading Harper's contributions, underscores that, "doubtless the Chicago University has produced both scholars and gentlemen."[20]

However, what distinguished Chicago for supporters such as Abbott was that "we may define that of the new type [of university] that President Harper has given to the world by the word service."[21] This interpretation claims that the scholarship that both the traditional college and the newer research universities incorporated as part of their missions was in the former case "as a means and measure of self-development," and in the latter "as an end in itself. . . ." By contrast, Chicago, trying to incorporate these features of scholarship and "self-development" so often held in tension and competition, "has regarded," scholarship "as an equipment for service."[22]

Chicago had its unique definition of mission and purpose, as is the case for any college or university. The way the mission of the University was created and its early footprint distinguished Chicago from numerous counterparts of its day. However, it is a stretch to portray Chicago as having invented service, albeit even as a byproduct of its heavy emphasis on scholarship and research.

We have previously noted the manner in which service—tending to the public good and to the commonweal, supporting the nation, and addressing the needs of individuals and society—has a long-standing history at the foundation and as fundamental values of the academy in America.

In this tradition, President Witherspoon, exercising leadership at Princeton in the 1760s through the 1790s, would not permit a latter day player like Harper and Chicago to contend that they had invented service as part of the basis of a college education. Witherspoon was an architect of the heritage that Harper and his colleagues, including Rockefeller, would inherit a century and a half later.

Nonetheless Harper's legacy is huge. The degree to which he blended service with a sense for the spiritual as integral to education is at the foundation of his leadership and of the fundamental values of Chicago.

Testifying to Harper's footprint, Abbott contends that as a memorial, "some appreciating friend will build for him the one monument he would desire above all others by putting in the center of the university campus a college cathedral which was his ambition to erect there, to symbolize and to nourish that spiritual life which he sought to make the inspiration and glory of the University, as equipment for service was its dominating purpose."[23]

What transpired in this era with Chicago as a focal point echoes a long history of religious purposes in the college and university in America. From Chicago back to days earlier than Witherspoon at Princeton, and at hundreds of colleges and universities, religious or spiritual impulses were cloaked in education's role to be of service to society, to the public good, and to the commonweal.

The founders and advocates of the University of Chicago embodied in the institution grand aspirations for what an education at the university level could do for students. Those most devoted to the Social Gospel believed that such an education had religious ends. They reached for a return to the religious connection in universities and colleges of a bygone era. Rudolph contends that in various forms this earlier heritage was established at Chicago and elsewhere, beginning in the early twentieth century and continuing for much if not all of it.[24]

That claim is not the conventional take of what was going on in the development of the university in America in the twentieth century. It is a contention subject to debate.

There is evidence supporting Rudolph's argument, i.e., the continuing presence of religiously affiliated colleges and universities in more than name through much of the twentieth century and the enduring religious affections of American society. However, there is other evidence—the materialism of the 1920s, the rapid expansion of the university following World War II in which governmental injections of support called a tune of practical education and outcomes—leading to a generally accepted claim that the academy in America in the twentieth century regularly bowed to the domination of secular forces.

However, the religious roots at the foundation of Chicago are of greater consequence than are readily observed on the surface. Conrad Cheery goes so far as to claim that Chicago was "An educational Zion continuously enlivened by the Protestant religion."[25]

Cheery corroborates Abbott's and Rudolph's contentions about the religious and spiritual aspirations fundamentally embedded in the mission and purpose of Chicago. This ambitious educational institution was a beachhead in the development of the American research university in the latter nineteenth century. What is less underscored about its famous profile is that Chicago possessed throwback traits, ones in a long-standing tradition of the Republic, and that these aspects of its foundation are ones not normally associated as undergirding the University.

The concept of Chicago as "An educational Zion continuously enlivened by the Protestant religion" is a considerable claim. How does Cheery make it stand up?

The partnership of Harper as founding president of Chicago with financial mogul John D. Rockefeller was the key to its meteoric rise as a premier research university. It is impossible to separate these two men from how Chicago was shaped, from its originating impulse, and from its emergence on the American higher education landscape. Who were these leaders joined in the launch of this university?

Harper and Rockefeller were devout Baptists "whose shared conviction about the need to Christianize the nation through educational institutions locked them together in common cause."[26] Harper was a complex figure, "a young man in a hurry, a person of immense energy often overcome by fatigue and depression who was able to spring back into action, an architectonic thinker capable of assembling a vast array of ideas and schemes (to the puzzlement of his contemporaries, some of whom referred to his university as 'Harper's Three-Ring Circus'), a popular teacher turned busy administrator. . . . These personal traits were matched by a comprehensive religious vision."[27]

In Cherry's estimation, "Harper's vision was openly evangelical, even messianic." To Harper's way of thinking, "The task of the American university, of the University of Chicago especially, was to fashion the American nation, and eventually the world, in the light of a religious understanding of democracy."[28]

That meant for Harper a grand vision, in this depiction one that unified the fortunes and expectations of America with those of the academy in messianic terms: "Democracy has been given a mission to the world, and it is of no uncertain character." This meant that "the university is to be 'the prophet of this democracy and, as well, its priest and its philosopher; . . . in other words, the university is the Messiah of the democracy, its to-be-expected deliverer.'"[29]

To Cherry, the scope of Harper's religion of the Republic is clear. Harper asserts, "Is democracy a religion? No. Has democracy a religion? Yes; a religion with its god, its alter, and its temple, with its code of ethics and its creed." Considering Harper's theology, Cherry interprets its social, ethical, and cultural implications: "The god of the religion is the whole of humanity; its altar is the home; its temple is the nation; its creed is human equality; and its system of ethics is the righteous defense of individualism."[30]

On one hand, Harper could be assailed for using a lens that fashioned a hugely parochial vision. But, in his day and even today, that vision of a westward march of history and the idea that American democracy and democratic creed constituted a religion of the Republic, in Cherry's notion a "civil religion of democracy," was and still is a commonly accepted theme and belief.[31]

At the same time, Harper did not allow these views to place him in a cul-de-sac. He was always tuned to the wider world outside the gates of the academy. The university, Chicago, and everywhere else, had a duty to press the expansion of knowledge and the frontiers of ideas. Even in terms of the relationship of his Divinity School to the institution of the University and the education it offered, the connection of the Divinity School was essential to Chicago's foundation. That relationship in no sense was to become parochial or polarizing.

This is Harper as a devotee of Cardinal Henry Newman.[32] Building on Newman's vision, Harper promoted the rationale for divinity and theological studies both to fit and to play a critical role in the scope and reach of curriculum and learning in a university. A curriculum that was engaged in divinity and religion "would offer breadth of social vision," in

Harper's words "'secured by mingling with men who have other points of view' in the university and thus would satisfactorily launch students into pluralistic modern America."[33]

Lest we overplay Harper's footprint, high profile and visionary leader that he was, Cheery believes he is in the mainstream of his times. In Harper we find a conventional convergence of beliefs and ideologies present in the Social Gospel and Progressive Era. Harper certainly asserted this ideology at a propitious moment and with all the heft of Chicago and of Rockefeller's considerable wealth in the mix to create a decisive moment for higher education in America. But Harper was not outside the conventional views of the day.

For Cherry this means that, while Harper was symbolic of the tenor and tempo of his times, he "is best understood neither as an originator nor as imitator, but, rather, as eponym. In his commanding messianic vision and his ambitious educational scheme, Harper was a figurative embodiment of an era when modernist, ecumenical Protestantism sought to determine the values of the whole of American culture through education."[34]

Harper's and Chicago's emergence on the higher education scene were a high tide, a renaissance of a long-standing American tradition of religion and spirituality in the academy. "Others preceded Harper in the ideas and plans of his educational mission," Cherry points out, "but none quite brought together in such a singular and energetic way the dreams and designs of *an educational Zion continuously enlivened by the Protestant religion.*"[35]

This is a vision evangelical to the core. The territory it imagines created the University of Chicago as a truly transformative place in style and substance. In the tradition of Perry Miller's "errand in the wilderness," to be a university that in Cherry's depiction is an "educational Zion continuously enlivened by the Protestant religion" is no small undertaking. But that is what Chicago was, and though adapting to circumstances over time, these religious and spiritual themes remain embedded at its core.

## THE INTRIGUING LEGACY OF THE UNIVERSITY EMPIRE: THE TWENTIETH CENTURY UNFOLDS

The advent of the University of Chicago was a watershed in the development of the college and university in America. The post-founding of Chicago chapter in the history of the academy in America has featured both integrated and centripetal developments during the more than a century since. Controversies and disagreements about the nature of the academy in America remain, as they always have been, embedded in the story.

Frederick Rudolph focuses on the polemics of what was at stake in the fortunes between the new research university and the long-standing liberal arts tradition embodied in the smaller liberal arts colleges. Less an "either-or" and more a "both and," Rudolph characterizes the shift in how the academy viewed itself and how others observed it as a change from "belief and opinion" in favor of "argument over evidence."[36]

Rudolph believes that "This distinction between belief and fact, between persuasion and argumentation, was essentially the distinction between the old college and the new university. It was the distinction between a certain morality, a world of settled conviction, a regard for the whole man, between these and a moral neutrality, a world of unsettled and tentative conviction, a regard for man as mind."[37]

Thus as the twentieth century unfolded, liberal arts colleges were no longer able naively to cling to simple notions of "a certain morality, a world of settled conviction." Some willingly and others less so, liberal arts colleges had no choice but to confront the complexities of the new century. Their fiber had to be stretched to accommodate not simply the knowledge explosion led by the research university, but the even greater pressures from an increasingly pluralistic and multicultural set of views in American society and in the world.

The battles however were not just those over morality versus a less settled set of convictions about knowledge and ethics that were the product of scholarly inquiry and the frontier of learning established in the research university. The conflicts for the liberal arts colleges, shared by the universities, were a throwback to the lines drawn over democratic vs. aristocratic ideals in the nineteenth century and even earlier. Rudolph contends these divisions were not clear black-and-white or either-or.

That is, ". . . what would be attempted," in terms of curriculum and rethinking of the principles of the academy, "in the 1920s was a clear return to aristocratic ideals—not for their exclusiveness, but for their suitability as standards of being for men and women in a modern democratic society." What remained at stake had long-existed: the idealistic hope to square the competing values of the old-time college with those of the German research university. Despite the differences in educational culture, "What would be attempted was a reconciliation between the aristocratic and democratic, between the English and the Germanic [view of the college], between the humanistic and the scientific."[38]

The conversation that Rudolph contends was initiated in the 1920s was an understandable response to the impact of the research university on the academy in America. The joining of that debate and argument has obtained for the better part of the century since. This discourse aspiring to discern coexistence in the tension between "the humanistic and the scientific" featured leaders in the world of educational philosophy such as Alexander Meilklejohn, Robert Hutchins, and John Dewey in the

1920s, to Jacques Barzun, David Truman, Daniel Bell, and James Bryan Conant later in the century.

These deliberations about the nature of the academy pivot on continuing notions about the role of education in the development of the character of the student. This throwback idea was not lost even among advocates for the research university such as Daniel Coit Gilman. For example, he famously invoked in his inaugural address at Johns Hopkins, that beachhead of the German university in the United States, that its object was "to develop character—to make men. It misses its aim if it produces learned pedants, or simple artisans, or cunning sophists or pretentious practitioners."[39]

Critics of what was happening to the liberal arts college and to liberal education viewed the research university and its advocates as boogeymen. However, leaders of the university, Gilman among them, were by no means the bad guys. In fact, the thread of what the colleges and vastly smaller universities had contributed to American education over more than two centuries was at least respected if not revered by founders and advocates of the research university.

The dust had barely settled on the founding of Chicago and the opening decade of places like Stanford, when leaders willing to assume responsibility to uphold the long-standing traditions of the college and the liberal arts began to have their say. Gilman again, though sitting astride the research university, was one who "got it" about the liberal arts and the mostly small colleges that remained committed to the propagation of liberal, progressive education.

Toward the close of his lengthy tenure as founding president at Johns Hopkins, Gilman was invited back to his previous home base at the University of California at Berkeley for the October 25, 1899, inauguration of Benjamin Wheeler as its president. Gilman concludes his address with a stand about the university and its place in the world and for civilization itself.

Gilman could have used this public occasion to argue the crucial role of the research university in exploring and expanding the frontiers of knowledge. He could have contended that the major universities of the day, of the ilk of his Johns Hopkins, Berkeley, and many others, were on the road of burying the small liberal arts colleges and the long-standing tradition of liberal education. But he did not go down that path. Rather he argued a classic defense of the liberal tradition and how it had been undergirded by the Progressive and Social Gospel eras.

Gilman exhortation was as profound as it was simple, "Let us study the progress of human civilization, remembering that by ideas the world is governed." The import of ideas is that:

> They are stronger than kings in council, or representatives in Congress; more enduring than Bills of Rights, or written constitutions, or govern-

ments, or treaties, or creeds: they bind together men of different
speech, of different races, of different parties; they give unity to human
purpose; they promote human progress: and . . . *universities are the*
*exponents of these civilizing ideas.*[40]

Gilman was a bridge builder. He was an educator who was able to connect thinking about the new research university, the home base of his
entire career, to the fortunes of the traditional liberal arts and liberal arts
colleges. Because of his role and his philosophy about higher education,
Gilman should be viewed as a saint by the world of liberal arts colleges.
However, the reach of thinking about all of higher education, its college
and university face, by leaders like Gilman and Harper, is that American
higher education always had its share of controversies and curmudgeons.

Much of the angst over the rise of the research university was long-
standing in the academy. The criticism and associated fears sharpened in
the latter nineteenth century because of anxieties sparked by assumptions
about the heightened involvement of barons of industry, commerce, and
the corporate world, men such as Rockefeller and Stanford.

However, proportionality and perspective are important. This era was
by no means the first time in the history of the nation's colleges and
universities that the rich and their wealth worked their way into prominence and came to be perceived as a threat in the foundation of the
academy in the eyes of fearful critics.

These jeremiads about corporate influence, control, and resulting bas-
tardization of the academy are at least as old as the beginning of the
twentieth century. In this arena, one of the most vociferous critics was
Thorstein Veblen.[41]

Even critics such a Veblen had to recognize that at a practical level, the
barons of industry and finance did not push their interests into the academy for no reason: they saw clear benefit of getting students educated
who would then quickly embrace and dedicate themselves to the business world. Nor did interested business leaders lack for willing partners
for their agenda inside the gates of the university.

The table was further set by the new generation of university leaders,
its presidents, symbolized by the Rockefeller-Harper alliance. Such a
partnership underscored how attractive as presidential timber these new
prospective leaders of colleges and universities were. The corporate, industrial and business world counterparts to this new breed of president
applauded a leadership style that they believed was essential to be
brought inside the gates of the academy.

Laurence Veysey connects these dots. He argues that the changing
characteristics of the university in America in the latter nineteenth century, especially the 1890s and the early decades of the twentieth century,
dictated changes in the tenor of presidential leadership. He suggests that
changes in the university's structure, its embrace of more universalistic

(rather than unique institutional) ideals, combined with an evolutionary expansion of academic bureaucracy, created increasingly larger academic institutions in which powerful, sometimes autocratic presidents became the rule.[42]

Thus it is not a surprise that we get the marriage (and still have today) of corporate leaders and a new breed of college presidents. These nineteenth and early twentieth-century barons of industry and commerce, so influential in the founding and the running of universities, developed a mutual attraction and fondness for university presidents who in Veysey's description were predictably "autocratic," and thus highly fit in leadership style and tone for what was believed required to push forward the fortunes of colleges and universities.

These influential founders, trustees, and supporters from the business world desired in their university presidents, large public figures who would cut sweeping leadership swaths. These men (almost exclusively) would establish their wills over their institutions. It mattered little if these leaders acted in uncompromising ways. No one worried or feared the fallout from an aggressive breed of presidential leaders. If they appeared detached and placed their campuses on trajectories that ignored the concerns and interests of entrenched constituents, and in the process diminished the role of faculty, so be it.

But there were countervailing critics of these developments. These detractors believed that the academy was subject to a hostile takeover by ill-informed, ill-equipped, and maliciously inspired barons of industry.

Veblen had great grist for his mill. His famous (or infamous depending on your persuasion) *The Higher Learning in America* is dedicated to castigating the era of the Gilded Age. He believed there were archenemies that had risen to the top of the heap with their undue social, political, and cultural interests and control. These nefarious forces had to be kicked out of the academy if it were ever to return to its fundamental roots and ideals.

Veysey characterizes Veblen as enraged by "the finger of business control in practically every aspect of the modern university: in the tendency to spend money on conspicuous buildings; in the growth of bureaucracy; in the prominence of fraternities and athletics; in what he (as an advocate of research) believed was the subordination of the graduate school to the undergraduate college; in the vocational courses; in the whole competitive search for prestige."[43]

The fallout from this development, Veysey's contends, is that the university and its presidents came to be more "tolerant," less "absolutistic." In this new version the university embraced an aura of "confidence" and an "air of respectability" different than in foregoing eras. Conveying this stature, the university's leaders "therefore embellished it [the university] with the attributes of dignity, both architectural and ceremonial."[44] This new "confidence" was different because it "clearly shifted," the meaning of the university "from the connotation of a stalwart defense of pious absolutes which it had possessed several decades earlier." [45]

The judgment was that the behavior and influence of these business moguls was corrosive and was growing more gravely with each passing day. Veblen's allegations and tropes about the university drew a faithful band around him like metal shavings to a magnet. These followers bought into Veblen's staunch belief that the influence of corporate, business executive, and financial barons was now shot through the landscape of the academy in America.

Such belief led the likes of John Jay Chapman at Harvard to declare "The men who stand for education and scholarship have the ideals of businessmen. They are, in truth, businessmen. The men who control Harvard to-day are very little else than businessmen, running a large department store which dispenses education to the millions. Their endeavor is to make it the largest establishment of the kind in America." [46]

Today's jeremiads about the encroachment of corporate and business moguls into the affairs of the academy approach at times the invective, but do not eclipse the vehemence of the likes of Chapman and Veblen. But whatever one chooses to think, concerns about the extent and sway of corporate entanglement in the academy are not new critiques without precedent, raised only in the few decades of the later twentieth and early twenty-first century.

The accusations of detractors like Chapman and Veblen had for a long time prior rained down on the college and university and its leaders, and has continued to do so for many decades after. Critics today sweepingly argue about the creeping effect of big money from big-moneyed people on the university. The problem is that the "sky is falling" complaint of these cynics ignores a crucial reality.

Corporate and business world influence in the academy did not arise out of nowhere as a brand new thing in the latter twentieth and early twenty-first centuries. Business and financial sector pressure has for better and worse been in the foundations of the college and university from their beginnings in America.

This historical context is crucial. Many faultfinders of today's academy fear a perceived contemporary threat from its entanglements with moneyed interests. The presumed new threat today results from the convergence of major business and corporate players with the running of universities and the selection of presidents, coupled with great angst over an alleged too-cozy relationship among these leaders in- and outside the gates.

These critics believe the incestuous relationship between money and the ideals of the academy can only lead to greater depravity and degeneration of its foundations. In fact, they believe the shape and direction of our colleges and universities have already changed as a result, and worse things are no doubt to come.

What we know, at least as far back as the Gilded, Progressive Era days, and arguably long before, is that there has long- existed an overlap of corporate and business sector sway in the operation and leadership of colleges and universities. This is not a newfangled thing arising for the first time in the contemporary era.

One may choose to fear this entanglement of business influence in the academy. Good people and wise observers of the college and university will debate whether this is a good or bad thing, often ending up agreeing to disagree. But by no means did this interlocking relationship start happening yesterday, or even only during the post-World War II decades.

Veysey pushes the theme of the dramatic shift in the structure of the American university in the latter nineteenth and early twentieth century. However, the question begged is whether these changes were inevitable. That is, would they have come about at some point or another regardless of any leader or any institution's aspirations or desire to embrace or reject them?

There is a seeming inevitability of the major forces of the latter nineteenth century. Industrialization, and the rise of a business and corporate structure fueling the America economy and industry sector were going to happen at some point. In one form or another we likely would have witnessed the social and political values of the Progressive Era, not to mention the beliefs of the Social Gospel era.

Those forces developed in this time period of American history. However, even if they had not occurred as they did, other features — increasing population, continuing issues spawned by socio-economic equities and inequities, the greater complexities in society and in the university, to name just a few — would have altered the landscape of the academy in America.

America is a nation shot through from its inception, and certainly in the westward expansion of the nineteenth century, by unbridled growth of space and population, development of economic wherewithal that is larger in every aspect. Certainly colleges and universities were destined to grow as they did throughout their histories. The potential was always there for this development to occur at ever-precipitous rates.

That is what happened as the centuries unfolded. The developments of the latter nineteenth to the twentieth century had a pronounced effect on the shape of the university. Those developments continued as the university and the nation moved through the post-World War II era and into the 1960s.

In those decades even greater growth and expansion were experienced, in population, industries, businesses, and an overall booming economy, than had been the case a half-century or more previously. But through it all and in the face of those changes, traditions and traditional views of the academy were never eclipsed or erased by the new world of the research university.

## THE IDEA OF THE COLLEGE ENDURES

Notwithstanding the evolution of the university and the changes in higher education it brought about in the latter nineteenth and early twentieth century, the concept of the college endured. These bastions of the heritage of the liberal arts, of liberal education, and of the idea of the college as known in America for well over two centuries were undeterred by the rise of the research university.

Navigating the presence of the research university, these colleges, formerly strongholds and defenders of the undergraduate experience and the liberal arts, were pressured to maintain traditional claims about what education should be. This challenge was even greater for the undergraduate colleges which were part of major research universities, and which were being continually challenged to become even larger centers of graduate research.

Between undergraduate colleges and research universities there existed tension, competition for mission and purpose, and confusion in the eyes of the public and even of those inside the gates. The strains for perceived status and position with the public was inevitable.

For both the college and the research university there was a timeless question that had to be answered: What is the value of education, particularly a higher education, in Robert Hutchins's parlance, the higher learning, in the first place? Why put students through the paces of an undergraduate educational experience and of navigating a coherent and uniform liberal arts curriculum that is dedicated to liberal education? The answer came from many quarters, of which two are paramount.

Numerous social, political, and cultural pressures have forever existed on education, especially on the academy, in America. Americans have sweeping expectations about the learning and knowledge that college and university undergraduates and graduate students will possess. Education should be designed, regardless the ideals underlying it, to produce practical, pragmatic, and popular outcomes for society and the nation.

However, albeit that education should have its "practical, direct contribution to society" face, undergirding that need is an equally longstanding American tradition in higher education: liberally educating students and forming their character for citizenship, for the exercise of professions, and for the conduct of their lives. Going back to the Colonial Colleges there was always the desire that education, the higher learning, would have at its core a critical task: the formation of the character in the college student.

We have heard Daniel Coit Gilman proclaim, in his inaugural at the inception of the German research university come to America in the form of Johns Hopkins, that the most critical purpose of the university is "to develop character—to make men."[47]

Gilman's argument is simple. Regardless the posture—the aspirations of moguls of business and industry or of the most enlightened social movers and shakers—of those calling the shots among their trustees and big-time donors, universities and colleges worth their salt are expected to assume responsibility to develop students of character. This means that the university must have front and center, in the education offered and in fulfilling its educational responsibility, a liberal education that its students then carry into society and into their contributions to the commonweal.

Gilman's view was picked up in the debates about the foundation and trajectory of the college and university in the early twentieth century by no less a light than Woodrow Wilson in comments at the beginning of his tenure as president of Princeton.

In contrast to the Veblen and his army brand of cynicism and fear mongering about the state of the academy, Wilson is a hardcore believer in the heritage of service, noblesse oblige, and commitment to the commonweal that the college and university in America was expected to produce. Flying in the face of fears that big money automatically corrupts the academy, Wilson argues for a positive role grounded in historic foundations for the university and the education it offers in the Progressive Era, regardless the influence of business and industry leaders in the academy.

Wilson's university had to straddle two worlds: that of Progressive Era values coupled with business influence, forthrightly expressed as the "relation of university education to commerce." "The most pleasant thing to me about university life," Wilson claims, "is that men are licked into something like the same shape in respect of the principles with which they go out into the world; the ideals of conduct, the ideal of truthful comradeship, the ideals of loyalty, the ideals of co-operation, the sense of *espirit de corps*, the feeling that they are men of a common country and put into it for a common service."[48]

In this understanding of the university, however it is elevated to a position of influence and whoever thinks they are influencing it, has to remain focused on the prize: its responsibility to prepare students for service to the commonweal and the common purpose of society. However, critics today can readily allege that Wilson's concept of the university is a relic of a throwback era. It is not what we experience today. Does the university any longer lay claim to the spiritual basis that underlay Wilson's *"espirit de corps"* in the academy?

Columbia University has historically been a bastion of the articulation of the value of a liberal education and the liberal arts. However, advocacy for these values in the academy has—no surprise here, as academics can argue about almost anything—not been without internal debates and pushes and pulls.

These controversies have included recurring deliberation about the purposes of education, and about the place of the humanities versus the scientific and the skill-building intentions of a college curriculum. But in debating these competing goals of education, Columbia is exemplary. As an institution of higher learning, Columbia reveals how even large, research-oriented universities have as much skin in the game of the traditions of liberal education as do the legion of small colleges, whose exclusive missions center on those principles and values.

One of the lead advocates within the Columbia orbit for traditional approaches to the college curriculum was John Howard Van Amringe, who was the dean of Columbia College (1896–1910). He overlapped with the opening decade of Nicholas Murray Butler's prodigious reign as president of Columbia University (1901–1945). Van Amringe strenuously battled Butler. Opposing the president, the dean sided with a long line of advocates for the traditional view of liberal education and the importance of the liberal arts.

One issue at stake in the debate about the "college" (including the college within the major university) versus the "university" was the degree to which the liberal arts would remain at the core of the curriculum. Here is where the rubber meets the road as faculty, deans, presidents, trustees and other key university and college constituents argue understandings about the purpose of the education that their individual institutions will offer.

These debates at Columbia and replicated elsewhere centered on pressure for professional and pre-vocational training, heavily enforced by graduate education at the university on one side, versus the liberal arts, humanities, and other instrumental courses on the other. However, when academics and others discuss the purposes of the academy and of a college education, it is always more than that. What naturally arises is a set of polemics, arguments existing much from the very beginnings of the academy in America.

Part of that "more" is revealed in what Van Amringe tackled in his battle with Butler. In stark contrast with his president, and echoing Gilman, Wilson, Meiklejohn, and others, Van Amringe's view was clear and absolute: the college ideal and "the purpose of the College . . . was not to make professional men and specialists but to 'make men.'"[49] For Van Amringe and the army of liberal arts and liberal education advocates on his side, the way men and women were made and character developed could only be accomplished by a liberal education and the way it inspired and undergirded the collegiate experience.

For a time in the latter nineteenth and early twentieth centuries, the fortunes of the goal to "make men," to "make women," to develop character and to teach and pass on traditions about morality and the ethical life appeared trapped in a zero-sum game. That is, when the liberal arts were pitted against an education that would turn out professionals, barons of industry, and the social need for trained practitioners in law, medicine, engineering, and other of the professions, only one side, likely the latter, would win out.

An army of today's critics believes that in the contemporary environment, large research universities are the clear winner in this contest of making professionals versus the making of men and women. These faultfinders are certain that the ambitions for practical outcomes, for a vocational curriculum and feeder majors and courses of study have indeed prevailed. The result of this wrangling has produced clear winners and losers. The major loser is the full-blown erosion of the foundation of the academy.

These detractors of what is going on in the academy suggest that few colleges and universities, including hard-core liberal arts colleges, any longer hold to the goal of making men and women, of building character, of confronting the moral and ethical issues of individuals and society. Even the strongest proponents of these ideals fear them to be in eclipse.

Despite public rhetoric, marketing strategies, and statements from educational leaders that attempt to convey a contrary view, in the minds of its worst critics the reality for liberal arts colleges is clear: They have capitulated to the social and public pressures to turn out students for careers and for high earning levels, not thinkers grounded in the ideas spawned by a liberal education and future citizens committed to the commonweal.

Over the last three to four decades, one turn or the other in the road of the development of the academy in America has led to prophesies of the demise of the liberal education at both the research and other major universities and at the liberal college presumed dedicated to that purpose. But these prophets nearly always turn out to be off the mark. The story is much more complex than these oversimplified assumptions about what has and will happen.

A frequently glossed-over belief is that the heritage of the academy as an institution of society that can and should develop character in the students who come through its gates has never disappeared from view. This foundation of the college and university persists into the contemporary era.

The historical *raison d'être* of the college qua the college, of the traditional undergraduate experience, and of transcendent values embedded in a liberal education remains well entrenched in the world of higher education in America. All this more than a half century and beyond from the era when Gilman, Wilson, Van Amringe and Meiklejohn, and even the irascible Robert Hutchins, were bedfellows in perpetuating this hope and vision.

In the mid-twentieth century, John Sloan Dickey as president of Dartmouth College (1945–1970) was a major voice for this traditional role of the academy. Dickey argued that the purpose of a college education was to prepare students with both "conscience and competence."[50]

These core features of an undergraduate education were mutually reinforcing. Dickey's argument is as simple as it is profound, one rooted in traditions begun in the Colonial Colleges. The college is duty-bound to prepare students as moral and ethical actors in society. At the same time, the college prepared students with knowledge, if not practical skills and the capacity to develop them, as they departed the gates of the academy into lives in the world. Advocates on either side of the false choice of conscience versus competence had to understand that both were at the foundation of the academy and of an undergraduate experience.

The research university in its American guise is unique on the world stage. When it came into being in its present form in the mid through the latter decades of the nineteenth century it sparked battles over the core purpose of the college and of the university. Those battles have persisted to the present day. However, these fights have also had a salutary effect because the debates have fostered essential discussion about the academy and its purposes in America.

None of this should be surprising. Those who wring hands about how these battles have played out in the past and will play out in the future have been wrong much more than right in their prophesies and fears.

The foundations of a college education in America have been shaped by the pressures that the research university exerts. However, those pressures and the outcomes of the ensuing battles about the purposes of education by no means indicate that the research university is a boogey man.

Despite the presence and growth of major universities during the last century and a half, the fortunes of liberal education and the liberal arts are not in eclipse at the dawn of the twenty-first century. In fact, those fortunes have more been strengthened rather than weakened by rational debates about what constitutes an undergraduate education and the undergraduate experience.

In the end, a robust case can be made that the Progressive and Social Gospel eras significantly shaped the rise of the research university in America. The reality is that these twin forces in society and culture, overlapping as the way they did, set much of the course and impact of the research university and subsequently the ways in which the liberal arts colleges not only survived, but thrived.

Unfettered, the research university could well have overridden the liberal arts colleges and the long-standing traditions of liberal education dating to the earliest days of the Colonial Colleges. However, that was not the case.

Like the liberal arts colleges, the research university faced pockets of resistance from forces outside its control that sought to shape what it would become. These pushes and pulls were uniquely an American phenomenon, coming as they did from competing academic and administrative forces from within; political movers and shakers from without; cultural, media, and social commentators and critics of all sorts; and of course moneyed interests both inside and outside the gates.

Amid all of these allied and rival forces, in a curious way the Progressive and Social Gospel eras prevailed. The ideas and ideals spawned in that era and the heir apparents to that legacy continue in the contemporary climate to shape and inform what the academy in America is; that is, an academy indeed shaped and measured by the influence of the research university, but by no means dominated by its impact and power. And an academy in its colleges and universities that embodies the rich heritage and long-standing traditions of the higher learning in America.

## NOTES

1. Frederick Rudolph, *The American College and University: A History* (New York: Alfred A. Knopf, 1968), 357.
2. Ibid.
3. Ibid., 358.
4. Ibid.
5. Laurence R. Veysey, *The Emergence of the American University* (Chicago: University of Chicago Press, 1965), x.
6. Ibid.
7. Ibid., 2.
8. Ibid.
9. Ibid., 237-38.
10. Ibid., 238.
11. Ibid.
12. Richard Hofstadter and Wilson Smith, eds. *American Higher Education: A Documentary History*, Volume II (Chicago: University of Chicago Press, 1961), 676.
13. Richard J. Storr, "The Public Conscience of the University," *Harvard Educational Review* XXVI, no. 1 (Winter, 1956): 71–84, 78.
14. Ibid., 79.
15. What follows is taken from Rudolph, 349–51.
16. Ibid., 350.
17. Ibid., 350–51.
18. Ibid., 351.
19. Ibid., 356.
20. Lyman Abbott, "William Rainey Harper," *The Outlook* (January 20, 1906): 110–12, 110. http://www.unz.org/Pub/Outlook-1906jan20-00110.
21. Ibid.
22. Ibid., 111.
23. Ibid.
24. Rudolph, 357.
25. Conrad Cherry, *Hurrying Toward Zion: Universities, Divinity Schools, and American Protestantism* (Bloomington, IL and Indianapolis, IN: Bloomington University Press, 1995), 13.
26. Ibid., 1.
27. Ibid., 2.
28. Ibid.
29. Ibid.
30. Ibid. Harper excerpts from his *The Trend in Higher Education*, 1–34.

31. Ibid., 2.

32. His classic work: John Henry Newman, *The Idea of the University* (Garden City, NY: Doubleday, 1959).

33. Ibid., 5.

34. Ibid., 13.

35. Ibid. Italics mine.

36. Rudolph, 451.

37. Ibid., 452.

38. Ibid., 453.

39. Daniel Coit Gilman, *The Launching of a University*. With New Forward by Francesco Cordasco (New York: Garrett Press, Inc., 1969), viii.

40. Ibid., 233, italics mine.

41. His major critique was offered in: Thorstein Veblen, *The Higher Learning in America: A Memorandum on the Conduct of Universities by Business Men* (New York: B. W. Huebsch, 1918). The part of the title after the colon is the give-away of his assumptions and fears.

42. Veysey, 263–68, 302–17, and 338–41.

43. Ibid., 347.

44. Ibid., 381.

45. Ibid., 382.

46. Ibid., 340. Quote from: John Jay Chapman, "The Harvard Classics and Harvard," *Science*, XXX (1909).

47. Gilman, viii.

48. Woodrow Wilson, *The Relation of University Education to Commerce* (Chicago, 1902), 29.

49. Daniel Bell, *The Reforming of General Education: The Columbia College Experience in its National Setting*. With Foreword by David B. Truman (New York: Columbia University Press, 1996), 18.

50. John Sloan Dickey. "Conscience and the Undergraduate," *The Atlantic Monthly* 195, no. 4 (April 1955): 31–35.

# SIX

## Battles over Liberty, Academic Freedom, and Free Speech

From its earliest days at Bologna and Oxford, the academy has been dedicated to the pursuit of knowledge, to the relentless exchange of ideas and intellectual thought, and to the pledge that the best of the cultural heritage it inherits is passed to future generations. These fundamental values are possible only when side-by-side there exist the broad principles of faith in academic freedom, commitment to the unending journey of academic and intellectual inquiry, and belief that, regardless desires to control them, ideas matter and must be heard.

Freedom of scholarly inquiry and the essentials of free speech in discourse are the principles that undergird the character of intellectual and academic inquiry demanded both within and outside the gates of the college and university. The concept of the university and the basis of a collegiate education are defined by the capacity of academic communities to adhere to these fundamental ideas.

Pursuit of these ideals within the academy is guided by principles that contrast to those of civil society and the civic order in the degree of freedom permitted and encouraged. Outside the gates of the academy, governmental, constitutional, and legal authorities can attempt with varying outcomes, to a larger extent than in the academy, to exercise restrictions and controls on free speech in the political and cultural discourse of society and the commonweal.

That is as it should be. As citizens, those inside the gates are governed by these constitutional and legal constraints on their speech. However, those inside the gates also hold to the dictates of the academy and to the demand that ideas born from scholarly and academic inquiry are not to be suppressed or curtailed regardless where they lead.

In the history of the university in America, there are two types of free speech and academic freedom instances. One comprises cases in which academic freedom is on the scaffold, but the result of the controversy is an affirmation of faculty rights (sometimes those of students and others), as well on the front of expression of their ideas in academic and scholarly discourse. In the instances of these dust-ups, those within the academy, whether they are joined or not by those outside its gates, applaud the outcome. Things went the way professors and academics desired, and academic freedom is upheld.

Of course there is the second, opposite type of occurrences regarding academic freedom; that is, where the response to what someone has said or done draws a reaction perceived to erode and to diminish the latitude of faculty and other members of an academic community. In these cases, appeals are made in various courts of public and academic opinion and of the legal and constitutional arena.

These appeals include internal college and university adjudicating bodies, e.g., unions, faculty senates, and/or their committee structures, and legal counsel, state and federal courts, and organizations such as the American Association of University Professors (AAUP). The AAUP itself was founded early in the twentieth century in direct response to a number of campus cases that reached a level that drove academics nationally to urge that an organization needed to be created to sit in judgment about matters pivoting on free speech, as well as academic freedom and liberty cases sparked by campus controversies.

When outcomes of academic freedom contretemps are judged to be negative, absent a change in the original finding, the losing side of academicians will roundly criticize what has happened. These episodes readily become casus belli. As such controversies arise they readily become grist for allegations from all sides, and aimed at their opponents.

Those believing themselves to be protecting the academy and faculty privilege will complain that the institution is under the control of forces that don't understand the colleges and universities. It matters little what is believed to be at the root of that lack of understanding. There are numerous reasons for this conclusion.

A frequent trope is the judgment that those exerting control over the university lack knowledge and commitment about the basic principles of academic freedom. There is always the fear that condemnations and stands against faculty voices result from bending over to please wealthy supporters who, offended by the ideas put in play, will take their money elsewhere. Maybe those in charge have simply rushed to protect long-held and passionate political viewpoints from criticism.

On the other side of parties offended over free speech and academic freedom issues are those who wish to exert political control over the college and university. Failing to get their way in a controversy, they will use what has happened as evidence of destruction of the purpose, stability, duty, and responsibility of these institutions of higher learning.

Ironically when things don't go their way, both sides use their judgments to excoriate colleges and universities of further depravity. The academy can find itself in a no-win situation, hedged in by these competing and complaining voices. However, regardless of how these parties respond to the outcome of academic freedom and free speech cases in the academy, the result combines to shape thinking, policies, and the nature of the college or university on these vital issues.

The battles over academic freedom, free speech, and liberty in the academy parallel to an extent the demands on the role of the university as "critic and servant." There are and will be competing values and points of view. However, in the case of critic and servant, even where sides in the debate would suggest that it must be one or the other, the mission of the college and university demands that it be both.

In the case of freedom of speech and of academic voice, the issue is more one of what limits, if any, should there be? Goldilocks's porridge comes to mind: Not too hot, not too cold, but just right. As we observe the history that has unfolded on these crucial matters of academic freedom and liberty, getting it just right is never easy, grows out of controversy and dissent, and even when apparently settled, is never fully secure.

How then has this history of free speech, academic freedom, and concerns over liberty played out in the academy in America? Who have been the key players? Who have been perceived at the time and with reference to the future as winners and losers? What have these battles and the parties to them done to shape the fabric and identity of the college and university in this country?

## THE NASCENT SEEDS OF
## ACADEMIC FREEDOM IN AMERICA

Players who based much of their thinking on liberal arts college counterparts from the Old World shaped the earliest years of the academy in America. Later on additional influences resulted from the advent of the German research university model (at least a variety of it) in the form of the founding of Johns Hopkins. These leaders sparked, confronted, and navigated their way through the earliest controversies over academic freedom, free speech, and liberty that arose in the colonial era and continued into the early decades and first century of the Republic.

There is an element of truth in that belief. However, as with every aspect of the shape and shaping of the college and the university in the America, the story is more complicated, has more twists and turns, and resists oversimplification.

The Colonial colleges displayed both observable disdain for what to-day we would consider the basics of academic freedom and free speech, and at the same time rudimentary acknowledgement for the diverse directions to which knowledge, learning, and intellectual inquiry could lead within the gates of the academy.

Evidence of this spectrum of denial and respect about academic freedom came in religious and theological litmus tests applied to anyone seeking to join the ranks of professors as well as demanded of those who served as administrators and trustees. The Massachusetts Bay Congregationalists split early on, those not persuaded of the majority view forced out of the colony, out of Harvard, and fleeing to the South.

Those early exiles of academic freedom—really religious freedom and denominational control, but as we know everything so intertwined in that era, creating a slippery slope for life in the academy—later founded Yale in response. But of course they too split into the Old and New Lights of the Congregational tradition in the Great Awakening, and the New Lights were further exiled. They went north and subsequently founded Dartmouth.

On similar grounds, Roger Williams was forced out by the Massachusetts Bay theocrats over issues of religious freedom and liberty. With Williams's theology and religious ideas firmly implanted in the Providence Plantations (later Rhode Island), Brown University (1765) became the first college of the then seven specifically to ban religious litmus tests for its faculty and for student enrollment. That proclamation at the heart of the Brown Charter stands as an early victory for academic freedom inside the gates.

Admittedly these were theological and religious dust-ups more so than direct controls about limits on the amount of free speech and academic freedom that could be tolerated in the academy. But the reality was that if religious beliefs, practices, and theological understandings could be constricted and even excised, then with that step what could be practiced and tolerated in the civil order and society, and as well as within the gates of the academy, was being curbed and controlled as well.

This was not academic freedom and speech as conceived today. However, these battles and the resulting outcomes were precursors that produced the fundamental formation of broad acceptance that standards of academic and intellectual inquiry had to be in place in these Colonial Colleges and should be adopted by those that would follow. But even these developments did not unfold in a simple, straight-line, always improving with no setbacks to academic freedom, liberty, and free speech. In reality, there were many ups and downs on the academic freedom front.

The early nineteenth-century ferment in American higher education included the injection of ideals from the German university long before the founding of Johns Hopkins. It is easy to think that the embrace of democratic values, and liberty and freedom in the emerging Republic, gave it a corner on these principles and beliefs. The assumption can follow that in both the era of the Colonial Colleges and in the Constitutional and Revolutionary War epoch, the young colleges of the nation were leading the world as bastions of freedom of thought and inquiry.

However, reports from abroad at the time provide countervailing signals. In the early 1800s many American college faculty went to European universities for doctorates, and advanced teaching and research experience. They returned to the New World with different takes on pedagogy, teaching, learning, and early research techniques and professorial duties than those with which they had left. Their experiences informed how these professors on their return approached the profession of faculty and altered expectations of what they were capable of doing in pursuit of learning and research.

For example, George Ticknor while at the University of Gottingen in Germany in 1815, notes the strong habits of discipline and learning that the German counterpart scholars exhibited, spending "fourteen to sixteen hours a day" at their craft, and that then produced a culture that stretched the envelope of public and university discourse.[1]

The effect of this culture revealed a crucial part of the foundation of the German university: "The first result of this enthusiasm and learning, which immediately broke through all the barriers that opposed it, was an universal toleration in all matters of opinion." The key issue and its impact on Ticknor's thinking about what we would call academic freedom was that, "No matter what a man thinks, he may teach it and print it, not only without molestation from the government but also without molestation from publick opinion which is so often more oppressive than the aim of authority."[2]

Ticknor is not done. He then contrasts what was evident in this German higher learning culture with the American scene and even elsewhere in Europe.

He claims this freedom to teach, and to write as one saw fit, "passes as a matter of course and produces no effect but that of stimulating the talents of their thinking men. Everyday books appear on government and religion which in the rest of Europe would be suppressed by the state and in America would be put into the great *catalogus expurgatorious* of publick opinion but which here are read as any other books and judged according to their literary and philosophical merit. They get, perhaps, a severe review or a severe answer, but these are weapons which both parties can use and unfairness is very uncommon."[3]

Ticknor was one of hundreds of American college professors who traveled to Europe for graduate education. Some of these path breakers left their campuses to study abroad and returned to the faculties they had left. Others went to Old World universities to get a research university education and came back to the United States to join the faculty of one of its higher education institutions. From those professorial positions they exerted great influence on the teaching, courses offered, and educational ethos of their campuses.

Thus the university-enlightened perspective that Ticknor brought back to the United States was multiplied with increasing frequency. The European academy continued to lure academics for graduate and doctoral education from America. That continued until the nation built and developed comparable research institutions in the latter decades of nineteenth and the early years of the twentieth century. It was only then that the nation was able to provide advanced, post-undergraduate education to its own scholars, professors, and academicians.

The service of Ticknor and his colleagues cannot be understated. They inspired in the American academy a more integrated approach to how ideas can and should be played out in the public square, given the influence of institutions and their faculty, inside as well as outside the gates of the academy. This outcome of more free-flowing academic and intellectual inquiry changed the prior preeminent American academic mindset that Ticknor, contrasting it with what was obvious from Germany, alleges had previously been firmly in place.

That is, absent the German and other European university model for academic freedom and free speech, the American approach up to that time was that the free play of academic and intellectual ideas was dealt with as Ticknor's *"catalogus expurgatorious."* In this rendering, the way American's approached academic freedom was to treat what professors did as a compendium of works and the ideas associated with them that were allowed systematically and in knee-jerk fashion—the implied assumption being at the direction of religious authorities—to be pushed aside and banned from public view, consumption, and discourse.

## CONTESTS ABOUT ACADEMIC FREEDOM: LESSONS FROM ROBUST DEFEATS AND PYRRHIC VICTORIES

College and university contests about academic freedom and free speech in America have always been extremely complex. The players and the positions they take are varied and often surprising. The pivotal episodes in the trek through these momentous cases that the academy has faced expose us to personalities who are attractive and to those who can be judged repellant, and at times even repulsive.

As sides are inevitably taken in these controversies, assumptions about the mixture of political, ideological, cultural, and social objectives held by combative parties surface and demand being subjected to cross-examination. This goes for us as historical observers. Following the actors in these historical episodes, we too will choose sides. We too will have viewpoints and judgments about what has happened, about what we believe to be at stake, and about the personalities in these battles over academic freedom and liberty in the academy.

Consequently, there should be no surprise to find ourselves attracted to otherwise strange bedfellows among historical figures whose positions can be judged as less than the best moral and ethical choice, or less than a close match up with our ideological suppositions, but who are nonetheless compelling for having taken a stand. However, if we are to be true to the claims of the fundamental principles of freedom and liberty in the academy, then we will at least feel drawn to, possibly compelled by their ideas, and thus choose to side with them even if they are on the opposite side of the fence from us.

## A STAND ON SLAVERY: PRESIDENT NATHAN LORD AND THE DARTMOUTH TRUSTEES

The period of 1830s through the 1860s was a time in the American college and university when the earliest major showdowns about academic freedom and free speech came to the fore. Litmus tests arose on a variety of social issues, among them slavery, abolition, and race relations and equity.

Tensions and controversies about slavery and the treatment of slaves were major national issues. They had been in the water beginning in the pre-Constitutional era, but then festered and broke into fuller public debate, protest, violence to a much greater degree after the Constitution essentially provided the legal undergirding for institutionalized slavery. That led to a redoubling of commitment by opponents of slavery in their efforts to abolish it.

These controversies and the battles of the pro and con sides about slavery presaged political correctness battles that came about over a century later in the 1970s. Despite what some thought to be progress on racial issues following the civil rights efforts of the 1950s and 60s, the ideological political correctness battles of the next decades, including to present times, have in similar fashion to the slavery debates been extensively waged over issues of racism, racial equality, and socio-economic status.

Democracy and democratic values were being scrutinized as the nation marched to the seeming inevitability of civil war. In the process, tests arose over what was proper and what improper in the stands that those inside the gates of the academy would be permitted make in the sensitive, highly politicized public discussion of these tense matters of slavery and race.

Though many college and university episodes can be cited regarding positions pro and con over slavery, the departure of Nathan Lord from

Dartmouth College in his dust-up with the trustees is one of the more dramatic.

Lord served the college beginning in 1821 when he joined its board, to 1863, the last thirty-five years beginning in 1828 as its president.[4] He was a Congregational minister and theologian. Using that foundation, Lord was one of many Christian clergy and lay people to use Judeo-Christian scriptures to argue justification of slavery.

Given his public stands, the New Hampshire Congregationalists following a meeting in May 1863, urged the Dartmouth Board to inquire "whether its interests do not demand a change in the Presidency. . . ." While the trustees in a meeting that July elected in response not to remove Lord, in his words the board's "disapproval of his actions [was] so strong that he felt impelled to resign."[5]

As Lord went out the door after the trustees accepted his resignation, he offered a verdict on what had transpired. In measured rhetoric, nonetheless a shot over their bow, he declared "the liberty respectfully to protest against their right to impose any religious, ethical, or political test upon any member of their own body or any member of the college faculty, beyond what is recognized by the charter of the institution or express statutes or stipulations conformed to that instrument, however urged or suggested, directly or indirectly, by individuals or public bodies assuming to be as visitors of the college, or advisers of the trustees."[6]

The pressure on Lord led to further push back about his right to make his voice known in the public square. His position of a justification for slavery in the Christian scriptures may not have been popular. But he had lots of company, even if there were also many opposed to his theological and Biblical contentions and conclusions.

Justifying his position, Lord stands on Constitutional guarantees of religious liberty and of freedom of speech. However, his refusal to be censured by the Dartmouth Board adheres in parallel to the mainstream of the classical tradition of academic freedom. On both fronts, Lord makes a robust defense:

> I do not feel obliged, when its exercise is called into question, to surrender my moral and constitutional right and Christian liberty in this respect, nor to submit to any censure nor consent to any conditions such as are implied in the aforesaid action of the Board. . . .[7]

In Lord's day, few would contest or wish to restrict a college president's use of the bully pulpit. Presidents had a free hand to make the kinds of claims that Lord did. Noteworthy is that even today college presidents, albeit with fewer academic freedoms than their faculty colleagues, still retain broad latitude, and often do make public utterances from their pulpits protected by tenets of academic freedom and free speech. This is particularly the case when the issues at hand fall in the realm of their scholarly and academic fields.

For Lord, such presumed freedom for presidents to make public comments based in the wheelhouse of their knowledge, and of their academic and scholarly disciplines, was clearly the case. He was a religious as well as college leader. He was a trained theologian and Christian thinker. Unpopular to some as his ideas were, Lord came to his conclusions about slavery from that foundation.

The Dartmouth Board and Lord's Congregationalist colleagues did not agree with his stance on slavery. The board in particular wanted to curb his public rhetoric, no doubt to protect the college's reputation. Regardless of the success of these two governing bodies in driving Lord out of the presidency and out of Dartmouth, neither group could have won the day in a court solely guided by the principles of academic freedom and free speech. There Lord's views, regardless their popularity or political correctness would, and should, be viewed as his right to hold and to speak about publicly.

The Lord episode presaged the litmus tests that college presidents, and other college and university faculty and leadership voices experience today. One need look no further than enumerable dust-ups over commencement and other public speakers on campuses in recent years. To what extent can a viewpoint that doesn't seem to fit the politically correct or mainstream opinion, such as Lord's, be tolerated then and now?

Though Lord's opinions about slavery and justifications for it might not be viewed as mainstream, he was not without fellow supporters singing from the same hymnbook. To what extent is he as a college president entitled to his opinion, particularly its public expression? Is this an example of a political, cultural, or social third-rail that lurches sufficiently far from the mainstream of moral and ethical sensibilities that a leader such a Lord would have to be silenced today as he was then, at least in terms of using his pulpit as a president to preach such ideas?

What are the arguments for who is in the right and who in the wrong in the episode of Nathan Lord at Dartmouth? The board along with the Congregationalists, taking a stand that slavery is immoral and inhumane, and that any attempt to justify it as a social institution has to be repelled? There is certainly moral and ethical ground for their posture, even if a portion of it was driven by the pragmatic need to protect Dartmouth's image and reputation, not to mention that of the Congregational church.

But in their stance, how much do they, especially the Dartmouth Board, end up eroding the principles—the Congregational leaders had no responsibility to defend—of academic freedom and free speech in the academy? What about Lord? He can be presumed to be a thoughtful man who dedicated nearly his entire life and career to foster the fortunes of Dartmouth College? To serve as long as Lord did has to be a reflection of exceptional leadership, well-matched style, and well-honed intellectual gifts for a college he had to have loved.

But as outcries over slavery grew in advance of the Civil War and with Lincoln's Emancipation Proclamation in 1863 (the Congregationalists acting as they did to push the Dartmouth trustees within two months of Lincoln's declaration), had Lord's beliefs about slavery become something that could no longer be tolerated? Did that judgment necessarily have to override allegiance to principles of academic freedom that would otherwise provide cover to permit him to say what he wished, however offensive to others?

The board didn't order Lord to resign. That was his choice. But they certainly drew a line around his ideas and made judgments about his right to utter them that made Lord's continued tenure, certainly in his mind, as their president untenable.

There are no easy or simple answers to these questions. Regardless where one stands on what happened to Lord, the issues surrounding his viewpoints and his departure from Dartmouth's presidency underscore the tangled web of complications at stake in controversies over free speech and academic freedom in the academy. For all the ins and outs in the Lord case, it is an example of a political correctness litmus test long before anyone thought of things in those terms. That is as reassuring—things have actually changed little—as it is disturbing—academic freedom and free speech in the academy are ever on the scaffold.

## JOHNS HOPKINS AND THE UNIVERSITY OF WISCONSIN THE WAY

Dartmouth was a prestigious college in the mid-nineteenth century, but the major research universities were coming to the fore in visibility and prominence. Compared to Dartmouth and the many small liberal arts colleges, the size and scale, higher profile with the public, including for the public institutions their citizen taxpayers, of the research universities made them ready hothouses for controversies over academic freedom, free speech, and liberty in the academy.

Given their footprint, but also because they were the new kid on the block, these research universities knew that every move, every utterance was under a public microscope. As institutions, and through their leaders, the new universities sought to convey their beliefs about the university writ large and to convince the public about the academic culture they believed they were committed to uphold. Any of the public rhetoric of the emerging research universities was aimed to make clear their beliefs about the academy and the role of research, the pursuit of knowledge, and the breadth of inquiry that they embodied.

Daniel Coit Gilman, first president of Johns Hopkins, made a strong case about the foundation of his university, but it was really a claim that befit all the colleague universities emerging on the scene. Gilman was viewed as one of the "Victorian" founders of the major universities of the latter nineteenth century.[8] The roster is familiar one, Gilman (1875–1901) at Johns Hopkins joined by the likes of Charles Eliot (1869–1909) at Harvard and Andrew White (1866–1885) at Cornell.

The label of the titans of the American college presidency can be over utilized and held as a benchmark, however inaccurate, of success. That is, anyone lasting in a college presidency for less than two, and preferably more toward three or four decades, then and now, has somehow failed. But for these three presidents, the tag of titans is apt.

They brought to America's shores the wisdom of the German universities they had either attended, or been exposed to by colleagues, or both. They used this reference point as the model for their institutions forever altering notions of what the university for America could be.

However, lest it be overlooked in the massive building they did at their universities, the vital ingredient these presidents brought to America was a broadened sense for what gets bandied about as academic freedom. The unique feature of the German model was deep-rooted reliance on the autonomy of professors over their work, and crucially that the judgment of the guild, the community of scholars and professionals had to hold sway. It was this comprehensive idea of the autonomy, latitude, and free rein of faculty that Gilman, Eliot, and White launched in the American landscape[9]

When Gilman addressed the Johns Hopkins trustees on January 30, 1875, the university had not yet opened its doors, the institution in the final stages of taking in its first students. Gilman argues that this about-to-happen university, "would not be worthy the name of a university, if it were to be devoted to any other purpose than the discovery and promulgation of the truth; and it would be ignoble in the extreme if the resources which have been given by the founder without restrictions should be limited to the maintenance of ecclesiastical differences or perverted to the promotion of political strife."[10]

At the door of the college and university the danger of collapse from its fundamental purpose endlessly lurks as a result of capitulation to the worst of ideological, including religious, and political forces.

Gilman knows that the lofty purposes of the university must hold. It cannot allow the petty attempts of competing parties with their much less than transcendent ideas and intentions to gain exclusive footholds on the mission and core beliefs of the academy. Nothing clobbers the ideals of academic freedom and free speech more swiftly and more fully than control by forces seeking to turn the academy into a political, social, and cultural institution of their design, and one that will as a result push an ideological platform.

Gilman had to navigate the ideological landscape of his day in and outside the gates of the academy. He marched to combat the dangers at hand in the preservation of academic freedom and free speech. In doing so he presages and sounds as though he is in the middle of today's political correctness era: "As the spirit of the university should be that of intellectual freedom in the pursuit of truth and of the broadest charity toward those from whom we differ in opinion it is certain that sectarian and partisan preferences should have no control in the selection of teachers, and should not be apparent in their official work."[11]

It takes heroic men and women to overcome the pettiness of these struggles in the academy over turf, control, and ideological turns of thought. In these face-offs, one tool at the disposal of college presidents and faculty leaders, not to mention trustees, alumni, and students, is firm commitment to the fundamental principles of academic inquiry, and of freedom of thought and expression that in the breach are at risk.

Gilman was one such leader. To underscore his point with the Johns Hopkins trustees, remember as they are all setting about the journey that would be this university, he adds a personal perspective. Gilman claims nothing less than "in a life devoted chiefly to the advancement of education I have found some of the best cooperators among those from whom I differed on ecclesiastical and political questions. . . ."[12]

The founders of a university have the advantages, though also the challenges, of confronting a blank slate. Like sports teams at the beginning of any new season, hope abounds. Nonetheless, they will face inevitable pitfalls that though warned about cannot be readily avoided. Their aspirations to stay true to mission can prove to be too idealistic. The expectations they hold and expect for collegiality and colleagueship often go unmet. The goals they hold for the institution may never be reached.

However, once a university or college is underway, then complexities and hard-fought battles truly begin. Such was the case of the University of Wisconsin a couple of decades into its institutional history. In this case a controversy over academic freedom and free speech produced a declaration that had lasting effect for Wisconsin—ending up etched in stone over its main administration building—as well as laying down an important marker for similar battles at other colleges and universities. The fallout from Wisconsin's crucible of free speech crisis provided an enduring compass for all the colleges and universities of America.

Conflicts and major controversies sparked inside the gates of the academy over academic freedom and free speech that get into the public view time and again result from remarks, utterances, and rhetoric and writing, intentionally provocative or otherwise, of faculty members. Students and the visibility of their public expressions can on occasion also produce negative public outcry.

However, student provocations commonly produce accusations that they have touched a political correctness third rail. Though not expressly intent using academic freedom and free speech, when called on the carpet they will seek refuge using these rights. The Water Buffalo episode at

Penn and much of the *Dartmouth Review's* most provocative activities and publications at Dartmouth come readily to mind.[13]

However, the greatest frequency and highest profile of campus free speech contretemps revolve around faculty. Professors can use their prominence and position, especially those tenured and more protected, to express opinions based on presumptive research, scholarship, and academic grounds to make public claims. These claims in the public square can spark debate, bring condemnation on the heads of faculty, and result in calls for their removal.

The free speech and academic freedom moments that get the most play and place faculty at the greatest risk are those for which controversy blows up over public judgments both outside and inside the gates. These are occasions fraught with questions about whether a professor's statements have stayed within the parameters of their field of academic study, or rather have wandered off into some other arena of political, social, and cultural controversy. In the latter case, the faculty member involved is judged as being on shaky ground.

It was a faculty member at Wisconsin that sparked its unparalleled moment of institutional conflict, drama, and decision over free speech, liberty, and academic freedom. It was an episode that reverberated throughout American higher education at the time and for decades and longer into the future.

Richard Ely was an economics professor at the University of Wisconsin in the 1890s.[14] Ely was a known liberal academic and ardent supporter of labor union activities in Madison and statewide. The University of Wisconsin's beliefs and creed had by the 1890s developed over four decades since its founding in 1848. Out of the Ely affair, Wisconsin created a lasting foundation for academic freedom, free speech, and liberty.

Ely became the target of the state's Superintendent of Public Instruction, what today would be a state Commissioner of Education, Oliver Wells. Wells, a Democrat, gained the post as superintendent after his party overthrew Republicans in the leadership of the State House. Wells complained to University of Wisconsin President Charles Adams and the Board of Regents about Ely's socialist philosophy, and his radical teaching and public rhetoric.

Wisconsin's leaders turned a deaf ear to Wells's allegations. But Wells persisted, going public with charges of what he viewed as Ely's "economic heresy," and "diabolical practices and teaching."

Ely had published a major book about socialism, a work in his scholarly realm of economics. Wells's cursory reading of Ely's book provided all the proof he needed to allege that Ely was nothing more than a threatening socialist with treacherous ideas that attacked America, its values and beliefs.

The university committee charged to resolve the accusations against Ely incorporated in their report what has become a classic phrase, not just for Wisconsin, but for any university worth its salt. Sounding the trumpet of the fundamental principles of the academy, the committee contended that, "Wisconsin should ever encourage that continual and fearless sifting and winnowing by which alone the truth can be found."[15]

The regents endorsed the report, officially exonerating Ely. Their statement reflected an unending, unlimited belief in the creed of academic freedom and inquiry. Years later Ely labeled the report the "Wisconsin Magna Charta."

The university must claim these core doctrines. But too repeatedly that is not the case. The university too easily casts aside their values as happened by contrast as we will see shortly at Stanford when Jane Stanford forced the termination of Edward Ross.

In their statement, the regents recognized the "vast diversity of views" of the state's citizens, the stakeholders in the university. Underscoring the absurdity of the implications of a successful prosecution of Ely, they argue that dismissing him "would be equivalent to saying that no professor should teach anything which is not accepted by everybody as true."

Further the board knew that, applied universally in the academy, such a step would cut the curriculum to almost nothing. They thus declared that expansion of knowledge and solutions to society's problems must be continually advanced. Professors, rather than being muzzled, must have free rein to explore knowledge and "should be absolutely free to follow the indications of truth wherever they may lead."

The coup de grace is the regents's affirmation of the "sifting and winnowing" that formed the core of Ely's judgment that their commentary about the affair constitutes a Magna Charta for Wisconsin and for the academy: "Whatever may be the limitations which trammel inquiry elsewhere we believe the great state University of Wisconsin should ever encourage that continual and fearless sifting and winnowing by which alone the truth can be found."[16]

The author of "sifting and winnowing" was not revealed at the time. This left historians and the Wisconsin family wondering for years who might have penned what became this classic phrase. It turns out that it was none other than Wisconsin's president, Charles Adams, a stand up moment for a university president.

## THE ROSS AFFAIR AT STANFORD AND
## THE UNIVERSITY OF CHICAGO'S RESPONSE

The University of Wisconsin's actions in the Ely case contrast starkly with how Stanford University handled a strikingly similar situation shortly after. Jane Stanford was co-founder of the university with her deceased husband Leland. On his death she had taken over sole control of the trustee-level leadership of the Stanford. She judged Edward Ross, like

Ely, to be a union-activist faculty member, to be a rogue professor. Out of personal animus and diametrically opposed political beliefs, Jane Stanford went after Ross and succeeded in forcing his firing.

The university's founding president, David Starr Jordan, was in the pocket of the Stanford's. They had personally selected and appointed him, and remained the driving force behind his early tenure in office. Jordan predictably capitulated to Jane Stanford's pressure.

Stanford University was in its first decade of existence. It did not yet have the hard-won traditions that Wisconsin possessed and that might have pushed events in a different direction.

As the events of Ross's demise unfolded the climate at Stanford was such that the faculty fearing what might happen to them, but for a few outspoken voices, said nothing in defense of their colleague and offered no negative comments about the process they were witnessing. The board also stood idly by as Jordan carried out Jane Stanford's autocratic move.

In his thinking about the Ross affair, Laurence Veysey characterizes it as seminal on the front of the evolution of thinking about academic freedom in America. He conveys a broad interpretation and contribution of the Ross incident to the evolution of the university and the college presidency. Veysey believes for better and worse that the events at Stanford led to the ways in which the university and the presidency evolved hand in hand in light of the heightened complexity and stakes in the game of higher education in America in the early twentieth century. [17]

As evidence of this claim, Veysey asserts that in capitulating to Jane Stanford, President Jordan let "institutional rather than personal" concerns dictate his actions because "he could never forget the endowment." [18] In an ideal world Jordan might have been persuaded to follow in the mold of President Adams at Wisconsin. But instead he caved in to the owner of Stanford.

The reality Jordan confronted was stark:

> As long as Mrs. Stanford lived, she could take away what she had given or she could change the character of the institution in some eccentric fashion. The vessel had weathered the severe gales of the mid-nineties: amid the new internal threats to its safety, the captain could not desert his post for any reason—friendship [with Ross], personal debt, or abstract principle [that of academic freedom]. In a crisis only the ship mattered. [19]

The upheaval that followed the Ross affair had a lasting and highly negative impact for Stanford University. Faculty morale suffered with multiple resignations of professors in the wake of Ross's forced departure by firing. Faculty compensation was stinted in large part because of Mrs. Stanford's (along with that of her partner Jordan) emphasis that the University build up the physical plant rather than fairly pay its faculty. [20]

The result for Stanford was that at the time of Jordan's retirement in 1913, the university:

> comprised a crazy-quilt of conflicting aspirations, each stalemated by the others. Whether the saving of the endowment—the one clear achievement of the past two decades—had been worth the price of so many gradually frustrated careers, highlighted by a surrender to obnoxious pressures, could more easily be answered after the fact than at the time.[21]

The late nineteenth and early twentieth centuries were a rough-and-tumble era, during which magnates of industry, commerce, and business—the likes of Leland and Jane Stanford at Stanford and John D. Rockefeller at Chicago—were about the business of founding and placing enormous financial wherewithal to start universities. An obvious concern with these folks at the helm as founders and trustees was that they would open the door for the even greater intrusion and influence of financiers and major donors into the missions and into day-to-day operations of these institutions. That meddling was most feared for its control over academic freedom and free speech.

William Rainey Harper was the first president at the founding of the University of Chicago in 1892. Stanford, founded two years earlier in 1890, was just nine years into its history when it became a proving ground for free speech in the American academy as a result of its handling of the Ross case. Among other things, Stanford's dealings with Ross spawned in its wake the founding of American Association of University Professors.

As Jane Stanford was forcing the termination of Edward Ross over his stands against railroads and other corporate interests, along with his pro-union politics, Harper sat in a fellow presidential perch from which to witness what was happening to President Jordan. From that vantage point Harper had well-informed eyes from which to judge Jordan's actions (and inactions) in response to Jane Stanford's orders, and the subsequent spillover across the country. Harper's response was that on his watch nothing like that would happen at Chicago.

Harper made his stance clear at the Decennial of Chicago in 1902, just two years after the contretemps at Stanford. On that occasion Harper presented "The President's Report: Administration." He took pains to recite in that report a statement made at a recent Convocation that was "adopted unanimously by members of the Congregation of the University, June 30, 1899."[22]

The warning bells from the West Coast university were ringing. To preempt any thought that Chicago could fall into a similar slough of despond, the "Congregation," its faculty went on the record stating bold convictions about free speech on their campus.

Harper points to the major assertions in this document: That the principle of freedom of speech in any aspect and on any topic or subject has from the founding of the University of Chicago been a fundamental standard and belief. No one in any official position at the university has raised a question of any instructor to justify and defend any public utterances made. Harper declares further no donors to the university, either individuals or the state, have a right to interfere with the faculty and their teaching. Simply stated the faculty of Chicago made patently plain that no person, agency or institution including the church can impede or attempt to countermand the search for truth and proclamations about it at the university.[23]

However, Harper wants even greater clarity to insure that there be no mistake in anyone's mind about his or Chicago's convictions. In short, among other differences with Stanford, Harper's wealthy underwriter in Rockefeller had not and would not operate the way the Jane Stanford had.

Bolstering that claim and protecting the bona fides of Chicago's founder and financial architect, John Rockefeller, Harper argues that there has been no interference in the academic life of the university. No donor, including all of its founding philanthropists, has made any attempt by word or deed to indicate dissatisfaction with the ways in which teaching and instruction were conducted at the university. Nor have these financial supporters tried to use their money as leverage to stop public expressions of opinion made by any professors or officers of the university.[24]

Who knows what would have happened to the Harper-Rockefeller partnership if the Chicago financier had attempted to do what Jane Stanford did. Nevertheless that was never close to the case.

Addressing the issue of faculty security in their appointments, something obviously breached in Ross's case, Harper acknowledges that prior to a faculty member's status becoming permanent—what we now label tenure but which did not yet exist—they could be severed for comments deemed harmful to the university. But even in these cases, for pragmatic as well as idealistic reasons, Harper wants to avoid the sacking of any professor.

He believes the damage done to the university when it forces the resignation of a faculty member is always far greater than any damage a professor might cause by public utterances. Even worse, such actions can call into question the university's judgment of granting permanent status to a professor in the first place.

Insisting on his creed of academic freedom and liberty, Harper argues that most crucial element necessary in the cultivation of the academic life of the academy and in the pursuits of the academic mind and intellect is spirit is the need for security from interference. Only with such protection are the scholars and teachers in a university or college able to do work that has the potential to be of benefit to society and its citizens. Again, given the choice of having this freedom versus its constraint, Harper is clear: "Freedom of expression must be given the members of a university faculty, even though it be abused; for, as has been said, the abuse of it is not so great an evil as the restriction of such liberty." [25]

Harper's and Chicago's position is simple and should be inarguable. However, not only at Stanford, but at many other colleges and universities before and since, that has not always been the case.

Too often, when they enter the fray of dust-ups over faculty academic freedom, academic leaders and the boards and governing bodies of these institutions take actions that do not square with Harper's view. Caught in controversies and searching for ways to escape, these leaders in the academy resort to reprimand, recrimination, and removal of professors (and students) judged to have gone beyond the pale with rhetoric or actions sparking public hullabaloos.

## TANGLES IN THE TWENTIETH CENTURY: CRISES AND CONFRONTATIONS IN THE MODERN COLLEGE AND UNIVERSITY ERA

As the twentieth century opened, higher education in America continued to feature controversial affairs over academic freedoms. After the Wisconsin and Stanford cases, notorious and hard fought as they were, the intensity of these episodes gathered steam.

As had always been the case, times of national crisis—and the twentieth century saw its fair share of them—exacerbate and inflame the tendency to bring all sorts of freedoms under attack. The targets are all sorts of citizens. When these attacks happen, special attention is readily focused on academics within the walls of colleges and universities for exerting what is deemed excessive privilege and for abusing these freedoms.

In these moments, critics are quick to claim that the rhetoric and actions of professors and students, and the refuge that they seek in academic freedom and free speech, is nothing more than a veneer. The critics believe that these denizens within the walls of the academy merely hide behind these high-sounding virtues as their last refuge as scoundrels.

The Revolutionary War, Civil War, World Wars I and II, the Cold War with its McCarthyism, the Vietnam War with President Nixon, his Vice President Spiro Agnew, and then-Governor Ronald Reagan making great hay decrying campus radicals among the professors and students of the land, and most recently in the post-September 11 era, fears about terrorism and national security have each created causes celebres and causes belli in the nation over freedom and liberty with significant rebound on American colleges and universities. [26]

During World War I Nicholas Murray Butler, president of Columbia University, took enumerable stands about national policy and international affairs, including pointing out who were and were not patriots. The debates tripped off at Columbia by Butler's presidential rhetoric and action about the parameters of free speech for faculty members reverberated throughout the country at other colleges and universities.

Butler was an autocratic, arguably a nearly dictatorial, leader. He was enormously active in politics and was never one to pull a punch. One who took Butler's bait was Lawrence Lowell, then president of Harvard. He embraced his equal presidential responsibility to tackle Butler's stands and actions in the public square.

Butler proved to be an elusive, slippery target regarding academic freedom and liberty. His rhetoric was one thing and his actions were quite another. Butler was a titanic figure in the college presidency, serving Columbia from 1902–1945, He hung onto power, blind, deaf, and declining in health even as an interim took over his position, but long enough for Butler to strong-arm the search process that produced his hand-picked successor with the appointment of Dwight Eisenhower.

But in the end it was Lowell and Harvard that got the better of Butler. His biggest problem was that despite his rhetoric, flowery and seemingly in the academic freedom camp, Butler's two major actions with faculty both in the heat of war and the run-up to another war tell a different story.

In 1917, Butler dismissed James Cattell from the Columbia faculty "officially because he opposed United States conscription policy," and due to his growing anti-militaristic and socialist set of political positions. But this final step in Cattell's removal resulted from continuing and building enmity between him and Butler for the better part of a decade.[27]

Things came to a head as the United States entered World War I. Butler made his position clear. It was one directed at Cattell and any of his ilk: "What had been tolerated before becomes intolerable now. What had been wrongheadedness is now sedition. What had been folly is now treason." [28]

In nearly identical language, as the run-up to World War II was in the winds in 1940, Butler argued that "those whose convictions are of such character as to bring their conduct in open conflict with the university's freedom," that they should "withdraw of their own accord." Pushing back against Butler's provocations about academic freedom, the Faculty Defense Group at Harvard issued a five-point statement about their position. The pivotal argument was that there was "no possible emergency so great as to justify a university or college in enforcing uniformity of faculty opinion in matters of national policy."[29]

Returning to Lowell's attack on Butler and the divergence of their philosophies about academic freedom, Lowell stresses that institutions must be very careful about restraining faculty members, even when they get outside their areas of academic and scholarly expertise, to make statements in the public square. Lowell's position stands squarely in the tradition of Harper's test of what Chicago had as its duty to faculty freedom.

Lowell amplifies Harper's ideas in a creative argument to place Butler and his heavy-handed approach into a corner of his own making. The box that Lowell maneuvers Butler into is rooted in a question: Would Butler or any university leader want to be accused of so infringing on academic freedom that the converse would apply as well: any utterance by any professor or any member of the community be viewed as de facto having the college or university imprimatur?

To Lowell, "If a university or college censors what its professors may say, if it restrains them from uttering something that it does not approve," Butler's tactic, "it thereby assumes responsibility for that which it permits them to say." Adding to the slap at Butler, Lowell concludes that, "This is logical and inevitable, but it is a responsibility which an institution of learning would be very unwise in assuming."[30]

Lowell is highly critical of Butler and of prevailing attitudes in the nation for making knee-jerk calls for greater restrictions on the principles of academic freedom and free speech in times of crisis and especially times of war. "It is sometimes suggested that the principles are different in time of war; that the governing boards are then justified in restraining unpatriotic expressions injurious to the country. But the same problem," Lowell asserts, "is presented in war time as in time of peace."[31]

The dilemma Butler creates is clear: "If the university is right in restraining its professors, it has a duty to do so, and it is responsible for whatever it permits." But Lowell quickly notes that, "there is no middle ground." In the final analysis, "Either the university assumes full responsibility for permitting its professors to express certain opinions in public, or it assumes no responsibility whatever, and leaves them to be dealt with like other citizens by the public authorities according to the laws of the land."[32]

The battles that leaders such as Butler and Lowell waged took place in a higher education arena that featured Stanford's blow up over academic freedom and Harper's promotion of principles to ensure the preservation of academic freedom at Chicago. The footprints of these major university players generated public discussion about academic freedom controversies. As a result, the academic community became more greatly concerned about what was transpiring. Concerns heightened about the need to build hedges around unbridled administrative and outside political meddling in affairs that best should reside in the wheelhouse for adjudication by university faculty.

Lowell's argument with Butler and his actions also transpired against the backdrop of the initial declarations of the newly founded American Association of University Professors (AAUP) in 1915. In the sweep of issues about academic freedom, free speech, and liberty in the academy in America, the founding and mission of the AAUP was unprecedented. No other single idea and initiative before or since has had an imprint larger than the AAUP's in confronting academic freedom and free speech issues on behalf of the academy.

The AAUP's "General Declaration of Principles" of 1915 is a groundbreaking statement about academic freedom. It is one that, though amplified and embellished over time, remains unmatched to this day in its scope and reach.

The declaration intentionally covers wide ground. However, its fundamental core principles warn about the danger to the academy of the rule of ideology and political correctness. The authors are even-handed in their alarm. They are equal opportunity critics of the constraints of ideology, whether driven by the progressive, left side of the political spectrum or from the right, conservative forces.

Ideologically politicized positions and personalities who hold them burden both private and public institutions. The AAUP Declaration notes that the stereotypes often associated with ideological and political assaults on academic freedoms often contradict commonly held assumptions. That is, the assault on private colleges and universities often comes from vested business and conservative interests—clearly the case at Stanford—when these forces are commonly assumed to be more interested in controlling public sector schools.[33]

Meanwhile public institutions, rather than being exclusively controlled as often thought by the ebb and flow of citizen influence, thought to be conservative at its foundations, have a different flank to protect. That is, they are frequently vulnerable to attack from the progressive side of the political spectrum, arguing that in the face of social and cultural changes, public colleges and universities are too slow to react, too entrenched, too protective and overall resistant to emerging issues and public needs.[34]

This latter problem is rooted in the assumption that this sluggishness in the face of social and cultural change results from unwieldy bureaucracies on the inside, and outside from political power brokers and machinery, public bickering, and inconsistency in governmental leadership and policies. This lack of responsiveness then makes public higher education less adaptable to changing needs and new challenges than it is expected to be, and also less so than how their private college counterparts are perceived.

These problems of the early twentieth century and of the authors of the AAUP Declaration of 1915 have changed in form but not in substance in the ensuing century. To this day, both public and private higher education institutions face complex, competing constituencies who can operate with little sense of compromise and little accountability, each with an agenda of sustaining dearly held convictions and beliefs. These realities compromise and divert educational mission and purposes.

The AAUP Declaration also tackles a long-standing and uniquely American conundrum: the tension between individualism and the rights and opinions of individuals on one hand, with the interests of society for democracy, civic values and goods, and the good of the commons on the other. It is a struggle with which Jefferson and his fellow founders wrestled mightily and worked earnestly to resolve. However, even as they did so, they knew that any resolutions were provisional and would further evolve with time, likely never reaching a point of perfection.

In a bold statement the AAUP hacks out territory designed to shape thinking about academic freedoms, and the ideal degree of free speech, opinion and liberties desirable in the academy. "Public opinion is at once the chief safeguard of a democracy, and the chief menace to the real liberty of the individual," the AAUP authors note. "It almost seems as if the danger of despotism cannot be wholly averted under any form of government. In a political autocracy there is no effective public opinion, and all are subject to the tyranny of ruler"; however, a similar and converse danger is that "in a democracy there is political freedom, but there is likely to be a tyranny of public opinion." [35]

The AAUP was the first nationally organized and recognized body to urge colleges and universities and all their constituencies, foremost faculty members, that it was a must for higher education institutions to be committed to sound policies and procedures. This required greater attention to governance, especially on the front of academic freedom, but also to all procedures and decisions involving hiring, promotion, tenure, and dismissal.

To accomplish this task, the AAUP advocated for nothing less than that the colleges and universities of America be duty-bound to the creed of the academy qua the academy. That is, if the academy was to be what it is ideally supposed to be, what then must it do? As a body they urged greater responsibility and accountability on all sides of controversies over academic freedoms, especially in prosecutions of allegations directed at professors.

Events building over decades, from Wisconsin and elsewhere—most precipitated by the Ross affair at Stanford—placed these issues over academic freedom and free speech squarely on the table for colleges and universities. Attention to these critical principles at the foundation of the academy formed the agenda that the AAUP placed at the center of its mission.

Despite the best-laid plans of organizations such as the AAUP and even the seemingly most enlightened policies at any college or university, violations of academic freedoms and liberties are ever in the picture. Contretemps over academic freedom always endanger the fabric of the academy, not merely the campuses involved, but with reverberations beyond them to other colleges and universities as well.

The AAUP's purpose is to advocate for universally accepted standards that work to shape institutional responses and verdicts in the face of controversies. The challenge the AAUP issued to all higher education institutions could not be more clear: judgments and decisions dealing with the tangled web of academic freedom had to be equitable, fair, and just, nothing less than adhering to the core beliefs and convictions of the academy.

The authors of the 1915 Declaration weigh in with their understanding of the university. As the first nationally recognized authority on the university, the AAUP's Declaration and all of its subsequent judgments and exhortations are directed toward undergirding the university to do what it does best: to be the university. The university is not in a race against society or given institutions with each other. By definition the academy is deliberative, wedded to its style and substance.

Thus the AAUP acknowledges that the university realistically will "indeed, likely always to exercise a certain form of conservative influence." The reason for that conservative nature is shaped by what the university is as an idea and ideal, and what it strives to do. To that end the university must be:

> committed to the principle that knowledge should precede action, to the caution (by no means synonymous with intellectual timidity) which is an essential part of the scientific method, to a sense of the complexity of social problems, to the practice of taking long views into the future, and to a reasonable regard for the teachings of experience.[36]

Issues of academic freedom have continually been on the front burner of colleges and universities. This has been especially true in the twentieth-century academy, beginning with the founding of the AAUP in the wake of one after another nettlesome episode, and knee-jerk reactions to the exercise of academic freedom and free speech by university leaders. These controversies became attenuated as the century drew to a close, and have not receded from public view as the twenty-first century marches on.

Free speech and academic freedom issues are ever-debated in- and outside the gates of the academy. It is obvious given the historical record that speculations will forever be bandied about over the question of whether the threats to these honored principles are greater today than in previous eras.

Each generation tends to draw the conclusion that no era has faced more dire challenges to academic freedom than it has. Thus there is likely no end to discussion about the contrast between what preceded "today" and how contemporary challenges are relatively viewed.

However persistent they are, these debates and battles must always be conducted by recognizing the existence of a fine but important line: that between free speech as a major component of academic freedoms within the college and university, and that of the free speech of citizens of the nation as expressed in the Constitution. That is, there exists a distinction in the safeguards about public expression and the liberty for citizens in the constitutional and governmental compacts established between the people and the state versus the principles of freedom of expression and speech in the academy.

These differing parameters of rights in and outside the academy were established in the academy as they developed in the colonial era and were made Constitutional with the founding of the Republic. These earliest distinctions between the rights to public speech of citizens and those of the denizens of the Colonial Colleges emerged as the democratic foundations of the colonial era evolved. That wrangling was fraught and freighted with battles about religious liberty and freedom, about how to balance individual liberties with the needs and security of the commons, and about who knew best how to govern a populace and community.

Those inside and outside the gates of the college and university need to discern the difference between rights of speech under the First Amendment of the Constitution, juxtaposed and distinguished as they are from the distinctive principles of academic free speech at play in higher education. Principles about speech within the academy are by nature not fully contained in the, albeit broad but still more necessarily restrictive, ideas about speech in the Constitution.

The argument that this division must be upheld is rooted in a fundamental stance of the academy. The college and university cannot permit those outside the gates to dictate what goes on inside. In the case of judgments about free speech, higher education institutions cannot allow their authority in this arena to be impeded and constrained. A separation of that power must be preserved. The autonomy of the academy must be maintained.

Reminding us about the feats of his "Victorian" presidents—Gilman, Eliot, and White—in expanding the idea of academic freedom in America, the historian Thomas Haskell takes up this argument that issues and concerns about academic freedom must be separated from the hedges of the First Amendment. His contention is that issues of academic freedom are not solely, actually in only a minor fashion, rooted in free speech. Rather, and this is the key rationale for the difference; they are rooted in fundamental and very different principles of the academy.

This interpretation of the reach of academic freedom defines it "as the capstone of the institutional edifice that Victorian reformers constructed in hopes of establishing authority and cultivating reliable knowledge."[37] What happened during the reign of the likes of Gilman, Eliot, and White in the latter nineteenth century was that the role of the professor at research universities, but subsequently at all colleges and universities, was changed and expanded.

In addition to performing exclusively as teachers, college and university professors were now expected to be on the road to become scholars, academicians, and researchers. The role of professor was promoted and advanced to much greater professional status. This meant that these new, more professional academician-professors were expected to bear increased responsibility to defend the academic freedoms at the foundation of their craft.

More than predecessor generations of professors, college and university faculty now had an even greater professional duty to guard academic free speech and liberty. They could not allow any critic, controlling interest, or ideological pressure to prevent them in any way from pursuit of research and scholarship, and the learning, knowledge and "truth" that it produced, regardless of where it might lead.

In his parlance of "establishing authority and cultivating reliable knowledge," Haskell declares the change marked by this evolving level of expectation and duty of college faculty. This new way of conceiving the profession of professor "implies a stronger linkage between academic freedom and professionalization than is commonly recognized today."[38]

The sea change that took place in this era of expanded expectations for college faculty is under appreciated, and at times ignored today.[39] The change in professional responsibility meant that professors now had, and had to accept, magnified duties to protect the academy and its principles.

Haskell believes those—presidents, faculty members, and trustees—charged with guarding academic freedoms in today's academy must not lose sight of this heritage. They cannot permit the line of free speech rights outside the gates, in society as a whole, and for its citizens to be collapsed with that of the broader free speech that those inside the gates enjoy. University faculty must use wisely and exercise responsibly their academic freedoms. If the university and its professors do not protect their prerogatives, who else should be expected to uphold these principles and values?

The principle of the academy's autonomy to control its affairs must be sustained. Judgments about free speech issues are a crucial part of that duty. Failure to assert this responsibility and obligation disastrously diminishes the fundamental foundation of the academy. This means that the collapse of First Amendment free speech rights with those of academic freedom has to be avoided at all cost. "Any effort to completely assimilate the former to the latter would be disastrous. Historically speaking, the heart and soul of academic freedom lie not in free speech," Haskell argues, "but in professional autonomy and collegial self-governance."[40]

Concluding this line of thinking, Haskell states that:

> Academic freedom came into being as a defense of the disciplinary community (or more exactly, the university conceived as an ensemble of such communities), and if it is to do the work we expect of it, it must

continue to be at bottom a denial that anyone outside the community is fully competent to pass judgment on matters failing within the community's domain.[41]

It is this territory that Haskell believes those beyond and within the gates of today's academy often fail to understand and to abide by. Failure to maintain this demarcation of free speech in versus outside the academy places its principles and beliefs at great peril.

## ACADEMIC FREEDOM'S PRECEDENCE IN THE SUPREME COURT: A BREAKTHROUGH CASE

Legal twists and turns related to Haskell's assertions shape a complex tale. However, given the decisive stakes, it is a story that must be grasped if the evolution of academic freedoms is to be fully understood. Notwithstanding Haskell's contention that his "Victorian" presidents and reformers engaged in a great breakthrough in understandings of academic freedoms, the legal system, and the courts have only in the last half-century weighed in on the Constitutional point of view of free speech in and outside the academy.

The pivotal court case that legally recognized academic freedom and free speech was Sweezy vs. New Hampshire in 1957.[42] The Sweezy case is a direct result of the McCarthy era loyalty oaths and similar pledges that came to be demanded as a result of McCarthy's screeds about subversive activities.[43] In the heat of that time, the State of New Hampshire passed the Subversive Activities Act. Under the act, all state employees were required to sign a statement indicating that they were not subversive persons.

Sweezy had delivered lectures on a couple of occasions at the University of New Hampshire and the State Attorney General called into question the content of those lectures. Sweezy refused to sign a statement that he was not a subversive and was subsequently prosecuted under the law.

The allegation was that he held and publicly expressed Marxist and Socialist views. During his hearing appearances, Sweezy cited the First Amendment right to free speech and association in his refusal to answer questions about the lectures, and about his political activities and about fellow citizens who associated with him.

The Attorney General petitioned for and got a state trial to force Sweezy to respond. When he continued to refuse, he was held in contempt. Sweezy appealed to the New Hampshire Supreme Court which, while finding that his rights of free speech and association had been violated, asserted that the state's interests outweighed those individual rights.

Sweezy consequently marched his case to the United States Supreme Court. The court by plurality, though not a five-justice binding precedent decision, agreed that Sweezy's "academic freedom" (the first time the court had ever invoked this principle) and his First Amendment rights had been infringed. The major finding was that however legitimate a state's concern, "subversive individuals and their activities does not trump the Bill of Rights."[44]

The resulting lines of demarcation from this case are essential to an understanding of the point at which free speech and academic freedom in the academy arrived after nearly four centuries in America. Prior to this benchmark Supreme Court case, the nation's colleges and universities had no definitive legal basis from which to defend themselves from challenges about the level of free speech and academic freedom they were asserting and securing for their communities.

It was only at that point, nearly two hundred years from the founding of the Republic, that the court and thus the U.S. Constitution "officially recognized the concept of academic freedom."[45] In retrospect it is remarkable that it took that long to get to a definitive legal rendering from the court about academic free speech.

Noteworthy is the fact that the United States Supreme Court a century and a quarter earlier likewise subsequently overturned a New Hampshire Supreme Court in a case analogous to Sweezy. In this instance the New Hampshire court backed then president of Dartmouth, John Wheelock's, attempt to rename Dartmouth from a college to a university and to permit the school to be transferred under state rather than private governance and control.

The New Hampshire decision in the Dartmouth case set the stage for Daniel Webster's victory on behalf of Dartmouth before the Supreme Court. In Webster versus New Hampshire, the court struck down Wheelock's position and affirmed Webster's classic line of defense that Dartmouth "is small college but there are those who love it. This case's finding asserted a similar position to that of Sweezy regarding state authority vis a vis a higher education institution

The opinions of two of the justices in the Sweezy decision are noteworthy. Chief Justice Earl Warren rooted the court's opinion in the link between the critical role of the intellectual quest in the academy and the connection of those endeavors to the fortunes of the nation.

First, Warren underscored and affirmed the foundation of the purpose of education in a democratic society that the founders of the Colonial Colleges and later forbearers of small liberal arts colleges and universities in the early nineteenth century developed. Second, he makes clear how freedom from outside constraints for both "teachers and students" in any academic inquiry is essential to learning and to the good of the commons.

Warren argued that, "to impose any straitjacket upon the intellectual leaders in our colleges and universities would imperil the future of our nation. No field of education is so thoroughly comprehended by man that new discoveries cannot yet be made. Particularly is that true in the

social sciences, where few, if any principles are accepted as absolutes."
Warren pressed the viewpoint that, "[S]cholarship cannot flourish in an
atmosphere of suspicion and distrust. Teachers and students must always remain free to inquire, to study and to evaluate, to gain new maturity and understanding; otherwise our civilization will stagnate and
die."[46]

In a concurring opinion, Justice Felix Frankfurter emphasized the degree to which a free society is dependent on free universities. "[T]his
means the exclusion of governmental intervention in the intellectual life
of a university. It matters little," Frankfurter declares, "whether such
intervention occurs avowedly or through action that inevitably tends to
check the ardor and fearlessness of scholars, qualities at once so fragile
and so indispensable for fruitful academic labor."[47]

Frankfurter makes a further major assertion about the academy in
America by providing a definition of the principles constituting academic
freedom and free speech. In so doing, he placed the court on the record
with its understanding of these key principles of the academy to a greater
degree of specificity that at any previous time.

"It is the business of a university to provide that atmosphere which is
most conducive to speculation, to experiment and creation" Frankfurter
argues. Regarding the environment that must be guaranteed to the university in order for its mission and purpose to be fulfilled, he cites the
values that have become a long-lasting definition of academic freedom:
"It is an atmosphere in which there prevail 'the four essential freedoms'
of a university—*to determine for itself on academic grounds who may teach,
what may be taught, how it shall be taught, and who may be admitted to
study."*[48]

Expounding about these fundamental values in the academy, Frankfurter declares that "inquiries into these problems," the academic quest,
the search for truth and knowledge, "speculations about them, stimulation in others of reflection upon them, must be left as unfettered as possible." The essential warning, yet also balance, in these considerations of
freedom in the academy is that "Political power must abstain from intrusion into this activity of freedom, pursued in the interest of wise government and the peoples well-being, except for reasons that are exigent and
obviously compelling."[49]

The message in Sweezy of the court to the academy clearly supports
autonomy for colleges and universities in their affairs of regarding the
pursuit of research, inquiry, and knowledge. Frankfurter gave the imprimatur for this purpose and quest by invoking the "the four essential
freedoms" of a university.

In the Sweezy case, the court for the first time addressed the matter of
academic freedom, and through Frankfurter's four freedoms affirmed
what the academy had always declared about its mission and purpose.
Autonomy from government or other civil interference in its academic

freedom and free speech serves both the best interests of America's colleges and universities and of the nation's political, social and cultural fabric.

## SPECULATIONS: THE STATE OF
## ACADEMIC FREEDOM AND ITS FUTURE

Sweezy vs. New Hampshire provided settled law about academic freedom and free speech in the academy. The case upholds the personal rights of individuals in the face of state and government pressure to compromise themselves and others. It removes forced loyalty oaths and asserts under the First Amendment that academic freedoms cannot be illegally constrained.

However, as the decades of the latter twentieth century unfolded after this landmark decision, college and university campus-by-campus handling of academic freedom and free speech controversies suggest a mixed review. As has historically been the case, times of national crisis in particular continue to amplify and place under harsh klieg lights the handling of free speech issues by higher education institutions, their leaders, and key inside and outside players and provocateurs.

National crisis sparked passionate debate about dueling positions on academic freedom between presidents Nicholas Murray Butler and Lawrence Lowell in the heat of World War I. Sweezy would have not been molested absent the face of McCarthyism, Red baiting and the Cold War.

Clark Kerr would have had a more lengthy tenure as Chancellor at Berkeley without tangles with Ronald Reagan, then Governor of California, about how to handle Vietnam War and racial campus protests of the 1960s. More recently the post-September 11 era we have examples of faculty outspoken in the public square, such as Ward Churchill at the forefront at the University of Colorado for his "little Nazis" comment about those killed in New York City. The handling of the Churchill case contributed in its wake largely to the resignation of Colorado president Elizabeth Hoffman.

From a twenty-first-century view of the sweep of the experience of higher education in America, one conclusion can be made: academic freedom has always been and remains fragile. Regarding individual freedoms and rights, whether those of citizens assuming protection under the First Amendment or other Constitutional provisions, or of those in the academy hoping for additional protection under the cloak of academic freedom and free speech, the reigning politics of the day on and off campus hold significant sway.

Against the backdrop of the early to mid- and even later nineteenth-century controversies over issues such as slavery, evolution, and Biblical literalism, historian Anthony Lucas stresses the fragility of the univer-

sity's duty to uphold academic freedom. Despite previous gains and occasions when the academy stood up to pressures to reduce academic
freedoms, Lucas's believes that "any suggestion that academic freedom
was well entrenched in nineteenth-century America begins," from the
latter twentieth-century perspective, "to look like a very dubious proposition."[50]

Fast-forwarding to the twentieth and now the twenty-first centuries,
the mixed nineteenth-century record regarding battles over academic
freedom at colleges and universities continues to hold. Lucas claims that
what happened during and after World War I, rapidly followed by what
happened in World War II and its aftermath, left in its swath continued
mixed messages about academic freedom. "Although it is true there were
many instances where there was resistance [to suppression of faculty
voices], in the main," Lucas contends, "when academe was pressured to
cleanse itself of suspected dissidents, colleges and universities readily
acceded."[51]

If Lucas is correct, then from mid-twentieth century on, even with
what appeared to be a settled court, if not a Constitutional guarantee, in
Sweezy, the academy in the least continually battles to get its house in
order. At worst, colleges and universities can be viewed as caving in with
greater frequency to prevailing political and social pressures of the day in
their upholding of fundamental principles about free speech and academic freedom.

A decade and a half into the twenty-first century, where does all of
this leave us regarding the stability or fragility of academic freedom, free
speech and liberty in the academy? A number of speculations arise about
where the academy is and where it may be headed as it continues to
wrestle with matters of academic freedoms.

First, when these matters of free speech and liberty both inside and
outside the gates of the academy are tied to periods of crisis, ensuing
controversies can extend over decades and longer as the crisis persists.
The opening years of the twenty-first century are already marked and
continue to be heavily influenced by the September 11 attacks. Those who
claim and wish to label the response to those attacks as a war on terror,
and even for those who don't buy that thinking, there is agreement that
the September 11 spillover will last for decades, if not longer.

Thus Americans are presently in another of these national times of
perpetual crisis, not unlike the Cold War that lasted more than forty
years. We know that when U.S. fortunes in the world become more visibly at stake—the two World Wars, Vietnam, and now the "War on Terror"—there is a predictable ensuing reaction to the rhetoric and activities
of members of the academy. In these instances public opinion—and it
doesn't need to be a majority—judging the position of individuals and
members of a college or university to be outside mainstream thinking,

and in any way criticizing the country and its policies and actions, will weigh in with negative reactions and consequences.

Father Theodore Hesburgh was Notre Dame's president from 1952 to 1987. He stated on many occasions that during the 1960s he carried a pocket necrology. It contained the names of presidents whose tenures were cut short either because critics felt that they did too little, or did too much—in that era in which it was very hard for college presidents to get it "just right"—in the face of campus protests. He claimed to have left off when he reached over two hundred. The heat of both foreign and domestic issues was unrelenting, and the free speech and liberty of not just presidents, but of many others on campuses, were infringed by one response or another to their rhetoric, actions or inactions, and public stands.

Second, from the mid- to late 1980s through a good portion of the 1990s, many campuses from the high profile—Universities of Pennsylvania, Michigan, Wisconsin, and Maryland—to less prominent universities and small liberal arts colleges, adopted speech codes and similar restrictions of public speech and behavior. These flirtations and concrete actions to control what were long-standing traditions of free speech in the academy resulted from the demands of campus political correctness partisans, and were both supported and decried by ideological forces in and outside the gates.

The fact that these flirtations existed, let alone that institutions of the academy would cave in to these forces, is a tale about the politics of the time and of the players. For example, at one school the faculty went so far as to consider putting in place a faculty committee that would review every syllabus for every course taught at the college. This was in reaction to student complaints that gained traction from the support of faculty members about the sources and readings being used in one professor's course.[52] The faculty had a proposal for the syllabus committee, but it never got to the floor of a faculty meeting and thus died a merciful death.

A current round of new issues are developing yet another battle of ideologies and political correctness. The colleges and universities of America are today faced with how they will wrestle with, accommodate, and push back on these assaults, and competing pressures and disputes about academic freedom, free speech, and liberty in the academy.

Some of these controversies are being newly created by extensions of interpretations and applications of provisions under Title IX. Others are being spawned by recent campus controversies over "trigger points:" content in courses that "may" trigger in some students negative reactions over religious or other beliefs or from emotional flashbacks to prior life experiences.

As federal legislation, Title IX was initially conceived to ensure equal opportunity and access for women in educational settings. The application of the law was especially directed in the areas of athletics and other extra- and co-curricular opportunities on campus regularly afforded to men, but now required to be available for women. Title IX's application has evolved to the point that it is now being used as a basis for a broad range of complaints at educational institutions.

Two contemporary examples underscore the reach of these issues provoked by Title IX and "trigger warning" controversies and their bearing on academic freedom and free speech for the higher education community.

The first case involved a feminist faculty member at Northwestern University, Laura Kipnis. Kipnis had written an article castigating what she viewed as misguided understandings about both sexual violence and trigger point warnings. She was concerned about an implicit infantilization of women as ethical and moral agents, and about stereotypes of men and women being incorporated in the conduct codes of Northwestern for both faculty and students. She feared a worrisome overlap of issues being lumped together in cases about sexuality, gender politics, and the emotional wellbeing of students.

Several students at Northwestern replied to her article by filing two Title IX complaints that under law necessitated investigation by Northwestern. Kipnis was cleared of the two complaints. But her tale is revelatory of the political temperature in today's academy.

Kipnis's article suggests that the university is caught up in an "obsession with helpless victims and powerful predators. . . . The result," she claims, is that "Students' sense of vulnerability is skyrocketing." [53] She questions the advent and application of trigger warnings and asks:

> But what do we expect will become of students, successfully cocooned from uncomfortable feelings, once they leave the sanctuary of academe for the boorish badlands of real life? What becomes of students so committed to their own vulnerability, conditioned to imagine they have no agency . . .

A related focus for Kipnis is on institutional policies and actions, and the reactions of today's academy to allegations about sexual improprieties. The Title IX complainants against Kipnis contended that her opinions regarding social and sexual behavior policies created a chilled and harassing environment for a student who might need to bring forward a complaint and a hostile milieu under Title IX regulations.

The ease with which the Title IX complaint was able to be filed, coupled with a prior petition to Northwestern's president "demanding 'a swift, official condemnation'"—a call for censoring suppression of her free speech—of the article only deepened Kipnis's concern for the core ideas of academic freedom about which she originally wrote. She was now determined to wade directly into what she viewed as a grand overreach of current applications of the legislation.

In a follow-up essay, also in the *Chronicle of Higher Education,* Kipnis once again underscored the core concepts of her own case and documented those of other colleagues who were also targeted under Title IX, especially the attack on her right to pen the initial critique. "I'd argued that the new codes infantilized students while vastly increasing the power of university administrators over all our lives," Kipnis notes pointing out the irony, "and here were students demanding to be protected by university higher-ups from the affront of someone's ideas, which seemed to prove my point. The president announced that he'd consider the petition."[54]

Her description of her experience also highlights the Star Chamber quality of the adjudication of these issues for faculty, ironically a style that is analogous to the kangaroo courts described by students in disciplinary cases on similar matters. Kipnis notes that in the Title IX complaint "I was being charged with retaliation . . . though it failed to explain how an essay that mentioned no one by name could be construed as retaliatory, or how a publication fell under the province of Title IX, which, as I understood it, dealt with sexual misconduct and gender discrimination."

Kipnis inquired of Northwestern's Title IX coordinator asking for clarification and details about the complaints, especially those that "appeared to violate my academic freedom?" She wanted to know "whether this was the first instance of Title IX charges filed over a publication. Was this a test case? From my vantage point, it seemed to pit a federally mandated program against my constitutional rights . . ."

Adding to the puzzle was how what appeared to be "intellectual disagreement," Kipnis's ideas in contrast to her accusers, was now "redefined as retaliation . . ." If this were in fact the case then "Wouldn't this mean that academic freedom doesn't extend to academics discussing matters involving their own workplaces?" But Kipnis contends that the replies to these simple questions were opaque, not specific and offered no procedure for the method by which the Title IX charges would be adjudicated.

In the face of this episode, Kipnis declares that, "Most academics I know—this includes feminists, progressives, minorities, and those who identify as gay or queer—now live in fear of some classroom incident spiraling into professional disaster." Faculty colleagues across the country wrote notes of congratulation and shared their fears. "My inbox became a clearinghouse for reports about student accusations and sensitivities," Kipnis reports, "and the collective terror of sparking them, especially when it comes to the dreaded subject of trigger warnings, since pretty much anything might be a 'trigger' to someone, given the new climate of emotional peril on campuses."

This leads to the larger question and conundrum: that as one climbs "the tenure ladder, the prize is academic freedom, the general premise being . . . that there's social value in fostering free intellectual inquiry."

But Kipnis warns, noting the larger problematic context in which academic freedom exists today, that "It's a value fast disappearing in the increasingly corporatized university landscape, where casual labor is the new reality." That is, that "Adjuncts, instructors, part-timers . . . simply don't have the same freedoms, practically speaking."

Though the concerns and issues Kipnis raised in the two essays were by no means original, her strong academic identity as a feminist scholar afforded no presumption of "good will" from her critics. She was charged for creating dynamics that threaten an environment essential to the safety of the university community. This allegation subsequently created a firestorm of controversy for Kipnis and Northwestern.

The reality of such treatment of academic liberty sets off alarm bells for academic freedom and free speech in the academy. The unsettling reality is that the complaints at Northwestern and elsewhere can proceed on such easy and ready avenues to litigation and other legal entanglements. Though brought forward by those who are contending for a moral good, the safety of the members of the community, the process and judgments reached in many cases can be needlessly tendentious and can lack fundamental fairness to those accused, as was the case for Kipnis.

These actions create an extraordinarily complex set of concerns for the academy that cannot be adjudicated by administrators and governing bodies alone. Faculties must take these matters with the utmost seriousness in order prevent an inarguable chill in the academic work place for faculty and for academe.

A second contemporary case involves the "trigger warnings" Kipnis excoriated and their unequivocal implications for academic freedom in the academy. Concern about pressure on faculty to provide "trigger warnings" for their courses and course content, and the prospect of mandates to do so at some colleges and universities led the AAUP to weigh in to protect the interests of faculty members.

The AAUP'S 2014 statement, ironically a year short of the one hundredth anniversary of its founding declaration, reveals the complexity of the "trigger warnings" issue. In it they point out the threat and chilling effect on academic freedom, free speech, and liberty for college and university professors. This is especially the case when a university caves to demands for mandatory policies as opposed to upholding faculty autonomy in the reaching of decisions about whether and when to issue such warnings.

The AAUP's considered thinking speaks for itself in its defense of the professoriate and the best interests of the academy. "A current threat to academic freedom in the classroom," they argue, "comes from a demand that teachers provide warnings in advance if assigned material contains anything that might trigger difficult emotional responses for students."[55]

The authors cite an Oberlin College proposed policy (tabled to permit greater faculty consideration at the time when the AAUP statement was written) as an example of "the range of possible trigger topics: racism, classism, sexism, heterosexism, cissexism (sic), ableism, and other issues of privilege and oppression."

However, the contrast with what should take place in the academy and in the intellectual setting of Robert Hutchins's idea of a "higher learning" could not be starker for the AAUP. "The presumption that students need to be protected rather than challenged in a classroom is at once infantilizing and anti-intellectual. It makes comfort a higher priority than intellectual engagement and—as the Oberlin list demonstrates—it singles out politically controversial topics like sex, race, class, capitalism, and colonialism for attention," the authors of the AAUP statement declare.

The impact on college and university faculty is obvious. "Trigger warning" pressures will make professors tend to avoid courses, topics, and content that could even remotely produce student complaints. Of course, the most affected group are untenured and other junior faculty, more highly exposed due to their less secure status against the slings and arrows of complaints. Nonetheless, the AAUP adds that, for all professors, "the demand for trigger warnings creates a repressive, "chilly climate" for critical thinking in the classroom."

With Oberlin as only one of numerous examples they could have cited, the AAUP notes that such "Institutional requirements or even suggestions that faculty use trigger warnings *interfere with faculty academic freedom* in the choice of course materials and teaching methods." Acknowledging that there can be cases of academic course material negatively affecting students, the right and responsibility for suggesting warnings must reside with faculty. By contrast, "Administrative requirements are different from individual faculty decisions. Administration regulation constitutes interference with academic freedom; faculty judgment is a legitimate exercise of autonomy."

For a century, the AAUP has stood to uphold the core beliefs and principles essential to the academy, and for its proper leadership and governance. The advent of trigger warnings is yet one more assault on the ideals that are at stake for the college and university, and one more moment for the AAUP to make a stand on behalf of college faculty nationwide.

In their statement the AAUP tackles the basic elements of what should constitute a college education, the "higher learning." To anyone who has thought about what constitutes education, the AAUP declaration about trigger warnings reminds us of the creed at the foundation of an education and of learning.

The core traditions of the academy, what is thought that a college education produces, are inarguably rooted, the AAUP notes, in firm commitment that "Some discomfort is inevitable in classrooms if the goal is to expose students to new ideas, have them question beliefs they have taken for granted, grapple with ethical problems they have never considered, and, more generally, expand their horizons so as to become informed and responsible democratic citizens." Trigger warnings are headed in one direction opposing that contention while the principles of the college push back from altogether another direction.

The AAUP's position is that trigger warnings lead to the infantilization of students. This is the same claim that Kipnis makes and for which she was being held account. The actions taken against her are evidence that the AAUP would cite as an infringement of academic freedom in these contests between the pro and con sides in the trigger warning debate.

"Trigger warnings suggest that classrooms should offer protection and comfort rather than an intellectually challenging education. They reduce students," the AAUP alleges, "to vulnerable victims rather than full participants in the intellectual process of education. The effect is to stifle thought on the part of both teachers and students who fear to raise questions that might make others 'uncomfortable.'"

The AAUP authors also "get it" regarding the overlap and conflation today of appeals for "trigger warnings" and the growing concerns about sexual violence on campuses. "It is probably not coincidental that the call for trigger warnings comes at a time," the report notes, "of increased attention to campus violence, especially to sexual assault that is often associated with the widespread abuse of alcohol." That may be true, but despite that they add, "Trigger warnings are a way of displacing the problem, however, locating its solution in the classroom rather than in administrative attention to social behaviors that permit sexual violence to take place."

In light of these recent early twenty-first-century controversies and contretemps about academic freedom and free speech, we return to Lucas's allegation. That is, that colleges and universities, at least since the McCarthy days, have tended to duck when confronting dueling forces in contests about academic liberty, be they within or from pressure outside the gates. In Lucas's parlance about mixed historical record, when push has come to shove, whenever "academe was pressured to cleanse itself of suspected dissidents, colleges and universities readily acceded." [56]

Does caving into pressure for institutionally mandated polices and restrictions about trigger warnings foisted on professors confirm Lucas's point of view? What is the effect of Kipnis's near institutional reprimand under a far reaching interpretation, though one unfortunately widely applied, of Title IX for writing an essay? The use of such a lever will get the attention of college professors and make them think twice before exercising free speech. That reality infringes academic freedom and forms another example of academe, in Lucas's mind, "readily acceding" to pressure to "cleanse itself."

We cannot be sure how cases similar to Kipnis and the AAUP's push back on "trigger warnings" will play out. Nor can we predict how similar cases both on the burner—continuing affirmative action and diversity battles, public speech by guest speakers on campuses, the politics over donors and their desire for influence—and unforeseen others will evolve. Whatever the issues are or will become, the fortunes of academic freedom and liberty in the academy are tied to how they will unfold.

The Kipnis case may never gain the high profile of that which Ward Churchill sparked on the backside of September 11th or certainly of Sweezy's battle which reached the Supreme Court. But the events that she confronted, and the extreme politics and ideologies at play reveal yet another round of how academic freedom and free speech are always at risk in the academy.

With such events in the contemporary mix, the logical question is "what's next?" If "trigger warnings" and a continual stretch of interpretations and applications of legal initiatives such as Title IX continue, it would seem that any pressure on academic freedom and free speech is possible.

We have seen many past examples of how free speech and academic freedom controversies can grow out of rhetoric and protests. When these episodes occur, whether from battles sparked by foreign and international entanglements of the United States in world and global affairs or by domestic, social-cultural ideological issues, inevitably there will be calls from critics of what is going on to curtail free speech as the remedy.

But as to the "what's next," as with any questions about the future, there is little point in getting into the game of prediction. However, what is clear is that, based on the history of these critical battles about academic freedom in higher education in America, we can be certain that controversies and assaults aimed at the academy over these core principles will unquestionably arise. At the same time, the stirring of public debate in these instances can be interpreted as good news, for it also means that the colleges and universities of the nation have maintained their autonomy and independence on the fronts of academic freedom, free speech, and liberty.

If the academy were to abandon that foundation and no longer maintain these beliefs about academic freedoms, no one would be at their doorstep bothering them about overreach and about the creation of problems that are inevitably part of the battles over those same principles. That is, to remain the academy, to perpetuate its identity and core purpose, it must maintain, in the words of Frankfurter, the "four essential freedoms" "of a university—'*to determine for itself on academic grounds who may teach, what may be taught, how it shall be taught, and who may be admitted to study.*'"[57]

# NOTES

1. Richard Hofstadter and Wilson Smith, eds. *American Higher Education: A Documentary History,* Volume I (Chicago: University of Chicago Press, 1961), 258.
2. Ibid.
3. Ibid.
4. Richard Hofstadter and Wilson Smith, eds. *American Higher Education: A Documentary History,* Volume II (Chicago: University of Chicago Press, 1961), 472.
5. Ibid.
6. Ibid., 473.
7. Ibid.
8. Thomas L. Haskell, "Justifying the Rights of Academic Freedom in the Era of 'Power/Knowledge,'" in *The Future of Academic Freedom,* ed. Louis Menand (Chicago: University of Chicago Press, 1996), 43–48. The interpretations that follow are drawn largely but not exclusively from Haskell's narrative.
9. Ibid.
10. Hofstadter and Smith, *American Higher Education: A Documentary History,* 845.
11. Ibid.
12. Ibid.
13. The Water Buffalo incident at Penn resulted from a male student yelling to a group of minority women students walking in the middle of the night past his dorm to shut up and stop "being water buffaloes." The comment was not a racist or racial slur and the student contended that he had no racist intentions. Rather he was merely trying to quiet some very loud student well into the early morning hours. Despite that, university disciplinary action was brought against him and he had to tender legal counsel to get himself back to Penn. At Dartmouth, the *Dartmouth Review* continually engaged in ad hominem attacks, taped faculty members in classes without their knowledge, and in their most aggressive action headlined an issue of their paper with "Ein Reich, Ein Volk, Ein Freedman" (mocking then President James Freedman), accusing the administration of packing conservative students on cattle trains and shipping them out of Hanover.
14. The material that follows is drawn from Theodore Herfurth, *Sifting and Winnowing,* 1949, Part I. http://www.library.wisc.edu/etext/WIReader/WER1035-Chpt1.html. The Ely affair at Wisconsin is also discussed in Stephen J. Nelson, *Decades of Chaos and Revolution: Showdowns for College Presidents* (Lanham, MD: Rowman & Littlefield), 45–46.
15. Herfurth, *Sifting and Winnowing.*
16. Ibid.
17. Laurence R. Veysey, *The Emergence of the American University* (Chicago: University of Chicago Press, 1965), 403.
18. Ibid.
19. Ibid.
20. Ibid., 406.
21. Ibid., 407.
22. Hofstadter and Smith, *American Higher Education: A Documentary History,* Volume II, 780.
23. Ibid.
24. Ibid., 781.
25. Ibid., 781–82.
26. Of particular note are the events leading to Kent State and Ronald Reagan's handling of a number of episodes at Berkeley and in the California University system. These are recounted in detail in Stephen J. Nelson, *Decades of Chaos and Revolution: Showdowns for College Presidents.* See especially, 17–18, 48–49 and 58–62.
27. Michael M. Sokal, "James McKeen Cattell, Nicholas Murray Butler and Academic Freedom at Columbia University, 1902–1923." *History of Psychology* 12, no. 2 (2009): 87–122, 87. Sokal alleges that Cattell was much an architect of his own demise.

However, his dismissal did follow on the heels of the dismissal of two other college faculty, even though these two as well could be viewed as having engaged in actions—refusal to merge Comparative Literature into English in one case, and allegations about flirtatious correspondence with a female employee by the other—that could be used as an excuse to sever them from the university. However, even though these two can be painted as agents provocateur, Sokal lays at Butler's feet much of blame because of his autocratic, detached leadership style and his penchant for such decisions as a demonstration of his power and office.

28. Ibid., 103. The Butler quote is from his Commencement Address, June 6, 1917, two months after United States entry into the war.

29. "Harvard Groups Condemn Butler's Columbia Speech: Defense Leagues, Teachers' Union, Deplores 'Fascism.'" http://www.thecrimson.com/article/1940/10/5/harvard-groups-condemn-butlers-columbia-speech/ (unpaginated).

30. A. Lawrence Lowell, *At War with Academic Traditions in America* (Cambridge, MA: Harvard University Press, 1934), 271. This quote and the ones following in fn. 31 and 32 were originally in Lowell's Report of President Lowell for 1916–17 presented to Harvard University. Excerpts of the report were also used in Lowell's essay "Discussions," *Educational Review*, December 1920 (New York: Educational Review Publishing Company, George H. Doran Company, Publishers): 431. His essay was juxtaposed with those of a number of other university presidents including Nicholas Butler on the subject of academic freedom and free speech.

31. Ibid.

32. Ibid.

33. Hofstadter and Smith, *American Higher Education: A Documentary History*, 869–870.

34. Ibid.

35. Ibid., 870.

36. Ibid.

37. Haskell, 53.

38. Ibid.

39. Ibid.

40. Ibid., 54.

41. Ibid.

42. Ellen Schrecker, *The Lost Soul of Higher Education: Corporatization, the Assault on Academic Freedom, and the End of the American University* (New York: The New Press, 2010). Her book's title gives away her point of view.

43. The following summary of the Sweezy case is based on Robert C. Cloud, "Sweezy v. New Hampshire, "Law and Higher Education," http://lawhighereducation.org/124-sweezy-v-new-hampshire.html.

44. Ibid., unpaginated.

45. Schrecker, 18–19.

46. Sweezy vs. New Hampshire, 354 U.S. 589 (1957), as cited by Schrecker, 19.

47. Schrecker, 19.

48. Ibid. Italics mine.

49. Justice Felix Frankfurter Opinion in Sweezy vs. New Hampshire in Robert K. Carr, Academic Freedom, the American Association of University Professors, and the United States Supreme Court, AAUP Bulletin, Vol. 45, No. 1 (Mar., 1959), 5–24, 19.

50. Christopher J. Lucas, *American Higher Education: A History* (New York: St. Martins Press, 1994), 305.

51. Ibid., 306.

52. This happened at Wellesley College in 1993 when Professor Tony Martin placed on a syllabus for one of his courses sources that alleged Jewish involvement in the American slave trade. This led to a campus kerfuffle that included Martin writing a vanity press book defending his position and decrying those who had vilified him. However, because he named names and excoriated what he viewed as his opponents in ad hominem attacks, the college's president, Diana Chapman Walsh, supported by

her senior cabinet, judged that Martin had gone beyond academic free speech by violating tenets of civility at the college. That judgment resulted "only" in censuring rather than censoring Martin in response.

53. Laura Kipnis, "Sexual Paranoia Strikes Academe," February 27, 2015, http://chronicle.com/article/Sexual-Paranoia-Strikes/190351/, np. The quotes that follow are taking from this essay.

54. Laura Kipnis, "My Title IX Inquisition," May 29, 2015, http://chronicle.com/article/My-Title-IX-Inquisition/230489/, np. The quotes that follow are taking from this essay.

55. This report was drafted by a subcommittee of Committee A on Academic Freedom and Tenure in August 2014 and has been approved by Committee A. http://www.aaup.org/report/trigger-warnings, unpaginated. The quotes below are taken from this document.

56. Lucas, 306.

57. Schrecker, 19. Italics mine.

# SEVEN

## The Disuniting of America and the University

*A Reprise of Academic Freedom and the Threat of Balkanization in the Quest for Pluralism and Diversity*

On the backside of World War II, after five plus years of warfare and international turmoil, America as a nation and its colleges and universities were at last able to return their attention to considerations other than war and its potential outcome. The post-World War II period for the college and university was to become a remarkably different time from previous eras. On the heels of the war, the decades of the late 1940s, 50s, and 60s for the academy featured both resolved and unresolved issues and problems inherited from the war years and those lingering from more distant previous decades as well.

The past always shapes the present and the future. World War II consumed the nation, requiring untold fiscal and human resources and investment, and robust commitment. Pent up demands and needs created post-war decades when new occasions arose, new duties were required. Opportunities for innovation and change swirled both auspiciously and inauspiciously, and often seductively, around the college and university. In short, the complexities of the post-World War II era intensified the ever-present strains on the university's mission and identity.

The massive changes and new initiatives of that era have been recounted in many histories of the college and university in America, and are taken into account as well in these pages. The short, though by no means exclusive list includes major investments in higher education ignited by national developments and social needs. The primary push came in the form of increased federal budgetary commitments for higher

223

education, complemented by state-by-state investment in public college and university education.

These new developments engineered by federal commitments in the immediate post-war years included: The GI Bill, funding tuition, and providing incentives to soldiers who had fought in World War II to resume, or for the first time enroll in college; investments in campus infrastructure through hefty support of federal dollars and grants designated for construction of new facilities, including dormitories to accommodate rapidly expanding enrollments, in large measure of returning GIs; government dollars to support research and development, and to address the engineering and scientific challenges brought about by the Cold War and the Space Race with the Soviet Union.

As the post-World War II era continued to unfold in the later 1950s and early 1960s, the faucet of federal dollars opened in the form of additional student tuition grants, loans, and aid. The civil rights era pushed onto the national agenda the need to address obligations for the educational needs of black Americans. Colleges and universities responded with major admissions outreach and recruitment programs, including the necessary financial aid to bring minority students to campuses in greater numbers.

However, further expanded federal assistance was required to adequately support the effort to close gaps in the education of black students, along with emerging concern about long-standing needs of socio-economically disadvantaged students aspiring to college. A major step in this direction was passage of the Higher Education Act of 1965 (part of Lyndon Johnson's Great Society program and reauthorized innumerable times in the fifty years since) that among other things incorporated the launch of the Pell Grant program (named after Senator Claiborne Pell of Rhode Island) of federal scholarship and aid for payment of college tuition costs for students in financial need.

The overall effect of these legislative initiatives and injections of massive dollars for higher education was enormous. For the first time in history, other than the one-time commitment of the landmark Morrill Land Grant program of the 1860s, the federal government was now in a regular, sustained role, directly supporting the colleges and universities of the land. But as we shall see, these injections and commitments proved not to be a unanimous success story.

These financial commitments were complemented by additional state taxpayer support for their individual public campuses. The states had local interest in the success of their land grant major research universities and of the other public universities growing in many cases from the normal schools of the mid-1800s and early 1900s, along with the burgeoning community college sector.

Throughout the post-World War II years, the country and the academy were becoming more pluralistic. Those citizens previously denied access, or at least fuller access, to higher education—minorities, the socio-economically deprived, as well as women—now found the gates of colleges and universities opened fully, or at least in some fashion, to them. The result was that over a period of less than twenty-five years from the mid-1940s to the end of the decade of the 1960s, the landscape of higher education in America changed dramatically, arguably in some cases being fundamentally reshaped.

The nation was becoming rapidly more diverse. It was continuing, though in fits and starts, to confront its mixed and not glowing history on the front of race, racism, race relations, and racial equity, and of women's and other minority rights. In order to keep pace, the world of higher education necessarily had to listen to and to follow nationally developing, even if widely contested, trends. This movement aimed at righting previous wrongs and at expanding efforts to incorporate all citizens more fully into the academy and society, and as contributors to the common good.

The history of pluralism is inevitably a grab bag of far-reaching promises and hopes, and of dashed dreams. Pluralism, and all that it means, fashions an ideal state of affairs, especially in any democracy and in democratic institutions. That is especially true as the ideal of pluralism leads to targeted embrace of previously denied sectors of citizens and leads newly arrived immigrants to more full participation in the body politic. This is the American commitment, unique in the world of civic duty and commonwealths and nations: *E pluribus unum*, out of many, one.

Commitments and goals for greater diversity and for expanded participation in a body politic are admirable. However, pluralism can also have a downside when ideologies capture "the one," investing in meeting the needs of individuals and their rights, but at expense of the "many." When that happens pluralism is highjacked, and the result is erosion of hard-won efforts at unity.

Thus, to what extent, if at all, do the college and university and the American nation presently confront precisely this problem? And if so when did pluralism, always embedded in the creed of the American Republic, become sufficiently pronounced to threaten unity and coherence in the academy and in society? If balkanization today threatens the college and university in America, when did that era begin? Or have disunity, balkanization, and polarized political camps always been with us in one form or another? If in fact such splintering and lack of a center that holds is the state of affairs in- and outside the academy, what if anything has been or might be done to address that condition?

America claims to be a nation of diversity and to embrace people from diverse countries around the world. Is "Give me your tired, your poor, your huddled masses yearning to breathe free," the signature invitation proclaimed by the Statue of Liberty, greeting everyone, but especially immigrants from all lands, a realized or even achievable ideal? Or is it simply nice rhetoric with little hope of being translated into reality?

## THE COLONIAL COLLEGES: THE EARLY FACE
## OF DIVERSITY IN THE AMERICAN ACADEMY

An argument can be made that the decades since World War II have featured heightened worries about the sway of pluralism, diversity, and balkanization in the academy and in the nation. However, an equal claim can be made that at least for the academy, and with little doubt for America as well, balkanization was in the water and has presented challenges from the very beginnings of the colonial era.

This state of affairs became more pronounced as the first Colonial Colleges proliferated to a total of nine and were then rapidly joined by numerous denominational and sectarian colleges in the late eighteenth and early decades of the nineteenth centuries. There appeared always to be some new leader, some new faction, a different way of doing things, all distinguished from and challenging what was viewed as tradition, or what had been.

At the origins of the American college, one of the early battle lines was a religious, theological ideological one. Prior to 1740, about a century into the history of the academy in the New World, only three colleges had been founded, in order: Harvard (1636), William and Mary (1693), and Yale (1701).[1]

This was not a large field of play and they were all quite small in size and scale. However, divisions over theological points of view developed early within the Puritan Congregationalists in the Massachusetts Bay Colony. That caused a fracture: the Congregationalists who later founded Yale departed as exiles to the lower Connecticut River Valley. Though not thrown out by Harvard per se, the ties between Harvard and the governing authorities of the commonwealth were in close accord. Consequently Harvard's culture and leadership had a hand in pushing their colleagues out.

Each of these first three schools was rooted in their founders' mainstream religious background, practice, and communities (Puritan, Anglican Congregational respectively). The divide within the Congregationalists deepened further with the Great Awakening in the 1730s and 40s, a split between the New Light revivalist preachers and followers, and the anti-revivalist Old Lights. This splintering, though occurring throughout New England, was most pronounced for the academy as reflected in what went on at Yale, where the Old Lights succeeded in restricting and then banning the New Lights from attendance and even from appearance on the campus.

Inspired by this experience of the defining role of religious beliefs and practice in the foundation of educational institutions established by a denomination, of the next six colleges coming on the map between the founding of Yale in 1701 and the Revolutionary War in 1776, four [Princeton (1746), Brown (1764), Rutgers (1766), and Dartmouth (1769)] were founded by "ministers and laymen with revivalist backgrounds and points of view."[2]

The revivalist fervor of these four colleges reflected and embodied the march toward religious freedom and liberty begun by Roger Williams in 1636 (same year as the founding of Harvard) when he founded the Providence Plantation colony after being forced out of the Massachusetts Bay Colony in 1633.

Princeton, Brown, Rutgers, and Dartmouth all had charters that "stated explicitly that the colleges were intended to serve Protestants of all denominations and forbade religious tests for admission." Douglas Sloan claims that one explanation for the stands made in their charters "has stressed that the charters gave expression to a real and growing sense of the need for religious freedom and denominational cooperation."[3]

This commitment to religious liberty and freedom was in turn driven by the presumption that, "Many of the revivalists also had a vision of an America unified in one great communal movement toward the realization of God's Kingdom on Earth."[4] Thus, even if a paradox, the desire to permit each group to go its own way religiously would result in their corporate spirit and commitments to produce a unity of the body politic, albeit presumed as all were Christian, that unified community would establish "God's Kingdom on Earth."

Thus despite religious diversity—and Thomas Jefferson and James Madison would argue as a beneficiary of the competing denominations—a unified body politic and commonweal was assumed and expected. In the context of these hopes of the Republic, religiously based and denominationally founded colleges and their cultures had to exert great care to at least regard highly, if not help to ensure, freedom and autonomy, at least rhetorically, for all citizens regardless the tightly held beliefs and creeds of the committed religious believers.

Thereby, in juggling sectarian beliefs with the demands of the Republic and to assert that they were open to all comers, leaders of colleges who were revivalist advocates of religious freedom and liberty were convinced that litmus tests in student admissions and faculty hiring had to be avoided. Likewise they were on guard about the slippery slope toward balkanization of their campuses and about the impact on national civic life of sectarian groups that were not committed to a unified society and to their role in it. These commitments informed the view that "Sectarian requirements for college attendance could only subvert such a vision," of a unified land and society, "God's Kingdom."[5]

The revivalists' convictions about religious beliefs and the common good were spawned by the persecution many had "experienced at the hands of the established churches and were determined to work toward greater separation of church and state."[6] All of these experiences and the revivalists' beliefs spilled into the culture and academic life of their colleges. When it came to the academy, many revivalists, "contrary to accusations then and since," did "have a high regard for learning and were not willing to subordinate it entirely to religious and sectarian ends."[7]

Consequently these early colonial origins and political theories in- and outside the gates of the college stressed caution about the dangers of balkanization. It was clear that the splintering of groups and factions with little commitment and interest in the unity of the commonweal would harm the common good. The hopes of the nascent Republic would as a result be at risk.

Though not all agreed or expressed concern, many colonial leaders including those of colleges viewed this risk as something to be feared. That is, sectarian and denominational factions, the theologically ideological competitors of the day, if driven to separatism and distinctiveness rather than toward unity, would erode the civic polity and the good of the commonweal. But by and large these factions recognized a responsibility for themselves and for their fellow citizens to avoid that disuniting outcome.

Hence, the earliest days colonial pluralism and diversity were viewed as hand in glove with the tough issues on the road to pursue the goal of a unified body politic. At the same time, as is always the case, that same pluralism and diversity created challenges to reaching social and cultural unity. Balkanization that would wreak havoc on unity and open the door to disunity lurked at every turn. However, one antidote to this dilemma was rejection of litmus tests and the establishment of efforts to insure an open door to the colleges of the land. These were signs that pluralism and diversity, essential as part of the American way, yet could be present under one tent in the academy and in society was well.

What would serve as a counterweight to the competing demands and interests of these citizens of pre-Republic society and of the early academics in the college was the "vision of an America unified," albeit wholly rooted in Christian beliefs, "in one great communal movement toward the realization of God's Kingdom on Earth."[8]

## GRAPPLING WITH BALKANIZATION IN
## THE NATION AND THE ACADEMY

A historical viewpoint is critical in developing a reasoned perspective about the issues and questions raised from the grappling of academy and the country with pluralism and diversity, and with the dangers of balkanization when a coherent center no longer holds. It is difficult, if not impossible to assess adequately how these dilemmas have been handled in the contemporary era absent the context of an understanding of how folks in previous eras viewed similar struggles in the times in which they lived.

That history over the last forty to fifty years reveals that pluralism and diversity become divisive when they come only in extreme designs advocated by the politics of ideology. This danger is that seemingly admirable goals—embracing diversity, recognizing that there is "the many" as well as the hope for "the one," and that social and economic equity should be sought and instilled—are schemed to the point at which they threaten social and cultural unity, and coherence both within and outside the gates of the academy.

The same argument regarding the quest for pluralism and diversity and all its connected challenges could be made concerning the closely related history of balkanization and the splintering of consensus and coherence. That is, previous eras to our own were presumed, and often romanticized by later generations, to have had a sufficient dedication and wisdom about unity to generate the capacity to hold the center. But that idealized version of events and of the role of key players is not always what it seems.

Thus, as historical observers we have to rely on the participants and commentators from other eras to inform what we are able to conclude about the times in which they lived. Regarding our inquiry, it is through the eyes of prominent figures in previous eras that we can gain an intimate view from which to characterize their times. This perspective includes the ways in which political and social events, and battles and tensions over pluralism and diversity, and whatever balkanization was created by ideological contests had an effect on the college and university.

Did those forces of pluralism and diversity, especially in ideological guises, conspire to wreak havoc on the academy? If so, when and how did that happen? Did forces of pluralism and diversity countervail core principles of the academy? Were the vital principles of the academy and the Republic placed at risk, or were they able to adapt to these changes? If pluralism and diversity produced fundamental changes, even to the extent of balkanization, was that for better or worse?

Snapshots of those bygone eras as well as those from our times serve to contrast the difficulties and demands of the quest for unity, "*E pluribus unum*," with the centripetal pressures exerted by diversity on one hand and pluralism on the other. Once again we confront the age-old American dilemma: balancing individual liberty and personal freedoms with the good of the commonweal, with a society that has coherence in its body politic, social order, and democratic governing principles.

To get a handle on these questions and states of affairs, we will cover questions of academic freedom, free speech, and the crafting of the collegiate curriculum similar to that in the previous chapter. We will also preview concerns tackled in the next chapter that will focus on the ideological battleground.

Issues and battles over academic freedom and over ideological pressures from within and from outside the college and university, at first appearing to be discrete affairs, end up blending into each other in the academy. Academic freedom and free speech, including its responsibility in curricular duties, and the role of ideological pressures are intertwined with the challenges of pluralism and diversity in the college and university. This is especially true in the wrestling about whether the center of the academy and of the Republic can hold. Thus the questions at hand in this chapter, taken together, cover two crucial chunks of ground.

First, the experience of disunity in the nation and in the university presents a discrete set of challenges to be addressed by the academy and throughout the Republic. Questions about the resulting threats of balkanization call for analysis and commentary. Second, inquiry concerning the impact of pressures created by a more pluralistic society and the accompanying demands for diversity in and out of the academy also serves as a bridge between concerns about academic freedom that we have addressed and about the ideological, political battles of the academy that we will tackle next.

## ACADEMIC FREEDOM AND PLURALISM AND DIVERSITY: A REPRISE FROM CHARLES ELIOT

Academic freedom in the academy is always navigated through the shoals of pluralism and diversity balanced with aspirations that the civic good and the interests of the commonweal are not compromised.

On one hand is the argument that the values and beliefs in the creed of pluralism and diversity trump other principles, including academic freedom. As an example of only one aspect of this danger, one must consider the challenges posed to academic freedom by the multicultural and diversity push to force changes in the collegiate curriculum on so many campuses in the late 1980s and 1990s.

On the other hand is the fear that the unity of the academy and the nation is put at risk by the voices of critics and naysayers inside the gates who no longer affirm the importance of coherence and unity. They and only they have the autonomy and protection of academic freedom and free speech to attack whoever and whatever they wish in the body politic and the nation as a whole. As only one example, think of the protests and criticisms in the 1960s and 1970s of the Vietnam War and of the military-industrial complex that professors in the academy mounted in the face of highly debated policy and actions of national government, and the corporate, industrial, and business establishments.

Toward the end of his forty-year tenure as president of Harvard, Charles Eliot weighed in about academic freedom. Eliot declared his thinking and philosophy in a published article subsequent to an address he made at a 1907 Phi Beta Kappa induction ceremony at Cornell University. His thoughts were published a few years after the Ross Affair in which Professor Edward Ross was forced out of Stanford by Jane Stanford's orders, carried out by its president, David Starr Jordan.

For decades and centuries before and since Eliot's time of the early twentieth century, American leaders and citizens have wrung their hands about a critical issue unique in the foundations and story of this nation. That is, the juggling of the creed and unifying interests of a democracy with the need to sustain the vitality of that same democracy's vision of freedom designed to guarantee that the thoughts, opinions, and actions of an increasingly diverse population are able to be wholeheartedly expressed.

Eliot proclaims what he and fellow leaders and citizens in and outside the academy had to grapple with, especially in a Constitutional American democracy barely over 125 years old. The balance of the right of free speech and disparate public opinions, with a commitment to a unified creed and belief that a democracy can have a center that holds, was not in Eliot's or any time an easy task. This tension was and always has been pronounced both in educational settings and in moments when denizens of the academy use academic freedom to venture into the public square.

Eliot claims, as though the country had not seen this movie before, that:

> the principal new difficulty is the pressure in a democracy of a concentrated multitudinous public opinion. The great majority of the people in a given community may hold passionately to some dogma in religion, some economic doctrine, or some political or social opinion or practise, and may resent strongly the expression by a public teacher, [using their academic freedom,] of religious, economic, political, or social views unlike those held by the majority.[9]

Eliot is concerned about the tyranny of the minority, something on which the political correctness critics of later in the twentieth century harped repeatedly. That ideological camp, in the 1980s to the present day, continually argued that marginal and minority interests, promoted by the few and catering to a small slice of the academic community, were holding sway. Eliot pushes the problem as he saw it a step further in a classical argument, always festering in the academy and in a nation-state. "This multitudinous tyrannical opinion is even more formidable to one who offends it than the despotic will of a single tyrant or small group of tyrants." Eliot argues:

It affects the imagination more because it seems omnipresent, merciless, and irresponsible; and therefore resistance to it requires a rare kind of moral courage. . . . For this difficulty there is no remedy except the liberalizing of the common people, or at least of the educated class.

Which in Eliot's mind is a duty of the university.[10] Then ahead of his time, Eliot notes with loathing an alternate solution. That is, "To be sure, there is another mode of preventing free teaching on dangerous subjects, which is quite as effective as persecution and much quieter, namely, the omission of all teaching on those subjects, and the elimination of reading matter bearing on them."[11]

This approach of avoiding controversial topics and engagement of debate and discourse altogether became prominent in the multicultural and diversity-political correctness debates of the end of the twentieth century. It has also come to the fore in the recent "trigger point" controversies about what college professors can or should do in the teaching of their courses.

Eliot doesn't name names. But his sights are no doubt on high-profile academic freedom cases of the day. "Many a professor in this country has felt acutely that he was not entirely free to publish in journals or books just what he thought on controversial subjects, if he put in connection with his signature his official title as professor. Doubtless some difficult cases of this sort," alluding to the firing of Edward Ross at Stanford and the charges against Richard Ely at Wisconsin but beaten back, "arise in which the reputation of an institution is unfavorably affected temporarily by the publications, or public speeches of one or more of its officers . . ."[12]

Eliot underscores the danger of institutional overreaction to perceived faculty miscreants which ends up being equal to any damage a professor could be alleged to have done: The problem of course is that ". . . no satisfactory defense against this kind of injury has yet been invented, since the suppression of such publications does infinitely more harm to the general cause of education than it can do good to the institution concerned."[13] Extending the example that the academy can and should provide for the nation, Eliot makes a suggestion based on his nearly forty years in the college presidency. "The government of a good college or university in the United States, which is free from denominational or political control," Eliot declares, "foretells the type of the best ultimate forms of human government."[14] For him, this comprises the principles of free speech, of an embrace of diversity and pluralism, without permitting special interests to take over in the academy, and it should be a model for the country.

Comparing college presidents and other college leaders to their counterparts in military, business, and government, Eliot further argues that leaders in the academy are the most ideal. He bases this contention on how well-equipped academic leaders, read presidents, are able, often with little choice, to deal with diversity and difference of opinion, and with the needs and voice of the individual juxtaposed to the fundamental requirements of the commons and a community. Eliot does not believe that leaders in other professional walks of life have the requisite agility and wisdom to juggle these competing, frequently presented as mutually exclusive, choices and demands born out of diversity, and diverse thinking and views.

Eliot points out that crucial in a democracy and in a nation is the necessity for leaders and the body politic to be able to juggle these disparate, often competing values. Counterparts of college presidents in other walks of life are too prone to be autocrats, despots, figureheads, or in the case of captains of industry who are "governed by motives, and pursue[s] ends, which are neither altruistic nor idealistic" to be able to juggle well the interests of the individual and their needs and liberties with the good of the whole.[15] It is college and university leaders, in Eliot's mind exclusively, who possess the know-how to fashion that critical balance.

What is it about leaders of a college that makes them distinctive from contemporaries in other sectors of business, industry, and government? It appears to Eliot that a portion of this difference is due to the culture and creedal beliefs of the academy. That culture of the academy requires an ideal balance (as should any institution and society, and especially those that claim democratic and consensus principles at their foundations), between the rights of individuals and expressions of their individualism with the unity that a coherent collective community, an organization, or nation-state demands.

The way any collective body, a body politic, a campus culture, a nation or group holds together is by belief in equality, in the common good but also the individual good of all, the American notion of life, liberty and the pursuit of happiness for all comrades and citizens. "At this moment the university administrator makes the best use now made of the powers of individualism on one hand, and of collectivism on the other, and," Eliot adds, "understands better than any other leader in the world that in order to have successful cooperative action on the part of thousands of human beings, special emphasis must be laid on brotherhood in that admirable trinity—freedom, equality and brotherhood."[16]

Eliot held high ideals, even if his prophecy about the academy leading the nation, even the world, has not turned out exactly as he had hoped. Even if less than the influence Eliot wished, the role and influence of the America college and university on the country, the government, and society remains nonetheless unsurpassed when compared to any other nation in the world. Furthermore, Eliot's description of the culture of a university is spot-on: "The American university gives an effective demonstration of the good results of the voluntary association in common work of many independent and unlike individuals possessing the maximum of goodwill . . ."[17]

No more apt description could be made for the attitude toward pluralism and diversity of the academy. However, Eliot gets out on a limb by
claiming "academic freedom," that core principle of the academy "is,
therefore, a good type of the considerate, humane freedom which will
ultimately become universal."[18] Eliot's vision for academic freedom to be
exported and universalized in the nation and the world is a grand idea.
But that of course did not happen in his time and has yet to happen in
ours, however worthy that aspiration may be.

## THE DISUNITING OF AMERICA AND THE ACADEMY:
## THE PROBLEM AND ITS PROSPECTS

More than two decades ago the noted historian Arthur Schlesinger, Jr.
addressed what he believed to be a "coming apart at the seams" of America and American society.[19] He was troubled about the drift posed by
debates within and outside the gates of the academy over diversity,
multiculturalism, and the ideological politics shot through the discussion. The result was the tearing of the fundamental fabric of society and
the nation.

In the 1990s, when Schlesinger took sides in the multiculturalism and
diversity debate, he was considered a dean among American historians.
He had been a liberal voice challenging the status quo in the protests and
civic discourse about the Vietnam War and civil rights three decades
prior. But now Schlesinger's attitudes about society, culture, and the nation led him to be a guardian at the gates, trying to protect the Republic,
democracy in America, and the traditional ways in the academy.

Schlesinger was primarily concerned about America as a nation, about
the creed of the Republic. However, he also knew that there exists a
symbiotic relationship of the nation's educational institutions and their
values with the state of affairs and future prospects of the nation itself.

Schlesinger believed that traditional principles and values were being
unfairly questioned, too easily ignored, and precipitously cast aside.
These beliefs constituted the fundamental creed in the foundation of
America, its democracy, and the commonweal and common good of the
Republic. The nation and its destiny are at risk if the unity on which it
depends becomes dashed by the disunity that surely results from tilting
too far from the broad center in an effort to meet the exclusive needs of
interest groups and constituencies. That balkanization would place the
Republic itself in danger.[20]

What to make of this? Schlesinger addressed overarching national and
societal questions, but they were also questions initiated and shaped in
the academy, frequently originating as ideas raised and nurtured from
within its walls. The litany of what was being wrestled with and con-

tended at colleges and universities was as comprehensive as it was fundamental to their core mission and purpose.

Was the drive to emphasize individual group, constituency-based, some would argue tribal, clannish, identities taking precedence over the identity of being first a citizen, of equals in a common enterprise, and of what it means to be an American? Could the goal of including "new" curricular material in schools, elementary through college, be accomplished without pushing out traditional, classical content and knowledge? Were the calls for a more diverse curriculum wreaking havoc with a traditional educational approach to teaching rooted in the fundamental foundations that ground a society?

There has always been a connection and interaction in the United States between the basis of what it means to be an American, of an American identity, and of how diverse constituencies in a democracy are able to carve out their various group identities, with the foundation and formation of the academy, the college and university in America. However, Schlesinger didn't lose hope.

The early 1990s were still a highly contentious time. The battering and influence of dueling constituencies, factions and polarities of the political correctness era, begun a decade or longer before, continued. Despite that Schlesinger declares that "The belief in a unique American identity is far from dead."[21]

With the multicultural curricular and other political correctness debates of the day on his front burner, Schlesinger judged and found of great concern the impact of the polemics that were being tossed about on the academy. Nonetheless, he remained sufficiently optimistic to see a way out of this forest. "The situation in our universities, I am confident," he concluded, "will soon right itself once the great silent majority of professors cry 'enough' and challenge what they know to be voguish nonsense."[22]

Schlesinger and his commentary could be characterized as curmudgeonly. However, his edgy judgments about what was going on in the society, culture, politics, and schools reveal realities that Schlesinger was witnessing, especially from the late 1970s to the early 1990s.

For example, while he gives some quarter to his opponents in the polemical jousting spawned by a State of New York report that called for a major injection of ethnic and non-Euro-centric material in the state's schools, he was highly critical of the report's conclusions and how emblematic of those times they were. In the face of the diversity and multicultural push of the 1980s and 90s embodied in what New York planned to do, Schlesinger was convinced that crucial aspects of the traditional education to which students should be exposed were being thrown overboard. Further, he believed that throwing out the old-fashioned content and learning would severely damage the fabric of the nation.

"The belief in the unifying force of democratic ideals finds no echo in the report, no doubt," Schlesinger suggests, "because the ideals were disqualified by their Eurocentric origin. Indeed, the report takes *no interest in the problem of holding a diverse republic together.*" If that weren't bad enough, Schlesinger notes the irony that even though there was some good that the multicultural emphasis might do, the reality was that, by dividing rather than uniting people and their ideas, "Its impact is rather to sanction and deepen racial tensions."[23]

Schlesinger is on the neoconservative side of the debate about diversity interests and minority group identity. He is committed to sustain the values, beliefs, and culture he believes to be vitally embedded in the fabric of America and of the academy. These values, in his opinion, had served the nation well and were the reason why the country is what it is. To Schlesinger, the balkanization that results from overly fixating on the needs of any constituency, and allowing it to become separated in the body politic to the point where it has little or no stake in the commonweal, is a threat to the Republic.

His fears were shared by those on his side of the fence in these multicultural battles. Their nightmare was that if the "new," the less traditional curriculum significantly displaced the tried and true—modest accommodation would be okay, though not believed necessary—Schlesinger's notion of "disunity of America" would result.

Although Schlesinger's views about changes taking place in schools and colleges would be judged as less-than-progressive in some quarters, his stand was rooted in deep concern about the Republic. For him and for traditionalists like him there exists an obvious connection between what America does with its educational system, with the curriculum in schools from secondary to the collegiate arena, and the good of the Republic. Faltering in the former—America's educational institutions and their culture—would produce serious negative consequences for the latter: the capacity to uphold and to sustain a Republic based in democratic values and principles.

Schlesinger's thinking was sparked by the tension emerging on college campuses at that time—and continuing to this day, twenty-five years later—between traditional commitments to free speech and inquiry, and protections for students alleging that they suffered discrimination and mistreatment. Although he could be accused of presenting a false choice, Schlesinger asks that "Presidents and deans begin to ask themselves, which is more important—protecting free speech or preventing racial persecution?"[24]

The puzzle for Schlesinger is that the answer to the choice raised by this question should be quite clear. That is, "The Constitution, Justice Holmes said, embodies 'the principle of free thought—not free thought for those who agree with us but freedom for the thought that we hate.'" Campuses should have better understood and heeded Schlesinger's question about what should happen when "the thought we hate under-cuts the Constitution's ideal of equal justice under law? Does not the First Amendment protect equality as well as liberty? How to draw a bright line between speech and behavior?"[25]

There is an enduring, robust link between the lively experiment of the academy in America and the experiment that is the Republic. Distinguishing the nation, but revealed in connected concerns about the state of the nation's educational system, including higher education, Schlesinger contends, "The Republic embodies ideals that transcend ethnic, religious, and political lines. It is an experiment, reasonably successful for a while, in creating a common identity for people of diverse races, religions, languages, cultures."[26]

However, the contemporary concern is that if Schlesinger's critique remains unchanged and has not been addressed twenty years after it was made, then one might question whether the experiment that is the American ideal is still able to transcend factions that are at odds at least and divisive at worst. That "experiment can continue to succeed only so long as Americans continue to believe in the goal. If the republic now turns away from Washington's old goal of 'one people,' what is its future?" Schlesinger questions, "—disintegration of the national community, apartheid, Balkanization, tribalization?"[27]

Schlesinger is a traditionalist, and even though he represents one part of the debate over issues of diversity, pluralism, and the threat of disunity, he does so grounded in principles that could well predict the long-range prospects for the nation and its colleges and universities. "The question America confronts as a pluralistic society is how to vindicate cherished cultures and traditions without," and here the critical point shot through Schlesinger's concern, "breaking the bonds of cohesion—common ideals, common political institutions, common language, common culture, common fate—that hold the republic together."

America's uniqueness is characterized by how it has sustained a creed demanding that it balance the rights of the individual with the needs of the commonweal, and that it permit diverse groups and people to enjoy freedom and independence, yet still adhere to the foundational unity of the Republic. Capturing that quest, Schlesinger turns to Frenchmen Hector St. John de Crevecoeur's observations about America, "What then is the American, this new man? . . . Here individuals of all nations are melted into a new race of men." Crevecoeur's answer to his rhetorical question leads Schlesinger to conclude: "Still a good answer—still the best hope."[28]

## THE CONTEMPORARY UNIVERSITY: CAN IT AVOID
## BALKANIZATION AND DYSTOPIA?

We have witnessed ways in which pluralism and diversity in the academy are able at times to play a complementary role rather than to function in a mutually exclusive zero-sum game with visions for the good of the whole. However, we also have seen how tensions are inevitable when the quest for pluralism and diversity, especially when pushed by strongly ideological forces, is juxtaposed and can readily come in conflict with the academy's fundamental commitment to academic freedoms and liberty.

If balkanization in the academy is to be avoided, these principles and passions undergirding the rights of individuals and the ability for diverse groups to develop independent identities must find ways to co-exist with each other. The common good must be sustained in the process. Because of the creed of the academy, all of these forces and interests must bend to sustain the core ideas of academic freedom. It is academic free speech and liberty that fundamentally define the shape of the college and university. This delicate and essential balance has been pursued from the colonial era through the decades of twentieth century.

The interplay of these ideals and values is unavoidable in the college and university. Because of their nature and the passions of their advocates, pluralism and diversity inevitably compete and battle at times with the desire for a united body politic.

At the same time all of these forces must figure out how to be shaped in a fashion that goes hand in glove with the university's commitments to teaching, research, and scholarship, and to its civic face and contributions in the public square. Handled wisely, as Eliot points to in the exemplar of the college leader, qua the president, these forces can co-exist and avoid becoming mutually exclusive. When these potentially dueling interests and passions are able to complement each other, they serve to build up the fabric of a college and university. When they fail to do so, one sure result is balkanization and dystopia.

However, the best ideals and hopes of the academy and in its best interests can be submerged and lost in the scuffle, however principled, of ideological controversies and wrestling. The most dangerous threat is that posed by warring political camps seeking to turn the university into something other than the university: a partisan establishment, a political party, a social movement, an institution catering to every social and societal demand, any or all which disregard the academy's primary mission and purpose.

As pointed out, from the get-go these tensions and troubles have been in the water of the college as well as the nation in America. However, at the end of the last century, and persisting in the twenty-first century, these ideological battlegrounds and their threat of turning the university into something other than the university inarguably became more pronounced both in and outside the gates of the academy.

Donald Downs is a historian with interest in the contemporary state of affairs in the college and university in America and the arenas of protest, the stature of administrative leadership, and the responses to tense, conflict-ridden events. Downs's focus grows out of personal experience: he was an undergraduate at Cornell University at the time of the black student takeover of Willard Straight Hall, the student union there in April 1969.

Decades later he investigated that episode as a historian. The result is a compelling narrative, much based on the recollections of key players, of the events and decisions that unfolded during the dramatic days of the students' actions and their aftermath.[29]

Downs has extensively probed controversies regarding free speech and liberty in the contemporary college and university.[30] He uses the label of "free speech and liberty" as the defining elements of academic freedom. He argues that adding "liberty" to understandings of academic freedom is important because it is frequently ignored or overlooked in discussions of free speech in the academy. "Liberty" for academics and in their academic culture is a comprehensive and overarching concept deserving considered deliberation.

He rivets on the nature of free speech and liberty episodes as case studies of what is happening on campuses across the country. Downs seeks to reveal what the contesting parties—presidents, administrators, trustees, faculty, and students—are doing and how they are behaving. Finally, he is focused on the extent to which primary principles and foundations of the academy are decisively on the scaffold as a result.

In the post-World War II, contemporary era, major events in the history of academic freedoms first cropped up when sparked by the Free Speech Movement (FSM) at Berkeley in the early 1960s. Through its protests and actions, the FSM triggered a battle at the heart of the university at Berkeley, but that also sent momentous and forceful waves nationwide, gaining the attention of academic leaders, faculty, commentators, and political figures across the country. Because what was going on in California was quickly viewed as radical and groundbreaking, in short order campus protests, inspired by events and tactics at Berkeley, sprung up at dozens of colleges and universities.

Albert Lepawsky was a Berkeley political scientist at the time of the FSM. Assessing what was transpiring on the campus, he felt strongly that all parties involved had to keep a grip. He urged student protestors and faculty colleagues and administrative leaders of the University, to maintain rational thinking. All factions and players had to be cautious about the potential for beware-what-you-wish-for scenarios being created by the FSM and the Berkeley community.

Lepawsky aired his thoughts penning an essay, "Intellectual Responsibility and Political Conduct." No doubt the youthful students wrote him off as an example, in the protest parlance of the day, of someone over thirty-five who shouldn't be trusted.

Nonetheless, Lepawsky's words were important then and echo through the decades since into the midst of political correctness battles over pluralism, diversity, and free speech today. The university needed to be true to itself: "an intellectual sanctuary within the greater society that is now in political flux." To Lepawsky the issue was clear: ". . . the university's prime mission resides not in political activity but in the cultivation of intellectual freedoms."[31]

Protests were fine, but they could not be permitted to seep into and damage the fundamental intellectual values and intellectual inquiry of the college and university. The fear was that the rhetoric of a mob mentality left unchecked would tear down the fabric of the academy and academic culture. "'Any conflict between the intellectual and political way of life must be resolved,' Lepawsky reasoned, 'in favor of the primacy of the intellectual over the political.'"[32]

As witnessed at Berkeley, if the academy is going to lead society, it leads with the intellectual as opposed to the political way of life, echoing Hoeveler's "politics of the intellect"[33] versus what I have labeled the "politics of ideology." The problem with aspects of the multicultural and diversity push in the academy, and this is what hands to the critics of the resulting political correctness all the fodder they need, is the confusion of these two forces; that is, to collapse thinking and discourse in the academy into the politics of ideology as opposed to a "politics of intellect."

Lepawsky judges what he saw at the origins of a major mass movement, advocating for greater free speech rights on a college campus, as fashioning, maybe reinventing the creed that the academy should adopt to deal with these critical issues of academic freedom and liberty. In the fifty years since his warning, America's colleges and university have variously adhered to his counsel, and at other times simply ignored it.

The Lepawsky critique regarding necessity of the "primacy of the intellectual over the political," the infection of politics into the intellectual life of the academy, is a backdrop for grasping many controversies in the decades since he uttered it. Throughout those years, the university's ability to handle, in ways grounded in the fundamental principles of the academy, the free speech conflicts it has confronted surely produces a mixed scorecard.

That story features oscillations, the back and forth of views of free speech born out, for just one example, in the speech codes of the late 1980s and early to mid-1990s. At many campuses these codes were implemented primarily to protect minority groups that feared and were subjected to what they viewed as demeaning, hateful, and harmful speech. Of course there was a grand irony in all of this. Those involved in the

FSM at Berkeley, arguing as they did for minority rights and views, would be appalled at the steps of colleges and universities to suppress speech just two decades after their strong efforts to secure free speech and liberty.

Fortunately for the sake of academic freedoms, within a few years or less most colleges and universities, often led by their presidents, moved back from the brink of infringing free speech at the hands of the overreaction of speech codes. For example, on her first day in office as president of the University of Pennsylvania in 1994, Judith Rodin threw out the speech code that her predecessor, Sheldon Hackney, had signed off on a number of years before as Penn wrestled with the "Water Buffalo" incident.[34]

Rodin's successor, Amy Gutmann, a forceful advocate of free speech and liberty, has maintained her predecessor's approach, originally under the moniker of "Penn Talks," as a way for the university community to handle controversies, differences, and conflicts among its members. Nonetheless, the issue of grappling to define harmful and hateful speech, and what to do about it even if you can define it, along with other concerns about academic freedom in the academy and how best to handle them, remain far from being resolved.

Despite handwringing otherwise, and mistakes such as the implementation of speech codes, "trigger point" warnings, and other conflicts that have resulted in restrictions of academic freedoms and liberty, the lack of resolution of these difficulties is as it should be. The academy is a vital center of intellectual inquiry and debate in society and the nation. When those within its gates push for new knowledge and new angles on "old" issues, conflict and controversy are likely to emerge.

However, as new controversies and issues crop up, as they always will, colleges and universities have responded with a great of lack of consistency. It has been two decades since the walk-back from the brink of speech codes as a purported solution to hate speech and to political argument alleged as offensive. However, restrictive and overreaching schemes proposed to remedy campus conflicts keep on coming, and with them come threats to academic freedoms and liberty as well.

Consequently back and forth swings resulting from the political pressures of interest groups and select constituencies continue to push campuses toward limits and restrictions on free speech. These actions and responses are undertaken just when it appeared that such reactionary steps were off the table. Perplexed by what he witnessed, Downs drills further into what is going on in the academy regarding free speech and liberty. His story brings up-to-date the ins and outs in the history of academic freedom at colleges and universities over the last three decades.

If this history of the academy in America in recent decades reveals that it is experiencing greater splintering and divisiveness than in previous eras, and is dealing with free speech in ways that belie the core beliefs and principles of the academy, what events have precipitated these actions and outcomes? What are the causes and why have they happened? What is the course of today's university regarding fundamental issues of academic freedom and liberty within the gates? If the university is "disuniting," along with the American nation as Schlesinger alleges, is there a pathway to turn away from "disuniting" and balkanization?

To gain a fuller picture of what is going on and to be able to assess the current campus milieu, Downs centers on selected campuses and on the players on all sides of these controversies in order to grasp current policies and public pronouncements about campus controversies over academic freedoms. That exploration produces case study examples of the assault on civil liberties at colleges and universities from the late 1980s to the middle of the first decade of the twenty-first century.

Downs is most concerned about what he views as the "dangers of unquestioned moral sentiment." Citing Dana Villa, a Notre Dame political scientist, Downs notes that "The implication of Socratic examination is that virtually every moral belief becomes false and an incitement to injustice the moment it becomes unquestioned or unquestionable," something he believes is happening regularly in the politically correct college scene.[35]

For example, there were a number of dust-ups over a sexual misconduct policy and discussions about it at Columbia in the late 1990s and early 2000s (and here we are in 2015 and these same reports could be delivered today as if they had no predecessors). Downs concludes that the "Columbia activists" who had advocated for stringent policies governing student behavior severely compromised the rights of the accused. In staking out their territory, these activist protesters "were so convinced of their own moral virtue that they considered any word of dissent to be immoral. Their righteousness blinded them to the importance of due process in the scales of justice," Downs recounts.[36]

Downs's inquiry ends a little more than a decade ago. As we have seen (in the previous chapter), since then issues of sexual harassment and battles over "trigger points," not on the radar until a few years ago, continue to roil. Claims persist that sexual misconduct is out of control and that the pleas of those claiming offense over activities in the life of campus communities are not being heeded. However, an unfortunate consequence, one Downs observed then and continues to fear now, is that the administrative reaction to these protests frequently leads to actions and policies antithetical to the core aspirations and purpose of the academy.

Lest his ideas be written off as just another jeremiad laid at the feet of the academy, Downs sees reason for hope in staunching the worst ideological and political excesses, which end up severely restricting free speech and liberty. One remedy he arrives at is that the university curriculum and other campus educational initiatives and approaches are one avenue by which, as they consider and develop disciplinary procedures and policies, university communities can find their way through the necessary balance of liberties, freedom, and justice.

Interestingly his optimism springs from an unusual source but one that, though not often turned to as Downs proposes, makes intuitive and practical sense. That is, to what extent is there a role for the college and university curriculum to set a more intellectually focused and, in the traditions of the academy, more free dialogue and discourse on campus?

Downs has suggested that new student orientation programs, rather than using required readings, should feature focused discussion about the parameters and demands of free speech and liberty in the academy. He is also interested in seeing, and recommends as highly valuable, that more attention be paid to courses taught by professors who understand the battle lines of contemporary politics, political correctness, and unchecked ideologies run amok. Is there a way for faculty, through their courses and teaching, even if in small measure, to alter the frame of campus discussion and to be a bulwark for more rational debate about contentious issues in the academy?

Downs finds a partial answer to the questions he raises from two campuses frequently noted for clashes over academic freedoms and liberty, both historically and in the contemporary era from the 1960s to present: Columbia and Berkeley. In an ironic twist, Downs suggests that we can find a solution at the academy's foundation to a threat at the heart of the academy itself.

He presents two cases that highlight the value of the intersection between the curriculum and courses offered at a university, with the individual and communal temperament required to address and better handle issues of speech, liberty, and civility in dialogue, and to promote more rational resolution of campus problems and controversies.

For example, at Columbia University in the late 1990s and early 2000s, when he investigated sexual harassment issues and policy changes, Downs found faculty and students who made the connection between curriculum and course offerings, and the tone of discourse on the campus. Citing its historical and traditional commitments, Downs suggests "Perhaps Columbia's exceptional commitment to liberal education—exemplified by the core curriculum requirement that features great minds of Western and other cultures—instills an appreciation of intellectual give-and-take."[37]

In the 1960s there was great pressure to liberalize the college curriculum. Many colleges and universities displaced required courses in favor of area requirements (i.e., students picking one or two from a list of eight or so courses in umbrella categories).

However educational the intention, one result of these changes was to splinter the previous core curricular experience of the first year of college, and sometimes even the second year. Students no longer had as much contact with each other within the peer cohort. However, Columbia maintained, in the vernacular of its students, its "Lit Hum" course, requiring all first year students to take, for multicultural reasons, two semesters of an updated version of the "old" Western civilization drill.

As a student at Gettysburg College I had a similar two-semester required course, "The Ideas and Institutions of Western Man," that existed for about two decades, from the mid-1950s to the early 1970s. As its broad title implies, the course covered history, philosophy, political theories and ideas, religious beliefs and creeds, and different and differing perspectives about culture and society, and about the ideas and ideals of political and body politic models and the shape of the commonweal.

Every first year student was in a class section, seminar fashion, each with about fifteen students, a cohort that remained intact for the entire academic year. Students studied together regardless of the section they were in, as all were covering the same material at the same time. This "forced" students in class and dorm discussions to thrash around political theory, philosophical ideas, cultural values, religious faiths, and the people and institutions that historically had left these imprints. The course reflected and set the background for discussion of the issues in campus discourse, including issues clearly at stake in contemporary ideological, political, social, and cultural controversies.

Would this have inoculated us as undergraduate students from some of the ideological, less-than-rational back and forth (not worthy of being called dialogue) that happens at times so readily in the current era of ideological polarities and political correctness? Did it make a difference then? Would it make a difference now? Downs claims that at least some at Columbia today believe such required course content holds the potential to make such a difference.

In the case of Berkeley, Downs found one course—there may be others—that embraces liberty and of discourse of ideas. The faculty member was Alan Ross a business and political science professor. Downs found that Ross's heavily enrolled course, offered annually, "tackles controversial public issues by regularly presenting prominent speakers from across the political spectrum." Speakers included figures such a Ward Connerly, a member of the state board of regents who became a lightning rod for his fight to pass "Proposition 209, the statewide initiative that eliminated race-based affirmative action in admissions and government hiring."[38]

Downs would never contend that these small dents in the assault on academic freedoms and liberty serve to solve the problem. However, he would contend that they show an avenue to address the losses that free speech has suffered and to highlight a semblance of a remedy.

THE SEDUCTIONS OF A UTOPIAN
VIEW OF THE ACADEMY

The battle lines and battlegrounds in the college and university in America have historically played out as contests of dueling visions about what ideals are going to shape the academy. It is not surprising that the colleges and later universities of the New World would pursue ideals fashioned by notions of a Utopian world. Such a concept of the university fit closely and purposefully for an academy sitting in the American nation that identified its place in the world and role as Messianic, a Chosen Land, a country with a Manifest Destiny, and for the Christian, nothing less than the Kingdom of God. Utopian visions were part and parcel of these dreams.

But of course, different parties and factions have differing ideas about what Utopia looks like. Utopians believe they have a solution that avoids the tyranny of either the majority or the minority. Even so, Utopians, to get where they want to go, arrogate to themselves the power that is critical to attain their chosen ends. Those who believe their vision is an ideal that must prevail will do what is necessary to control and to fashion culture and institutions, in this case the academy, in that image. That is what Utopians, particularly those in the academy, do.

Mercifully, debate about the nature and shape of the college and university in America has not played out quite so starkly. Nonetheless, its history is littered with leaders, players, and advocates who believe their way is the only way.

One true Utopian about the university was Robert Hutchins, president of the University of Chicago from 1929–1951.[39] Hutchins is a major figure in American higher education, though he also wandered into the world of secondary education and its preparatory value for entrance into, in his phrase, the "higher learning." However, the reality of his presidential tenure and public influence is that while there was a lot of bluster, a lot of intentional sparking of controversy, few of his ideas and concepts were ever embraced at Chicago or elsewhere.[40]

For example, judging an ill-informed public and what he nearly considered barbarians at the gates of the academy, Hutchins is clear: "I do not need to tell you what the public thinks about universities. You know as well as I, and you know as well as I that the public is wrong." Partially defending the university against the assaults of an unknowledgeable populace, but at the same time decrying the faults of the university itself, he adds, "The fact that popular misconceptions of the nature and purpose of universities originate in the fantastic misconduct of the universities themselves is not consoling."[41]

Among figures in American higher education, Hannah Gray is a most remarkable figure. Her entire life has been committed to the academy, beginning as a professor, continuing through the administrative ranks as

a dean, and serving as interim president of Yale between the distinguished tenures of Kingman Brewster and Bart Giamatti. Gray went on to
a fifteen-year tenure (1978–1993) as president of the University of Chicago. Still teaching today in her mid-eighties, she is a remarkably long-
standing denizen of the university, and her commentary about the academy is uttered from this highly informed perch.

Gray succeeded Hutchins as Chicago's president a couple of decades
after his departure. She is critical of both her predecessor's autocratic and
dictatorial style, and also of the substance of his ideas for the academy
and for the shape of the university.

Gray's critique begins with an example of what she views as a mis-
guided Hutchins's proposal. She then extends that to the even larger
discussion about the shape of the university.

The focus of Gray's story is Hutchins's roll of the dice with Chicago's
trustees in 1944, when he argued that they vest in the president all authority for the academic life, program, and policies of the university.
Aiming at the all-too-powerful senior, tenured faculty, Hutchins suggested that he could be trusted to use this autocratic authority in a way
that would lead to "a more democratic community by reducing the preponderant power of the senior faculty and extending the same rights to
those previously excluded from the faculty senate."[42]

In that speech to the trustees, Hutchins went even further, and this
leads Gray to a rebuke of her predecessor's leadership and the kind of
world of the university he was trying to create. She views Hutchins's
claim that, "The whole scale of values by which our society lives must be
reversed if any society is to endure. We want a democratic academic
community because we know that if we have one we can multiply *the
power which the University can bring to bear upon the character, the mind, and
the spirit of men. . .*" as valuable, if an overreach, in highlighting the influence that the university can actually exert.[43]

But more important to Gray is what Hutchins's rhetoric reveals about
the ideological nature of his philosophy and intent. His goals are admirable and shared by many, including Gray. But the pathway he intended
to employ to reach them was antithetical to the principles of the academy
itself. In the upside down world of Hutchins's mind, Gray believes his
intent was "to impose an ideological conformity threatening to the intellectual freedom at the core of the university."[44] Thus the irony is that
Hutchins, though portraying himself as a protector of the gates and a
defender of an ideal of the university, sought nothing other than the
mutually exclusive establishment of his ideal.

To an extent, Hutchins has to be given his due as an interpreter of the
academy. Gray realizes that the history of the university is mixed, pointing out that it was not originally a liberal arts oriented institution—something for which she acknowledges Hutchins fought.[45] However, she also
knows that this mixed history is frequently selectively picked over by

ideologues to justify or to denounce contemporary assumptions and predilections. "The ideas associated with that image [of the university] have taken on quite different meanings, shades of meaning, and quite different embodiments at different times. The history of the idea of the idea of the university is one," Gray notes, "of continuing reinterpretation, in which the strongly felt need to assert a continuity with the past confronts the project of giving new life and form and purpose to the higher learning under circumstances quite remote from that past." Factions always try to shape the academy to suit their purposes. Any claim can find fertile ground when "The past was continually cited to legitimize later ideas, and it was continually altered and given modern face by doing so."[46]

However, as a warning about how interpretations and understandings of the university are sometimes promoted by those selling a slice of what the university should be, Gray finds Hutchins instructive. Here was as an idealist who would have liked to think he could convince others, even opponents, with the most persuasive arguments about what the university is and should be. However, at the end of the day, Hutchins was just another interlocutor and, given the intentionally high public profile he created and promoted, his ideas demand at least as much and indeed more scrutiny than those of others.

Gray passes judgment on Hutchins's Utopian visions by turning to no less a source than the originator of the idea, Thomas More. She claims that More's famous *Utopia* in 1536 (interestingly just one hundred years before the founding of Harvard) initiated the liberal arts critique and its establishment as a beachhead in the university. For Utopia to work, the Utopians had to be a fully, liberally educated people, well steeped in the humanities and the classic works. Here More provides a portion of the basis for much of Thomas Jefferson's thinking two hundred years later.

More's language, based as it is in his aspirations for the University of Oxford of his day, can equally be transported to many moments in the history of the academy in America, including the pressures of the latter twentieth and early twenty-first centuries. Gray finds More's advice to the populace of his day compelling. That is, the citizen "could not expect the whole crowd of academics to possess the wisdom, temperance, and humility," rather he must warn them that the "decay of learning" must be prevented, "and learning will perish if the university continues to suffer from contentions of lazy idiots, and the liberal arts are allowed to be made sport of with impunity."[47]

Gray believes that More's picture of how the academy should be shaped is spot-on. Its care and tending cannot be turned over willy-nilly to even the most informed and dedicated participants—primarily its faculty and other leaders—because yet they may lack the necessary "wisdom, temperance, and humility" to sustain its fundamental principles and beliefs.

Unfortunately, even those, primarily faculty and academics, to whom we have little choice but to entrust the foundation of the college and university, cannot always be depended upon to carry out that duty in ways vitally crucial for the university to be the university. It is their responsibility to prevent it from becoming something else, not the wholly distinctive institution it must be.

Anyone who has spent any time in the academy knows that the best-intentioned people can slip into diversions and meaningless rhetoric and actions that are antithetical to and place at risk the university's core purposes and mission. Consequently, the foundation of the university hangs in the balance.

The dangers abound. The litany of threats is long: Hutchins and his ideas, speech codes, dismissals of the likes of Ross at Stanford and Ely at Wisconsin, intentions to use multicultural initiatives as a back door to remake the university as a social action institution dedicated to social justice, are but a few examples of the debates and actions that can erode the foundations of the academy.

Gray is concerned about Hutchins's and any Utopian thinkers' ideas about the academy. They may on the surface appear compelling. Nevertheless, Utopians by nature and definition are radical. That makes them what they are. However respectable, a Utopians ideas about a vision of utopia translate to an ideal that can be chased but rarely, if ever, institutionalized. One need look no further in America than to the handful of mid-nineteenth-century Utopian experiments, such as the Oneida community, which rarely lasted more than a few decades, and many just a few years.

The citizens, thinkers, and leaders of that era, as is frequently the case, were largely formed in reaction to dilemmas and turmoil in culture and society, which were, in those times, the revolutions of 1848 and related tumult in Europe and around the world, including in the United States. As we have seen, anxieties and fears about crises and perceptions of crises frequently spawn radical solutions.

Hutchins was no different. Two world wars and a massive depression in his lifetime fed Hutchins's contention that "The whole scale of values by which our society lives must be reversed if any society is to endure," and that in his phrase the University of Utopia would lead the way in overcoming depravity and reaching that more perfect state.[48] As we will shortly see, the 1960s were another such era of crisis which produced cries for the university to be society's salvation.

It is such knee-jerk reactions and rhetoric that lead to Gray's skepticism and trepidation about a Utopian idea of the university, including that of her predecessor, Hutchins (not to be belabored, it is unusual for a college president to criticize so publicly a predecessor in the office, though Hutchins's self-crafted image and notoriety makes him an unsurprising target to take on). Gray believes that attempts to push the college and university to be a Utopia, while likely to fail, can nonetheless exact damage to the image of the academy.

Certainly everyone in the academy holds one or another ideological point of view and will work to shape the university according to those beliefs. However, the danger spawned by Utopian ideals and ideology in the university is very real. The primary cause for concern is that these attempts to shape the academy in the image of philosophies, religious beliefs, political theories, cultural analyses, and social understandings, however well intentioned they might be, fall well outside a mainstream view of the college and university.

The reality of ideological differences sets up an on-going battle of radical Utopian visions of the academy versus those, who though ideological, possess political and educational philosophies that are broadly in the mainstream. Despite Utopian pressure from whatever end of the political spectrum, the college and university avoids disunity and is significantly strengthened when the more "traditional" arguments about what the university is carry the day in that contest.

What is it then that constitutes that mainstream? How can we know it when we see it? The idea of the university is complex, and the beliefs and values that undergird the university are complicated. The concept of the university is always fraught with politics from all sides, and from within and without. But the formation of the academy in ways true to its foundation and core principles and beliefs, is also not rocket science.

Cardinal Newman's thoughts about the university were a set of original and systematic formulations about what the university should be.[49] They have stood the test of time. Newman and those who have followed in his footsteps, even while modifying his ideas, are broad thinkers about the university and its foundations. They seek to incorporate into the university elements that give it definition, but at the same time do not confine it. Their closely held ideas do not create problems for the university because these mainstream ideas don't conflict with, rather they support and complement, what the university should be in the first place.

Hutchins was out of that mainstream, despite protestations to the contrary. He was a self-appointed provocateur. He knew precisely what he was doing. That is why in the spirit of More's understanding of Utopia and Downs's notion that ideological ideas frequently take open debate and dialogue off the table, Gray is accurate in her criticism and in underscoring the danger that Hutchins's positions contain.

Gray then fast-forwards to the 1960s regarding the Utopian quest in American higher education and its continued foibles. She claims that what happened in that tumultuous decade vis-à-vis Utopian impulses is: "What emerged as to some extent new in the sixties and beyond was a belief that the university or college itself should represent a kind of Utopian community, not of the ivory tower removed from its surroundings, but of an exemplary counterpoint to the world out there, not only in its educational program, but in its internal policies and social organizations as well."[50]

The path undertaken in that era of change and reaction to protests produced a Utopian impulse that "in whatever form, has become yet another idea of a university, and one that links the idea of what is to be taught, and why it is to be taught in a liberal arts program, very closely to the purposes of social reform."[51] It was easy to get caught up in what the 1960s represented, what Gray calls "The vision of the 1960s as the golden age of the research university . . ."[52]

However, there is a seduction about this era for those who lived through it and certainly for those who overly romanticize it decades since. Both those examining that time exclusively as historians and those who experienced firsthand the times of the 1960s as they unfolded need to exert great care with any conclusions about what was going on. As William Bowen, then president of Princeton and one of Gray' presidential colleagues in the 1980s, characterized, "it seems clearer and clearer that that decade [the 1960s] was an aberration in almost every respect."[53]

There is significant evidence to support Bowen's assessment of the 1960s. The convergence of social, political, and cultural upheaval, tension, and strife all packed into a decade, give or take a few years, was unprecedented for American society and for the college and university.[54]

Campuses and their leaders had never seen anything like what was happening in both substance and ferocity and the haste with which opposing sides challenged each other. The conflicts and conflagrations over the Vietnam War, civil rights and racial tensions, socio-economic disparities, and campus social and residential life were rampant. College presidents, trustees, faculty leaders, and others invested in the university had to make up much of their reactions in policy decisions and rearguard actions literally on the fly.

At the same time as further confirmation of Bowen's point of view, federal and state support had reached its zenith in the early to mid 1960s after years of growth beginning in the aftermath of the Second World War. Levels of spending and massive investments in infrastructure, student financial aid and loans, and faculty research had, like the protests that began to accompany those expenditures in the early 1960s, never been seen before.

But that support in people and institutional budgets at those 1960s levels by any designation: per capita to student enrollment, faculty, and citizens, and in constant dollars, has not been reached since and is very unlikely to be seen again in even the longest-term future.

In continuing her critique of the contemporary university, Gray sets her sights on issues of political correctness, academic freedom, and the press for pluralism and diversity. Some goals associated with these pressures and ideals are admirable. In some cases those ambitions are reachable with at least modest levels of progress.

However, again there are seductions wrapped in Utopias and Utopian thinking. Gray warns that efforts such as those in the 1960s, demanding that the university and what and how it teaches be linked "to the purposes of social reform," all those encroachments eroding the prospect for the university simply to be the university, always create a dangerous path, and one that inevitably leads to undesirable outcomes.

Gray places this impetus to divert the mission of the university in historical context. She suggests, "Over their history, universities have been asked to enforce many different shades and kinds of conformity and different versions of what we now call 'political correctness.' Pressures of this sort have come not only from the outside; they are often internal ones as well."[55]

As witnessed in the recent decades of the end of the last century and the beginning of this, "They can be explicit, as in the case of rules about speech, or more generally and subtly part of an accepted environment that fosters a certain form of orthodoxy or sense of limits or lives with the dominance of particular schools of thought."[56] The problems that the academy encounters as a result of stretching the boundaries and purpose of the college and university are so evident that they hardly need restatement.

However, the way in which an experienced leader and educator such as Gray highlights the threat makes it worthy of emphasis. "Those members of the academy, however well-meaning, who embrace such an environment in the name of some higher good will soon find." Gray warns, "weakened institutions of higher education and eroded conditions of academic freedom, both for the individual and for the university itself."[57]

This is the dystopian vision that Cardinal Newman feared in the mid-nineteenth century and that a century later Kenneth Minogue railed against.[58] This is a vision and potential outcome of what the university could become that transforms it as something other than the university. In the face of that threat, leaders of the academy throughout history and their counterpart contemporary stewards of the university, such as Gray and her late twentieth-century colleagues, are duty-bound to mount stanch defense and opposition.

There is a further "be aware what you wish for" irony and twist to this part of our story and to Gray's critique. That is, the further danger that the university exposes itself to by capitulating and caving in to special interests and political ideologies, be they from the political Left or Right.

As noted previously, when the academy is compromised and eroded in this fashion, its identity and special status in society as the university qua the university is lost. This danger creates two complementary and interlocking problems.

First, the leadership of the university, and its goals and aspirations are likewise compromised. Second, external criticisms and the polemical forces behind them are given a boost and perceptions of their influence are magnified. In this milieu of the over-politicizing of the university, because of judgments hurled at it from all sides, it becomes ". . . harder also to recognize and act on the principle that universities in their institutional capacity have the obligation to nurture and respect the differing individual convictions of each member."[59]

Thus there is a grand irony, unwittingly or not, inspired by the progressive and reformist-minded Left (though if the shoe were on the other foot, the Right would likely create similar problems with their agenda). That is, the overreach in the quest for diversity, equity, and social progress by the forces pushing that agenda and simultaneously criticizing the university for its lack of responsiveness actually make it tougher for the university to address that agenda and interests because the battle itself leaves the fundamental foundations and core of the university tattered and eroded.

The distinctiveness of the university, the distinguishing characteristics and parameters of what it is and should be, and by definition what it cannot afford to morph into, must remain unmistakably demarcated. It is the clear delineation of what the university is that shapes its ability to carry on as it has historically, and to be for society in any era what citizens, the nation, and the world reasonably expect it to be.

Given her years of serving and watching the college and university in America, Hannah Gray holds a longer-term outlook than any other commentator today about the university. The Clark Kerr Lectures, honoring Kerr's leadership and contributions to higher education as president of Berkeley from the late 1950s through much of the 1960s, provided the opportunity for Gray to construct these ideas about the line the university must not cross, even as it is pulled by social forces, advocates, and pressure groups. She knows well that for the university to be and to endure as the university, it must preserve a distinctive institutional definition of its mission and purpose.

The problem with the competing and at-odds ideological factions in and around the university is that:

> The insistent demands for universities to make a difference in every important good cause that merits attention will only divert them endlessly from the central contributions that are theirs specifically to make. So, too, does the idea that the university's ultimate goal is to exemplify social virtue.[60]

Stressing this claim, Gray cites her colleague Kerr who noted that "The presence of the university carrying out its normal functions changes society fundamentally, but" and here Kerr's critical assertion particularly for a leader who confronted the contentiousness of his era and one whose tenure was no doubt cut short as a result, "*the attempted manipulation of the university, for the sake of specific political reforms, changes the university for the worse more than it changes society for the better.*"[61]

Kerr is fervent about what happens to the university when it goes down the path of political, one can certainly add any social, cultural, or other reform and movement. These reformist pressures are a major seduction. Utopian visions in the academy and for the university to be a Utopia are designs on the shape of the college and university, of the academy. As a consequence, its leaders must, because of the stakes at hand, use any tactics to avoid going down that path.

Kerr's leadership perch at Berkeley in the Free Speech Movement, and other pushes and pulls of the 1960s, produces an outlook that is decisive. In those days, Berkeley was being compelled to bend to the views of protestors and often was unable to resist their pressure and demands.

But whatever Kerr feels can be reasonably laid at his feet for caving in to these political demands during his tenure as president, four decades later he urges a robust definition of the university as the university, an institution of society and of the nation that has a duty to preserve its heritage and tradition. To accomplish that end, the university must repel those who would have it do otherwise.

Gray is equally concerned as Kerr about how seductive these internal and external forces that hold the potential to divert the university from its core purposes and mission, its very identity, can be. The university must resist distractions that lure it into arenas outside the basis of its uniqueness as a foundational institution in society. Navigating the poles of what the university should be with what others might wish to shape it to be is convoluted. That complexity is rooted in the a priori tension between the rights and identity of the individual on one hand versus the essentials of the commonweal and body politic that those individuals in common constitute on the other.

This American and democratic public ethos has long been a requisite consideration for the college and university in this Republic. The pushes and pulls of that political culture can be addressed in ways that do not deter or divert the academy from its purposes. However, that goal can be accomplished only by carefully drawing lines in the sand, in the tending to the rights of individuals versus the obligations of the commons, to civic duty and polity.

For Gray, the challenge within the gates of the academy, and as it is able to serve as an example to those outside, cannot be more resounding. The test is an experiment as old as the founding British Charter for the establishment of the Providence Plantations, later Rhode Island, in the seventeenth century to de Tocqueville's observations of democracy in America in the nineteenth.

This lively experiment in and outside of the college and university is a balancing act between commitment to the commonweal, to have principles and beliefs that create bonds between diverse people and constituencies on one hand, while on the other to recognize differences in beliefs and values, to tolerate them civilly, and to permit competing impulses to live in tension and irreducible lack of resolution. Addressing the tension, Gray uses the heritage of the university: it must be both. In the end, to tilt too far into the pathway of "foster(ing) a certain form of orthodoxy or sense of limits or lives with the dominance of particular schools of thought" is a mistake, even a fatal error for the academy.[62]

In this vein Linda Pratt, president of the AAUP in the early 1990s, captures the campus scene roughly a decade into the latter twentieth century, ideological political correctness battles that began in the late 1970s and early 1980s. She notes that although some might think that era a historical artifact, in fact the Red Scare tactics of the McCarthy era had by no means died out, cropping up in offspring in a different guise three and four decades later. Pratt notes that by 1990, "Academic practices and values, always subject to misunderstanding by those outside the academy were increasingly suspected of having a political agenda designed to undermine traditional American values."[63]

What was happening in this public debate and arena of latter twentieth-century political correctness was that "The polemics that ensued did little credit to any tradition of scholarly debate and dialogue. If the attacks of many nonacademic critics seemed unfair and misinformed, the defense from those within universities," Pratt hastens to note, "was often ragged and hasty." Thus even as the university attempted to defend against critics on the outside, the academy was far from unified on the inside. "Almost invisible in the midst of the public controversy was the extent to which arguments were as divisive and contentious within the academy as they were on the outside," laments Pratt.[64]

It is inevitable that we are drawn to comparisons between and among different historical eras. Thus it is commonplace given the apparent tensions of recent years to ask questions about whether things are worse today than what has been experienced in previous times.

Are matters of pluralism and diversity, and the connected threats to academic freedoms and to an academy allowing itself to be disunited as a result of an inability to maintain as a common sense of purpose any worse in the last two or more decades than they were in the 1950s at the peak of McCarthy's attacks in- and outside the academy? Has the front of ideological conflicts with all their contentiousness and animosity changed dramatically over the last seventy years since McCarthy, let alone from any previous eras that could be brought up?

One response to these questions and to the jeremiads of those who perseverate about what they view as the plight of the college and university in America today is found in a major theme that we have been plumbing in these pages. That is, the more things change, the more they stay the same. For anything in the contemporary arena that appears new, perplexing and beyond the bounds of anything previously experienced, there are notable and equally puzzling and perceived as dangerous, historical examples that our forebears in every era have confronted and sought to overcome.

Connected to this theme is the reality that ideology, ideological pressures and camps, including those with progressive agendas to advance pluralism and diversity, have ever been in the midst of the academy. Those forces were more homogenous in previous eras. Nonetheless, there were camps and they were ideological, even if their differences and divisions in points of view were more negligible than is perceived to be the case today.

But those ideological pressures and their mutually exclusive points of view nonetheless existed in bygone eras. The march of ideology and the divisiveness it produces were feared by as many observers in these previous eras as there are those who equally justifiably fear them today.

The quest for the university, especially if it is to remain the university, as with many other aspects in the history in of the college and university in America—its presidents and other leaders, their decisions, institutional policies, the shape of curriculum, and program initiatives—is to maintain balance. Overreaching in mission and purpose into areas in which the university simply does not belong is a prescription for erosion of what the university is designed and destined to be.

Leaning too far, even marginally, in the direction of any dueling and polarized political forces, Left, Right, or some other Utopian design, likewise mistakenly diverts from the necessity of maintaining that balance. Moreover, in today's early twenty-first-century social and cultural politics in government and society, that task is made all the more difficult because of those who indulge in partisan and divisive rhetoric. When targeting the college and university, these critics are drawn to make public hay from their proposals to impose forced choices on the academy, and worse are rewarded for doing so.

It is often remarked that in the words of Shakespeare, "what's past is prologue."[65] In the history and life of the college and university in America, its shape and shaping, nothing could be closer to the truth.

## NOTES

1. Douglas Sloan, *The Great Awakening and American Education: A Documentary History* (New York and London: Teachers College Press, 1973), 19.
2. Ibid.
3. Ibid., 28.
4. Ibid.
5. Ibid.
6. Ibid.
7. Ibid.
8. Ibid.
9. Charles W. Eliot, "Academic Freedom," *Science* (July 5, 1907): 1.
10. Ibid., 2.
11. Ibid.

12. Ibid., 6.

13. Ibid.

14. Ibid., 10.

15. Ibid., 12.

16. Ibid.

17. Ibid.

18. Ibid.

19. Arthur Schlesinger, Jr., *The Disuniting of America* (New York: W. W. Norton and Company, 1992).

20. Schlesinger sits in a long-standing tradition dating to colonial times and its colleges in America and argued throughout the nineteenth century and longer. For only one example, see Michael Sandel, *Democracy's Discontent: America in Search of a Public Philosophy* (Cambridge, MA: The Belknap Press of Harvard University Press, 1996), 164–67. Sandal features among others a dean of American education, Horace Mann.

21. Ibid., 19.

22. Ibid., 18. The notion of the "silent majority" may appear to be an odd turn of phrase, not simply because it echoes the Nixon-Agnew rhetoric about those they tried to rally against protestors in the late 1960s and early 70s but more so because we don't often think about academics, college professors being readily silent. Rather that they are and can speak publicly about their reactions to issues and events. However, in this case in the mid to late 1980s and the 1990s (before and after Schlesinger penned this comment), the chilling effect of the advocates for multicultural education and the pressure for greater diversity indeed worked to silence many otherwise outspoken critics among faculty in the academy.

23. Ibid., 69, Italics mine.

24. Ibid., 113.

25. Ibid., 113–14.

26. Ibid., 118.

27. Ibid.

28. Ibid., 138.

29. Donald Alexander Downs, *Cornell '69: Liberalism and the Crisis of the American University* (Ithaca, NY and London: Cornell University Press, 1999). The Cornell episode is examined in Stephen J. Nelson, *Decades of Chaos and Revolution: Showdowns for College Presidents* (Lanham, MD: Rowman & Littlefield, ACE Higher Education Series, 2012). See Chapter Three, "Cornell and Kent State: Inevitable Disaster and Tragedy?"

30. Donald Alexander Downs, *Restoring Free Speech and Liberty on Campus* (Oakland, CA: The Independent Institute, and Cambridge: Cambridge University Press, 2005).

31. Ibid., 8.

32. Ibid.

33. J. David Hoeveler, *Creating the American Mind: Intellect and Politics in the Colonial Colleges* (Lanham, MD: Rowman & Littlefield Publishers, 2002), x.

34. See Endnote 13 in Chapter 6.

35. Ibid., 105–106.

36. Ibid., 106.

37. Ibid., 72.

38. Ibid., 108.

39. Among Hutchins voluminous writings was Robert M. Hutchins, *The University of Utopia* (Chicago: University of Chicago, 1953) in which he laid out a shape of the academy in America as rooted in Thomas More's Utopian notion and vision

40. A full discussion of Hutchins's legacy is presented in Stephen J. Nelson, "President Robert Hutchins' Designs on Education and the University: Imposing Provocateur or Mediocre Prophet?," paper presented at EERA Conference February 2014.

41. Robert Maynard Hutchins, https://president.uchicago.edu/directory/robert-maynard-hutchins.

42. Hannah Holborn Gray, *Searching for Utopia: Universities and Their Histories* (Berkeley: University of California Press, 2012), 17.

43. Ibid., italics mine.

44. Ibid.

45. Ibid., 32.

46. Ibid., 33.

47. Ibid., 37.

48. Ibid., 17.

49. John Henry Newman, *The Idea of the University* (Oxford: Clarendon Press, 1976) and Jaroslav Pelikan,, *The Idea of the University: A Reexamination* (New Haven, CT: Yale University Press, 1992).

50. Gray, 54.

51. Ibid.

52. Ibid., 65.

53. Ibid., 65, endnote 2, found on 105.

54. For a full recounting of the decade of the 1960s, see Stephen J. Nelson, *Decades of Chaos and Revolution: Showdowns for College Presidents* (Lanham, MD: Rowman & Little-field, ACE Higher Education Series, 2012).

55. Gray, 86.

56. Gray, 86.

57. Ibid., 86–87.

58. Kenneth Minogue, *The Concept of the University* (Berkeley: University of California Press, 1973). Though Minogue was not the first one, he warns as clearly as any that if we do not let the university be the university, if we allow it to be turned into some other social, political or organization entity, then it loses the very label of university and can be treated only was whatever it is that it has morphed into.

59. Gray, 87.

60. Ibid., 94–95.

61. Ibid., 95, (endnote 1 from found on p. 111). The Kerr quote is from Clark Kerr, *The Uses of the University*, 5th ed., (Cambridge, MA: Harvard University Press, 2001), 133. Italics mine.

62. Gray, 86.

63. Louis Menand, ed. *The Future of Academic Freedom* (Chicago: University of Chicago Press, 1996), Forward by Linda Pratt, vii.

64. Ibid.

65. William Shakespeare, *The Tempest*.

# EIGHT

# The Contemporary Ideological World of the McCarthy Era to Present

*Political Rightness and Wrong-Headedness*

The lively experiment that is the college and university in America is characterized by the claim that throughout its history the key struggle and the tempered triumph has been the maintaining of its normative and fundamental foundation as the academy. That means the principal beliefs and values that constitute the university as the university have been sustained through centuries of wrangling and debate, and generations of college presidents, faculty, trustees, and others whose leadership has undergirded this endeavor.

This definition and shape of the university reflects the beliefs of thinkers who have thought at length about what the concept of the university should be. Among those are Cardinal Newman's nineteenth-century assertion that the university must adhere to "first principles" in order to maintain its identity.[1] About a hundred years later, Kenneth Minogue offered complementary arguments about what the university must do to maintain its core purpose and identity.[2]

Minogue witnessed the upheavals on college and university campuses in the United States and in his home, Great Britain in the 1960s and early 1970s. He believed those events threatened and eroded the foundations of the university. What was most disturbing was the decay unleashed by uncompromising ideological thinkers and camps.

The essentials necessary for the university to remain as the university pivot on a number of assertions. First, Minogue notes, "universities have many beneficial side effects which have sometimes led states to embrace them enthusiastically. But to take any of these side effects as the function of universities would be a distortion of their character." He enlarges the arena of debate adding that, "The prevalent functional view of universities is part of a general debasement of the very word of 'education.'"[3]

Second, Minogue views the university as a complex institution. That means "Any attempt to characterize universities in terms of a single criterion will inevitably be wrong." He declares that the academy must not be reduced to a single criterion based on well intentioned, but, as he argues, "wrong" notions. Minogue opposes those who advocate that universities must choose only one identity from choices like "centres of civilization, intellectual powerhouses, areas of 'social criticism' and all the rest." [4] It was fine for the academy to embody these and other elements as part of its purpose. But no one element, or even combination of a couple, could be allowed to rule the roost.

Third, Minogue recognized the overlap of ideologies with what, by any definition, are religious passions. Minogue declares that " . . . if we look a little below the surface of many modern ideological conflicts about education . . . we shall soon find, beneath the intellectual trappings and the parade of rationality, the unmistakable presence of religious passions." [5]

Minogue believes that while the university can allow ideologies to be debated within its gates—in fact this must certainly transpire in an ethos of free and open debate and discussion—those ideologies cannot be permitted to gain a foothold of control. Those with political agendas, desires for social reform, or other civic interests, no matter how principled or valuable to society, cannot be allowed to shape the university in that image and to those ends. If that were to happen, the university would no longer be the university, but rather an institution wholly different.

The history of the college and university in America is not one of straight-line clarity and pursuit of the Newman-Minogue ideals. There have always been intrusions and bumps in the road. There are always those who wittingly and unwittingly have sought willy-nilly to change the academy into something else other than the university. But they have remained primarily on the margins and have not prevailed. This has been the case in the academy from the present ideological battleground of the politics of Left and Right, back in time, as we have and will note further, to the earliest days of the Colonial Colleges.

These political and ideological formulations threaten the identity and foundation of the university. Despite these political, cultural, social pressures, the college and university in America managed, by a combination of good fortune and intentional design, to adhere to the classic and fundamental understanding of the university.

Principles of free speech and liberty go to the heart of Newman's view that the university stands for the intellect and for the pursuit of the intellectual foundations of knowledge. Those principles cannot be secured absent academic freedoms. Thus, a critical measure of the state of the academy is the state of academic freedom at the basis of the university.

## THE ROAD TO THE PRESENT STATE OF
## IDEOLOGICAL CONFRONTATIONS

Major changes in the shape of the American college and university in the last century and longer have resulted from the leading institutions, those with the biggest profiles, creating decidedly influential positive and negative examples for public consumption and scrutiny. As a consequence of their ever-growing scale and complexity, America's educational institutions leave increasingly sizeable footprints on the landscape of higher education and of society, culture, and politics in United States.

The pro side of the ledger features the good that colleges and universities do. A few of these imprints are: research that serves vital national needs and interests, such as the Space Race with the then Soviet Union and more recently in fields of energy production and environmental, climate change challenges; the opening of the doors to education for returning World War II soldiers through the GI Bill, coupled with initiatives to recruit and the financial support essential for previously shut out populations to make their way to higher education; advances in medicine and health care; and public contributions through training educators, social workers, clergy, and religious leaders of all faiths, and those committed to public service, as political and governmental leaders.

On the con side of the equation we have witnessed: the encumbering weight of mammoth, even if necessary, bureaucracies; polemical battles among ideological camps over political correctness; similar politically motivated arguments about curriculum and controversies over how professors teach, and what and whether students are learning; contentious arguments about the mission of the college and university; athletic scandals and questions about the sums of money involved in mounting major college sports; and the entanglements of legal cases and legislative brouhahas over affirmative action, grant overhead spending, sexual harassment and assault, and free speech.

The colleges and universities of America have in the last hundred years become vastly bigger and more sophisticated in their leadership, research, teaching, and services and amenities for students. But the increasingly more prominent image and more pronounced scale of the academy has in recent decades, analogously, but more than in previous times, produced its share of critics and attention-getting jeremiads of judgment and broadside on the con side of the ledger.

Questions about higher education abound: the cost to students and the debts they incur in order to attend; the priorities and choices made in investments in infrastructure and support services as opposed to concentration on the academic mission and purpose, however debated that enterprise; the political leanings that critical commentators are convinced influence the content of the courses taught and the class discussions that professors conduct, including the caliber of their teaching; designs and schemes raising institutional profiles in a scramble for athletic prominence; and how much time and leadership capital presidents and senior college and university leaders spend in chasing dollars.[6]

But bigger questions shape the larger framework within which the academy in America is viewed and how it functions. To name just a few: ideological and political correctness, the degree to which there should be restrictions and if so what kind on speech and behavior, and the political views of presidents even in the bully pulpit, and of faculty, students, and of those invited and given the platform to speak on campus.

All in all, the contemporary college and university environment is at least as politicized and ideologically driven as at any time in its history, if not arguably more so. Considerable aspects of those controversies, though by no means all, pivot on issues of academic freedoms, free speech, and liberty. In addition there is the even larger question of how the university and college is able to maintain the fundamental identity at the foundation of its heritage in the face of ideologies that would pull it willy-nilly in the direction and bending to the expediency of their competing and mutually exclusive points of view.

This evolution in the university's size, scale, and complexity precipitated the formation of the American Association of University Professors, now celebrating the one hundredth anniversary of its founding and its groundbreaking 1915 Declaration. Indeed there was a long history of free speech and academic freedom concerns in earlier times. But it was only when the university evolved into its late nineteenth and early twentieth-century guise that the issues sparking the founding of the AAUP reached a fever pitch and impact.

At that point those issues that in Newman's phrase were "first principles" could no longer be left for defense exclusively by the ranks of leaders and faculty, each at their individual colleges and universities. Concerns about academic freedoms and liberty, and the accompanying pressures of politics and ideologies that threatened faculty and the foundation of the academy reached such a point of gravity and high public profile that there was no choice except for them to be addressed by an organized national body.

Hence the founding of the AAUP heralded the mid- to late twentieth century and now the twenty-first-century brand and iterations of those antecedent campus contretemps. Reaction to immediate events confronting leading professors and academics in the early twentieth century led them to formulate an organized and institutionalized response to what they witnessed. In the face of assaults on academic freedom and free speech it became crucial to have an organized counter voice and a counter set of claims. Since that time, the AAUP has served as a bulwark against the intrusion inside the ivory tower of ideological forces and players from whatever part of the political spectrum.

In earlier years, the impact of episodes of political pressure brought to bear by society on academic expression and speech within the university and college ranks was not as magnified as what developed in the cases that took place at Wisconsin in the 1890s and Stanford in the early twentieth century. Nonetheless, these cases and the overall evolution of storms around the university in the latter nineteenth and early twentieth century confirm that the contemporary ideological battleground had its precursors in the longer-term history of the academy in America.

Consequently, to understand more fully the state of the ideology and politics in the present situation of the college and university in this century, and including its earlier roots in the previous, we need to glance back in history to the seedbed of ideological challenges and confrontations in the academy in America.

## COLONIAL AND EARLY REPUBLIC
## ROOTS AND HERITAGE

The nation's founders formulated a religious basis with Christian but more so Deist roots to shape the body politic, especially its aspirations in a democracy. In that quest, an unavoidable issue was how to handle the pull of individual conscience and principles in the agreements and disagreements among "men," in Madison's language, in the Memorial and Remonstrance Against Religious Assessment, (1785).[7]

People and factions would, because of innate differences and diversity of opinions, have disagreements, this inherent in freedom of conscience and religion. The question was: what were reasonable parameters and expectations for individual and public debate and disagreement, something the academy would surely seek to embody and expect?

Madison's social and political philosophy was conceived to apply broadly to all human affairs, not only to those with a religious basis. Furthermore, because of the overlap between the commonwealth and the affairs of education in the colonial era, Madison's ideas about creeds, beliefs, convictions, and ideological (read in his and the founders dilemmas and parlance, religious) differences and controversies echoed in the affairs in the academy.

Madison opposed "A Bill establishing a provision for Teachers of the Christian Religion" under consideration by the Virginia legislature. Citing the existing "Virginia Declaration of Rights," Madison declares the predicate that, "If 'all men are by nature equally free and independent,' all men are to be considered as entering on equal conditions; as relinquishing no more, and therefore retaining no less, one than another of their natural rights."[8]

He continues that if the "equal title to the free exercise of Religion according to the dictates of Conscience" is violated, or "If this freedom be abused, it is an offense against God, not against man: To God, therefore, not to man, must account of it be rendered."[9] Madison's thoughts are directed toward the arena of religious ideas, convictions, and passions. However, given the overlap of governmental and educational institutions, his notions about "natural rights" are broadly applicable to the rights of individuals regarding their convictions and beliefs in any social and political setting, including within the gates of the college.

These are Enlightenment, and democratic ideals and virtues that lie at the foundation of the college and university in America, just as they do in that of the nation. An array of civil and political beliefs, including those time-honored in America: rights to religious liberty and freedom, free speech and assembly as well as others in the Bill of Rights, the Constitution, and in various other amendments concerning individual and civil rights, were readily imported into the foundation of the college and university. It is these values and beliefs that contribute to the uniqueness of how the academy is both shaped and viewed in the nation's landscape.

Robert O'Neil, former president at the University of Virginia and a legal scholar, has considered at length issues about academic freedom, free speech, and individual liberty in the academy. O'Neil concurs in the connection between Madison's ideas about conscience and convictions and the culture desired in the college and university. He invokes Madison's "wise caution that 'it is proper to take alarm at the first experiment on our liberties.'"[10] O'Neil suggests a number of actions that can be undertaken better to secure academic freedom, not least collaborations where the interests of the normally polemic and warring factions of the political Left and Right coincide.

O'Neil is especially concerned that "Those beyond the campus," who so often knee-jerk in reaction to highly publicized cases, "need to appreciate why the silencing or dismissal of a single faculty crackpot or nutcase potentially affects the entire community" in terms of the overall quality of academic inquiry, education, learning, and "the capacity of the academic community to advance knowledge and pursue the eternal quest for truth."[11]

"That, after all, is what academic freedom is all about, and that is why it matters to those who are not professors as much as to those who are. The sooner citizens at large appreciate that equation," O'Neil urges, "the better they will be prepared for an uncertain future, as will be the academic community."[12]

The college and university is a complex entity, in many ways an organism with interlocking, related but independent parts. Many within its gates and certainly many critics on the outside do not fully comprehend and appreciate how fragile the academy can be when those unaware and unsympathetic about how and why it exists fail to give the academy the leeway to function as its mission dictates.

O'Neil's opinion is that this tendency to misread and to misunderstand the academy is something of which both the Right and the Left are guilty. He believes that it is in their mutual interests to work to understand the ground rules and to treat each other as guided by and with acknowledgement of the academy's basic parameters and assertions about public and civil discourse.

This hoped for coming together of opposing factions and flanks calls for those on different partitions of the political and ideological fences within the university to affirm the inherent dangers when their differences of ideology and politics are not worked out rationally and civilly. These polemical forces must also recognize the virtues of different viewpoints. Simultaneously, they must work to reduce the most extreme, even reckless of those ideas that divide them. O'Neil posits that their ability to square the circle of ideas and dug-in positions that threaten the common good could be accomplished without sacrificing critical protections of individual rights and liberties.

However, O'Neil's hopeful prospects fly in the face of realities about how ideologies have functioned in the academy in the last forty or more years. O'Neil's position about a way out of contentious, and often irrational debate and positions is based on the idea that there is or can be common ground of mutual self-interest found between the dueling forces of the political and ideological Left and Right. While that hope is desirable, it is quite optimistic.

Nonetheless, as we continue to look retrospectively at the seedbeds of contemporary polemical factions in the academy, there is at least some cold comfort in the fact that whatever is going on ideologically in the academy today developed from analogous precursors years ago.

Douglas Sloan views the roots of cultural and accompanying political loggerheads in American society and their influence on the views and treatment of education in America to an extent originating in the Great Awakening of the 1730s.[13] That contention can be extended to the Second Great Awakening, less than a hundred years later.

The battles of the Awakenings were religious and theological. They were struggles between the Protestant revivalist forces and their traditional, more hide-bound anti-revivalist counterparts. The differences between these factions played out in assumptions about society and how it should be shaped and maintained. But because of the weighty influence of religion and religious thinkers and passions in American colonial and national life of the day, the implications of these confrontations spilled into many aspects of society and culture, including into thoughts and assumptions about education.

In America, "Educational institutions had always provided one of the central bulwarks of civilized life . . . but their function was traditionally one of maintaining and strengthening an already accepted ideal of social organization. In the Great Awakening a subtle but extremely important shift began to take place," Sloan observes, "from an essentially conserving to a more dynamic view of the role of education in society."[14]

This shift in beliefs about the meaning and value of education meant that the traditional view of it as a stabilizing, consistent, conserving, and conservative force and institution in society was now contested. That challenge arose from views that the shape of education and its institutions from school to college was, in Sloan's words, "more dynamic." Consequently there was an evolution toward a more up-for-grabs debate about education, what its content and culture should be, and what and how it should contribute to society, and to the civic polity and good.

The major change that this debate between the poles of the Awakenings produced was a new balancing of how an education was conceived and a reshaping of conceptions about what education was supposed to do. "The social uses of education were increasingly conceived, not primarily in terms of maintaining the given society," what the Harvard's of the day were clearly designed and expected to do, "but of creating a new social order that did not yet exist," Sloan declares.[15]

In the era of the eighteenth and early nineteenth centuries, the ideological tension was between the traditionalists, on one hand, and their view of sustaining society and culture as it had been, and on the other, the newer viewpoints of forces seeking to use education to transform society. Although today's opposing ideologies of Left and Right do not base their beliefs in the Protestant religious beliefs and values of two and three centuries ago, they battle similarly with each other. Both possess cultural beliefs and values that are tantamount to and often based, al a Minogue's ideas, on the overlap of ideology and religious passions, in religiously geared concepts, even if they would not want to admit so.

The forces on today's neoconservative Right seek preservation, maintenance of the traditions and traditional curriculum and culture of the academy. Those on the Progressive Left seek the transformation of society, the use of the college and university for egalitarian, social justice, and minority advancement ends. Thus, the Right and Left line up respectively much like the anti-revivalist, tradition-minded Awakening forbears on one side polemically, against the revivalist challengers with a message of transformation and dynamism, and change on the other.

Sloan's view supports the claim that, because the Awakening raised core questions about education and society, and about education's role in culture and cultural formation, the debate begun in those times has cast a lingering shadow. We are left to judge whether that shadow is a good or bad thing.

But Sloan is not afraid to judge. He finds instructive implications of this debate and the change it signaled. For example, as a result of the Awakening, "Americans divided and the divisions persisted. From this perspective the Awakening was the initiation of a grand cultural dialogue that has yet to be completed. And, perhaps, the Awakening has a final meaning for our own time as a warning against allowing positions to polarize and harden to the extent that men cease to talk, regardless of how irreconcilable the lines of disagreement may appear." [16]

The landscape and vantage point of Sloan's time was the immediate backside of the ideological and political battles of the 1950s, beginning with McCarthyism through the protests and upheaval of the 1960s and early 70s. [17] From his time forward to today, the scene is little if any different and the battle lines continue. And Sloan's idea, "that grand cultural dialogue that has yet to be completed," obtains as much today as it did nearly fifty years ago when he made that assertion.

Sloan frames the key questions of his era with prescience about what lay ahead. His list is applicable to the continued wrestling and grappling with the contemporary ideological divide and debate over political correctness, the content of intellectual discourse, and whether that dialogue and debate can any longer be had in a rational and civil manner.

What are those questions for Sloan? How much are they confronting us today as compared to when he posed them five decades ago? "How to preserve and honor the tradition of accumulated knowledge—built up patiently and painstakingly over the course of generations—while at the same time remaining open to creative innovation and spontaneous inspiration? How to safeguard culture's frail hold on ordered and rational knowledge while empowering it with vital emotional and aesthetic experience? How to connect objective knowledge *about* with personal, subjective knowledge *of*? How to relate and adjust the frequently conflicting claims of immediate, pragmatic social problems and the long-range strategies and goals of a larger social vision? How to uphold standards of excellence and simultaneously remain responsive to popular tastes, and demands?" [18]

Little else needs to be said other than that these questions frame the horns of the present dilemma. And if O'Neil's hope for convergence of diverse, diffuse, and conflicting camps is overly optimistic, Sloan's questions, if all sides could find their way to grapple with them, could inform and shape the debate and discourse in the contemporary ideological battleground.

## THE CONUNDRUMS AND CURMUDGEONS OF
## CONTEMPORARY CAMPUS BATTLES

In the late 1970s and early 1980s, the Right wing political camp both in- and outside the gates of the academy began to use the label political correctness to belittle and disparage Left wing, Progressive forces in colleges and universities across the country. Political correctness critics on the Right pointed to what they believed to be a nearly universal lock of the Left wing in all aspects of campus and student life, and the dangerous domination of the Democratic political party in both administrative and faculty appointments and ranks.

The charge is that higher education suffers from a vacuum of politically conservative leaders from presidents, deans, and trustees to lower ranking staff, as well as most critically in the professorial ranks. The political tilt in one direction includes student bodies that are monochromatic, upended only occasionally by a conservative outlier or two. These critics are certain that colleges and universities are shot through with litmus tests, and are bound and determined unalterably to stamp their political leanings and convictions not only within campuses themselves, but infiltrating society and the nation as well.

The litany of offenses that progressive forces in the academy had wrought included a range of programs and policies. To name just a few: minority advancement and recruitment initiatives and incentives designed to expand diversity (and allegedly as a consequence, diluting desirable credentials) in student bodies and faculty ranks; rumblings about divestment from university portfolios in corporations with investments in the alleged apartheid regime in South Africa; the establishment of policy and politically geared centers and think tanks with liberal biases and beliefs; and continued curricular reforms designed to make courses, course content, and pedagogy more multicultural and diverse.

The Left pushed back against these charges using their own batch of contending tropes. They denied all of these accusations. The Left was not monolithic. It featured many slices and shades of individual differences, rather than a one-size, must-fit-all batch of political beliefs and values. There were assertions that the criticisms were unfair, often ad hominem (which in many cases they were). There were defenses based on the claims that the ideas, formulations, and policies that the Left were proposing in the life of colleges and universities reflected mainstream thinking of the heritage and purposes of the academy, not a fringe, factional set of schemes.

However, an aspect of the allegations of control, whether and to what degree they were true, prompted crucial questions. What if the roles of Left and Right were reversed and the shoe was on the other foot? In going about their business and using their leverage to shape the culture of the academy, was the liberal, Progressive Left ignoring the prospect of what the legacy of their influence would leave behind?

In other words, if the Left were indeed presently in a dominant and domineering position, able to get their way, what would happen if they were on the outside looking in? What if they were consigned to the minority position with little power? What ammunition would they in turn use in the uphill climb to reclaim territory? Wouldn't they likely throw at their enemies on the Right what the Right was now throwing at them?

Ron Dworkin, a philosopher and legal scholar, rivets on the cautionary tale of this highly ignored prospect of the shoe being on the other foot. He believes that academic freedom is at the forefront of the political correctness controversy, and decries critics on both sides who abuse this principle of the academy by using it as a dodge and a refuge of the scoundrel.[19]

Hiding behind academic freedom, both the Left and the Right feel they have license to trample other values at the foundation of the academy—civility, rational discourse, mutual respect for intellect and ideas—that are part of what makes the university the university. The tragedy is that both sides of the political and ideological divide on the contemporary campus use these principles of the academy, including and foremost academic freedom, as cudgels to strike at their opponents and to protect their own turf.

Polemics and polarized points of view in the academy have forever been with us. However, the battles on the contemporary campus are fed heavily by outside meddling. Today's rapid and relentlessly nonstop, due-to-technology-boosted communications make easier unrestrained invective, ad hominem attacks, and uncivil rhetoric at levels previously not seen.

Playing willy-nilly with the core principles and values of the university is an extremely dangerous game. Its effect erodes the foundations of the academy and creates the prospect that what is wrought can come back to bite you. "If critics of academic freedom succeed in teaching the public at large that that ideal is overrated, and may be set aside in the interests of attractive social goals," Dworkin warns, "the lesson will be studied in other than egalitarian constituencies."[20]

This is "the shoe is on the other foot" conundrum: "If some people think racial and gender equality are urgent goals, others—and there are more of them—think it more urgent that the decline in family values and traditional virtues be halted, and they will be glad of a chance to dictate that university curricula emphasize those virtues and avoid texts that ridicule them. . . . I am, I agree only repeating an old liberal warning. But it is a warning that cannot be repeated often enough." That warning and the fear about the damage it does to academic freedom is that "Censorship will always prove a traitor to justice."[21]

Dworkin's contemporary public intellectual counterpart, Edward Said, turns to Cardinal Henry Newman in search of an alternative to his colleague's dystopian prospect: that is, the danger that foundational and fundamental principles of the university will be sacrificed on the scaffold of dueling political parties parading their ideological points of view. Said focuses on academic freedom but with a different angle than Dworkin, one that is more comprehensive: Newman's idea about the "intellectual culture" that constitutes the foundation of the university.[22]

"Intellectual culture" is an umbrella and transcendent idea that includes and incorporates academic freedom but also consists of other of Newman's "first principles" that govern and shape the academy. All who are members of the university community, including the most extreme ideological camps and poles, must buy into this concept of the intellectual foundation on which everything in the academy is based. This concept is a social contract: Individuals and groups in the university are duty-bound to agreement that "intellectual culture" shapes the parameters in which they live, think, and act, and to which they will make contributions.

Said's hopes are lodged in the idea of the university that Newman believes was an institution that "has this object and this mission: it contemplates neither moral impression nor mechanical production; it professes to exercise the mind neither in art nor in duty, its function is intellectual culture." For the university to be the university, its identity and foundation must be grounded in "intellectual culture." This is the essential foundation that Newman declares as a "first principle."

Whatever the arguments between camps and factions in the university, the only way out of the spin of recrimination and response is for the sides to acknowledge the necessity of an "intellectual culture." Warring factions can have their battles and battle-worn positions. However, if they are to be citizens of the university, they must consider first and comply with the requisites of that intellectual basis and culture. Unfortunately, in today's academic arena, that is not always the case. Despite that, and in the face of it, presidents, professors, and other leaders have a duty to make this compact clear, and to urge campus debate and dialogue within its parameters.

One barrier in the search for a common ground, an agreed middle in which contending views can be played out, is that ideologies tend to despise relativism. That is because they are locked into and very certain, or must appear so, about their judgments and declarations. Reduced to its simplest form this is a battle over authority and power of the university. Consequently the stakes are high: the desire to be more persuasive than the other side is decisive in order to prevail.

The problem for any ideological faction is that the university, its "intellectual culture," is about seeking information and knowledge. Thus, at its foundation, the academy embraces relativism because all sides of all issues are up for grabs and should be openly discussed. Juxtaposed to this thinking, ideologies in the academy, and outside as well, abhor relativism. There is a pox on both houses, the Left and the Right. Making that point, Said turns to Newman's classic line about the Bugaboo of Relativism: "Not to know the relative disposition of things is the state of slaves or children."[23]

Subsequently, both sides in the ideological battleground stand warned about both what they might wish for in their wars with each other. What happens if their opponents are in control of the power and authority of the university? How do they handle and acknowledge the university's values, its "first principles," which finally trump any of their particularistic points of view? Said argues that the "profound truth in what Newman says is . . . designed to undercut any partial or somehow narrow view of education whose aim might seem only to reaffirm one particularly attractive and dominant identity, that which is the resident power or authority of the moment."[24]

In many cases, the ideologies competing in the marketplace of today's academy stand to do the opposite, that is, to have a "view of education" that has as its aim "only to reaffirm one particularly attractive and dominant identity, that which is the resident power or authority of the moment."

This is juxtaposed to what Newman expected of the academy: "the power of viewing many things at once as one whole, of referring them severally to their true place in the universal system, of understanding their respective values, and determining their mutual dependence."[25] That is the mission and purpose of the college and university that must endure and which its leaders must defend. This is doubly true in the face of ideological factions and their actions that left unfettered and to themselves, would erode that foundation.

## HOW THE UNIVERSITY FIGHTS BACK: CAN "FIRST PRINCIPLES" SAVE THE DAY?

We have noted the distinguishing value and characteristic of Newman's idea and concept of the university. That is, the view that the university must establish and maintain a foundation of "first principles," and that its heritage is one of establishing and sustaining an "intellectual culture." The question for the academy historically as well as in the present day is whether the beliefs and values, the creed of the university to hold to "first principles" and to shape an "intellectual culture," can be and remain its fundamental foundation. Can this underpinning be the bulwark that saves the day? That guarantees that as an institution, the university can be the university, not something wholly different?

Robert O'Neil notes the "essential nature of a university" and its "distinctive character" is that it is "the one and only institution in American society that is unambiguously committed to the question for truth and the advancement of knowledge and within which no avenue to those ends may be closed, blocked, or declared to be 'off limits.'" However, he quickly adds that this "recognition does not, however, automatically make the case for protecting academic freedom in general."[26]

That lingering problem exists because the university is, as Minogue asserts, a complex institution and because the battles of academic freedom, who is it that secures it, who might be assaulting it and why, are equally complex matters forever at hand in the academy.

O'Neil's picture of the contemporary university includes close attention to issues of academic freedom and academic speech, and how those crucial principles, especially in recent decades, have been intertwined in the ideological battles on campuses. One fairly recent (though Dartmouth College was subjected to the student-led, but significantly outside funded by alumni and others, *Dartmouth Review* engaging in surreptitious surveillance and recordings of faculty in the early 1980s) dust-up and conundrum has presented itself in the form of conservative forces prompting undergraduates to record the presumed political and other ramblings of university faculty.

Most of these efforts have produced little or nothing. However, O'Neil notes that on the backside of September 11, 2001, the AAUP established a Special Committee on Academic Freedom and National Security in Time of Crisis. That committee "could envision no legal safeguard against such reprehensible practices [of students recording professors]. Nor would the group have wished to invoke such recourse even if it existed."[27]

The AAUP report noted that, "as private entities' outfits dedicated to trying to nitpick faculty in the classroom are nonetheless 'protected by the First Amendment from state censorship so long as they stay within lawful bounds. They are sheltered by the same freedom of expression that we seek for ourselves [the academic community], and they are equally subject to public rebuke.'"[28] Nevertheless, despite the requirement of extending academic freedom even to the worst actors in the academy in order to preserve those same rights and freedoms for all, O'Neil yet sees volatile waters.

He is clearly distressed by the pressures applied by conservative groups and forces such as David Horowitz for an Academic Bill of Rights (ABOR).[29] The large issue, in which these contretemps over who is doing what in the halls of the academy, is the question of whether, as a solution, colleges and universities will be faced with state or federal legislation. This step would inject public adjudication and control over faculty and their normal and expected duty and jurisdiction over academic life and affairs.

Citing J. Peter Byrne, law professor at Georgetown University, O'Neil argues that a core principle of the academy concerns "determining on academic grounds who teach and what may be taught."[30] The step of legislation that would take this control of recruiting, selecting, and hiring new colleagues, of shaping the curriculum, and of the specific choices of content in their courses out of the hands of professors would be a treatment that is worse than the disease.

The prospect of outside forces moving in to legislate either pro or con about student recordings, and thus surveillance of faculty in the classroom, remains hypothetical to this point, despite pressures from ABOR to the contrary. However, O'Neil is not sanguine about the degree to which the constitutionality of such legislation would be readily or easily thrown out. If such legal steps were taken and if they could not be overturned, their existence would alter the course of academic affairs and faculty control over what has long been believed to be their exclusive province.

Byrne, on the other hand, is convinced that constitutional grounds would prevent such a take-over of academic authority from the faculty ranks. Whether his view would be sustained, O'Neil holds out some hope in Byrne's argument that ABOR and similar initiatives, "'violate [academic freedom] on its face' because the legislation is prima fascia flawed because it holds the 'indisputable premise that faculties have [any] obligation to be viewpoint neutral regarding substantive disputes within their disciplines.'"[31]

This hope that legal intrusion can be avoided or overturned rests on the notion that "Although neutrality may be constitutionally obligatory when it comes to institutional allocation of student activity fees, the same is hardly true for professors: 'university faculties need not and, perhaps, should not be [neutral].'" Byrne also asserts that courts would treat such legislation proposed by the Right precisely as they have the initiatives from the Left for speech codes about harassing and politically incendiary campus rhetoric: by showing "little patience with novel mechanisms to regulate speech on campus."[32]

If this were the case, the autonomy of the college and university would be preserved along with that of its academicians, teachers, and scholars. The result: the academy would be the winner as the competing ideological sides would both be the losers

O'Neil's conclusion rests on the idea that "bias and balance" in the academy is a false choice. That is, "even the most ardent champion of faculty autonomy could not claim in good conscience that a quest for better balance is inherently inimical to academic freedom; indeed there is a powerful argument that broader tolerance for diverse viewpoint serves the interests of academic freedom."[33]

There are inevitably differences of opinion in and outside the gates of the academy about whether viewpoints uttered from the faculty side of the house are sufficiently broad and diverse. However for O'Neil the bottom line is clear: "The critical issue is far less whether any steps may be taken to redress apparent imbalance than who should initiate those steps and what specific steps might be consistent with academic freedom."[34]

The AAUP is a major bastion to which those in the academy can turn for advocacy on the front of academic freedom and its connection to ideological frictions on and among campuses. Even the most contemporaneous of issues are subject to criticism and advice from the work of the AAUP. The starting point of their arguments and declarations is for balance and for the critical necessity to avoid taking up sides in the academy.

The AAUP's 1915 Report on Academic Freedom and Academic Tenure upholds values undergirding academic discipline, authority, and autonomy. "'Any university which lays restrictions upon the intellectual freedom of its professors,' notes historian Thomas Haskell about the AAUP stance, 'proclaims itself a proprietary institution, and should be so described when it makes a general appeal for funds.'" This means "any institution that withheld from its faculty the rights of academic freedom in the interest of serving a propagandistic function could not claim the authority of a true university and would deserve the support only of fellow sectarians, not that of the general public."[35]

However, college and university professors are not innocent bystanders simply waiting for their colleges and universities, with support from organizations such as the AAUP, to defend their profession and territory. They not only have skin in the game but, more indispensably, also have the duty and obligation in the search for knowledge not to mount the soapbox of personal biases, which are not backed up by research and scholarly evidence. Doing otherwise taints and undermines core professional principles of their professions and of the academy.

This sense of duty that faculty are expected to assume and exert as their professional responsibility, and the degree to which they have or haven't done that, goes to the nub of the political correctness debates of the last forty or more years. Thus if faculty were to speak without, in the AAUP's words, "'fear or favor,'—and equally important, be *seen* as speaking thus, so as to earn the deference of the general public—they would not only have to purge themselves of interest, insofar as possible, but generally distance themselves from all influences extrinsic to their work."[36]

Namely, when faculty cannot lay aside personal agendas in their teaching (thus also avoiding the bugaboo of student surveillance that would invade the privacy of the classroom) and research in terms of avoiding bias, rather truly searching for knowledge, they do a disservice to themselves and their profession, and to the entire academy. It is a slippery slope for those faculty who fall into the trap of allowing firm convictions about ideological positions to end up framing and limiting the full play of ideas in the marketplace in and outside the gates of the academy. The ironic result is the infringement of the very academic freedom on which they and their colleagues rely to do their work.

## FINDING A WAY OUT OF POLITICAL CORRECTNESS BATTLES: POLITICAL RIGHTNESS, WRONG-HEADEDNESS, AND ANTI-INTELLECTUALISM

Over the last four decades, a number of critical issues and events have shaped the college and university. Much of this shape-shifting has occurred on a number of fronts: free speech and liberty, the pressures applied from the voices of pluralism, the increased political pressures for diversity—with their pros and cons—and the centripetal forces that balkanize academic life and culture.

There is a diversity of responses to the state of affairs and the high-wire dangers that face the college and university. Some commentators are optimistic. Others land on the pessimistic side about the fortunes of higher education in the face of ideological struggles. Still others merely report what they see and don't seem to have an opinion, despite the stakes.

Regardless of their thoughts, perceptions, and prognostications, whether it is Byrne, O'Neil, Dworkin, or the aspirations of the AAUP or a combination that have it right, the academy continues to face the true challenge and divisiveness of the ideological divide. The personalities and contentions at the poles—Right and Left—in ideological campus debates and contests are matters with which the academy must contend.

These are realities from which there is no clear path of escape, and given the historical persistence of ideological battles in the American higher education experiment, it is naïve to expect them to go away. The matter is better framed as how the most radical and irrational justifications of dueling, partisan camps and factions can be minimized. That end can only be accomplished through a cultural foundation of civility, of rationality, and of full and not limited debate and discussion that are engaged in the richest traditions of the university.

Donald Downs is a historian, observer, and one experienced in the academy over a lifetime spanning fifty years. His handle on the political rightness and wrongness of the contemporary political correctness saga focuses on the complexity and confusions that have marked this era in higher education. Downs judges from a number of angles what he perceives to be taking place in the ideological battleground.

First, as any historian, Downs has beliefs and assumptions. But despite that bias he is able to let facts speak for themselves and leaves judgments to the reader. His case illustrations are studies and investigations of key political players and parties to events at numerous campuses across the country.

Second, he issues jeremiads, but that is a long-standing tradition that the academy has ever faced from critics within and without its walls about its problems, policies, and actions. Downs joins that group, but with a hope that the academy can find its way through these challenging political and politically motivated difficulties.

Finally, Downs's proposed solutions are grounded in and designed to maintain the creed of the academy. While the proposals and rhetoric are idealistic, he is not disingenuously offering ideas expecting they will be summarily dispatched. Rather Downs's suggestions about how colleges and universities can navigate the political divides are rational, concrete, and realizable.

Downs believes there has been a contemporary shift in the handling of issues of liberty and speech in the academy. He alleges that the culture of the college and university has been altered such that fear about the reaction to speech or academic honesty has led professors, as well as students, to keep their mouths shut, remain quiet, detached, and on the sidelines despite the contributions they might otherwise make.

This change in thinking results from the notion that "The right not to be offended was now ascendant in many domains of American society, especially its universities, where it was linked to various other causes. The problem is that the pursuit of truth and intellectual engagement wither and die," Downs declares, "if we grow afraid to offend or anger by presenting our honestly held ideas and beliefs—especially when the antioffense principle is enforced by sanctions backed by administrative power."[37]

When the "right not to be offended" is exploited and trumps everything else in the arena of free speech and academic freedom a double whammy results. Principles previously assumed to be untouchable are shunted aside while in the same stroke the values of the academy are corroded. This is precisely the problem that critics of political correctness decry: that the actions of colleges and universities become overwrought in order to placate the complaints of the minority. The result: the creed of the academy is eroded and the interests of the majority of its constituents are thwarted and suppressed.

What has been turned upside down in society and the academy is that "In today's polity, we appear to have forgotten that citizenship and the character virtues that it presupposes are the foundations on which meaningful equality is attained, not the other way around." Further, that mistake leads to a dire trap: "Victimology undermines citizenship by infantilizing its would-be beneficiaries, rather than treating them as responsible adults. Applied to free speech, victim ideology treats individuals as inherently incapable of handling the rigors of open discourse,"[38] Downs laments.

This analysis about the ethos of the college conjures up further inquiry. What has the academy in recent decades permitted to happen in guiding its affairs, principally in its duty toward intellectual and academic culture? If Downs is correct, by extension there should be little surprise about how and why university policies and decisions have unfolded as they have. These changes become most evident in differences within the gates of the college and university about how community is shaped and formed, and how student behavior and discipline are handled.

"This assumption," about the ideology of victimology and the infantilization of students to Downs, "is not surprising, given the conflation of speech and action that characterizes much of the free speech theory championed by such ideology. "In such a politically and ideologically infused climate, what then comes to pass is that "Victimology represents the conjunction of a debilitating form of identity politics and the broader trend that social theorist Philip Rieff identified as the 'triumph of the therapeutic.'"[39]

Based on these contentions, Downs sets the table for further concerns about the critical issues in the academy and in the nation, especially as they connect to Arthur Schlesinger's ideas about the forces that lead to "disuniting."[40] These alarms center on the vital importance of dialogue and debate in a democracy, whether in a nation or in the academy. That debate leads Downs deeper into the puzzle that is academic freedom and free speech in today's college and university.

Free and open debate, the byproduct of commitment to the principles of free speech and liberty, are the antidote that prevents any one special interest, any one ideology, to account for nothing but its own special interests. That call for commitment to dialogue runs counter to the position of those whose who believe their points of view to be beyond debate or question. When ideological advocates find themselves backed into that corner, the frequent response is to retreat into a refusal to engage the body politic and to be an active part of it.

When the university as a community, likewise for a nation, relies on discussion and dialogue to address matters of difference and diversity, it directly challenges the inferred claims of special interest and ideological groups that points of view other than theirs are not entitled to exist at all. Finally free and open debate in the public square is an antidote to the march toward balkanization in any college or university, again equally in the nation.

Downs is alarmed about a number of issues that pivot on claims that lead to erosion academic freedoms and liberty in the academy. His concern is that these issues addressed improperly, or at worst not addressed at all can lead, and he would argue have already led, to balkanization on campuses and unfettered threat to the academy in America.

A large part of the political correctness arena, the rightness and wrongness of where things are headed for the college and university,

resides in notions about the current course of the academy and its programs, policies, and approaches to education. To an extent this is a "the
sky is falling" set of questions. And if so, what is it that we are doing
about it? What is the history of the relationship of American society to its
higher educational system?

Contemporary events and clashes in the academy viewed through a
historical lens can serve to make us less perplexed about what we confront, i.e., that present times are not the first in which these battles have
happened. Present challenges are not as unique as we think.

John Searle is another long-standing denizen of the academy in the
tradition of O'Neil, Byrne, Dwokin, and Menand. He provides guidance
and context about the tense confrontations of political correctness. Searle
possesses a close up and in-depth view of the academy, having first cut
his teeth as an undergraduate at the University of Wisconsin opposing
the election of Joseph McCarthy, and later teaching at Berkeley as a
young faculty member, joining the Free Speech Movement (FSM) there in
the mid-1960s.

In the early 1990s, looking over ten years or so of political correctness
debates, and in words applicable to the fears that political correctness is
only the tip of the iceberg of a disintegration of the academy in the two
plus decades since, Searle argues "I cannot recall a time when American
education was not in a 'crisis.'" [41]

That crisis has relatively simple roots. "Since we do not have a national consensus on what success in higher education would consist of, no
matter what happens some sizable part of the population is going to
regard the situation as a disaster," Searle contends. The reality is that "As
with taxation and relations between the sexes, higher education is essentially and continuously contested territory." To which Searle adds,
tongue-in-cheek and urging a deep-breath from all sides: "Given the history of crisis rhetoric, one's natural response to the current cries of des-
peration might reasonably be one of boredom." [42]

The major debate of Searle's day in the late 1980s and early 1990s was
focused on the canon, the traditional and often required texts in a college
curriculum. This was the debate about dead, white males and whether
their prominence should be so exclusively maintained in texts and readings that regularly appear on professors' syllabi, and thus be forced on
students. Concerns about educational content were raised because of a
lack of works of women, minority, and other interest group writers and
scholars. By including these voices of diversity, the curriculum is expanded and diversified.

Searle took a clear side in the debates. In the canon battles that were
taking place, he argues that, "There is a certain irony in this [debate over
white male domination] in that earlier student generations, my own for
example, found the critical tradition that runs from Socrates through the
Federalist Papers, through the writings of Mill and Marx, down to the

twentieth century, to be liberating from the stuffy conventions of the traditional American politics and pieties."[43]

To Searle there was a hegemony that preceded the one being debated in the 1990s. That was what he and his generation of the 1950s and 1960s had reacted against what they viewed as the oppressiveness of a national and nationalistic, America is always right, viewpoint. Their critique and way out of that box was to turn to the very canon that was now under assault.

Thus in a remarkable irony, Searle notes, "Precisely by inculcating a critical attitude, the 'canon' served to demythologize the conventional pieties of the American bourgeoisie and provided the student with a perspective from which to critically analyze American culture and institutions. Ironically, the same tradition is now regarded as oppressive. The texts once served an unmasking function; now we are told that it is the texts that must be unmasked."[44]

Arguments over the canon have taken place throughout the history of the college and university in America. Think, for example, of the earliest battles in the Colonial Colleges that though theological were the same set of issues about whether the canon in one era can remain unchanged as it is challenged by newer, more diverse understandings in the next.

On the other hand, Searle voices the opinion of those who fear that the baby gets thrown out with the bath water. That means enormous care needs to be taken by academicians and university leaders as they assess what should be considered in versus what is considered out of the curriculum and in individual courses that professors teach. However, continually as the university addresses those challenging and often polemical debates, it must do so absolutely sustaining the authority and duty of faculty over that curriculum and their courses.

By the end of the 1990s, the curriculum battles were for the most part settled, or had withered and died. Even major campus battlegrounds in curricular controversies such as Stanford and Columbia modified what they were doing by adding more diverse content, authors, and subjects in required first year Western civilization courses. These changes on the whole were met with satisfaction from a good number of critics, even as they continued to anger "traditionalists," people like Searle, on the other side.

However, the issues these curricular clashes raised did not go completely away. Today they are more likely to be battled out over "studies" departments, concentrations, and majors (black, Afro-American, women's, gender, LGBT, and other), and the faculty hired specifically to teach in these areas viewed as outside the traditional canon. This of course continues to beg Searle's point that in his education the "'canon' served to demythologize the conventional pieties . . . " The lingering question is whether Searle's point of twenty years ago is still the case today.

Searle etches a comprehensive view examining the recent history of college and university curriculum from his early college days to present. His focus is on the status of the canon and what critics sought as replacements for it.

Nevertheless, there exists an even larger context from which to view how and why American society and culture reached the moment and divisiveness of the political correctness controversies, especially as played out at college and university campuses. That background is that the political correctness debates of the 1970s to present have occurred in the midst of a long-standing American tradition of cultural and social biases about education and about politics. That pattern is one of America as a nation with a thread and continual outbreaks of anti-intellectualism.

This trope characterizing the nation's anti-intellectualism has endured throughout successive generations, spanning decades and even centuries. Persistent allegations of an anti-intellectual tradition in the American nation have evolved such that they provide the populace with an unavoidable set of assumptions and description of events, policies, and institutions of the nation.

First coined by Richard Hofstadter, anti-intellectualism in his parlance is "resentment of the life of the mind, and those who are considered to represent it; and a disposition to constantly minimize the value of that life."[45] To those inside the gates of the academy anti-intellectualism forms a present threat. In addition, anti-intellectualism is a perfect cudgel for those on the outside to use over the heads of denizens and leaders on the inside.

To get a further handle on this larger context of the anti-intellectual tradition, Irving Howe goes back a decade or more before political correctness raised its head. Howe, a literary and social critic and political activist, tackles the picture of what has been going on in American higher education since the appeals of the 1960s for "relevance" in the curriculum and for the education of undergraduate.

The problem with relevance is that it is "a notion hard to resist (who wishes to be known as irrelevant?) but proceeding from an impoverished view of political life, and too often ephemeral in its excitements and transient in its impact."[46] Howe focuses on the faddish quality built into the curricular reform efforts of the 1960s, cast around as they were in a time of unprecedented turmoil and conflict in society.

Those seeking to make college and university curricula more "relevant" simultaneously sought a closer connection of a higher education with the needs (seen as cropping up everywhere) of society. However, at the same time advocates for relevance also wanted to make academic life in a college more individualized, therefore less concentrated on a sense of a common educational and learning quest for students as well as faculty, and a refuge from the presumed constraints of the canon.

Howe's reflections on these times and pressures lead to conclusions not unlike Hofstadter's classic conception about anti-intellectualism in America. "American culture is notorious for its indifference to the past. It suffers," Howe alleges, "from the provincialism of the contemporary, veering wildly from fashion to fashion, each touted by the media and then quickly dismissed."[47]

This penchant for faddishness in American society and inside the gates of the academy is even more extreme today than twenty plus years ago when Howe penned these words. The danger he saw then is even more prevalent today: that "the past is the substance out of which the present has been formed, and to let it slip away from us it to acquiesce in the thinness that characterizes so much of our culture."[48] This is a full-throated endorsement of Searle's concern about what happens in the absence of a canon that at least provides a common ground of understanding even if not agreement for students and thinkers.

Howe stresses the problem that is created when society and it educational institutions fall into the trap of ignoring the best of the past. When these institutions and the people in them fail to study the past and to incorporate it into a framework of knowledge and thinking of citizens, Howe argues that a negative effect results for the ways in which the commonweal and those same institutions, including the academy, are shaped.

Further, Howe joins his ideas to the quest for the college and university to be both servant and critic. "Serious education must assume, in part, an adversarial stance toward the very society that sustains it—," because Howe contends "a democratic society makes the wager that it's worth supporting a culture of criticism." Howe is clear about the challenge: "if that criticism loses touch with the heritage of the past, it becomes weightless, a mere compendium of momentary complaints."[49]

Indeed as Howe points out, the contemporary face of anti-intellectualism has a robust imprint, interwoven as it has been with the emergence of political correctness, on the milieu of American society and of the academy in the last sixty plus years since the McCarthy era. However, there are even earlier roots of the relic of anti-intellectualism in the nation's history.

The first major high tide of anti-intellectualism in the American nation and culture (though certainly not its origin) was in the 1830s, emerging with candidacy, election to the presidency of Andrew Jackson, and the political and social views of Jacksonian philosophy. Jackson and politicians who followed him "exhibited relative disdain for what later were to be called 'eggheads' in favor of 'virile' and practical leaders."[50] The Jacksonian era was a time when practicality and pragmatism held sway, qualities that persisted not only into the twentieth century, but also even to today.

However, the political correctness of the late twentieth century, continuing into the twenty-first, has origins that go back even further into the nation's founding. We return to the territory of the era of the Great Awakening. Drawing lessons from that time, Seymour Martin Lipset notes how seminal religious affections and associations in sects and denominations in turn shaped beliefs about human behavior, about society and about the body politic. He pushes this contention into the realm of ideology and the ways both liberals and conservatives have used this American ideology born in the Great Awakening over centuries and into contemporary times.[51]

Lipset believes that the colonial heritage and the Great Awakening shaped the culture of the Republic such that in the longer-term view of history "The United States is the only country in which the majority of the citizens have adhered to the sects, those which the British refer to as the 'dissenting' or 'non-conformist' denominations, rather than to groups that are or once were state churches."[52]

What this culture means for American society and for its colleges and universities is that the social practice and mores of this religious and theological inclination produced "The sectarian emphasis on moralism is reinforced by elements derivative from the fact that the United States defines its *raison d'être* ideologically." Lipset then adds a clincher, quoting Richard Hofstadter about America: "It has been our fate as a nation not to have ideologies but to be one."[53]

This is the ideology of "Americanism" and it is one that both the political Left and the political Right have fought over for centuries. The battle lines are clear: "The emphasis on Americanism as a political ideology has led to a Utopian and absolutist orientation among American liberals and conservatives." Sharing this burden and the cudgels that it provides has led both sides of the political spectrum and divide to "seek to extend their version of the good society. Those who reject American values are incorrect, are un-American and may be denied rights."[54]

These diametrically opposed political sides have, whether aware of it or not, been fighting over this ideology of "Americanism" during the contemporary era of political correctness. The corner on the market they seek to control is not a jingoistic or overwrought patriotic (though it has some elements of the latter) rallying around the nation, right or wrong. Rather it is a battle for prominence as the holder of the keys, and by implication to be able to shape the transcendent, essential, and correct "morality," of American society and of the academy.

That morality is rooted in Lipset's assertion that "The American sectarian religious ethos has assumed, in practice if not in theology, the perfectibility of humanity and the obligation to avoid sin," as opposed to the major churches that accept "the inherent weakness of people and the need for the church and the polity to be forgiving and protecting."[55]

Thus there is a plausible way, one grounded in history and historical examples, to examine what the sides of Left and Right are doing in today's politically correct setting. To be precise, the ground that is being contended is begged by the question: Who has the correct path to "perfectibility of humanity," versus some other power, be it the church, the government, or any other institution, ironically including the academy, that accepts "the inherent weakness of people"; or that provides for the need for forgiveness and protection?

Lipset concludes his thoughts about political rightness and wrongness invoking a 1975 statement at Yale University developed by a Committee on Freedom of Expression, chaired by the noted American historian C. Vann Woodward. This committee was charged with helping Yale, and given its prestige other college and university faculty and leaders as well, to navigate the tense struggles of the 1960s and early 1970s.

That committee attempted to get at the root of a classical American dilemma and balancing act: the need for respect and civility in a university or any community on one hand, with the university's and society's particular need in a democracy to guarantee individual free expression. The Yale group concluded that, "even when some members of the university community fail to meet their social and ethical responsibilities, the paramount obligation of the university is to protect their right to free expression."[56]

The Yale statement makes clear the horns of the dilemma, but also provides critical direction and advice about what the university's obligations are: "If the university's overriding commitment to free expression is to be sustained, *secondary social and ethical responsibilities must be left to the informal processes of suasion, example, and argument.*"[57]

## CAN THE ACADEMY "ESCAPE FROM THE IDEOLOGICAL PRISONS"?

Life for the college and university in the immediate post-World War II years on the front of ideological battles became more complicated as the academy dealt with political rightness and wrongness, the political correctness conundrums of the latter twentieth and early twenty-first centuries. The position of ideological individuals and groups about how society should be fashioned differed widely. These polemics of differences were more intense and received greater public attention beginning in the early 1950s than had been the case in prior decades and centuries.

Much of this increasingly complicated pressure stemmed from the confluence of four issues on the nation's agenda. These issues were in the forefront of the social and political platforms shared by many citizens of the nation and by constituents of diverse and clashing groups, especially in the academy but also outside the gates.

The first issue was a greater emphasis than in previous times on pluralism—to what extent would the nation embrace its rhetoric of "give me
your tired, your poor," and of "_e pluribus unum._" America was assumed
to have out a welcome mat and to bring into the fabric of the nation a
broad diversity of people, and by extension the college and university.
Regardless of any group, racial, ethnic, gender or other differences, all
were to be welcomed.

Pluralism was in theory supposed to work out and to be successful,
especially in a democracy, its aspirations able to be accomplished even if
with tensions and conflicts. However, dueling political correctness camps
came to think otherwise and to create a great divide between them about
the meaning, efficacy, and acceptability of pluralism.

A second problem in the post-World War II years connected to the
problem of pluralism was increased visibility and accompanying debates
in the arena of diversity. Populations, especially racial and ethnic minorities, the socio-economically disadvantaged, and women, previously shut
out of American society, its politics, governments, workplace employment, housing, and educational opportunities—K–12 and higher education—were at the door seeking access and a share in the rewards of the
commonweal.

But as with pluralism, contending political parties and campus factions, in- and outside the gates of the academy, found little agreement
about the problems, whether there even were problems, and what to do
about them.

Further complicating matters, and also connected to both pluralism
and diversity are issues of equality, a third factor in the tangled web of
political and social issues that came more to the forefront for the nation
and the academy in the mid- to latter twentieth century. As with the
assumed American claims about pluralism and diversity, the 1960s protests about equality also challenged whether the nation would be true to
its creed: all are created equal, endowed by their Creator with unalienable rights, life, liberty, and the pursuit of happiness.

A final element in the mix of the flurry of post-World War II changes
that complicated the political culture and made more intense political
correctness debates was the emergence of the "post" everything era. To
wit, coming into the public consciousness and discussion, the platform
for discussion of social and political issues in America was defined in
terms of post-Modernism and post-Protestantism (some claimed post-
religious, i.e., "God is dead" as declared on a 1960s cover of _Time_ magazine). This environment led to complicated issues and concerns being
reduced to simple pros and cons, further reduced to appearance as black
and white.

In such an environment, critical thinking challenged and criticized
long-standing premises and established mores, ethical assumptions and
beliefs. This critique of society and culture created a vacuum of morality

and values. Into that breach came those demanding moral replacements and often through the use of sheer demagoguery. Both sides of the political correctness divide made careers out of presenting themselves as the saviors, filling this vacuum that creates a society and academy that is in disarray, and lacks moral fiber and a moral compass.

These four factors created a complex culture of politics and academic thinking than had previously been witnessed pre-World War II. This environment, with all of its entanglements and competing, mutually exclusive demands, jump-started ideological thinking. Social and political culture, and advocates for competing positions were provided with new grist for their mills. This in turn altered how issues were framed, how sides were chosen, leading by the late 1970s, but also born out of the Sturm und Drang of the 1960s, to the coining of the term political correctness.

Though not the only precipitating pressure leading to the choosing of sides and the hardening of positions, diversity and multiculturalism simultaneously became a cause celebre on one side, the Progressive Left, and a red flag on the other side, the neoconservative, Right wing, of the political correctness divide. The seeds of disagreements over diversity and multiculturalism were planted in the minority recruitment, curricular innovation, financial aid, and "studies" program challenges and controversies of the 1960s and early 1970s.

Those battlegrounds were partially resolved but in large measure kicked down the road to become even more inflamed in the 1980s and early 1990s. The goals of multiculturalism and of the demands for diversity are admirable. However, advocates of those goals occasionally resisted engaging any discussion about their positions, in part because of the invective and ad hominem attacks mounted by their opponents.

At the risk of violating political incorrectness, Eric Mack wades into this complicated territory. He points out that "the university *must*, to be true to its mission—establish mechanisms for the evaluation of how fully its members satisfy the diverse aspects of this complex demand," for multiculturalism and diversity. However, it must do so in ways that insure "its members contribute to (or show due promise of contributing to) the process of inquiry and debate by which its goal is advanced."[58]

For Mack the core of the problem is what happens when issues, especially ones of potential or real controversy, are cordoned off, siloed, and insulated from criticism and discussion? Or what happens when those issues are viewed as third rails that few professors, leaders, or commentators on the Left especially, but occasionally even on the Right as well, wish to avoid at all costs.

Mack's contention is that if "intellectual worth" is not viewed as something that can be evaluated with "validity across all racial, ethnic, or gender lines," if these "forms of intellectual worth . . . were incommensurable all the way down," then "Clearly this would require the dissolution of anything like the evaluation process." That should be the modus operandi required of a university. However, the failure to do so puts at risk its mission and its way of doing business.[59]

The danger is clear: When the university caves to political correctness it equally loses its identity as the university in a fashion similar to what happens when it becomes exclusively a social, political, and cultural institution of change.

Maintaining dialogue and rational discussion in the academy across these divides over diversity is no simple task. Mack cites the great thinker and experienced denizen of the ivory tower—professor and academician for decades, administrator at Columbia in the tense and tight 1960s—Isaiah Berlin. Berlin commented about "the analogous problem of transcultural understanding: 'Unless we are able to escape from the ideological prisons of class or nation or doctrine, we shall not be able to avoid seeing alien institutions or customs as either too strange to make any sense to us, or as issues of error, lying inventions of unscrupulous priests . . .'"[60]

The problem is that life in the academy in the middle of the political battleground lends itself to Berlin's "ideological prisons of class or nation or doctrine." Mack drills down into this morass in light of Berlin's ideas.

"If today's friends of diversity were equally responsive to the significance and limits of diversity, then two hallmarks of that tradition," Mack argues, "the liberal social order and the liberal university would have more auspicious futures." However, that prospect pivots on the counter impasse that " . . . at its base the current ideology of diversity, the new Counter-Enlightenment, denigrates the possibility of common epistemological norms and of rational dialogue among representatives of differing racial, gender, or national groups."[61]

Mack views this denigration as corroding the establishment of a common framework for comprehending human values and aspirations, and the ambition of ordering relationships within the university or within society at large in ways that are just for all.[62] In other words, in his view the manner in which advocates of diversity make their claims creates an environment in which rational dialogue and critique are less possible and that these foundation stones of the academy could cease to exist. In an added irony, the quest to fashion society and the academy as "just for all" is kicked to the curb by the very camp—proponents of diversity—that would claim that as a major goal.

Thus a dystopian outcome presents itself. "This is not a formula for increased harmonious existence among individuals or groups, either within the university or within the wider society. Rather it is a formula for factional strife, irresoluble tribal conflict, and rule by interest-group manipulation and coercion," Mack laments.[63]

A slice of the diversity debate and of the on-going tribal conflict that Mack underscores is a battle-line over the questions of minority versus majority interpretations of history and current events. This debate is also coupled with a set of assertions pro and con about the degree to which those of any race, gender, or other minority status require for positive affect only leaders, mentors, teachers, and writers of their own kind.

Multiculturalists tend to take this point of view. Namely that education should feature not only diverse curriculum and attention to diversity within content areas, but also that minority teachers are necessary to educate minority students, whether in the early grades or much later in the collegiate educational years.

Arthur Schlesinger does not agree with this contention about who can best educate whom. "Great artists, thinkers, leaders are the possession not just of their own racial clan," Schlesinger alleges, "but of all humanity."[64]

Building on this assertion and joining Philip Rieff's thoughts above about the "triumph of the therapeutic," Schlesinger presses the case that "The use of history as therapy means the corruption of history as history."[65] Schlesinger's evidence for this assertion is simple yet profound: "All major races, cultures, nations have committed crimes, atrocities, horrors at one time or another. Every civilization has skeletons in its closet."[66]

In the face of the skeletons in everyone's closet, "Honest history calls for the unexpurgated record. How much would a full account of African despotism, massacre, and slavery increase the self-esteem of black students?" Schlesinger rhetorically asks. His answer cuts to the chase: "Yet what kind of history do you have if you leave out all the bad things?"[67]

If the academy in America has an escape route from the confines and bondage of the most extreme forms of political correctness on one side, and the politically motivated critics of those progressive, leftist agendas on the other, it is only through relying on its foundation: the college and university qua the college and university.

To do this, academic freedom and responsibility have to be at the forefront. And the balancing act is between the tyrannies of both the majority and the minority. Both sides in the political correctness debates would claim that they too wish to avoid becoming a tyranny of the minority or of the majority. However, both sides seek and are more than willing to use this leverage when it is to their advantage and suits their purposes.

The twin injunctions of responsibility and restraint are critical traits that college and university faculty must regard, pay homage to, and exert extreme caution about when they exercise academic freedom. Robert Post and Matthew Finkin acknowledge that these are realistic concerns, but caution that they cannot be pushed too far lest academic freedom itself collapses.[68]

Post and Finkin argue "there is a fundamental distinction between holding faculty accountable to professional norms and holding them accountable to public opinion." This tension is a severe one, in which "The former exemplifies academic freedom; the latter undermines it." "Even though institutions of higher education in fact depend on public acceptance," Post and Finkin note, "they cannot shackle scholars to the 'generally accepted beliefs' of those 'persons, private or official, through whom society provides the means for the maintenance of universities.'"[69]

Here again is the balancing act of the university as servant and critic and that applies to all within its gates, but especially faculty members. Those who have been the "architects of the American idea of academic freedom" knew that while faculty have to be "professionally responsible," as they exercise that responsibility they "should be insulated from the *pieties of public opinion.*"[70]

In today's early twenty-first-century climate, the "pieties of public opinion" appear similarly in the 1915 "Declaration of Principles on Academic Freedom and Academic Tenure" of the AAUP at its founding, when it warned about the "tyranny of public opinion."[71] The question for the college and university at present and as a prospect for the future is: Is the tyranny of public opinion worsening or is it merely always a threat, as is the tyranny of the minority (and as pointed out, the two are often coincident) in a democracy?

Nothing more aptly concludes this journey through the post-McCarthy years to present in the political, social, and cultural wrangling in the American college and university than the 1940 AAUP Statement of Principles on Academic Freedom and Tenure: "*Institutions of higher education are conducted for the common good* and not to further the interest of either the individual teacher or the institution as a whole. *The common good depends on the free search for truth and its free exposition.*"[72]

Here is a guide and a prescription for an "escape from the ideological prisons" of the academy and American society. This statement of the AAUP is drawn from Cardinal Newman's notions of an "intellectual culture." It reflects Minogue's thinking that constitutes his "concept of the university."

To have that truly "intellectual culture," to be the university as the university, the pathway is clear: "If the university's overriding commitment to free expression is to be sustained, *secondary social and ethical responsibilities must be left to the informal processes of suasion, example, and argument.*"[73]

## NOTES

1. John Henry Newman, *The Idea of the University*, I. T. Kerr, ed., (Oxford: Clarendon Press, 1976).

2. Kenneth Minogue, *The Concept of a University* (Berkeley: University of California Press, 1973).

3. Ibid., 3–4.

4. Ibid., 7.

5. Ibid.

6. For a full discussion of this latter problem of fund raising and the hunt for dollars, see Stephen J. Nelson, *Leaders in the Labyrinth: College Presidents and the Battleground of Creeds and Convictions* (Westport, CT: ACE/Praeger, Greenwood Publishing, 2007), 7–22.

7. James Madison, "Memorial and Remonstrance Against Religious Assessments," 1785, http://press-pubs.uchicago.edu/founders/documents/amendI_religions43.html.

8. Ibid., unpaginated.

9. Ibid.

10. Robert O'Neil, *Academic Freedom in the Wired World: Political Extremism, Corporate Power, and the University* (Cambridge, MA: Harvard University Press, 2008), 281.

11. Ibid.

12. Ibid.

13. Douglas Sloan, *The Great Awakening and American Education: A Documentary History* (New York and London: Teachers College Press, 1973).

14. Ibid., 47–48.

15. Ibid., 53.

16. Ibid.

17. For extensive discussion about the era of the 1960s and 70s, see Stephen J. Nelson, *Decades of Chaos and Revolution: Showdowns for College Presidents* (Lanham, MD: Rowman & Littlefield, ACE Higher Education Series, 2012).

18. Sloan, 52. Italics the author.

19. Ron Dworkin, "We Need a New Interpretation of Academic Freedom," in *The Future of Academic Freedom*, ed. Louis Menand (Chicago: University of Chicago Press, 1996).

20. Ibid., 195.

21. Ibid.

22. Edward Said, "Identity, Authority, and Freedom: The Potentate and the Traveler," in *The Future of Academic Freedom*, ed. Louis Menand (Chicago: University of Chicago Press, 1996), 224, from Newman's *The Idea of a University* (1853, 1858) (New York: Doubleday and Co., 1962), 149

23. Ibid., 225, in Newman, 138.

24. Said, 225.

25. Ibid., Newman, 158.

26. Robert O'Neil, *Academic Freedom in the Wired World: Political Extremism, Corporate Power, and the University* (Cambridge, MA: Harvard University Press, 2008), 4.

27. Ibid., 248–49.

28. Ibid., 249.

29. Ibid., 250–56.

30. Ibid., 256–57.

31. Ibid., 256.

32. Ibid., 256–57.

33. Ibid., 260.

34. Ibid.

35. Thomas L. Haskell, "Justifying the Rights of Academic Freedom in the Era of 'Power/Knowledge,'" in *The Future of Academic Freedom*, ed. Louis Menand (Chicago: University of Chicago Press, 1996), 58.

36. Ibid., 59.

37. Donald Alexander Downs, *Restoring Free Speech and Liberty on Campus* (Oakland, CA: The Independent Institute and Cambridge: Cambridge University Press, 2005), 14.

38. Ibid., 44.

39. Ibid.

40. Arthur Schlesinger, Jr., *The Disuniting of America* (New York: W. W. Norton and Company, 1992).

41. John Searle, "The Storm Over the University," in *Debating P. C.: The Controversy Over Political Correctness on College Campuses*, ed. Paul Berman (New York: Dell Publishing, 1992), 85.

42. Ibid., 85–86.

43. Ibid., 94.

44. Ibid., 94–95.

45. http://www.thedailybeast.com/articles/2014/03/09/richard-hofstadter-and-america-s-new-wave-of-anti-intellectualism.html, unpaginated.

46. Irving Howe, "The Value of the Canon," in *Debating P. C.: The Controversy Over Political Correctness on College Campuses*, ed. Paul Berman (New York: Dell Publishing, 1992), 162.

47. Ibid.

48. Ibid.

49. Ibid.

50. Stanley Rothman, "Tradition and Change: The University Under Stress," in *The Imperiled Academy*, ed. Howard Dickman (New Brunswick, NJ and London: Transaction Publishers, 1993), 33.

51. Seymour Martin Lipset, "Sources of Political Correctness on American Campuses," in *The Imperiled Academy*, ed. Howard Dickman (New Brunswick, NJ and London: Transaction Publishers, 1993).

52. Ibid., 71–72.

53. Ibid., 72.

54. Ibid.

55. Ibid., 71.

56. Ibid., 91.

57. Ibid., Italics mine.

58. Eric Mack, "The Limits of Diversity: The New Counter-Enlightenment and Isaiah Berlin's Liberal Pluralism," in *The Imperiled Academy*, ed. Howard Dickman (New Brunswick, NJ and London: Transaction Publishers, 1993), 112.

59. Ibid.

60. Ibid., 113.

61. Ibid., 121.

62. Ibid.

63. Ibid., 121–22.

64. Arthur Schlesinger, Jr., *The Disuniting of America* (New York: W. W. Norton and Company, 1992), 92.

65. Ibid.,93.

66. Ibid.

67. Ibid.

68. Matthew W. Finkin and Robert C. Post, *For the Common Good: Principles of American Academic Freedom* (New Haven, CT and London: Yale University Press, 2009).

69. Ibid., 154. Quotes are from Arthur O. Lovejoy, *Academic Freedom, in Encyclopedia of the Social Sciences*, eds. Edwin R. A. Seligman and Alvin Johnson (1930), 383–85.

70. Ibid., 154–55, italics mine.

71. Ibid., 150.

72. Ibid., Frontispiece, Italics mine.

73. Seymour Martin Lipset, "Sources of Political Correctness on American Campuses," in *The Imperiled Academy*, ed. Howard Dickman (New Brunswick, NJ and London: Transaction Publishers, 1993), 91. Italics mine.

# Conclusion

## A Coda: The Concept of a University
## in America and the Culture We Deserve

The college and university in America is nearly four hundred years old, launched at the founding of Harvard in 1636, an anniversary just two decades away. The academy has changed dramatically since those few dozen students gathered in and around John Harvard and in Cambridge less than two decades after the first settlers landed on the shores of what was to become the Massachusetts Bay Colony. It took nearly 150 years for the number of higher education institutions, the Colonial Colleges to expand their ranks to a total of nine, at that point with an enrollment toted up among them probably not greater than that of one mid-sized liberal arts college today.

Who in the seventeenth century could have envisioned universities the size and scale of the University of Michigan today, with its two nearly separate campuses that not only comprise Ann Arbor but also fully consume it? Who at the founding of Harvard could have imagined that same University of Michigan being described by one of its late twentieth-century presidents, James Duderstadt, as a "multi-national, entrepreneurial conglomerate"?[1] And Michigan is only one of dozens of such major, gigantic research universities, counting among them but leaving many out: The University of Pennsylvania, Ohio State, Berkeley, Cornell, Johns Hopkins, Chicago, the University of Maryland, Columbia, New York University, and the list could go on.

The founders of Harvard could equally not have come close to imagining even the scale, organizational and bureaucratic complexity, broad curriculum, and grand student amenities of enumerable "small" liberal arts colleges, so closely built on the originating Harvard and classic British models.

There has clearly been a massive evolution in the scope of America's colleges and universities over these nearly four centuries. However, along that road and in the relative terms of history, the First and Second Great Awakenings arguably had as much influence on the shaping of the college and university in America centuries ago as the major technological changes of the latter twentieth and twenty-first century have had in recent times. Changes have been wrought over time. But never has there

291

been a revolution in the direction, mission, and purposes of the nation's higher education institutions.

Thus, one conclusion over and throughout the history of the college and university in America is that the more things change, the more they stay the same. External forces and pressures come and go, be they from political leaders and trends, social and culture critics, or from those who make a parlor game of firing jeremiads and of meddling in the affairs of the academy. All the while, the university retains its shape and form, and it remains on its chosen course.

Sometimes these demands and sways on the college and university lead to constructive and progressive change. In other cases the impact in both the short and long run can be negative. In still other instances, presidential, faculty, and other academic leaders and trustees of the academy have been remarkably skilled and sufficiently sophisticated to be able to duck, feint, and kick challenges aside and down the road so that, whatever the consequences might have been, especially when they were certain to be harmful, they are minimized or avoided altogether.

Many themes in the history of the academy in America have been on the stage for much if not all of the unfolding of our story. We have delved into a number of these in detail. That list, which could be added to, in concise form includes: "disinterested learning" (pure, liberal education vs. vocationalism and professionalism), "faculty power and governance," academic authority and freedom," "curricular conservatism," "educational aims and ideals," "inclusivity and elitism," "knowledge as social construction," "academic conventions," and "rights and rituals."[2]

The historian, Christopher Lucas, formulated these issues and concerns more than twenty years ago. They remain in place in the ensuing two decades, and, given the endurance and persistence they have shown in the past, they likely will continue to be critical in the shaping of the college and university in America for decades, and even in centuries to come. While he does not include the label of political correctness and ideological passions per se, the issues he lists have been shot through those ideological battles for a long time, and particularly in the last fifty years.

## THE POLES OF DEBATE ABOUT THE SHAPE OF THE COLLEGE AND UNIVERSITY

The nation's colleges and universities have been shaped and have fashioned themselves between two poles. Both poles have sought to be victorious with their ideas of the university.

The problem both poles face is that their ideas square off against the concept of the university, and the ideals that undergird this idea. Both poles care little about that foundation, because their goal is to push particular and particularistic agendas.

Both sides in the conversation about what the academy should be are persistently visible with their arguments and insistent on their points of view. For good and ill, they have a remarkable capacity to sustain their positions. Despite setbacks and defeats, they have the ability to present themselves in different guises, to find new iterations of their messages, and to be resurrected by descendants in decades, and sometimes centuries, in the future.

What are the philosophical positions of these opposing poles? Who are these competing parties and factions that seek to shape and create the college and university in their image? Though caricatures, a description of them goes something like this.

On one side are traditionalists, in today's parlance neo-conservatives (not to be confused with foreign policy neo-cons). This side believes that the college and university lost its way. Whatever it once was, along the line the academy and its foundations changed for the worse. Although they don't finger exactly when, they argue that this change happened earlier rather than later in its history. Because traditionalists decry the decay they see happening in every and any historical era, their allegations include but also transcend what is happening today. However, their jeremiads are always clear that today's changes are always more corrosive than anything that took place in past.

What are the horrors that have occurred?

The college and university has abandoned its sense of heritage and the duty to maintain fundamental beliefs and principles. The canon was abandoned. Bureaucrats, their professionalized image and their bureaucracies have corrupted the university's foundations, infected how it is run, and what it conveys its in the public square. The university has been taken over by minions who have no clue about what the higher learning is. Political manipulators overpowered the province of the faculty, of professors, especially their duty and responsibility for the curriculum. Students became less serious about intellectual and academic pursuits. In connected fashion, student behavior and discipline ran amok (and the caliber of the students severely declined).

At the pole on the other side of this equation are the progressive, liberal thinkers. They want to break away from the traditionalists. They condemn the views of the neo-conservatives as hide-bound, elitist, and blind to the need for change and to the face of the challenges of today. In the mind of the progressives, the mission and purpose of the university must be constantly updated, even if that means selectively throwing overboard beliefs and values of predecessors and prior generations of faculty, leaders, and students.

The progressives want social justice and believe the academy has to have a significant hand in that quest. The academy's mission should even be grounded in pursuit of that goal. They want every inequity in society solved. Colleges and universities should be the institutions of society to rectify the wrongs of inequality and inequity. Everyone inside the gates should be protected from anything that they find offensive or disconcerting. No one should be harmed socially or psychologically within or by any attack from outside the gates. Constraints and infringements on academic freedom sometimes must be sacrificed for the greater good of protecting the diversity and multicultural agenda.

Progressives and liberals want to tinker. They believe the curriculum can always be improved and updated for the demands of today, even if that means in the process leaving behind previous content, however important to history and tradition, including where necessary what previously was believed to constitute the essentials of knowledge.

As poles apart as these viewpoints and factions are, their ideas and contentions have been in the water of the academy in America from the get-go. Whatever consternation they cause, their concerns and viewpoints raised are essential to the vitality, the dialogue, and the direction of the academy.

The critical issue at stake for the college and university to remain the college and university is that it continues to be able to juggle and to balance these competing ideologies, and their ideas and principles. That is, amid the controversies and distinctions of political position, there needs to be a center that holds. The university's foundation must be based on weightier, transcendent values, beliefs and convictions, rooted in the university qua the university, rooted in Cardinal Henry Newman's "first principles."

It is these principles that must be sustained in every era and passed on to the next. If either of the poles in this ideological battleground got its way, there would be no "first principles" ala Newman, and there would be no center that could hold. Collapsed in this fashion the university, as Kenneth Minogue points out, is no longer the university but simply some other institution, however important that institution might be and what it might do, in society.[3]

* * *

College presidents are critical shapers and shakers of the academy. The presidential bully pulpit has always been a crucial platform for their ideas. Although only a small sample, three presidents of the last sixty years are noteworthy for ideas about the longed-for hopes and expectations for what the university is and how it can become what it needs to become. These are voices about the fundamental principles in the foundation of college and university and about what it must do in order to have a future as robust as its past.

There is a lengthy litany of critical issues in the life of the academy. This list includes obstacles that must be overcome and the rich heritage that must undergird the future pathway that ensures that the university remains the university. Numerous hallmarks have overtime contributed to and altered the shape of the college and university in America. The themes that emerge make the history of the college and university unique and distinctive.

These presidents and their ideas provide touchstones about what is known, understood, and crucial in the history that will continue to unfold for the college and university in America. Three presidents—John Dickey of Dartmouth, Bart Giamatti of Yale, and John Sexton of New York University—express concerns about the foundation of the academy in distinctive ways reflective of their times, interestingly separated from each other by about twenty-five years.

They utilize these touchstones of the history of the college and university to craft impressions about the current and future state of the academy in America.

Their ideas address where the college and university stands, and the challenges and crises it has faced over the last decades of the twentieth and in the early years of the twenty-first centuries: Dickey: the purpose and ideal of the college and the value of the liberal arts and a liberal education; Giamatti: the fundamental value of free and open dialogue in the navigation of controversies and disagreements in the university; and Sexton: the university's duty to push back against dueling ideological factions, especially in a politically correct world, and to maintain a civil climate and an arena of free speech conducted with rationality and respect.

## THE PURPOSE OF A COLLEGE EDUCATION:
## THE UNITING OF CONSCIENCE AND COMPETENCE

John Sloan Dickey served as the president of Dartmouth College from 1945–1969. Ten years into his tenure Dickey published in (of all places and wouldn't it be lovely to see this today) *The Atlantic Monthly*, "Conscience and the Undergraduate." He claimed that both "conscience" and "competence" had to be viewed as instrumental in an undergraduate education. One without the other would not do if the college student were to be fully educated as an undergraduate.

The college had to "find a significant, even unique, mission in the duality of its historic purpose: to see men [and women] made whole in both competence and conscience." The rhetorical but compelling question: "Is there any other institution at the highest level of organized educational activity that is committed explicitly by its history and by its program to these twin goals?"[4] While Dickey doesn't deny the necessity, even the desirability, of educational preparation for competence, the critical value and the task of the college are "to keep competence civilized."

There is an understandable tension created by those who view undergraduate education as the setting that provides competence and pathways to vocations, to professional lives. Of course, those on the other side of the coin are fearful that emphasis on a college education as preparation for the professions, for life in the real world, debases, even destroys the loftier, more transcendent aims of the liberal arts: education for the sake of education, and an education that in Dickey's terms will shape and inspire conscience.

However, Dickey believed, rather than cordoning off the needs of professions from the goals of a liberal education and of an education in conscience, that the risk of mixing the two purposes of education was ". . . worth taking because I am increasingly persuaded that the cause of liberal education will not be overrun by vocationalism if the college holds to its birthright and remains committed as a matter of purpose to serious concern with the issues of conscience." Absent that commitment, the danger is clear. "To create the power of competence without creating a corresponding sense of moral direction to guide the use of that power is bad education," Dickey exhorts.

Life in- and outside the gates of the academy is an ever-changing landscape. Dickey acknowledges that the pillars on which the academy in America had relied in prior eras were no longer in place. Those pillars were: "1) the tradition of preacher presidents, 2) a curriculum heavy with religion and moral doctrine, and 3) compulsory church and chapel." These "constitutional elements in the life of these [independent, liberal arts] colleges permeated all that these institutions were and did." By 1955, all three were wiped out, the only exceptions being religiously dominated colleges, most of which within a decade or two had also abandoned these "constitutional elements."

"Nothing comparable was substituted for the outmoded agencies, and this gap in the context of purpose," Dickey believed "remains an uncorrected weakness on most undergraduate campuses today." He argues that to cave into this reality was "bad education."

That is, the future of a moral basis and conscience in education is in jeopardy if either: "1) the college's historic commitment to furthering the moral and spiritual growth of an undergraduate truly ceased with the passing of these particular witnesses, or 2) in serving this purpose," the unreliable choice being that "we can rely exclusively on the ebb and flow of its awareness in individual teachers and administrators rather than on the more traditional combination of men plus the prod of institutional form and purpose." This latter point is most telling. Dickey did not believe we could run the risk of simply relying only on the "ebb and flow" of whether teachers and administrators in any generation understand and are committed to the moral foundations of education.

Dickey pressed his board for a critical statement designed to make clear his position about a Dartmouth education. They delivered, stating that the college's "moral and spiritual purpose springs from a belief in the existence of good and evil, from faith in the ability of men to choose between them and from a sense of duty to advance the good." This is religious, theological language, pushing for discernment and by commitment from faculty and students, designed to sort expectations of what should be the nature and outcome of an education.

Dickey heralds the trustees for a response to the eclipse of the three pillars that had featured in and sustained the academy over the previous three centuries of its existence in the United States. And he turns to his turn-of-the-century predecessor, William Jewett Tucker, Dartmouth's last preacher-president, who set the table for Dickey's contentions about an undergraduate education: *"Do not expect that you will make any lasting or very strong impression on the world through intellectual power without the use of an equal amount of conscience and heart."*

The academy has proven to uphold both broad preparation for life and for pursuit of the life of the mind. Dickey stands in a long tradition of shapers of colleges and universities committed to this combined purpose of education. He makes clear that it is not competence versus conscience, rather that "it is the human interplay between these two poles of purpose that gives liberal education its orientation to the light and brings to the undergraduate grown a man those liberating and civilizing qualities men never quite define nor ever quite deny."

### THE DANGERS OF IDEOLOGICAL DIFFERENCES: CODIFICATION VERSUS DIALOGUE AND THE HOLDING OF THE CENTER OF THE ACADEMY

The historic role of an exchange of ideas on college campuses faced compromises in the 1960s and 1970s related to institutional handling of rational, open discourse and dialogue in the academy. Competing poles in the political climate of the times led to the politically correct environment that stifled the core principles of free speech and liberty.

In this environment, disagreements and mutually exclusive positions of competing factions reached not-before-seen levels of intensity and acrimony. Controversies came in waves, sparked and magnified by critics, and by the opposing political poles of Left and Right both in and outside the gates.

What was at stake was whether colleges and universities would be able to continue navigating their affairs within the canopy of a broadly defined and agreed-to center that can hold. Absent a consensus about fundamental principles of debate and dialogue, the university was destined to become a centripetal institution, rudderless, vulnerable, and unable any longer to the face critical issues and crises with rational thinking and collegiality.

Bart Giamatti was the president of Yale University from 1978 to 1986. Political correctness was in its nascent stage. Ideologies peppering campuses in the preceding decades were becoming more firmly entrenched in the life of the academy. Anticipating the battles that would emerge over political correctness before it even had that name, Giamatti was prescient about what the academy would have to juggle in handling diversity concerns and in resorting to "solutions" like speech codes.[5]

Giamatti saw a dangerous drift toward codifying and legislating as the way to resolve differing points of view, as contrasted with the messy thrashing out of divisive matters through debate and discourse. He called this approach "codification," the tendency for "the codification of us all."[6]

On the horizon of Giamatti's time were arrays of developments that came to shape the 1980s. These included speech and harassment codes and more recently dust-ups over "trigger points," i.e., the need for professors somehow to anticipate negative student reactions to course materials and class discussions, and for litmus tests concerning public speakers and pressures to draw lines around who can speak and who cannot.

Underscoring the hypocrisy of the academy in handling battles over values, Giamatti lamented that ". . . the values universities say they cherish and foster and promote have not always been fostered, cherished and promoted within them. . . ."[7] He hoped for change in that "codification" would end up being only "a transitory phenomenon; that . . . we do not depend upon law for all our ideals; that we do not believe codes are more than ghostly sketches of consensus. . . ."[8]

Giamatti warned present and future generations of college and university leaders—presidents, trustees, and faculty—that they would have to deal with these issues of the threat to consensus and with a heightened development of political correctness. To defend the academy, leaders would have to repel these damaging forces and to ameliorate their destructive effects. However, he recognized that this task would not be easy: "In such matters we do best when we remember institutions change so they may endure, endure with a sense of their purpose and dignity, which sense is what differentiates endurance from mere survival," Giamatti exhorts.[9]

THE UNIVERSITY AS SANCTUARY: CIVILITY AND
DISCOURSE IN THE CONTEMPORARY IDEOLOGICAL ERA

John Sexton, president of New York University from 2002 to present, tackled the political correctness debates and the ideological divide controversies of the latter twentieth and early twenty-first centuries that had begun to emerge during Giamatti's watch. Sexton stresses both the gravity of these divides as well as the ways the academy can and should navigate them. Invoking Judeo-Christian and medieval notions about the physical and psychological "space" that defines the temple or the church, he argues for the "university as sanctuary."[10]

"Increasingly, our great universities are modern sanctuaries, the sacred spaces sustaining and enhancing scholarship, creativity and learning," Sexton argues. The notion of "sanctury" signals "both the specialness of what our great universities do, and the fragility of the environment in which it is done. What makes these sanctuaries special," Sexton declares, "is the core commitment to free, unbridled and, ideologically unconstrained discourse in which claims of knowledge are examined, confirmed, deepened, or replaced."[11]

In this way the university counters the "powerful evidence that the quality of dialogue in much of our society increasingly is impoverished — that, just when there is a need for more nuanced reflection and discussion, civil discourse seems ever less able to deliver it."[12] However the danger remains that "the polarization and oversimplification of civic discourse have been accompanied by a simultaneous attempt to capture the space inside the university for the external battle."[13]

Like Giamatti, Sexton takes aim at both the political Left and Right. "This trend does not arise from one political side or another, but from a tendency to enlist the university not for its wisdom, but for its symbolic value as a vehicle to ratify a received vision."[14] The university cannot permit itself to fall into this dangerous trap. The damage of politicization of the university is a major dilemma facing American higher education. To Sexton these are the stakes: political battles about the university and brought into the "ivory tower" as proxy battles to be fought within the university risk its very survival.

In this contemporary landscape and culture, fundamentalists of all stripes—political, cultural, and religious—are in great ascendency. This ratchets up the rhetoric of ideological debates to unprecedented levels. The result in Sexton's view is that whether played out on television and other media, or directly inside the gates, what the university and American society are subject to is "a coliseum culture that reduces discourse to gladiatorial combat."[15]

It bears repeating that ideologies possess the look of religions, and hold their beliefs and convictions with the passion and commitment of true religious believers. Sexton sheds light on this situation, claiming that these "theological politics" reveal, "the tendency of more and more of my fellow citizens literally to derive political views from maxims of religious faith, maxims at best untestable in civil discourse and sometimes at odds with observable reality."[16]

These theological politics are coupled to a "more pervasive dogmatism" that reflects the following: "the resulting appetite for simple an-

swers is nourished in a feedback loop involving the media and civic
leaders, and breeds a discourse by slogan (equally untestable in civil
dialogue) and a powerful civic dogmatism." This dogmatism produces
"those who would restrict free inquiry on campus or impose regulations
requiring that the composition of the faculty conform to their notions of
'balance.'"[17]

The tragic result of all of this battling is that *"The dogmatic in effect
believe that they already have arrived at their final intellectual resting place,
which is why they are so at odds with the nature of the university."*[18] If the
university is to remain the university, it cannot permit such dogmatism
to rule.

The questions raised by this contemporary milieu and its bearing on
the university are numerous: How do you engage those that disdain
dialogue and discourse? Absent rational discourse how are understandings reached among competing ideas and positions? What is the pathway
to solutions to alter a climate that is this corrosive to the historical foundation of the university?

In response, Sexton argues that "Instead of the occasional invitation to
an academic to have seven minutes on 'Crossfire,' the university can
invite the public into a very different process for testing and shaping
ideas."[19] However, the problem that remains in battling ideological
camps is that they "cannot contribute [to discourse] because they treat
their conclusions as matters of dogma and, therefore, expound their positions," Sexton laments, "in declaratory form; they live in an Alice in
Wonderland world—first the conclusion, then the conversation."

These dualing factions "cannot participate meaningfully in the dialogue, because they will not engage it; the exercise is a serial monologue
in which they state and restate but never revisit or rethink their positions.
*Thus, the kernel of truth in the political correctness debate: ideological conversa-
tion is of little or no value."*[20]

## CHALLENGES IN THE FUTURE OF THE
## COLLEGE AND UNIVERSITY

The challenges ahead for the college and university in America will be
equally boundless as any that have been faced in the past. Regarding
recurrent crises of the university, John Gardner, public servant and federal cabinet official, presciently declared nearly fifty years ago, "If the college or university is to preserve its character as a community and forge
for itself a distinctive identity and role in the vast clutter of scholarly,
scientific, and instructional activities that will characterize our evolving
technological society, it will have to have a considerable measure of internal coherence and morale."[21]

If anything, the splintering and individualizing (as well as isolating) effect of technology has been even greater than Gardner could have figured in the late 1960s. But it also has by no means wrecked the college and university.

Gardner adds that for there to be that level of "internal coherence and morale, . . . trustees, administration, faculty, and students are going to have to admit that they are all part of one community—distasteful as that may be to some of them—and they are going to have to ask what they can do individually and collaboratively to preserve the integrity and coherence of that community and to regain command of its future."[22] Commenting about any nation or society, but equally applicable to the academy, Barzun underscores Gardner's point contending that, "When the general will does not habitually prevail over particular wills, nothing is left but the arbitrary acts of improvised centers of power."[23]

Another challenge that the university in America continues to face, both in the 1960s of Gardner's day and today, is the degree to which the liberal arts and especially the humanities can be sustained in the core and requirements of the undergraduate curriculum, and in the breadth of the education students receive.[24]

Debates about the liberal arts reveal long-standing arguments about higher education in America. These discussions and the sides that ganged up in this debate have been around since the Colonial Colleges. However, the issues captured under the umbrella of the role and place of the liberal arts became more critical and a more crucial focus with the advent of the research university and the heightened emphasis on education beyond the undergraduate years, as well as for advanced training for the professions.

There has always been this tension—the Dickey issue—in the college in America between education for the sake of education, and education as preparation for the trades and professions. This has been the case from the colonial era through later eras, when the demands arose for a college education to provide preparation for work in the industrial, commercial, and corporate economy that emerged from the Industrial Revolution of the mid to late nineteenth century. This emphasis has continued as the university has had to confront and adapt to the growth and complexity of the commercial, technological, and innovative changes in the economy of twentieth and now the twenty-first centuries.

As we have seen, there are many examples throughout the ages of this battle of the liberal arts versus education for the practical, professional, and business needs of society and the economy. To reiterate only a few: the Yale Report of 1828 clearly wrestled with this issue.

It was the modus operandi for Francis Wayland's attempts in the late 1820s and into the 1830s to make over Brown University as an educational institution more dedicated to workforce and workplace competence and preparation.

Continuing battles ensued from the 1920s to the 1950s over concerns about how well (many thought nowhere near enough) colleges and universities were contributing to national needs in world conflicts against Fascism, Nazism, Communism, and other threats of those decades. The solution in this case: much greater emphasis on science, technology, and the practical domestic and geo-political arts involved in war and peace.

Finally, the last fifty and more years have been marked by a succession with some overlap of suggested initiatives and also kicking cans down the road regarding curricular battles over relevance in the 1960s, through the multicultural demands and debates of the 1970s, to present times. Even as those unfolded, concerns over the demands for workplace preparation have continued to provide a backdrop for all these larger arguments about the purposes of a college and university undergraduate education.

However, throughout all of that history there exists a nagging conundrum that cannot be simply swept under the carpet. How this puzzle and the challenges it comprises are resolved pivots on two critical issues: First, how we understand the heart of the matter of the purpose and intent of a higher education, the higher learning; and second, what we believe about how those aspirations, met or unmet, filter into and shape the very society, the type of nation in which we live.

David Truman had a long and distinguished career in higher education. He was in the middle of the extensive debates about curriculum (and also the major student protests about the war and racial issues) during the 1960s as dean of Columbia College and Provost at Columbia, and later serving as president of Smith College.

Concerning a college education, what should transpire for students? What is the faculty's duty to insure the best education they might offer? What are the choices they face in trying to accomplish that end?

Truman argues that considering "training in the skills that lie at the core of a specialty" and questions about where the liberal arts fit in that picture "is not the specious one of 'breadth' versus 'depth,' which implies a nonsensical choice between superficiality and competence. The central problem is rather relevant breadth versus a limited and dangerously irresponsible competence."[25]

The further inescapable concern is that, "Such personal competence," Truman echoing Dickey warns, "may be equivalent to social incompetence; it may either ignore the moral and political consequences of what the specialist does or may permit him to make decisions on behalf of the society for which he is in fact unequipped."[26] Herein lies the larger problem for individuals and for society: How are people educated? What is it that we would like to think students, particularly undergraduates, have learned in the "big picture" for their lives? And thus, what is the impact on society and the greater good of the commons concerning what those students will do for good or ill, whether intentionally or by default?

The intensifying necessity in the latter twentieth and twenty-first centuries for specialization at the college and university level, in the content of the curriculum, and in the type of students produced as they labor through their college education, should come as no surprise. The demands of the nation and of American society have become more exacting, especially in the last century.

Thus the academy had to get progressively more up-to-speed with the claims on it from outside the gates in order to continue fulfilling its long-standing and expected role for the public good. To be comprehensive in its role, it had to do this by graduating rising generations of students not only to become political, social, cultural, and religious leaders, but more critically to produce students who would be business, corporate, and industrial movers and shakers, as well to fill the ranks of ever-important professions in medicine, law, and engineering.

How to do all of that without the college and university morphing into an institution altogether different from its heritage, that is the university as the university, was and remains a tricky proposition. No one appreciated more the trickiness of this duty of the academy than Jacques Barzun.

Barzun was long-standing member of the academy as a professor, one time provost and thinker about what the college and university is and how it can maintain its status and presence in society. He served administratively side-by-side with Truman at Columbia in the tumultuous 1960s and in discussions over the curriculum at the university, subsequently returning full-time to the faculty as he turned over the provost's chair to Truman.

Barzun uses the word culture, or more precisely "cultivation" to describe what distinguishes universities from among even other similar institutions in the world of arts and culture.[27] He suggests that:

> If a visitor from outer space were to ask any well-informed American, on a campus or at some artistic gathering. Tell me how I can find the best evidences of high culture in this country, the answer would very likely be, Go to our colleges and universities.

Even though other cultural and artistic institutions would likely be named as well, Barzun is convinced "that universities would be mentioned first."[28]

The problem for Barzun, however, is that this person from outer space would be disappointed upon observation of our universities. That is because the visitor would find "extraordinarily bright people, often very learned people, dedicated to the *idea* of a particular art," but that these experts and specialists would be so caught up in their own field that they would be "too busy handling their cultural assignment to cultivate themselves within it or beyond it."[29]

The college and university has not done its job of "cultivation" when the education offered to students produces such shortsighted ways of seeing the world around them. This failure diminishes the lives of students in terms of what they are able to contribute to society, and to the very education they receive. In such an educational world, even the arts and the humanities "are no longer valuable for their direct effect on the head-and-heart; they become valuable as professions, as means of livelihood, as badges of honor, as goods to be marketed, as components of the culture industry," Barzun laments.[30]

A piece of this problem, maybe the horse that has left the barn, is rooted in Barzun's belief that the challenges for the humanities were magnified when colleges like lemmings raced over the cliff in reframing the curriculum on the grounds of the value of electives. This battle was fought out over decades in the eighteenth century and spilled well into the twentieth. Today, liberal arts colleges and universities that believe they sustain the essence of a liberal education feel they can only do so by permitting a choice of courses within umbrella categories of requirements.

However, this curricular structure only papers over the conundrum Barzun sets up. He views what was goes on in the academy as a battle between knowledge for "professional or vocational use," on one hand, and "social or moral (or philosophical or civilizing)" on the other. Barzun declares that "One is know how, the other is cultivation." He then claims that, "for some hundred years [i.e., beginning in the late 1800s] American colleges and universities have innocently confounded the two. . . ." The problem is that these two ends "require distinct uses of subject matter and of the mind, and they cannot be fused into one."[31]

## THE COLLEGE AND UNIVERSITY IN THE FUTURE

One of the famous and enduring Yogi Berra-isms is that "it's tough to make predictions, especially about the future." Mindful of this advice, historians, or anyone for that matter, who wade into the territory of scoping out the future, do so at their peril.

The safer place to be is on this side of history, which is where we have been in our journey through these pages and this narrative. It is much easier to sit in the present and to argue how assuredly, along the historical path, the destination in which we unmistakably had to land is the present. Or stated another way, we can claim with Louis Menand that "History is the prediction of the present. Historians explain why things turned out the way they did. Since we already know the outcome, this might seem a simple matter of looking back and connecting the dots." However, Menand quickly points out, "But there is a problem: too many dots. Even the dots have dots. Predicting the present is nearly as hard as predicting the future."[32]

Thus for any "dot" in the past, any number of outgrowths and evolutions might have or could have happened. What did occur and any dispositives about what could have been different are open to continuing speculation.

For example, we trace the inauguration of the German research university to the founding of Johns Hopkins University in the mid-nineteenth century. This doesn't mean that if Johns Hopkins had not been founded, there would have been no research university. Other major universities existed in the Hopkins era, and though it catapulted itself ahead of them by rule of its design, absent Johns Hopkins, the University of Michigan or any number of other fledging but rapidly growing universities might have assumed the seat as the founder of the research university in America.

An aspect of the college and university in America that contributes comfort about how we develop a picture of what higher education will look like in the future is that, as we have stated: for the academy in this country, the more things change, the more they stay the same.

In addition, as we sit in the present and have a past on which to look back, while care must be taken about how we judge what we see, that does not mean that we are incapable of drawing any conclusions. As Barzun remarks:

> The judgment as to what took place during a past era is naturally easier to make than the judgment as to what is happening now. But it is again possible to draw guidance from history and take an inventory of significant activities and institutions so as to gauge the degree to which fruitful novelty is keeping pace with obvious destruction.[33]

Debate has persisted for centuries over liberal education, the liberal arts, and the possible eclipse of those traditions at the hands of high-pitched demands for scientific, engineering, business, vocational and professional course work, academic departments, and "schools." Likewise, the tensions and stresses of ideology have been there forever. This has been true from the "politics of the intellect"[34] in the Colonial College era to Sexton's "theological politics," in the twentieth and twenty-first centuries.

These ideological and other battles for the soul of the university continually arise as well as change over time. Some of these ideological problems remain remarkably similar, even in content. But throughout, in disparate and distant eras, squabbles about academic freedom, free speech, and liberty in the academy and how these values are treated and responded to by those outside the gates refuse to go away.

All these persistent issues that are battled inside as well as outside the gates of the academy are set against a uniquely American civic framework. That is, an American society and culture, and its politics, which are defined by the rights and responsibilities of the individual, the citizen, on one end, versus the necessities and insistence on commonly agreed principles and assumptions to guide a civil society and the body politic on the other.

Tocqueville pondered at length this unique and distinctive quality in the American ethos in the mid-nineteenth century. It had existed for two centuries prior to his visit to American and his groundbreaking *Democracy in America*, and it continues today as a scaffold for political, social, and cultural discourse in- and outside the gates of the college and university.

These two commitments to both the individual and the commonweal, and the conundrums of free speech undergirded by the democratic principles underlie not only the nation, but the foundation and convictions of the university. In both settings, potential conflicts and tension between the individual and the state, and the limits, if any, placed on free speech inevitably come into sharp, often tense contention in times of national crisis.

Again, the type of the crises change, but their effect changes little. Be it the Revolutionary War, the Civil War, the geo-political demands of two world wars, and more in the twentieth century or the struggle against terrorism in the twenty-first. Be it battles over those international involvements, or domestic fights about equality and equity across racial, gender, ethnic, and other distinguishing lines of the multicultural groups that inhabit America, the role of wealth, and concern about the environment. The effects are the same. Regardless the impact of these factions and forces on the university, its role as critic and servant doesn't change. For the betterment of society, the academy must perform its role and duty to be both.

Concerning these issues and their relative presence and play in years, decades and even centuries to come, the specifics of time and place, and of the content of the face-offs and battlegrounds, apropos warnings about predicting the future, cannot be known.

However, it is clear that the college and university in America in the future will be called upon on a number of fronts in the educational, political, cultural, and social life of the Republic. The academy will be expected to affirm its core beliefs, principles, and convictions. Colleges and universities will have claims placed on them to be critics and servants to the nation and to the community. Higher education will need to possess and if lacking be committed to gain the resources of learning, knowledge, and research that only colleges and universities possesses.

The expectation in the future as it has been in the past is that the academy cannot simply hold these values and the products of the labor of faculty and students close to their vests. Rather both national expectations as well as the internal motivations tied to its mission and purpose will move colleges and universities to contribute to the common good, as only they among the institutions of society are able and expected to do.

Finally, echoing where the journey through this saga of the college and university in America began, the academy will continue in the future to have a relationship to religion.

That relationship will feature institutionally structured and organized connections to religious institutions, as well as serendipitous and opportunistic individual involvement and association with an array of churches, synagogues, mosques, denominations, sectarian groups, and smaller sects and cults. The liaison with religion will include the normative and formative role of religious values in its diverse constituents. And these beliefs and points of view inexorably filter from these religiously committed and inspired individuals and groups into the fabric of the academy.

In addition, by nature in college and university settings and in defending its territory, religion unavoidably raises questions and produces stand-offs over how faith and spiritual beliefs and convictions are treated in the academy's distinct culture of teaching and learning, research investigation, refusal of absolutes, academic inquiry, and the search for knowledge wherever all of those lead. At the same time religious controversies grounded in faith and belief systems will battle with each other in the same fashion as other ideologies in the academy.

Mindful of the danger in making predictions, one might be made on this front. That is, it is quite possible that aspects of the encounters and conflicts between and among disparate religious groups and organizations will gain momentum and conceivable intensity in the future.

Space here prevents the development of a full picture of these potential difficulties. Nonetheless, suffice it to say that there are national and international, global conflicts and battles between religious faith systems and that those are and will play out within university communities. The hope is that cool heads will prevail. But given the intensity of beliefs and core religious differences that lead to threats and fears on the national and international stage, those conflicts cannot simply be barred from equally unfolding inside the gates of the academy.

However, side-by-side with particularistic, sectarian religious commitments and passions sits the religion of the Republic. Its theology and core principles will continue to shape the nation's identity and purpose, and its values and beliefs will remain, in the future as they have in the past, a significant feature of the college and university's foundation.

To recap briefly, the relationship of religion to the college and university in America has evolved over centuries. An original, fervently denominational, nearly exclusively Protestant control over colleges—albeit for a handful of early Roman Catholic higher education institutions—was gradually replaced by a more Judeo-Christian collection of commonly agreed upon religious values. Later this Judeo-Christian tradition gave way to a more syncretistic, multi-religious (not unlike multicultural) alignment of faith systems in the academy.

My contention is that this more diverse composition of religion as viewed and understood within the gates has been supplanted by a default to another long-standing theme: that of the religion of the Republic. This religion and its values have run as a thread underneath the surface values and principles of the academy, yet informing them throughout the history of the college and university in America. This religion of the Republic, the civil religion in America overlaps significantly and thus connects to the core values of the university: equality, freedom, treating others as we would want to be treated, liberty, and assertion of democratic values for the good of the commonweal.

At one level this trend is no different from and clearly overlaps with notions of "*E Pluribus Unam*" as a core value and essential foundation of the American democratic landscape. The religion of the Republic provides unifying values and convictions. These are sufficiently universal that most people can agree to and embrace them, even as they simultaneously maintain individual and group religious identities, formed and shaped in their differing and conflicting faith communities.

Although not using the label of the religion of the Republic, Arthur Schlesinger underscores the transcendent values and beliefs shot through America. "The republic embodies ideals that transcend ethnic, religious and political lines. It is an experiment, reasonably successful for a while," Schlesinger hedges, "in creating a common identity for people of diverse races, religions, languages, cultures.[35]

Schlesinger's hesitation is rooted in concern that, "the experiment can continue to succeed only so long as Americans continue to believe in the goal. If the Republic now turns away from Washington's old goal of 'one people,' what is its future? —Disintegration of the national community, apartheid, Balkanization, tribalization?"

Indeed in upholding the lively experiment of the academy and of the nation, the drift toward disintegration absent the aspirations to be "one people" has forever been a threat. This is particularly true in trying times of crisis and conflict, such as Schlesinger witnessed. However, the same could be argued in any era. This threat of turning away from the commitment and sacrifice to be "one people" will no doubt be a characteristic challenge in the future of the college and university. The college and university has managed to put its stamp on *E Pluribus Unum* in the past. Its continuing capacity to make that affirmation in the future is plausible, if not likely.

## MINOGUE'S "SECRET UNIVERSITY"

Kenneth Minogue's "concept of a university" has informed our narrative throughout. As a coda to our coda, his thoughts about "The Secret University" recapitulate much of what has been suggested about the college and university in America.[36] Examination about the shape of the university is incomplete absent Minogue's ideas, which offer a penultimate contribution to our narrative and add clarity to what it is that we are talking about when we think about the idea of the university.

For Minogue, "the true identity of universities is buried deep under an accumulated lumber of moral pieties, political doctrines, misleading legends about the past, and irrelevant aspirations towards changing the whole character of human existence." The problem that arises out of that pile is the potential to misconstrue the university: "The place of universities in society has become a public question, and as befits a public question it has fallen into the hands of publicists keen to appropriate a valuable resource to the purposes of their commonplace commitments."[37]

In contrast, the difference between the university and the world around it could not be more profound: "Once this lumber has been removed, however, the academic world appears as a vast imaginative realm whose range is immensely greater than anything to be found amongst the shifts and schemes of the practical world, because (unlike the practical world) it is not tied down to the limitations of action."[38]

Pressures and events ever lurk at the gates of the academy. No one knows this more than Minogue. "It is generally some sense of urgency which brings us back into practice, and it is always the voice of urgency which tempts us to see universities as parts of 'Society' (and having a duty to contribute to it)," he cautions:

> rather than as independent institutions cutting across the grain. Few are the academics so completely absorbed in their work as to be immune to those bold pronouncements by which practical men explain to us our duty in terms of the function, role, purpose, or true character of the university. And as we have seen, even quite perceptive accounts of the concept of university may come to be twisted in this direction.[39]

In the end, Minogue's argument is "that it is important to distinguish the academic from the intellectual." The contrast between the "intellectual" and the "academic" is beyond debate. Unfortunately, confusion both within and without the gates of the academy about the difference between them leads to a distortion of how we comprehend the concept of the university. "Intellectuals are unmistakably inhabitants of the practical world. They quite legitimately," Minogue makes evident, "embrace causes, conduct vendettas, suppress inconvenient evidence, strike moral postures, succumb to intellectual fashions, scheme, feud, and sign petitions."[40]

But intellectuals are dangerous beyond simply how they operate in the practical world: "if the class of intellectuals could ever agree on some set of truths, they would not hesitate to impose it upon universities. Intellectuals are the source of those passionate ideas which periodically

seize the imagination of the masses, sometimes even capturing governments, and then demand to be declaimed from the lecture rostrum as
final truths."[41]

Minogue's conclusion about "the concept of a university" is unbend-
ing: "The only thing that universities ought to do is the only thing they
can do: sustain the academic world." Timelessly what the university provides to both those inside and outside the gates is crucial: "though we
commonly recognize that the university, being an international institution, transcends national frontier, we do not so easily recognize its far
more important transcendence of the most elusive and parochial of all
provincialisms: that of the present moment."[42]

\* \* \*

We have reviewed the history of the American college and university in
every era of its evolution as a crucial institution beginning in the life of
the Colonies and the early foundations of the country to continuing in the
later creation as a nation and a Republic. The influence of the college and
university as a center for academic culture, and its role as critic and
servant continued in the ensuing two centuries, and especially in recent
decades.

We also know that the academy in the United States is unique in
countless respects and characteristics when compared to counterparts
around the world, including differences with its heritage in the colleges
and universities of the then "Old World."

The college and university has succeeded in America due in large
measure to the organizing principles and beliefs that undergird the nation: freedom, equality, the rights of citizens, a press for the common
good and for responsibility in the public square, and "life, liberty, and the
pursuit of happiness." Admittedly these values have come late to the
party for many citizens.

However, the core beliefs of the country have willed out. Doors have
opened, even if glacially and in fits and starts, to citizens and groups
previously denied the rights and privileges of life in a Republic. This has
happened because the nation's creed and its principles of equity, equal
access, and an emphasis on merit will not permit those doors to be closed
forever.

The nation's colleges and universities have embraced these core values as well as their own "first principles." The academy in America has
been instrumental in building up society and culture both inside and
outside the gates. The university in America has fulfilled its historic mission and traditional purpose: to inspire Newman's "culture of intellect,"
and to understand the best of the culture that it inherits, to improve it and
to pass it on to succeeding generations.

That task has relied as it always must on the academy's most critical commitments and values: teaching from the best and brightest professors, the engagement of learning by students, openness to discussion and dialogue about any and all ideas, a relentless and unending search for knowledge and truth, pursued wherever they lead.

The academy has had its share of jeremiads foisted on it by both well-intended, but also malicious critics. It will continue in the future to be the target of these complaints and of those who believe that the best days of the college and university are behind it, not the prospect of a coming future.

Nonetheless, this reality needs to be placed in context. Indeed there is a tendency for observers in any era to view that unfolding of events and the actions of the major players and leaders lead to one and only one conclusion: the sky is falling. However, Barzun notes how relative such perceptions inevitably are. We need to be mindful of his counsel as we think about the present state of the university and the nation and culture in which it resides. That is "Sooner or later, the sophisticated person who reads or hears that Western civilization is in decline reminds himself that to the living, 'the times' always seem bad. In most eras voices cry out against the visible decadence; for every generation—and especially for the aging—the world is going to the dogs."[43]

The college and university will always face the challenge to navigate successfully the choices between tradition and change, and between what can and should be dearly held and what may need to be jettisoned in light of present and coming tests and demands. Some change is inevitable and should not be feared. Barzun's counsel is that we should:

> ask why that same phenomenon [that things are getting worse] recurs; in other words, the historical-minded should look into the meaning and cause of the undying conviction of decline. One cause, one meaning, is surely that in every era some things are in fact dying out and the elderly are good witness to this demise.[44]

The formation of the academy in America is a distinctive saga. This saga demands continual reexamination and revisiting in every generation and in every era. It is a saga that endures.

It is a history that only when we are able to get our arms around it and to gather a firmer grasp of it, are we able to have a more enlightened and nuanced sense for the story of the shape and shaping of the college and university in America.

## NOTES

1. James Duderstadt, Personal Interview, March 6, 1995.
2. Christopher J. Lucas, *American Higher Education: A History* (New York: St. Martins Press, 1994), 300–16.

3. Kenneth Minogue, *The Concept of a University* (Berkeley: University of California Press, 1973).

4. John Sloan Dickey, "Conscience and the Undergraduate," *The Atlantic Monthly* 195, no. 4 (April 1955): 31–35, http://www.theatlantic.com/past/docs/issues/95nov/warring/conscien.htm, unpaginated. The quotes that follow are Dickey's from this article.

5. A. Bartlett Giamatti, *The University and the Public Interest* (New York: Atheneum, 1981), 180–84. The assertions attributed to Giamatti that follow are drawn from these pages.

6. Ibid.

7. Ibid., 183.

8. Ibid., 183–84.

9. Ibid., 184.

10. John Sexton, "The University as Sanctuary," draft of paper provided by the President's Office, New York University. Also delivered in part as a speech, "The University as Sanctuary," February 17, 2004, at Fordham University. The notes that follow are taken variously from each version and will be indicated accordingly.

11. John Sexton, "The University as Sanctuary," draft of paper provided by the President's Office, New York University, 3–4.

12. Ibid.

13. John Sexton, "The University as Sanctuary," February 17, 2004, delivered at Fordham University, 5.

14. Ibid.

15. John Sexton, "Dogmatism and Complexity: Civil Discourse and the Research University," President's Office, New York University, August 2, 2005, (unpaginated).

16. Ibid.

17. Ibid.

18. Ibid., Italics mine.

19. John Sexton, "The University as Sanctuary," draft of paper provided by the President's Office, New York University, 6–7.

20. Ibid. 14–15. Italics mine.

21. John Gardner, "Agenda for the Colleges and Universities: Higher Education in the Innovative Society, in *Campus 1980*, ed. Alvin C. Eurich (New York: Delacorte Press, 1968), 8.

22. Ibid.

23. Jacques Barzun, *The Culture We Deserve*. ed. Arthur Krystal (Middletown, CT: Wesleyan University Press, 1989). 166.

24. Ibid. Barzun's chapter "Exeunt the Humanities," 109–19, is a thorough statement about the need for the humanities in a liberal education, but also about the profound threats to the existence of the humanities as the twentieth century came to a close.

25. Daniel Bell, *The Reforming of General Education: The Columbia College Experience in its National Setting*. With Foreward by David B. Truman (New York: Columbia University Press, 1996), xix.

26. Ibid.

27. Barzun, 50.

28. Ibid., 6.

29. Ibid.

30. Ibid., 7.

31. Ibid., 111.

32. Louis Menand, "Thinking Sideways: The one-dot theory of history," *The New Yorker* (March 30, 2015): 73–79, 73.

33. Barzun, 163.

34. J. David Hoeveler, *Creating the American Mind: Intellect and Politics in the Colonial Colleges* (Lanham, MD: Rowman & Littlefield Publishers, 2002), x.

35. Arthur Schlesinger, Jr., *The Disuniting of America* (New York: W. W. Norton and Company, 1992), 118.

36. Minogue. The final chapter of *The Concept of A University*, "The Secret University," 220–26.

37. Ibid., 220.

38. Ibid.

39. Ibid. 221.

40. Ibid. 222.

41. Ibid.

42. Ibid., 223.

43. Barzun, 161.

44. Ibid.

# Bibliography

Abbott, Lyman. "William Rainey Harper," *The Outlook* (January 20, 1906): 110–112, Retrieved from: http://www.unz.org/Pub/Outlook-1906jan20-00110.

*Addresses at the Inauguration of Professor Noah Porter as president of Yale University*, Noah Porter Inaugural Address. New York: Charles Scribner and Company, 1871.

*American Association of University Professors*. Retrieved from: http://www.aaup.org/report/trigger-warnings.

Bailyn, Bernard. *Education in the Forming of American Society*. Chapel Hill: University of North Carolina Press, 1960.

Barzun, Jacques. *Education in the Forming of American Society*. Chapel Hill: University of North Carolina Press, 1960.

———. *The American University: How it Runs, Where it is Going*. New York: Harper and Row, 1968.

———. *The Culture We Deserve*. Edited by Arthur Krystal. Middletown, CT: Wesleyan University Press, 1989.

Bell, Daniel. *The Reforming of General Education: The Columbia College Experience in its National Setting*. New York: Columbia University Press, 1996.

———. *The Reforming of General Education: The Columbia College Experience in its National Setting*. With Forward by David B. Truman. New York: Columbia University Press, 1996.

Bellah, Robert. "Civil Religion in America," *Daedalus* (Winter 1967): 1–21.

Brinton, Crane. "Many Mansions." *The American Historical Review* 69, no. 2 (January 1964): 309–326.

Cameron, J. M. *On the Idea of a University*. Toronto: Published in Association with the University of Saint Michael's College by University of Toronto Press, 1978.

Carr, Robert K. "Justice Felix Frankfurter Opinion in Sweezy vs. New Hampshire. Academic Freedom, the American Association of University Professors, and the United States Supreme Court," *AAUP Bulletin* 45, no. 1 (March 1959): 5–24.

Caspar, Gerhard. "The Search to Know—What? Reflections on the Purposes of the University Curriculum Workshop." *The Van Leer Jerusalem Institute* (May 27, 2010): 1–14.

Chapman, John Jay. "The Harvard Classics and Harvard," *Science* XXX (1909).

Cherry, Conrad. *Hurrying Toward Zion: Universities, Divinity Schools, and American Protestantism*. Bloomington, IL and Indianapolis, IN: Bloomington University Press, 1995.

Clark, Burton R. *The Distinctive College: Antioch, Reed and Swarthmore*. Chicago: Aldine, 1970.

Cloud, Robert C. "Sweezy v. New Hampshire," *Law and Higher Education*. Retrieved from: http://lawhighereducation.org/124-sweezy-v-new-hampshire.html.

Conrad Cherry, *Hurrying Toward Zion: Universities, Divinity Schools, and American Protestantism*. Bloomington, IL and Indianapolis, IN: Bloomington University Press, 1995.

Delbanco, Andrew. *College: What It Was, Is, and Should Be*. Princeton, NJ: Princeton University Press, 2012.

———. "Conscience and the Undergraduate," *The Atlantic Monthly* 195, no. 4 (April 1955): 31–35.

Dickey, John Sloan. "Conscience and the Undergraduate," *The Atlantic Monthly* 195, no. 4 (April 1955): 31–35. Retrieved from: http://www.theatlantic.com/past/docs/issues/95nov/warring/conscien.htm.

Diggins, John P. "Consciousness and Ideology in American History: The Burden of Daniel J. Boorstin." *The American Historical Review* 76, no. 1 (February 1971): 99–118.

Downs, Donald Alexander. *Cornell '69: Liberalism and the Crisis of the American University*. Ithaca, NY and London: Cornell University Press, 1999.

Dworkin, Ron. "We Need a New Interpretation of Academic Freedom," in *The Future of Academic Freedom*, edited by Louis Menand. Chicago: University of Chicago Press, 1996.

Eliot, Charles W. "Academic Freedom," *Science* (July 5, 1907): 1–12.

Finkin, Matthew and Robert C. Post. *For the Common Good: Principles of American Academic Freedom*. New Haven, CT and London: Yale University Press, 2009.

Franklin, Benjamin. "Articles of Belief and Acts of Religion." Retrieved from: http://franklinpapers.org/franklin/framedVolumes.jsp?vol=1&page=101a.

Gardner, John. "Agenda for the Colleges and Universities: Higher Education in the Innovative Society," in *Campus 1980*, edited by Alvin C. Eurich. New York: Delacorte Press, 1968.

*General Education in a Free Society*. Report of the Harvard Committee. Cambridge, MA: Harvard University Press, 1945.

Giamatti, A. Bartlett. *The University and the Public Interest*. New York: Atheneum, 1981.

Gilman, Daniel Coit. *The Launching of a University*. With New Foreward by Francesco Cordasco. New York: Garrett Press, Inc., 1969.

Gray, Hannah Holborn. *Searching for Utopia: Universities and Their Histories*. Berkeley: University of California Press, 2012.

Harvard. "Faculty Rebukes Whitefield," Boston, 1774. Retrieved from http://declaringamerica.com/harvard-faculty-rebukes-whitefield-1744-exerpt/.

Harvard. "Groups Condemn Butler's Columbia Speech: Defense Leagues, Teachers' Union, Deplores 'Fascism.'" Retrieved from: http://www.thecrimson.com/article/1940/10/5/harvard-groups-condemn-butlers-columbia-speech/.

Haskell, Thomas L. "Justifying the Rights of Academic Freedom in the Era of 'Power/Knowledge,'" in *The Future of Academic Freedom*. Edited by Louis Menand. Chicago: University of Chicago Press, 1996.

Hawkins, Hugh. *Between Harvard and America: The Educational Leadership of Charles W. Eliot*. New York: Oxford University Press, 1972.

Herfurth, Theodore. *Sifting and Winnowing*, 1949, Part I. Retrieved from: http://www.library.wisc.edu/etext/WIReader/WER1035-Chpt1.html.

Higham, John. "Hanging Together': Divergent Unities in American History," *The Journal of American History* 61, no. 1 (June 1974): 5–28.

Hofstadter, Richard and Wilson Smith, eds. *American Higher Education: A Documentary History*, Volume I and II. Chicago: University of Chicago Press, 1961.

Hoeveler, David J. *Creating the American Mind: Intellect and Politics in the Colonial Colleges*. Lanham, MD: Rowman & Littlefield, 2002.

Howe, Irving. "The Value of the Canon," in *Debating P. C.: The Controversy Over Political Correctness on College Campuses*, edited by Paul Berman. New York: Dell Publishing, 1992.

Hutchins, Robert M. *Education for Freedom*. Baton Rouge: Louisiana State University Press, 1943.

———. *No Friendly Voice*. Chicago: University of Chicago Press, 1936.

Kemeny, John G. Convocation Address, September 17, 1978.

Kerr, Clarke. *The Uses of the University*, 5th ed. Cambridge, MA: Harvard University Press, 2001.

Kipnis, Laura. "My Title IX Inquisition," May 29, 2015. Retrieved from: http://chronicle.com/article/My-Title-IX-Inquisition/230489/.

———. "Sexual Paranoia Strikes Academe," February 27, 2015. Retrieved from: http://chronicle.com/article/Sexual-Paranoia-Strikes/190351/.

Lewis, Harry R. *Excellence Without a Soul: Does Liberal Education Have a Future?* New York: Public Affairs, 2006.

Lipset, Seymour Martin. "Sources of Political Correctness on American Campuses," in *The Imperiled Academy*, edited by Howard Dickman. New Brunswick, NJ and London: Transaction Publishers, 1993.

———. *The First New Nation: the United States in Historical and Comparative Perspective.* New York: Basic Books, Inc., 1963.

Lowell, Lawrence A. *At War with Academic Traditions in America.* Cambridge, MA: Harvard University Press, 1934.

———. "Discussions," *Educational Review*, (December 1920). New York: George H. Doran Company, Publishers, 431.

Lucas, Christopher J. *American Higher Education: A History.* New York: St. Martins Press, 1994.

McClosky, Herbert. "Consensus and Ideology in American Politics." *The American Political Science Review* 58, no. 2 (June 1964): 361–383.

McCosh, James. *The New Departure in College Education: Being a Reply to President Eliot's Defence of it in New York, February 24, 1885.* New York: Charles Schribner's Sons, 1985.

Mack, Eric. "The Limits of Diversity: The New Counter-Enlightenment and Isaiah Berlin's Liberal Pluralism," in *The Imperiled Academy*, edited by Howard Dickman. New Brunswick, NJ and London: Transaction Publishers, 1993.

Madison, James. "Memorial and Remonstrance Against Religious Assessments," 1785. Retrieved from: http://press-ubs.uchicago.edu/founders/documents/amendI_religions43.html.

Martin, Lipset, S. *The First New Nation: the United States in Historical and Comparative Perspective.* New York: Basic Books, Inc., 1963.

Mascriatra, David. "Richard Hofstadter and America's New Wave of Anti-Intellectualism." Retrieved from: http://www.thedailybeast.com/articles/2014/03/09/richard-hofstadter-and-america-s-new-wave-of-anti-intellectualism.html.

Mead, Sidney E. *The Lively Experiment: The Shaping of Christianity in America.* New York: Harper and Row, 1963.

———. "The Nation with the Soul of a Church," *Church History* XXXVI. (September 1967): 1–22.

———. *The Old Religion in the Brave New World: Reflections on the Relation Between Christendom and the Republic.* Berkeley, Los Angeles, and London: University of California Press, 1977.

Menand, Louis. "How the Deal Went Down: Saving Democracy in the Depression," *The New Yorker* (March 4, 2013): 69–74.

———. "Thinking Sideways: The one-dot theory of history," *The New Yorker* (March 30, 2015): 73–79.

———. *The Future of Academic Freedom.* Chicago: University of Chicago Press, 1996.

Miller, Perry. *Errand into the Wilderness.* Cambridge, MA: The Belknap Press of Harvard University, 1964.

Minogue, Kenneth. *The Concept of a University.* Berkeley: University of California Press, 1973.

Moore, LeRoy. "Sidney Mead's Understanding of America," *Journal of the American Academy of Religion* 44, no. 1 (March 1976): 133–153.

Morrison, Jeffrey. *John Witherspoon and the Founding of the American Republic.* Notre Dame, IN: University of Notre Dame Press, 2005.

Nelson, Stephen J. *Leaders in the Labyrinth: College Presidents and the Battleground of Creeds and Convictions.* Westport, CT: American Council on Education Praeger, Series on Higher Education, 2007.

———. *Decades of Chaos and Revolution: Showdowns for College Presidents.* Lanham, MD: Rowman & Littlefield, ACE Higher Education Series, 2012.

————. "President Robert Hutchins' Designs on Education and the University: Imposing Provocateur or Mediocre Prophet?" Unpublished paper delivered at the Eastern
Educational Research Association Conference, February, 2013.

Newman, Cardinal John Henry. *The Idea of the University*. Garden City, NJ: Doubleday,
1959.

————. *The Idea of the University*, edited by I. T. Kerr. Clarendon Press: Oxford, 1976.

————. *The Idea of a University*, edited by John Henry Turner. New Haven, CT: Yale
University Press, 1996.

O'Neil, Robert. *Academic Freedom in the Wired World: Political Extremism, Corporate Power, and the University*. Cambridge, MA: Harvard University Press, 2008.

Pelikan, Jaroslav. *The Idea of the University: A Reexamination*. New Haven, CT: Yale
University Press, 1992.

Purcell, Jr., Edward A. *The Crisis of Democratic Theory*. Lexington, KY: University of
Kentucky Press, 1973.

Rothman, Stanley. "Tradition and Change: The University Under Stress," in *The Imperiled Academy*, edited by Howard Dickman. New Brunswick, NJ and London: Transaction Publishers, 1993.

Rudolph, Frederick. *The American College and University: A History*. New York: Alfred
A. Knopf, 1968.

Said, Edward. "Identity, Authority, and Freedom: The Potentate and the Traveler," in
*The Future of Academic Freedom*, edited by Louis Menand. Chicago: University of
Chicago Press, 1996.

Sandel, Michael. *Democracy's Discontent: America in Search of a Public Philosophy*. Cambridge, MA: The Belknap Press of Harvard University Press, 1996.

Schlesinger, Jr., Arthur. *The Disuniting of America*. New York: W. W. Norton and Company, 1992.

Schrecker, Ellen. *The Lost Soul of Higher Education: Corporatization, the Assault on Academic Freedom, and the End of the American University*. New York: The New Press,
2010.

Searle, John "The Storm Over the University," in *Debating P. C.: The Controversy Over
Political Correctness on College Campuses*, edited by Paul Berman. New York: Dell
Publishing, 1992.

Sexton, John. "Dogmatism and Complexity: Civil Discourse and the Research University," President's Office, New York University, August 2, 2005.

————. "The University as Sanctuary," draft of paper provided by the President's
Office, New York University.

Shakespeare, William. *The Tempest*.

Shapiro, Harold. *Tradition and Change: Perspectives on Education and Public Policy*. Ann
Arbor: University of Michigan Press, 1987.

Sloan, Douglas. "Harmony, Chaos, and Consensus: The American College Curriculum," *Teachers College Record* 73 (December 1971): 221-251.

————. *The Great Awakening and American Education: A Documentary History*. New York
and London: Teachers College Press, 1973.

Sokal, Michael M. "James McKeen Cattell, Nicholas Murray Butler and Academic
Freedom at Columbia University, 1902-1923." *History of Psychology* 12, no. 2 (2009):
87–122.

Storr, Richard J. "The Public Conscience of the University," *Harvard Educational Review*
XXVI, no. 1 (Winter 1956): 75, 71–84.

Sweezy vs. New Hampshire, 354 U.S. 589 (1957).

Miller, Thomas, ed. *The Selected Writings of John Witherspoon*. Southern Illinois University, 1990.

Thorstein Veblen. *The Higher Learning in America: A Memorandum on the Conduct of
Universities by Business Men*. New York: B. W. Huebsch, 1918.

Veysey, Laurence, R. *The Emergence of the American University*. Chicago: University of
Chicago Press, 1965.

Wilson, Woodrow. *College and State: Educational, Literary and Political Papers (1875–1913)*, Vol. II. Edited by Ray Stannard Baker and William E. Dodd. New York: Harper and Brothers, 1925.

———. *The Relation of University Education to Commerce.* Chicago, 1902.

Wriston, Henry. "A Critical Appraisal of Experiments in General Education," in *The Thirty-Eighth Yearbook of the National Society for the Study of Education, Part II, General Education in the American College*, edited by Guy Montrose Whipple. Bloomington, IL: Public School Publishing Co., 1939.

# Index

Adams, Charles Kendall, 159–160, 195, 196, 197
Agnew, Spiro, 105, 200, 256n22
American Association of University Professors (AAUP), 184, 198, 202, 203, 204, 205, 217, 218, 262–263, 272, 274, 288
American Civil Religion, 37, 45, 48; Civil Religion, 1, 27, 36, 37, 41, 45, 46, 47, 167, 308
Angell, James, 64–65, 66, 67, 73, 88, 91, 145

Bailyn, Bernard, 85, 86, 87–88, 110n14
Baptists, 6, 34
Barzun, Jacques, 13, 14, 15, 76, 142–143, 144, 169, 301, 303–304, 305, 311
Beecher, Lyman, 147
Bell, Daniel, 56, 76, 169
Bellah, Robert, 37, 45, 46
Berlin, Isaiah, 286
Bill of Rights, 37, 208, 264, 272
Bologna University, 5, 40, 183
Boston College, 34
Bowen, William, 250
Brewster, Kingman, 246
Brinton, Crane, 41–42, 50
Brooklyn College, 70
Brown University, ix, 3, 12, 31, 34, 45, 99, 114, 124–126, 127, 133, 138, 186, 227, 301
Butler, Nicholas Murray, 76, 98, 99, 177, 201–202, 211, 220n27, 221n30
Byrne, J. Peter, 273, 275, 278

Cameron, J. M., 103–104, 105, 106
Caspar, Gerhard, 75, 76
Cattell, James, 201
Chapman, John Jay, 173
Chase, Philander, 64

Cheery, Conrad, 166, 168
Churchill, Ward, 211, 219
Civil War, the, 7, 8, 15, 22, 48, 64, 66, 67, 91, 99, 132, 144, 153, 155, 157, 160, 192, 306
Clark University, 163
Clark, Burton, 47
Cold War, the, 8, 70, 98, 104, 105, 211, 212, 224
College of William and Mary, 2, 12, 17, 226
Colonial Colleges, 1, 2, 5–6, 7, 9, 11, 12, 16, 18, 19, 20, 21, 22, 23, 27, 28, 29, 31, 40, 41, 42, 43, 50, 63, 75, 113, 114, 115, 116, 117, 120, 132, 137, 156, 157, 175, 179, 186, 187, 206, 209, 260, 279, 291, 301, 305
colonial era, 4, 18, 20, 28, 44, 51, 185, 206, 226, 238, 263, 301
Columbia University, 45, 70, 76, 90, 98, 141, 176–177, 201, 242, 243, 244, 279, 286, 291, 302, 303
Conant, James Bryan, 98, 99, 169
Congregationalists, 2, 6, 12, 28, 34, 61, 186, 190, 191, 192, 226
Connerly, Ward, 244
Cornell University, 22, 30–31, 32, 65, 91, 159, 193, 231, 239, 291

Dartmouth College, 22, 43, 58, 109, 114, 117–118, 119, 120, 178, 186, 190, 191–192, 209, 227, 272, 295, 297
*Dartmouth Review*, 58, 194, 220n13, 272
de Tocqueville, Alexis, 10, 45, 46, 116, 253
Declaration of Independence, 37, 42, 115
Deist, 38, 263
Delbanco, Andrew, 76, 77–78, 81, 106–107, 108

Dewey, John, 13–14, 15, 169
Dickey, John Sloan, 178, 179, 295–297, 301, 302
Diggins, John, 57, 58
Downs, Donald, 239, 241, 242–243, 244, 249, 275–277
du Crevcour, Jacques, 10
Duderstadt, James, 291
Duke University, 34
Dwight, Timothy, 147
Dworkin, Ron, 269, 270, 275

E pluribus unam, 308
Eisenhower, Dwight, 201
Eliot, Charles W., 64, 65, 91–92, 128, 129, 130, 131, 134, 135, 136, 143, 193, 206, 231–234, 238
Ely, Richard, 195, 232
Emancipation Proclamation, 192
Emerson, Ralph Waldo, 107, 108
Enlightenment, 41, 42, 50, 52, 57, 71, 76, 85, 107, 116, 264, 286

Finkin, Matthew, 287
Finney, Charles, 147
Flexner, Abraham, 70
Frankfurter, Felix, 210, 219
Franklin, Benjamin, 10, 38–39, 137
Free Speech Movement (FSM), 239, 241, 253, 278

Gardner, John, 73–74, 300–301
Georgetown (College) University, 29, 30, 34, 273
Gettysburg College, 34, 244
GI Bill, 8, 104, 224, 261
Giamatti, Bartlett, 246, 295, 298, 299
Gideonse, Harry, 70–72, 82n31
Gilman, Daniel Coit, 65, 66, 67–68, 73, 75, 76, 91, 170–171, 175–176, 177, 178, 192–193, 206
Gray, Hannah, 78–79, 80, 245–247, 248, 249–251, 252, 253
Great Awakening, 31, 43, 58, 59, 60, 63, 186, 226, 265, 266, 282, 291; First Great Awakening, 6, 44, 59, 291; Second Great Awakening, 6, 20, 28, 30, 31, 32, 34, 59, 60, 64, 147, 155, 157, 265, 291

Great Society, 224
Gutmann, Amy, 241

Hackney, Sheldon, 241
Harper, William Rainey, 145, 162, 163, 164, 165, 166, 167–168, 171, 198–200, 202
Harvard Redbook, 5, 98
Harvard University, xv, 1, 2, 3, 5, 11, 12, 16, 19, 22, 32, 34, 38, 40, 41, 43, 64, 65, 88, 91, 98, 119–120, 128, 129, 130, 133, 143, 149, 154, 156, 173, 186, 193, 201, 226, 227, 231, 247, 266, 291
Haskell, Thomas, 206, 207–208, 220n8, 274
Hawkins, Hugh, 91–92
Hesburgh, Father Theodore, 213
Higham, John, 46–50, 53n40
Hoeveler, J. David, 18–23, 60, 240
Hoffman, Elizabeth, 211
Hofstadter, Richard, 280, 281, 282
Holmes, Justice Oliver Wendall, 89, 236
Hooker, Thomas, 28
Horowitz, David, 272
Howe, Irving, 281
Hutchins, Robert, 57, 68–73, 78–80, 82n31, 95–96, 97, 98–103, 135–138, 140–141, 143, 144, 164, 169, 175, 178, 245, 246, 247, 248, 249

Illinois College, 61
Industrial Revolution, 48, 64, 153, 154, 301

Jackson, Andrew, 63, 89, 90, 281
Jacksonian, 63, 64, 89, 90, 119, 128, 136, 155, 158, 161, 281
Jefferson, Thomas, 10, 16, 17, 29, 96, 97, 101, 137, 204, 227, 247
Jewish, 33, 37, 221n52
Johns Hopkins University, 22, 30, 33, 65–66, 75, 91, 128, 154, 170, 175, 185, 186, 192, 193, 194, 291, 305
Johnson, Lyndon, 224
Jordan, David Starr, 197–198, 231
Judeo-Christian, 30, 33, 36, 47, 61, 190, 299, 307

Kemeny, John, 109, 111n59

Kenyon College, 34, 64
Kerr, Clark, 211, 252–253
Kipnis, Laura, 214–219

Lafayette College, 141
Lepawsky, Albert, 239–240
Lincoln, Abraham, 89, 132, 192
Lipset, Martin Seymour, 42, 282, 283
Lord, Nathan, 189–192
Lowell, Lawrence A., xv, 201–202, 211
Lucas, Anthony, 211–212, 218
Lucas, Christopher, 292
Lutherans, 6, 34

Mack, Eric, 285, 286
Madison, James, 10, 227, 263–264
Marshall, Justice John, 118
Marx, Karl, 278
Maryland, 28, 40, 213
Massachusetts Bay (Colony), 1, 2, 3, 11,
    12, 13, 16, 28, 40, 226, 227, 291
McCarthyism, 8, 15, 200, 211, 267
McCloskey, Herbert, 57
McCosh, James, 128–130, 131, 134, 135
Mead, Sidney, 2, 3, 4, 24n7, 32, 37, 39,
    40, 41, 42–45, 46, 47, 50, 86, 119, 120
Meiklejohn, Alexander, 133–135, 138,
    141, 144, 177, 178
Menand, Louis, 89, 278, 304
Mennonites, 6
Methodists, 6, 34
Mill, John Stuart, 278
Miller, Perry, 11, 12, 168
Minogue, Kenneth, xii, xiii, xvn2, 69,
    251, 257n59, 259–260, 266, 272, 288,
    294, 308, 309
Moore, LeRoy, 4, 5, 24n7
More, Thomas, 247
Morrill Land Grant Act, 22, 30, 48, 62,
    118, 153, 159
Muslim, 33, 39

national university, 17, 66, 97
New Hampshire, 43, 118, 190, 208, 209,
    211
New York University, 291, 295, 298
Newman, Cardinal John Henry, xiii,
    34, 35, 44, 105, 120, 138, 167, 249,
    251, 259, 260, 262, 270–271, 288, 294,

310
Nixon, Richard, 105, 200, 256n22
Northwestern University, 214, 215, 216
Novak, Michael, 4–5

O' Neil, Robert, 264, 265, 267, 272,
    272–273, 275, 278
Oberlin University, 147, 216–217
Ohio State University, 291
Oxford University, 183, 247

Palmer, Alice Freeman, 163
Palmer, George Herbert, 92
Pell, Claiborne, 224
Phi Beta Kappa, 107, 231
Porter, Noah, 130–132, 134, 135, 144
Post, Robert, 287
Pratt, Linda, 254
Presbyterians, 6, 61, 114, 116
Princeton University, 67, 93, 114–116,
    117, 124, 128, 129, 130, 143, 154, 157,
    165, 176, 227, 250
Progressive Era, 7, 48, 49, 90, 154, 155,
    156, 163, 164, 168, 174, 176
Protestant Reformation, 28
Providence Plantations, 12, 186, 253
Purcell, Edward, 13, 14, 15
Puritans, 1, 2, 3, 12, 13, 16, 28, 39, 156

Quakers, 28

Reagan, Ronald, 105, 200, 211, 220n26
religion of the Republic, 1, 3, 4, 5, 6, 7,
    8, 9–10, 20, 27, 36–38, 39, 41, 45, 46,
    48, 52, 57, 77, 167, 307–308
Revolutionary War (American), 1–2, 7,
    114, 187, 227, 306
Rhode Island, 2–3, 12, 24n6, 28, 40, 186,
    224, 253
Rieff, Philip, 277, 287
Rockefeller, John David, 162, 165, 166,
    168, 171, 198, 199
Rodin, Judith, 241
Roman Catholic, 28, 30, 34, 35, 37, 307
Ross, Edward, 196–197, 198, 199, 204,
    231, 232, 248
Rousseau, Jean Jacques, 41
Rudolph, Frederick, xi, 31–32, 55–56,
    63, 64, 81n2, 81n16, 118–119, 141,

154, 155, 156, 157, 158, 162, 163, 166, 169
Ruggles, Samuel, 90, 93
Rutgers University, 70, 114, 227

Said, Edward, 270
Schlesinger, Jr., Arthur, 234, 235–237, 242, 256n20, 256n22, 277, 287, 308
Searle, John, 278–280, 281
September 11th, 15, 97, 100, 200, 211, 212, 219, 272
Sexton, John, 295–299, 300, 305
Shapiro, Harold, 83, 84, 85, 89, 109
Shils, Edward, 56
Sloan, Douglas, 59, 60, 121, 144–149, 227, 265, 266–267
Social Gospel, 7–8, 48, 90, 91, 154, 159, 163, 164, 166, 168, 170, 174, 179, 180
Soviet Union, 224, 261
Stanford University, 33, 75, 76, 154, 161, 170, 196–199, 200, 202, 203, 204, 231, 232, 248, 263, 279
Stanford, Jane, 76, 196–198, 199, 231
Stanford, Leland, 161, 171
Storr, Richard, 90, 160
Sturtevant, Julian, 61, 62
Sweezy vs. New Hampshire, 208

Tappan, Henry, 30, 32–33, 35, 127, 128
Ticknor, George, 64, 187–188
Title IX, 213–215, 218, 219
Truman, David, 169, 302, 303
Tucker, William Jewett, 297
Turner, Frederick Jackson, 10

United Church of Christ, 34
University of California, Berkeley, 65, 67, 170
University of Chicago, 33, 68, 78, 95, 135, 157, 161, 162, 163, 166, 167, 168, 198, 199, 245, 246
University of Colorado, 211
University of Gottingen, 187
University of Michigan, 30, 83, 88, 91, 127, 159, 291, 305
University of Notre Dame, 30, 34, 213, 242
University of Pennsylvania, 45, 241, 291

University of Virginia, 17, 97, 264
University of Wisconsin, 194, 195, 196, 278

Van Amringe, Howard, 177, 178
Veblen, Thorstein, 70, 171, 172, 173, 176
Veysey, Laurence, 157–158, 171–172, 174, 197
Vietnam War, 5, 104, 200, 211, 231, 234, 250
Villa, Dana, 242

Warren, Earl, 209
Washington, George, 17, 66–67, 97, 139, 237, 308
Wayland, Francis, 124–127, 128, 131, 301
Webster, Daniel, 43, 118, 209
Wellesley College, 221n52
Wells, Oliver, 195
Wheeler, Benjamin, 67, 170
Wheelock, Eleazor, 118
Wheelock, John, 118, 209
White, Andrew, 31, 32, 65, 91, 145, 159, 193, 206
Whitefield, George, 52n23, 119, 120
Whitehead, Alfred North, 39
Williams, Roger, 2, 12, 24n6, 28, 186, 227
Wilson, Woodrow, 93, 94, 115, 143–144, 176, 177, 178
Winthrop, John, 2, 11, 12
Wirth, Lewis, 56
Witherspoon, John, 114–116, 117, 124, 157, 165
Woodward, C. Vann, 283
World War I, 98, 201, 211, 212
World War II, 8, 98, 99, 104, 137, 166, 201, 212, 223, 224, 261, 284, 285
Wriston, Henry, 34, 99–101, 102–103, 104, 138–141

Yale Report of 1828, 89, 90, 91, 121, 122, 123, 124, 127, 128, 132, 147, 301
Yale University, 2, 12, 61, 120, 121, 122, 123–124, 125, 130, 133, 147, 154, 163, 186, 226–227, 245, 283, 295, 298

Lightning Source UK Ltd.
Milton Keynes UK
UKOW02n1327110416

272029UK00001B/26/P